Schoolwide Physical Activity

A COMPREHENSIVE GUIDE TO DESIGNING AND CONDUCTING PROGRAMS

Judith E. Rink

University of South Carolina

Tina J. Hall

University of South Carolina

Lori H. Williams

The Citadel

Human Kinetics

Library of Congress Cataloging-in-Publication Data

Rink, Judith
  Schoolwide physical activity: a comprehensive guide to designing and conducting programs /
Judith E. Rink, Tina J. Hall, Lori H. Williams.
     p. cm.
  ISBN-13: 978-0-7360-8060-6 (soft cover)
  ISBN-10: 0-7360-8060-0 (soft cover)
  1. Physical education and training--Curricula. 2. Curriculum planning. 3. Sports for children--
Health aspects. I. Title.
  GV363.R549 2010
  372.86--dc22

                         2009041880

ISBN-10: 0-7360-8060-0 (print)
ISBN-13: 978-0-7360-8060-6 (print)

The Web addresses cited in this text were current as of October 1, 2009, unless otherwise noted.

Acquisitions Editor: Sarajane Quinn; **Developmental Editor:** Melissa Feld; **Assistant Editor:** Rachel Brito; **Copyeditor:** Joyce Sexton; **Indexer:** Alisha Jeddeloh; **Permission Manager:** Dalene Reeder; **Graphic Designer:** Bob Reuther; **Graphic Artist:** Julie L. Denzer; **Cover Designer**: Keith Blomberg; **Photographers (cover):** Upper left: iStockPhoto, Right: © Human Kinetics, Bottom left: © Human Kinetics; **Photographer (interior):** See photo credits on page 328; **Photo Asset Manager:** Laura Fitch; **Visual Production Assistant:** Joyce Brumfield; **Photo Production Manager:** Jason Allen; **Art Manager:** Kelly Hendren; **Associate Art Manager:** Alan L. Wilborn; **Illustrator:** Tim Offenstein; **Printer:** Sheridan Books

Printed in the United States of America   10   9   8   7   6   5   4   3   2   1

The paper in this book is certified under a sustainable forestry program.

Human Kinetics
Web site: www.HumanKinetics.com

United States: Human Kinetics
P.O. Box 5076
Champaign, IL 61825-5076
800-747-4457
e-mail: humank@hkusa.com

Canada: Human Kinetics
475 Devonshire Road Unit 100
Windsor, ON N8Y 2L5
800-465-7301 (in Canada only)
e-mail: info@hkcanada.com

Europe: Human Kinetics
107 Bradford Road
Stanningley
Leeds LS28 6AT, United Kingdom
+44 (0) 113 255 5665
e-mail: hk@hkeurope.com

Australia: Human Kinetics
57A Price Avenue
Lower Mitcham, South Australia 5062
08 8372 0999
e-mail: info@hkaustralia.com

New Zealand: Human Kinetics
P.O. Box 80
Torrens Park, South Australia 5062
0800 222 062
e-mail: info@hknewzealand.com

E4729

Contents

PART III   The Secondary Physical Activity Program   233

PART IV Wellness Programs 307

CD-ROM Contents

The accompanying CD-ROM contains printable figures, tables, sidebars, and text from the book. These elements are all marked with a CD-ROM icon in the book.

In addition, the CD-ROM contains a wealth of activities and resources for the classroom teacher—over 200 games, dances, and integration activities, as described below.

Integrating Physical Activity Into Academics (Chapter 5)

Language Arts
Math
Science
Social Studies

Transitional Activities for the Classroom (Chapter 5)

Playground Activities for Recess (Chapter 6)

Simple Activities for Young Children
Playground Favorites
Basketball Games
Common Recreational Games
Other Fun Playground Activities

Low Organization Outdoor Games (Chapter 7)

Active Listening Games
Tag Games
Target and Net Games
Territorial or Invasion Games

Classroom Games (Chapter 7)

Cooperative Games (Chapter 7)

Games From Other Countries (Chapter 7)

Dance and Rhythmic Activities in the Elementary School (Chapter 8)

Folk Dances
Rhythmic Activities, Novelty Dances, and Line Dances

Fitness Activities (Chapter 9)

Flexibility
Aerobic Capacity
Aerobic Capacity, Muscular Strength and Endurance
Muscular Strength and Endurance

Intramurals for the Elementary School (Chapter 11)

Fielding Games
Target and Net Games
Territorial or Invasion Games

Preface

The problems attributed to poor diet and lack of physical activity have caught the nation's attention. Because schools house all children a large portion of the day, schools have been targeted for solutions, and many have responded by changing their nutrition policies as well as initiating programs to increase students' physical activity.

The Centers for Disease Control and Prevention (2008) recommends that children obtain at least 60 minutes of moderate to vigorous activity daily. The National Association for Sport and Physical Education recommends daily physical education for children. Some schools have the resources to provide daily physical education, but most do not. Schools that do not have daily physical education need to find alternatives for students under the auspices of a planned physical activity program.

Physical activity programs are not the same as physical education programs. Physical *education* programs are instructional; they teach students the skills they need in order to be physically active. Physical *activity* programs are not instructional; they engage students in moderate to vigorous physical activity for health and wellness.

Schoolwide Physical Activity will help classroom teachers, physical education teachers, and administrators at both the elementary and secondary levels design and conduct school physical activity programs. The perspective is that physical activity programs are the responsibility of the entire school (administrators, classroom teachers, and physical education teachers), not just physical education teachers.

Physical education teachers often conduct programs at the secondary level, but it is assumed that classroom teachers play a major role in physical activity programs at the elementary level. Teachers at the elementary level will learn how to conduct good recess programs, incorporate physical activity throughout the school day, integrate physical activity into academic work, and reinforce opportunities for physical activity outside of school. Physical education teachers and administrators at the elementary level will learn how to prepare and supervise both paraprofessionals and classroom teachers and work with the community. At the secondary level the focus is on creating a vision of a good physical activity program and how to achieve it so that every student in the school is regularly involved in physical activity. The introductory material is applicable to all school levels, and there are separate sections for elementary school and secondary school. The last chapter describes programs for adults.

Each chapter begins with an outline of the content and ends with a chapter summary, checks for understanding, and lists of suggested readings, references, and Web sites. A CD-ROM with activities and resources for the classroom teacher (over 200 games, dances, and integration activities) accompanies the book. All material marked with a CD-ROM icon 🔘 is available on the CD-ROM.

Various resources are available free of charge to instructors who adopt this book for their courses; these resources are available at www.HumanKinetics.com/SchoolwidePhysicalActivity. Following is a description of each ancillary:

- The **instructor guide** includes a course syllabus for a classroom teacher course and course syllabi for physical education teachers to use in a variety of curricula. All units in the syllabi are accompanied by suggested student learning experiences.

- The **test package**, created with Respondus 2.0, includes a bank of over 200 questions. With Respondus LE, a free version of the Respondus software, instructors can create printed versions of their own tests by selecting from the question pool; create, store, and retrieve their own questions; select their own test forms and save them for later editing or printing; or export the tests into a word processing program. Instructors or institutions may purchase an upgrade to the free software from Respondus. With the upgrade, instructors can create and manage exams through a variety of course management systems, including Blackboard, eCollege, and WebCT.

■ The **presentation package** includes a comprehensive series of PowerPoint slides for each chapter. The presentation package has 500 slides that can be used directly with PowerPoint and used in printing transparencies or slides or making copies for distribution to students. Instructors can easily add to, modify, or rearrange the order of the slides.

PART I

Introduction

Physical Activity and the School Program

OVERVIEW

This chapter is designed to set the stage for the rest of the book by describing the need for physical activity programs in the school as part of a comprehensive effort to improve the physical activity levels of children, adolescents, and adults.

CHAPTER OUTCOMES

This chapter will help you

- understand the importance of a physical activity program in the school;
- explore the reasons for lack of physical activity with today's youth;
- identify the contributions of a school physical activity program to the total mission of schools;
- identify the factors related to participation in physical activity;
- identify the national recommendations for physical activity for children, adolescents, and adults;

- identify the efforts and responsibilities of the community, family, federal and state government, and schools in developing a physically active lifestyle; and
- identify the characteristics of a good physical education program and a good physical activity program and distinguish the purposes of the two.

IN THIS CHAPTER

Intuitively, most people know that being physically active is good for you. Our growing understanding about how the body works and the physiological effects of physical activity on the body has provided us with a knowledge base to document those benefits, as well as the negative effects of the lack of physical activity. In 1996 the surgeon general published *Physical Activity and Health: A Report of the Surgeon General*. Like the report issued in 1964 on smoking, the surgeon general's report on physical activity was designed to call attention to a national crisis in health. The report documented the effects of a lack of physical activity on health, including premature death and increases in chronic disease (particularly diabetes). With little evidence of change, in 2001, Surgeon General David Satcher released *The Surgeon General's Call to Action to Prevent and Decrease Overweight and Obesity* (U.S. Department of Health and Human Services [USDHHS], 2001). Satcher addressed the health issues involved in the obesity epidemic and outlined strategies to increase physical education and provide healthier food options in the schools.

Major and continuous increases in the number of obese children and adults in this country over the past 50 years have been attributed not only to poor nutrition but also to lack of physical activity. The prevalence of overweight children among those aged 6 through 11 has more than doubled in the past 20 years, increasing from 7% in 1980 to 18.8% in 2004 (Council on Sports Medicine and Fitness and Council on School Health, 2006). Inactive children and adolescents have a greater likelihood than others of becoming inactive adults.

Children and adolescents who are overweight are more likely to be overweight or obese as adults (USDHHS, 2004). Obesity is the second leading cause of premature death (next to smoking) and is responsible for well over 400,000 deaths each year (Mokdad et al., 2004). While lack of physical activity can be directly connected to premature death, perhaps more importantly it is connected to chronic diseases that are ongoing and *preventable*.

The lack of physical activity is a health problem not only in terms of premature death and the prevalence of chronic disease that affects our quality of life. Lack of physical activity and the increased health costs connected to taking care of large numbers of people with chronic diseases are a major burden on our economy. The percentage of our gross national product being spent on health care increases every year.

The Problem

The lack of physical activity is a multidimensional problem, associated with changes in our lifestyles, changes in school policies, and changes in the communities in which we live. All of these have contributed to a lack of physical activity of children and adults; and because there is no one cause, there is no one easy solution.

Lifestyle Issues

One of the major problems we have living in this century is that the technological advances of the past century were designed to remove physical activity from our lives, to make life easier for us. If we want to increase physical activity, we will need to find ways to put it back into our lives and find time in our schedules for it. How many of us are willing to give up our "remotes"? How many companies are willing to put the copy machine on a different floor so that employees will have to walk to get copies made? How many employees are willing to walk into the next office to talk with an office worker as opposed to e-mailing? How many of us spend 20 minutes looking for the closest parking space? How many of us allocate a very small portion of our day to physical activity?

Push mowers for lawns have been replaced with riding lawn mowers heretofore reserved for large acreages of land. All appliances are automatic and require little physical labor. Jobs that used to be done around the house and outside are now considered too technical or too time-consuming for the home owner. So we hire professionals to do everything from washing our house to painting the inside. Many middle-class home owners use cleaning services.

Children who used to take off their going-to-school clothes and put on their going-outside-to-play clothes are relegated to the inside, either because their parents work or want to know where they are or because neighborhoods are considered too unsafe to allow children to be outside. The TV, video gaming systems, the Internet, and computers have replaced many active "play" activities and dominate unscheduled time for all ages. Children who watch the most TV and have the least physical activity are the most overweight (Anderson et al., 1998). Youth and adolescents have been captured by video games that occupy a great deal of their unscheduled time. It is not uncommon to find many teenagers at the controls of these games until wee hours of the morning.

We have spent a good part of our lives trying to figure out how to remove physical activity from our lives and now we need to think about how to put it back.

School Programs

School programs have likewise undergone major changes. While periodically school programs experience a back-to-basics movement, the more recent emphases on academics and the No Child Left Behind national legislation (U.S. Department of Education, 2002) have caused schools to look for ways to increase the time children spend in the academic portion of the curriculum. One of the ways schools have chosen to do this is to decrease time spent in physical education and other subject areas considered nonacademic. Although most states require physical education, few have mandates for how much time should be devoted to these programs or how they should be conducted (National Association for Sport and Physical Education [NASPE], 2006). Only Illinois has required daily physical education, and major loopholes and "waivers" have increased the number of children not being served by the mandate in that state.

Where schools do have physical education, the amount of time students actually spend in physical education varies a great deal from school to school even within a state. At the elementary school level, physical education time varies from 30 minutes per week to 150 minutes per week, and this time is not always with a specialist in physical education. At the middle school, the time varies from 80 minutes per week to 225 minutes per week; at the high school level, the time also varies considerably. Most states require only one or two years of high school physical education, and a large number less than that or none. Even in states that require physical education, 58% allow substitutions, and many students at the elementary level are being pulled out of their physical education classes to receive remedial help in academics. The reduced participation in physical education has been partially blamed for the increase in obesity levels in students. As physical education time has decreased, obesity levels in students have increased.

Community Changes

In neighborhoods where children once walked to school, cars line up in the morning and afternoon waiting to drop children off and pick them up—some living only a few blocks from the school. Neighborhood schools have been replaced in many cases by larger, more cost-effective buildings, placing students farther away from their school. Few schools have sidewalks leading to their doors from the communities that surround them. Small community shopping areas within walking distance of many residents have been replaced with large mega shopping centers accessible only by car. Those who do at least plan on building exercise into their lives and can afford it, do so at "gyms" and fitness centers that they ride to. Most people who sign up to exercise at fitness centers inevitably abandon their efforts within a short time due to "busy schedules." All of these changes have resulted in the need to find ways to build physical activity back into the lives of both children and adults.

The Contributions of Physical Activity

While awareness of the importance of physical activity to health has certainly increased, what most people do not understand is how important physical activity is to the well-being of children and youth in areas other than health. Although these contributions may not receive as much press, they are equally important.

Growth and Development

Children and adolescents are growing and developing as physical beings. Regular physical activity is essential to their growth and development. Regular physical activity helps build strong bones and muscles, helps control weight, and may play a major role in improving blood pressure and cholesterol levels (NASPE, 2008). Strong bones develop as a result of weight-bearing activities and those that stress the bones. Active children have a higher bone mass and are less likely to have problems (osteoporosis) later in life. The development of all systems of the body is affected by the level of physical activity of children and adolescents.

Social and Emotional Well-Being

Play is an important human behavior. While the forms of play change throughout the life span, the need for playful activity does not. There is evidence that motor skills used in play and learned early in life enhance a child's ability to participate in activities later in life (Malina, 1996). Physical play is a critical contributor to the development of children's social skills and the well-being of adults. Elementary schools that have eliminated recess (see chapter 6), as well as home environments that do not provide children opportunities to go out and play, deprive students not only of the opportunity to be physically active but also of the opportunity to develop the social skills they will need as an adult.

Physical play is important to our emotional well-being. Studies show that regular physical activity in childhood and adolescence reduces stress and improves self-esteem. We are physical beings, and as such we need to move. Each culture has accepted forms of play. Children who do not learn to participate in the accepted forms of play of their culture are at a disadvantage socially as children and later as adults. Such learning not only takes care of our physical body but also facilitates emotional well-being.

Cognitive Functioning and Academic Performance

A common misperception of educators is that if they take time out to provide students with the physical activity they need, the students will not do well academically. Actually there is more and more evidence that physical activity enhances cognitive functioning (Castelli et al., 2007); time spent in increased physical activity during the school day does not decrease academic performance but instead actually increases it (Dwyer et al., 1983; Sallis et al., 1999; Shephard, 1997; Strong et. al., 2005). Children need breaks from sedentary activity.

Physical activity is a great medium for learning other content areas and should be used to actually teach academic content. When physical activity is provided for children during the school day, they are more attentive and teachers have fewer behavior problems (Pellegrini, Huberty, & Jones, 1995; Strong, et al., 2005).

Beginning research with adolescent-aged students also indicated that students who participated in vigorous activity for at least 20 minutes three times a week had higher grades (Sibley & Etnier, 2003; Pellegrini & Bohn, 2005; Tremblay, Inman, & Williams, 2000). Higher grades are attributed to the increased attention that students have when they are not bored and not forced to spend an entire day in sedentary activities.

Physical Activity, Exercise, and Fitness

Unless you are in a health or physical education field, the terms physical activity, exercise, and fitness probably mean the same thing to you. Actually these terms have quite different meanings that will be useful for our discussions of appropriate physical activity. Physical activity is any bodily movement produced by skeletal muscles that results in energy expenditure. Exercise is a subset of physical activity that is planned, structured, and repetitive and is done to improve or maintain physical fitness. Physical fitness is a set of attributes that are either health or skill related. Health-related fitness includes cardiorespiratory endurance, muscular strength and endurance, flexibility, and body composition; skill-related fitness includes balance, agility, power, reaction time, speed, and coordination (Caspersen, Powell, & Christenson, 1985).

For young children the relationship between fitness and physical activity is not high (Payne & Morrow, 1993), and the recommendation of most professionals for this age group is to focus efforts on increasing physical activity and not fitness. In one sense if students are active in appropriate physical activity, fitness will follow. Fitness becomes more important as students enter adolescence, but the emphasis should be on the development of health-related fitness components as defined in table 1.1. Chapters 9 and 16 describe appropriate fitness programs for the elementary and secondary student, and chapter 17 discusses appropriate programs for adults.

Factors That Affect Physical Activity

There are many factors that affect the level of physical activity of children and adolescents. Where you live, whether you are a girl or a boy, how old you are, what race you are, your socioeconomic status, whether you are successful in physical activities, and whether you enjoy your physical education class all affect your level of participation in physical activity. The following list summarizes

TABLE 1.1

The Components of Health-Related Fitness

Fitness component	Definition	Typical activities
Cardiorespiratory endurance	The ability of the cardiovascular system of the body to supply oxygen to the muscles	Running, jogging, sustained work, swimming, cycling, step aerobics
Muscular strength	The amount of force exerted by a muscle group in a single contraction	Weight training, heavy lifting
Muscular endurance	The ability of a muscle group to keep working	Number of repetitions of a heavy load in weight training
Flexibility	The ability of a joint to move freely through a full range of motion	Stretching exercises
Body composition	The ratio of body fat to lean body tissue	Cardiovascular exercises that burn calories over a period of time

these relationships (USDHHS, Centers for Disease Control and Prevention, 1997, available online at www.cdc.gov/HealthyYouth/physicalactivity/guidelines).

- Girls are less active than boys.
- Older children are less active than younger children.
- Black older students are less active than white students.
- Students who have confidence in their physical abilities are more active.
- Students who perceive the benefits of physical activity as positive (fun, learning new skills, social interaction, and so on) are more active.
- Students with active parents are more active.
- Students who have convenient access to places to be active are more active.

These factors have been used to formulate recommendations for developing school and community programs to increase physical activity and particular efforts to target specific at-risk groups of young people. As you learn more about what constitutes a good physical activity program in the school, you will recognize deliberate efforts to use these ideas to develop both policy and programs.

National Recommendations for Physical Activity

Physical activity does not have to be strenuous to be beneficial. This is good news, because it is difficult to get a population to become active if they think they have to push themselves to the point of hurting to achieve the health benefits of physical activity. Researchers over the past decades have identified minimal levels of physical activity essential to the well-being of children and adolescents. Most of these recommendations distinguish levels of physical activity by using the terms "moderate" and "vigorous" to describe the intensity level of effort required by a person to do the activity. There are several methods of measuring the intensity of activity, including using target heart rate and perceived exertion; but these terms are better understood on the basis of the relative intensity of the activity. The talk test is a simple way to measure relative intensity. As a rule of thumb, if you're doing moderate-intensity activity you can talk, but not sing, during the activity. If you're doing vigorous-intensity activity, you will not be able to say more than a few words without pausing for a breath. Following are examples of activities classified as moderate intensity or vigorous intensity based on the amount of energy used by the body while doing the activity.

It is difficult to get today's youth active and away from sedentary activities.

Moderate Intensity

- Walking briskly (3 miles [4.8 kilometers] per hour or faster, but not race walking)
- Water aerobics
- Bicycling slower than 10 miles (16 kilometers) per hour
- Tennis (doubles)
- Ballroom dancing
- General gardening

Vigorous Intensity

- Race walking, jogging, or running
- Swimming laps
- Tennis (singles)
- Aerobic dancing
- Bicycling 10 miles per hour or faster

- Jumping rope
- Heavy gardening (continuous digging or hoeing)
- Hiking uphill or with a heavy backpack

Figure 1.1 presents the physical activity pyramid, used by many educators and health professionals to help people understand the types of physical activity appropriate for different ages. Children, adolescents, and adults should get the majority of their physical activity from lifestyle activities (Level 1) and at least some from either the active aerobics or active sport and recreation categories (Level 2). It is also important to maintain flexibility and muscular strength by engaging in activities that make you stretch and overload the muscles (Level 3). A sedentary lifestyle with long periods of inactivity (Level 4) is to be avoided at all ages.

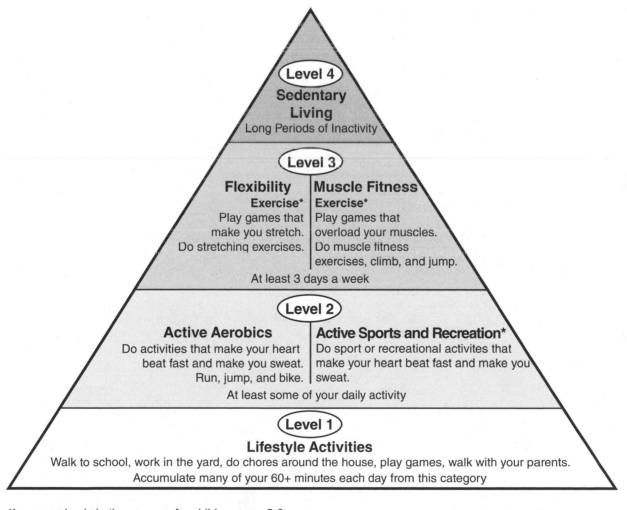

Level 4
Sedentary Living
Long Periods of Inactivity

Level 3

Flexibility
Exercise*
Play games that make you stretch.
Do stretching exercises.

Muscle Fitness
Exercise*
Play games that overload your muscles.
Do muscle fitness exercises, climb, and jump.

At least 3 days a week

Level 2

Active Aerobics
Do activities that make your heart beat fast and make you sweat. Run, jump, and bike.

Active Sports and Recreation*
Do sport or recreational activites that make your heart beat fast and make you sweat.

At least some of your daily activity

Level 1
Lifestyle Activities
Walk to school, work in the yard, do chores around the house, play games, walk with your parents.
Accumulate many of your 60+ minutes each day from this category

*Less emphasis in these areas for children ages 5-9.

Figure 1.1 The physical activity pyramid.

Recommendations for Children

Unlike adults, most children if given the opportunity will engage in physical activity. If children are to grow and develop as they should and establish the skills and desire for a lifetime of physical activity, adults need to provide appropriate opportunities for children to be active. Recently published guidelines issued by the USDHHS for physical activity of children and youth stress the need for at least 60 minutes of physical activity a day and stress the importance of some of that activity falling into activity levels that are also bone strengthening and muscle strengthening (*Physical Activity Guidelines for Americans*, 2008).

Children do not need to engage in sustained vigorous activity. Rather, vigorous activity should come in short bursts that are accumulated throughout the day. Optimal benefits will occur if children participate in bouts of physical activity lasting at least 15 minutes. Table 1.2 describes the differences between continuous and intermittent kinds of activities.

The physical activity that children participate in should be age appropriate. When children reach 10 to 12 years of age, many will begin to engage in more sport-related physical activity and may choose to jog or become a runner. The important idea is that children should make the decision about what vigorous activities they want to engage in and that these choices should not be forced on them. The following are some important concepts related

Summary of Physical Activity Guidelines for Children and Youth

Children should do 60 minutes (1 hour) or more of physical activity daily.

- **Aerobic:** Most of the 60 or more minutes a day should be either moderate- or vigorous-intensity aerobic physical activity, and should include vigorous-intensity physical activity at least three days a week.

- **Muscle strengthening:** As part of their 60 or more minutes of daily physical activity, children and adolescents should include muscle-strengthening physical activity on at least three days of the week.

- **Bone strengthening:** As part of their 60 or more minutes of daily physical activity, children and adolescents should include bone-strengthening physical activity on at least three days of the week.

It is important to encourage young people to participate in physical activities that are appropriate for their age, that are enjoyable, and that offer variety.

Department of Health and Human Services, *2008 Physical Activity Guidelines for Americans*

TABLE 1.2

Examples of Appropriate Intermittent and Continuous Physical Activity

Activity type	Intermittent	Continuous
CHILDREN		
Moderate activities	Low-intensity games such as hopscotch and Four Square; playing low-activity positions in sports such as goalie in soccer or the outfield in softball; and some chores and yard work	Walking to school, bike riding, and some chores and yard work
Vigorous activities	Active games involving running, chasing, and so on; playing sports	Self selected activities such as jogging
ADOLESCENTS		
Moderate activities	Playing golf, hand washing the car, Frisbee tossing and catching, jogging and walking	Dancing, basketball, shooting hoops, jogging/walking combination, raking leaves, mowing lawn (power mower)
Vigorous activities	Football, Ultimate, moving and pushing furniture	Race walking, jogging or running, swimming laps, mowing lawn (hand mower), singles tennis

to physical activity for children from the NASPE report (2004b):

- Children usually have a relatively short attention span for tasks compared to adults, which means that long-duration activities do not capture the attention of this age group.
- Children are concrete rather than abstract thinkers. The idea of "future health" is usually not effective in motivating this age group to be active. They need evidence of success.
- Children are typically active intermittently and need frequent periods of recovery.
- High-intensity physical activity has benefits over moderate activity, but may reduce persistence among some people including children and youth.
- Self-efficacy (a feeling that you can be successful) in physical activity is one of the factors that is strongly associated with lifetime physical activity adherence. It is important to build feelings of efficacy early in life.
- Children and youth who have active parents and family members and do regular activities with them are more likely to be active than those who are not active in the family setting. Active children most often come from active families.
- Just as children and youth can learn the habit of regular activity involvement, they can learn to be inactive if they are not given opportunities to be active when young.

Recommendations for Adolescents

A consensus statement (Sallis, Patrick, & Long, 1994) on physical activity for adolescents recommends a minimum of 30 minutes of moderate physical activity on most days of the week and involvement in more vigorous activity on at least three days per week for 20 minutes. This guideline for adolescent activity includes one recommendation based primarily on the Lifetime Activity Model (30 minutes of moderate physical activity most days of the week) and one recommendation based on the Exercise Prescription Model (20 minutes of more vigorous physical activity three days a week); it differs from the recommendations for young children in suggesting that vigorous physical activity should be continuous.

Participation in all types of physical activity declines strikingly as age or grade in school increases. Many children who were active at the elementary school level become inactive teenagers. Only about one-half of U.S. young people (ages 12-21 years) regularly participate in vigorous physical activity. One-fourth report no vigorous physical activity (www.fitness.gov/adoles.htm, June 12, 2008).

While most of the activity for the adolescent may be at Level 1 of the physical activity pyramid (figure 1.1), the activities of adolescents should start moving into Level 2 in sport and recreational "play" activities. Adolescents can be expected to sustain

Adolescents can prepare for a lifetime of skills with physical activity.

Lifetime Activity and Exercise Prescription: What's the Difference?

There are two orientations toward fitness. The *lifetime activity* orientation stresses involvement in physical activity and an active lifestyle (e.g., games, sports, yard work). The *exercise prescription* model focuses on exercise for the sole purpose of developing and maintaining fitness (e.g., jogging, curl-ups, weight training).

longer bouts of more intense activity and will need to attend to Level 3 activities.

Recommendations for Adults

The recommendation in the surgeon general's report for adult physical activity is similar to that for adolescents: a minimum of 30 minutes of moderate-intensity physical activity per day (such as brisk walking) on most days of the week or a minimum of 20 minutes of vigorous-intensity physical activity (such as jogging or running) on three days a week. In addition, adults should have some resistance, strength-building, and weight-bearing activities. An ideal program would incorporate strength training two days a week. Strength training activities, such as weightlifting, maintain and increase muscle strength and endurance. A goal to reach toward is completing six to eight strength training exercises, with 8 to 12 repetitions per exercise (USDHHS, 1996).

The Solution

Getting a population active after most of our efforts have been directed toward making life easier is not going to be easy or quick. However, the surgeon general's report on smoking decades ago led to important progress in what was also considered a major health crisis and an impossible task. No single change in the culture that surrounds us will be a "cure-all" for what has taken decades to develop. The solution will require the efforts of communities, schools, and parents; and successful efforts will be those that are facilitated with policies at the national, state, and local levels. Figure 1.2 is a presentation that Lori Rose Benson, director of the Office of Fitness and Health Education for the New York City Department of Education, made to a U.S. House of Representatives subcommittee on the efforts of the New York City School system to cope with the lack of physical activity in that system. You will recognize in the presentation the comprehensiveness of the effort and the magnitude of the problem. The fact that Benson was asked to testify is also an indication of how important the lack of physical activity is perceived to be by our federal government.

The Role of the Community

Most physical activity among young people occurs outside the school setting. Changes in community planning are part of a comprehensive effort to put physical activity back into people's lives. Where

there are walking trails, people walk. Where there are bicycle lanes, people bike. Where there are sidewalks, children are more likely to walk to school. Where there is a playground, children play. Where there are opportunities for families to be active together, families are more likely to be active together. Community centers, playgrounds, churches, and recreational programs that offer a wide variety of activities for children and youth and include minorities and low-income groups in their planning are more likely to increase the level of activity of the population of a community.

The Role of Government Policy

As with most national health issues, government policy at the national, state, and local level has a major role to play in combating the problem of obesity. This section briefly describes some of the critical policies affecting physical activity.

School Wellness Programs   In 2004, legislation called the Child Nutrition and WIC Reauthorization Act of 2004 was passed at the federal level (PL 108-265); the act directs school districts to formulate and develop wellness policies. Each district must have a plan that involves wellness, comprehensively including both nutrition and physical activity, and sets goals for nutrition education, food provision, and physical activity for students and employees. Chapter 2 in this text is devoted to the school wellness program targeted by this legislation.

No Child Left Behind   The No Child Left Behind legislation (2002) was designed to improve academic performance of students throughout the country by creating accountability for standards and student achievement. One unintended consequence of this legislation was that the emphasis on academic achievement in the schools pushed policy makers at the state and local levels to reduce time spent in areas other than "core" subjects in the curriculum (physical education, music, art), as well as to eliminate other opportunities that students had during the school day for physical activity (recess) and breaks from academic content. The revisions of this legislation hopefully will take some of the pressure off academic achievement testing and create opportunities for students to be more active.

Federal Grants   The Carol M. White Physical Education Program is commonly known as PEP grants. This federal program provides grants to initiate, expand, and improve physical education programs for K through 12 students in order to

FIGURE 1.2

Example of a Comprehensive Effort to Increase Physical Activity

Testimony of Lori Rose Benson Before House Committee on Education and Labor, July 24, 2008
Good morning, Chairman Miller and members of the Committee on Education and Labor.

I am Lori Rose Benson, director of the Office of Fitness and Health Education for the New York City Department of Education. From my experience in meeting the fitness and health challenges of New York City's 1.1 million students, I have three key messages that I hope inform your thinking and your work:

- There is no magic formula for addressing the national childhood obesity epidemic, but we must address this issue immediately, vigorously, and comprehensively.

- Schools can play an important role in improving student fitness levels, but they are only one part of a larger problem that includes family refrigerators stocked with high-calorie foods, well-worn couches opposite TVs, and lack of community opportunities and facilities for family fitness activities.

- We must create and nurture a culture of fitness that includes, but is never limited to, athletics and traditional sports with clear accountability standards tied to appropriate assessments.

Last week my bosses, Mayor Michael Bloomberg and Schools Chancellor Joel Klein, appeared before this committee to highlight the successes of New York City's education reforms. Their support for closing our city's student achievement gap also extends to tackling the tough issues surrounding physical education and its relationship to student health and academic performance.

Under their leadership we are making great strides toward providing quality fitness and health instruction for every student, male or female, able-bodied or not, sports fanatic or couch potato. My office is building the capacity of schools to provide students with the knowledge, skills, and increased opportunities for moderate to vigorous physical activity that are essential for fitness.

If there is no magic bullet, are there programs and strategies that can be part of the solution? Absolutely. National health standards tell us that children need 60 minutes of moderate to vigorous physical activity every day. I encourage schools to look at required physical education classes, before- and after-school opportunities, and moments of physical activity in classrooms.

Movement in classrooms is an exciting development in school fitness. In New York City we have trained over 1,200 teachers in 80 elementary schools using the Nike "Let Me Play" curriculum in classrooms. Regular classroom teachers are leading their students in fitness activities that complement, not supplant, teaching in core academic subjects. We're showing teachers that including activity in the regular classroom day gets students "ready to learn" and also teaches that lifelong fitness habits are essential for good health.

We also introduced the Physical Best curriculum, a program of the National Association for Sport and Physical Education, for physical education classes. This is a health-related fitness education program for kindergarten through 12th grade. The emphasis is on empowering students to develop the knowledge and skills to take responsibility for their own personal fitness, to discover which physical activities are the best fit for them.

We support that curriculum with hundreds of free year-round professional development opportunities for administrators and teachers. Creating school buy-in for fitness requires creating a culture of healthy fitness that goes beyond traditional ideas of "gym class."

Just as there is no magic formula for attacking childhood obesity, there is also no one-size-fits-all formula for schools delivering physical education. My team works with almost 1,500 schools to solve problems with facilities, scheduling, and staffing.

As this committee and the House consider setting new national standards for minutes of physical education, I encourage you to also consider that increasing minutes of instruction by itself does not necessarily create a quality program or more minutes of moderate to vigorous physical activity.

Here's another New York City example. We created the first ever city-wide middle school sport and fitness program, called CHAMPS, which stands for Cooperative Healthy Active Motivated Positive Students. Instead of the thrill of victory and the agony of defeat, we offer students a range of 1,000 traditional and nontraditional sports and fitness programs in 200 middle schools. If you like baseball, basketball, or track and field, we've got a program for you. Not interested? What about dance, crew, Double Dutch, or yoga?

(continued)

(continued)

School districts also need to consider how they can effectively interact with local public health agencies to inform families about requirements for healthy fitness. Under Mayor Bloomberg's leadership in New York City, the Department of Education and the Department of Health and Mental Hygiene are collaborating in new ways to pool resources and work together to leverage changes in health and fitness habits.

One of our most successful collaborations will soon generate national attention. Last year about 640,000 public school students in all grades took home NYC Fitnessgram reports in one of nine home languages. We took decades of research done by the Cooper Institute of Aerobic Research and Human Kinetics and adapted their report to the needs of our students. NYC Fitnessgram measures components of health-related fitness: aerobic capacity, muscular strength and endurance, flexibility, and body composition.

The data from these student reports is shared with the Department of Health, which is creating the country's largest longitudinal Web-based database of student fitness. We are beginning to look at how fitness levels influence student's core academic achievement. We continue to tailor our professional development to demonstrate for teachers how their instruction bolsters student fitness levels.

This year Chancellor Klein included completion of NYC Fitnessgram reports as one of the criteria used in principals' annual job performance reviews as part of his accountability initiative. The expression, "talk the talk, but walk the walk" now has a whole different layer of meaning in fitness education.

In closing I want to echo something else the mayor and chancellor stressed in their appearance last week. New York City is on the right track when it comes to physical education. Excellence and equity are the cornerstones of our approach to teaching and learning. But the fact remains that only 53 percent of students are at a healthy weight. The immediate and long-term personal and social consequences for that fact are devastating in terms of health care costs, education, and employment opportunities for our students.

As you consider legislation, I encourage you to look at schools as a tool and lever for changes in *fitness.* Let me leave you today with an interesting question. Try asking your colleagues, family, and friends for their answers. The range of answers is interesting, I assure you.

The question is, "When you were in school did you like gym class? Why, or why not?"

Here's my answer: "I am a native New Yorker and a proud graduate of public schools. But I hated gym class. I felt fat, awkward, and unsuccessful. I hated team sports, and that's all there was to do."

The United States must create future generations who answer this way: "Physical education changed my life. I found activities that I was good at, things that I enjoyed doing. Teachers showed me how those activities contributed to good health, and that's still an important part of my life. My teachers taught me, and now I teach my children."

Thank you for this opportunity to speak today, and I would welcome your questions today or at any time in the future.

help them make progress toward meeting state standards for physical education. Funds may be used to provide equipment and support to enable students to participate actively in physical education activities. Funds also may support staff and teacher training and education (U.S. Department of Education, 2008).

State Legislation State legislators throughout the country have begun to recognize the problems caused by lack of physical activity and have passed a wide range of legislation related to increasing opportunities for physical activity. Such legislation has included provisions like the following:

- Increasing physical education time in schools
- Requiring high school participation in physical activity
- Requiring schools to provide physical activity time during the school day
- Requiring recess in the elementary school
- Requiring new housing developments to include sidewalks, particularly around schools
- Increasing opportunities at state parks and recreational centers for physical activity
- Funding bicycle paths and walking trails
- Taking soft drink machines out of schools and monitoring the school lunch programs

Recommendations for School and Community Programs Promoting Physical Activity Among Young People

1. Policy: Establish policies that promote enjoyable, lifelong physical activity among young people.
2. Environment: Provide physical and social environments that encourage and enable safe and enjoyable physical activity.
3. Physical education: Implement physical education curricula and instruction that emphasize enjoyable participation in physical activity and that help students develop the knowledge, attitudes, motor skills, behavioral skills, and confidence needed to adopt and maintain physically active lifestyles.
4. Health education: Implement health education curricula and instruction that help students develop the knowledge, attitudes, behavioral skills, and confidence needed to adopt and maintain physically active lifestyles.
5. Extracurricular activities: Provide extracurricular physical activity programs that meet the needs and interests of all students.
6. Parental involvement: Include parents and guardians in physical activity instruction and in extracurricular and community physical activity programs, and encourage them to support their children's participation in enjoyable physical activities.
7. Personnel training: Provide training for education, coaching, recreation, health care, and other school and community personnel that imparts the knowledge and skills needed to effectively promote enjoyable, lifelong physical activity among young people.
8. Health services: Assess physical activity patterns among young people, counsel them about physical activity, refer them to appropriate programs, and advocate for physical activity instruction and programs for young people.
9. Community programs: Provide a range of developmentally appropriate community sport and recreation programs that are attractive to all young people.
10. Evaluation: Regularly evaluate school and community physical activity instruction, programs, and facilities.

The Role of the Family

If efforts to increase activity are to be successful, what students do at home and what they see their parents do at home are going to play a major role. Active students generally have active parents. Parents not only should be made aware of the need to encourage physical activity; they will also need assistance regarding what to do to help their children be active. The NASPE has published a pamphlet for parents, *101 Tips for Family Fitness Fun* (2006), that describes what parents can do to increase the physical activity of their children. Media, schools, communities, and health agencies have enacted major campaigns to "get America moving" that target parents as well as children and students.

The Role of the School

While schools can't be the only mechanism to change the activity patterns of students, they should play a major role in the effort. Children and adolescents spend a lot of their waking hours at school and all are required to attend, giving schools a captive audience for change. The development of a physical activity program in the schools is the focus of this book.

Coordinating Efforts

From the discussion throughout this chapter, it should be obvious that those communities that coordinate their efforts and bring all the targeted groups together to enact change will be more successful. The USDHHS and Centers for Disease Control and Prevention document "Guidelines for School and Community Programs to Promote Lifelong Physical Activity Among Young People" (1997) recognizes the advantage of collaboration in establishing the 10 guidelines presented in the sidebar. Schools have often operated in a vacuum apart from community efforts to improve the physical activity of children and youth. The perspective of this text is that schools must play a major role in these efforts, which will require coordination with the community and is further discussed in chapter 4.

Physical Education and the School Physical Activity Program

The school physical activity program should be a comprehensive effort to increase the level of physical activity of students both in school and out of school. The cornerstone of a comprehensive school effort to increase the physical activity levels of students is a good physical education program. The NASPE recommends that students have daily physical education including 150 minutes per week at the elementary level and 225 minutes per week at the secondary level. Children and adolescents need physical activity every day. Because few children have physical education every day, other school programs have to accept responsibility for providing the needed activity. Although in one sense it is desirable to include physical education in any discussion of providing physical activity for students in schools, in terms of the conduct of the programs and given that few schools offer daily physical education, it makes more sense to see these two programs as having different purposes.

> The purpose of a good physical education program is to educate students for a physically active lifestyle.

> The purpose of a good physical activity program is to provide students with their daily needs for physical activity.

Quality Physical Education Programs

Quality physical education programs are designed to give students the skills, knowledge, and dispositions to lead a physically active life. Such a program is an instructional program taught by a specialist as an important part of a school curriculum. A physically educated person (NASPE, 1992)

- *has* learned skills necessary to perform a variety of physical activities,
- *knows* the implications of and the benefits from involvement in physical activities,
- *does* participate regularly in physical activity,
- *is* physically fit, and

- *values* physical activity and its contributions to a healthful lifestyle.

The Physical Education Content Standards

Like all content areas in the school curriculum, physical education programs are guided by a set of national standards (figure 1.3). These standards define what a student should know and be able to do as a result of a school physical education program. It is important for all school personnel to understand the standards so that they can facilitate their attainment and understand the instructional nature of the program.

The School Physical Activity Program

The school physical activity program needs to be a coordinated effort on the part of all school personnel to provide students with their daily needs for physical activity and do so in a way that increases the propensity for participation. It should also be the responsibility of the school to reinforce participation. This will require schools to

- plan and conduct activities during the school day that provide physical activity for students,
- plan and conduct before-school and after-school programs that provide students with opportunities to be physically active,
- plan and conduct special school and community events that encourage physical activity,
- plan and conduct programs to educate parents on the importance of physical activity and involve families in physical activity,
- provide good adult role models for physical activity, and
- have teachers in all programs reinforce student participation in physical activity.

Effective physical activity programs will be planned by a multidisciplinary team. Using the comprehensive school health program and the required school wellness policies is an ideal way to initiate a good school physical activity program. Both of these are discussed in chapter 2. The manner in which these goals are achieved will vary from school level to school level and from school to school. This text is designed to give you the skills to plan, conduct, and evaluate the school physical activity program. This text is organized primarily into elementary and secondary programs.

FIGURE 1.3

The National Content Standards
for Physical Education ⊙

- **Standard 1:** Demonstrates competency in motor skills and movement patterns needed to perform a variety of physical activities.
- **Standard 2:** Demonstrates understanding of movement concepts, principles, strategies, and tactics as they apply to the learning and performance of physical activities.
- **Standard 3:** Participates regularly in physical activity.
- **Standard 4:** Achieves and maintains a health-enhancing level of physical fitness.
- **Standard 5:** Exhibits responsible personal and social behavior that respects self and others in physical activity settings.
- **Standard 6:** Values physical activity for health, enjoyment, challenge, self-expression, and/or social interaction.

SUMMARY

1. Lack of physical activity is a major health crisis in this country with implications for the quality of our lives as well as the economic health of our people.

2. Lifestyle changes and the decrease in physical education and physical activity opportunities in the schools over the years are major causes of lack of physical activity.

3. Physical activity makes a major contribution to the growth and development of children, their social and emotional well-being, and their cognitive functioning.

4. Where you live and your gender, age, race, success in physical activities, and socioeconomic status all affect your degree of physical activity.

5. Young children should accumulate at least 60 minutes of physical activity a day.

6. Adolescents should accumulate at least 30 minutes of moderate to vigorous physical activity a day or at least 20 minutes of vigorous physical activity on three days of the week.

7. The recommendations for physical activity for adults are the same as those for adolescents.

8. The community, school, family, and federal or state governments all have a major role to play in increasing physical activity, and these efforts should be coordinated.

9. The role of the school is to establish a good physical education and physical activity program.

CHECKING YOUR UNDERSTANDING

1. Why is a physically active lifestyle important to children? Adults?

2. What are the causes of a lack of physical activity on the part of youth and adults?

3. What contributions does physical activity make to child development?

4. What is the role of schools in increasing physical activity?

5. What are the national recommendations for physical activity for children? Adolescents? Adults?

6. What responsibility do the community and family have for increasing physical activity?

7. What is the difference between a school physical education program and a school physical activity program?

RESOURCES

Centers for Disease Control and Prevention: Physical Activity
www.cdc.gov/physicalactivity

The Robert Wood Johnson Foundation
www.rwjf.org

The President's Council on Physical Fitness and Sports
www.fitness.gov

After School Physical Activity
www.afterschoolpa.com

Physical Activity for Adults Over 50, Walking Programs, Exercise, and Fitness
www.aarp.org/health/fitness

Health Topics: MedlinePlus
www.medlineplus.gov/healthtopics

Allison, K.R., & Adlaf, A.M. (2000). Structured opportunities for student physical activity in Ontario elementary and secondary schools. *Canadian Journal of Public Health, 91*(5), 371-375.

American College of Sports Medicine. (1988). ACSM opinion statement on physical fitness in children and youth. *Medicine and Science in Sport and Exercise, 20*(4), 422-423.

American College of Sports Medicine. (1995). *ACSM's guidelines for exercise testing and prescription* (5th ed.). Baltimore: Williams & Wilkins.

Beighle, A., Morgan, C.F., Le Masurier, G., & Pangrazi, R.P. (2006). Children's physical activity during recess and outside of school. *Journal of School Health, 76*(10), 516-520.

Castelli, D., Powell, K., & Christenson, G. (2007). Physical fitness and academic achievement in third and fifth grade students. *Journal of Sport and Exercise Psychology, 29*(2), 239-252.

Corbin, C.B., & Pangrazi, R.P. (1996). What you need to know about the surgeon general's report on physical activity and health. *President's Council on Physical Fitness and Sports Research Digest, 2*(6), 1-8.

Corbin, C.B., Pangrazi, R.P., & Franks, B.D. (2000). Definitions: Health, fitness and physical activity. *President's Council on Physical Fitness and Sports Research Digest, 3*(9), 1-8.

Dietz, W.H. (1994). Critical periods in childhood for the development of obesity. *American Journal of Clinical Nutrition, 59*(5), 955-959.

Dietz, W.H. (1998). Health consequences of obesity in youth: Childhood predictors of adult disease. *Pediatrics, 101*(3 Pt 2), 518-525.

Fairclough, S., & Stratton, G. (2005). Physical education makes you fit and healthy: Physical education's contribution to young people's physical activity levels. *Health Education Research, 20*(1), 14-23.

Flegal, K.M., Carroll, M.D., Ogden, C.L., & Johnson, C.L. (2002). Prevalence and trends in obesity among US adults, 1999-2000. *Journal of the American Medical Association, 288*(14), 1723-1727.

Gruber, J.J. (1985). Physical activity and self-esteem development and children: A meta analysis. *American Academy of Physical Education Papers, 19,* 30-48.

Kohl III, H.W., & Hobbs, K.E. (1998). Development of physical activity behaviors among children and adolescents. *Pediatrics, 101,* 549-554.

Mahar, M.T., Murphy, S.K., Rowe, D.A., Golden, J., Shields, A.T., & Raedeke, T.D. (2006). Effects of a classroom-based program on physical activity and on-task behavior. *Medicine and Science in Sports and Exercise, 38*(12), 286-294.

Model School Wellness Policies. National Alliance for Nutrition and Activity. Available at www.schoolwellnesspolicies.org. Accessed June 25, 2007.

Moore, L.L., Lombardi, D.A., White, M.J., Campbell, J.L., Oliveria, S.A., & Ellison, R.C. (1991). Influences of parents' physical activity levels on activity levels of young children. *Journal of Pediatrics, 118,* 215-219.

Morgan, C.F., Beighle, A., & Pangrazi, R.P. (2007). What are the contributory and compensatory relationships between physical education and physical activity in children? *Research Quarterly in Exercise and Sport, 78*(5), 407-412.

Mota, J., Silva, P., Santos, M.P., Ribeiro, J.C., Oliverira, J., & Duarte, J.A. (2005). Physical activity and school recess time: Differences between the sexes and the relationship between children's playground physical activity and habitual physical activity. *Journal of Sport Science, 23*(3), 269-275.

Must, A., & Strauss, R.S. (1999). Risks and consequences of childhood and adolescent obesity. *International Journal of Obesity Related Metabolic Disorders, 23* (Suppl 2), S2-S11.

Nader, P.R., Sellers, D.E., Johnson, C.C., Perry, C.L., Stone, E.J., Cook, K.C., et al. (1996). The effect of adult participation in a school-based family intervention to improve children's diet and physical activity: The child and adolescent trial for cardiovascular health. *Preventive Medicine, 25,* 455-464.

National Association for Sport and Physical Education. (2000). *Appropriate practices for elementary school physical education.* Reston, VA: Author.

National Association for Sport and Physical Education. (2002). *Co-curricular physical activity and sport programs for middle school students.* Reston, VA: Author.

National Association for Sport and Physical Education. (2002). *Guidelines for after school physical activity and intramural sport programs.* Reston, VA: Author.

National Association for Sport and Physical Education. (2003). *What constitutes a quality physical education program?* Reston, VA: Author.

National Association for Sport and Physical Education. (2006). *101 tips for family fitness fun.* Reston, VA: Author.

National Association for Sport and Physical Education. (2006). *Recess for elementary school students.* Reston, VA: Author.

Ornelas, I.J., Perreira, K.M., & Ayala, G.X. (2007). Parental influences on adolescent physical activity: A longitudinal study. *International Journal of Behavioral Nutrition and Physical Activity, 4,* 3.

Pangrazi, R.P., Corbin, C.B., & Welk, G.J. (1996). Physical activity for children and youth. *Journal of Physical Education, Recreation and Dance, 67*(4), 38-43.

Pate, R.R., Small, M.L., Ross, J.G., Young, J.C., Flint, K.H., & Warren, C.W. (1995). School physical education. *Journal of School Health, 65*(8), 312-318.

Powers, H.S., Conway, T.L., McKenzie, T.L., Sallis, J.F., & Marshall, S.J. (2002). Participation in extracurricular physical activity programs at middle schools. *Research Quarterly for Exercise and Sport*, 73(2), 187-192.

Public Health Service. (1991). *Healthy people 2000*. Washington, DC: U.S. Government Printing Office.

Ridgers, N.D., & Stratton, G. (2005). Physical activity during school recess: The Liverpool sporting playgrounds project. *Pediatric Exercise Science*, 17, 281-290.

Sallis, J.F. (1994). Influences of physical activity of children, adolescents, and adults or determinants of active living. *President's Council on Physical Fitness and Sports Research Digest*, 1(7), 1-8.

Sallis, J.F., Alcaraz, J.E., McKenzie, T.L., Hovell, M.F., Kolody, B., & Nader, P.R. (1992). Parental behavior in relation to physical activity and fitness in 9-year-old children. *Sports Medicine*, 146, 1383-1388.

Sallis, J.F., & McKenzie, T.L. (1991). Physical education role in public health. *Research Quarterly for Exercise and Sport*, 62, 124-137.

Sallis, J.F., McKenzie, T.L., Alcaraz, J.E., Kolody, B., Faucette, N., & Hovell, M.F. (1997). The effects of a 2-year physical education program (SPARK) on physical activity and fitness in elementary school students. *American Journal of Public Health*, 87, 1328-1334.

Sallis, J.F., Patterson, T.L., McKenzie, T.L., & Nader, P.R. (1988). Family variables and physical activity in pre-school children. *Journal of Development and Behavioral Pediatrics*, 9(2), 57-61.

Sallis, J.F., Simons-Morton, B.G., Sothe, E.J., Corbin, C.B., Epstein, L.H., Faucette, N., Iannotti, R.J., Killen, J.D., Klesges, R.C., Petray, C., Rowland, T.W., & Taylor, W.C. (1992). Determinants of physical activity and interventions in youth. *Medicine and Science in Sport and Exercise*, 24 (Suppl), S248-S257.

Trost, S.G., Pate, R.R., Sallis, J.F., Freedson, P.S., Taylor, W.C., Dowda, M., & Sirard, J. (2002). Age and gender differences in objectively measured physical activity in youth. *Medicine and Science in Sports and Exercise*, 34(2), 350-355.

U.S. Centers for Disease Control and Prevention. (2001). Increasing physical activity: A report on recommendations of the task force on community prevention services. *Morbidity and Mortality Weekly Report*, 50 (RR-18), 1-16.

U.S. Department of Health and Human Services. (2004). *Physical activity and the health of young people*. Atlanta: Centers for Disease Control and Prevention.

U.S. Department of Health and Human Services, Centers for Disease Control and Prevention. (2002). Prevalence of overweight among children and adolescents: United States, 1999. Atlanta: National Center for Health Statistics. Available at www.cdc.gov/nchs/products/pubs/pubd/hestats/overwght99.htm.

Vincent, S., & Pangrazi, R.P. (2002). Does reactivity exist in children when measuring activity level with pedometers? *Pediatric Exercise*, 14, 56-63.

Welk, G.J., Morrow, G.J., & Falls, H.B. (Eds.). *Fitnessgram reference guide*. Dallas: Cooper Institute.

Welk, G.J., Wood, K., & Morss, G. (2003). Parental influences on physical activity in children: An exploration of potential mechanisms. *Pediatric Exercise Science*, 15, 19-33.

Whitehead, J.R. (1993). Physical activity and intrinsic motivation. *President's Council on Physical Fitness and Sports Research Digest*, 1(2), 1-8.

Whitehead, J.R., & Corbin, C.B. (2000). Self-esteem in children and youth: The role of sport and physical education. In K.R. Fox (Ed.), *The physical self: From motivation to well-being* (pp. 175-203). Champaign, IL: Human Kinetics.

World Health Organization. (2001). *Obesity: Preventing and managing the global epidemic. Report of a WHO consultation on obesity, 3-5 June 1997, Geneva*. Geneva: World Health Organization. WHO/NUT/NCD 98.1.

REFERENCES

Anderson, R., Crespo, S., Bartlett, L., Cheskin, L., & Pratt, M. (1998). Relationship of physical activity and television watching with body weight and level of fatness among children: Results from the third National Health and Nutrition Examination Survey. *Journal of the American Medical Association*, 279, 938-942.

Caspersen, C.J., Powell, K.E., & Christenson, G.M. (1985). Physical activity, exercise, and physical fitness: Definitions and distinctions for health-related research. *Public Health Reports*, 100(2), 126-131.

Castelli, D., Hillmann, C., Buck S., & Erwin, H. (2007). Physical fitness and academic achievement in third and fifth grade students. *Journal of Sport and Exercise Psychology*. 29, 239-252.

Council on Sports Medicine and Fitness and Council on School Health. (2006). Active healthy living: Prevention of childhood obesity through increased physical activity. *Pediatrics*, 117, 1834-1842.

Dwyer, T., Coonan, W., Leitch, D., Hetzel, B., & Baghurst, T. (1983). An investigation of the effects of daily physical activity on the health of primary school students in South Australia. *International Journal of Epidemiologists*, 12(3), 308-313.

Malina, R.M. (1996). Tracking of physical activity and physical fitness across the lifespan. *Research Quarterly for Sport and Exercise*, 67, 48-57.

Mokdad, A., Marks, J., Stroup, D., & Gerbending, J. (2004). Actual causes of death in the United States, 2000. *Journal of the American Medical Association*, 291(10), 1238-1245.

National Association for Sport and Physical Education. (1992). *Outcomes of a quality physical education program*. Reston, VA: Author.

National Association for Sport and Physical Education. (2004a). *Moving into the future: National standards for physical education* (2nd ed.). Reston, VA: Author.

National Association for Sport and Physical Education. (2004b). *Physical activity for children: A statement of guidelines for children ages 5-12*. Reston, VA: Author.

National Association for Sport and Physical Education. (2006). *Shape of the nation report*. Reston, VA: Author.

National Association for Sport and Physical Education. (2008). *Comprehensive school physical activity program* [Position statement]. Reston, VA: Author.

Payne, V.G., & Morrow, J.R. Jr. (1993). Exercise and VO2max in children: A meta-analysis. *Research Quarterly for Exercise and Sport*, 64(3), 305-313.

Pellegrini, A. & Bohn, C. (2005). The Role of Recess in Children's Cognitive Performance and School Adjustment. *Educational Researcher*, 34 (1), 13-19.

Pellegrini, A.D., Huberty, P.D., & Jones, I. (1995). The effects of recess timing on children's playground and classroom behaviors. *American Educational Research Journal*, 32(4), 845-864.

Sallis, J.F., McKenzie, T.L., Kolody, B., Lewis, M., Marshall, S., & Rosengard, P. (1999). Effects of health-related physical education on academic achievement: Project SPARK. *Research Quarterly in Sport and Exercise*, 70(2), 127-134.

Sallis, J.F., Patrick, K., & Long, B.L. (1994). An overview of international consensus conference on physical activity guidelines for adolescents. *Pediatric Exercise Science*, 6, 299-301.

Shephard, R.J. (1997). Curricular physical activity and academic performance. *Pediatric Exercise Science*, 9, 113-126.

Sibley, B. A., & Etnier, J. L. (2003). The relationship between physical activity and cognition in children: A meta-analysis. *Pediatric Exercise Science*, 15, 243-256.

Strong, W., Malina, R., Blimkie, C., Daniels, S., Dishman, R., Gutin, B., Hergenroeder, A., Must, A., Nixon, P., & Pivarnik, J. (2005). Evidence based physical activity for school-age youth. *Journal of Pediatrics*, 146(6), 732-737.

Tremblay, M.S., Inman, J.W., & Williams, J.D. (2000). The relationship between physical activity, self-esteem, and academic achievement in 12 year old children. *Pediatric Exercise Science*, 12(3), 312-323.

U.S. Department of Education. (2002). Public Law 107-110. The No Child Left Behind Act of 2001. Washington, DC: U.S. Government Printing Office.

U.S. Department of Education. (2008). Carol M. White Physical Education Program. Available at www.ed.gov/programs.

U.S. Department of Health and Human Services. (1996). *Physical activity and health: A report of the surgeon general*. Atlanta: U.S. Department of Health and Human Services, Centers for Disease Control and Prevention, National Center for Chronic Disease Prevention and Health Promotion.

U.S. Department of Health and Human Services [USDHHS]. (2001). *The surgeon general's call to action to prevent and decrease overweight and obesity*. Atlanta: U.S. Department of Health and Human Services, Centers for Disease Control and Prevention, National Center for Chronic Disease Prevention and Health Promotion.

U.S. Department of Health and Human Services. (2004). Section 204 of Public Law 108-265—June 30, 2004, Child Nutrition and WIC Reauthorization Act of 2004.

U.S. Department of Health and Human Services, Centers for Disease Control and Prevention. (1997). Guidelines for school and community programs to promote lifelong physical activity among young people. *Morbidity and Mortality Weekly Report*, 46(RR-6), 1-36.

U.S. Department of Health and Human Services, Centers for Disease Control and Prevention. (2008). Physical activity guidelines for americans. Available at www.health.gov/paguidelines. Accessed September 2009.

2

The School Wellness Program and Physical Activity

OVERVIEW

Schools alone cannot solve the obesity epidemic and other health concerns in the United States. However, it is reasonable to assume that without school policy and program change, the present trends will continue. In 2004, federal legislation required all school districts involved in a federally funded meal program to establish a district wellness policy by the 2006-2007 school year (U.S. Department of Health and Human Services [USDHHS], 2004). The purpose of this chapter is to guide the reader in establishing an effective school wellness program.

CHAPTER OUTCOMES

This chapter will help you

- interpret national- and state-level policy, programs, and actions related to physical activity;

- identify national-level organizations and their critical role in school wellness programs;

- determine state-, district-, and school-level progress toward creating nutrition, physical education, and physical activity policy;

- determine how to create collective efficacy and stakeholder support;

- explore the meaning, purpose, and justifications for establishing a school wellness program;

- identify how to form a school wellness committee and coordinate a school wellness program;

- describe the process of developing, implementing, and evaluating a school wellness plan;

- assimilate ideas from success stories for avoiding potential barriers; and

- explore potential funding opportunities.

IN THIS CHAPTER

Improving the health status of children has long been a fundamental component of education in the United States. Guiding students toward healthy and active lifestyles is therefore not a new role for schools. However, in many school districts, a commitment to this role has either disappeared completely or taken a back seat to academic accountability—a decision that has proven counterproductive. Research now supports the idea that providing opportunities for physical activity will increase academic performance and decrease behavior problems. Stakeholders initiating systemic change in our nation's health status support the belief that schools can and must promote healthy eating habits, quality physical education, and multiple opportunities for physical activity.

At the turn of the 21st century, the U.S. Department of Health and Human Services (USDHHS), the Institute of Medicine, the Centers for Disease Control and Prevention (CDC), and other leading health organizations identified overweight and obesity as a critical public health risk that was reaching an epidemic level. In 2001, Surgeon General David Satcher released *The Surgeon General's Call to Action to Prevent and Decrease Overweight and Obesity* (USDHHS, 2001). Satcher addressed concerns about the health issues involved in the obesity epidemic and outlined strategies to increase physical education and healthier food options in the schools. In response, Action for Healthy Kids (AFHK), a partnership of more than 60 national organizations and government agencies representing education, health, fitness, and nutrition, was launched at the Healthy Schools Summit in 2002. Action for Healthy Kids began the initiative to improve nutrition and increase physical activity in schools.

Also in 2002, Congress charged the Institute of Medicine (IOM) with developing an action plan to decrease the number of obese children and youth. The committee of 19 experts in child health, obesity, nutrition, physical activity, and public health examined environmental factors to identify approaches for prevention. The committee took on the challenge and in September 2004 released a report, *Preventing Childhood Obesity: Health in the Balance,* that identified causes and influences as well as strategies for change on the part of the following:

- Federal, state, and local governments
- Industry and media
- Health care professionals
- Community and nonprofit organizations
- State and local education authorities and schools
- Parents and families (for more information, visit www.iom.edu)

The following were IOM recommendations specific to schools:

- Improve the nutritional quality of foods and beverages served and sold in schools.
- Increase opportunities for physical activity both during and after school.
- Implement school-based interventions to reduce children's screen time.

- Develop and implement programs for staffing and teaching about wellness, healthful eating, and physical activity (IOM, 2004).

In 2003, a report from the Healthy Schools for Healthy Kids, sponsored by the Robert Wood Johnson Foundation, justified the need for states to develop and implement policies for nutrition and physical activity. The recommendation was for states to establish a baseline requirement for schools, with encouragement to *exceed* the requirements.

Providing what some have termed the launching pad for the school wellness movement, the Child Nutrition and WIC (Women, Infants, and Children) Reauthorization Act of 2004 required all school districts involved in a federally funded meal program to establish a district wellness policy by the 2006-2007 school year. Specifically, school wellness policies were to include

- goals for nutrition education,
- goals for school meals programs,
- nutritional guidelines for all foods available on campus during the school day,
- goals for physical activity,
- goals for other school-based activities designed to promote wellness, and
- a plan for measurement and evaluation (USDHHS, 2004).

State-, District-, and School-Level Response

Nationwide education efforts, while influential, do not always have a direct effect on schools. The United States, unlike many other countries, does not have one recognized education system; rather it has 50 state-level education systems with distinct sets of regulations, governance systems, and traditions. Each state determines how to balance authority and responsibilities between state and local districts, often giving major responsibilities for policies governing schools to individual school districts throughout the state.

The lack of a national authority over educational policy has meant that the response to the Child Nutrition and WIC Reauthorization Act of 2004 and other initiatives differs across states, districts, and individual schools. The National Association of State Boards of Education (NASBE) in 2007 documented that at least 48 states had met some of the intended expectations of the legislation. Forty states produced or provided policy guidance documents and resources to help local school districts create wellness policies. At least 19 state legislatures, boards of education, and agencies adopted requirements for policy evaluation and accountability. Three states, Arkansas, Rhode Island, and South Carolina, developed particularly compelling policy

The school has a responsibility to provide nutritious meals.

strategies by integrating local wellness policies with the general education accountability system (e.g., school report card). This action was intended to ensure that schools address nutrition and physical activity and that these issues carry the same status as academic and other important areas. Arkansas, Rhode Island, and South Carolina's initiatives demonstrate a commitment to promoting healthy and active students. Although the data cited here reflect that most states are making some effort to aid districts, according to the AFHK report (2008), only 54% of local school districts are actually meeting the minimum federal requirements. This percentage reflects slow progress in initiating new wellness and physical activity programs in schools.

A summary report on the physical education and physical activity components of the School Health Policies and Programs Study (SHPPS) of 2006 (Lee et al., 2007) indicates that improvements, though in some cases limited, have occurred in most states and districts since 2000. The SHPPS is conducted every six years and is arguably the most comprehensive study of U.S. school health policies and programs at the state, district, and school levels. An analysis of the data from 2000 through 2006 indicates the following changes on the state level:

- The percentage of states that employ a state-level coordinator for physical education or a named administrator increased from 68.6% to 88.2%.
- The percentage that require or encourage districts to follow national standards or guidelines for physical education increased from 59.2% to 76%.
- The percentage that require physical education teachers to have an undergraduate or graduate degree in physical education increased from 51.5% to 64.7%.

At the district level the following changes occurred:

- The percentage of districts that require or encourage schools to follow national standards or guidelines for physical education increased from 65.6% to 81.4%.
- The percentage that have adopted a policy mandating or recommending elementary physical education increased from 82.6% to 93.3%.
- The percentage that require regularly scheduled recess increased from 46.3% to 57.1%; the percentage that require a minimum of 30 minutes of daily recess increased from 25.5% to 38.5%.

- The percentage that wrote policies not allowing exemption from recess for behavior issues increased from 19.2% to 36.5%.

School-level data from the 2006 SHPPS report are separated into physical education and physical activity. Data of interest for school-level physical education indicated the following:

- A low percentage of schools met the National Association for Sport and Physical Education (NASPE) weekly recommendation of 150 minutes of physical education in elementary school and 225 for middle and high school. Only 3.8% of elementary schools, 7.9% of middle schools, and 2.1% of high schools reported meeting the minimum number of minutes. These numbers have not significantly increased or decreased since 2000.
- A pupil/teacher ratio was established for physical education classes in only 36.5% of the schools. The median maximum ratio reported was 29 to 1.

The following data on physical activity were reported:

- 43.6% of elementary schools, 66.8% of middle schools, and 22% of high schools provided physical activity breaks during the school day.
- 44.3% supported or promoted walking or biking to and from school.
- Physical activity clubs or intramurals were offered by 49.5% of elementary schools, 48.5% of middle schools, and 44.8% of high schools.
- 54.6% of schools paid staff to run before- or after-school programs.
- 22.9% provided transportation home for students participating in after-school physical activity.
- 35% charged a fee for after-school physical activity, and 86.1% waived fees based on specific income limits.

The *Shape of the Nation Report* (2006) was produced with a partnership of NASPE and the American Heart Association (AHA). The report is derived from a questionnaire completed by state physical education coordinators or the named administrator. Of note, most states have very general or minimal requirements, as they delegate policy responsibilities to local school districts. *Shape of the Nation*, reporting on all 50 states and the District of Columbia, indicates the following:

- 36 states mandate elementary school physical education.
- 33 states mandate middle or junior high school physical education.
- 42 states mandate physical education for at least one year in the high schools.
- 18 states grant exemptions or waivers from physical education.
- 27 states permit students to substitute other activities such as ROTC, interscholastic sports, or marching band for physical education.
- Only two states, Illinois and Massachusetts, require physical education in every grade (K-12). New Jersey and Rhode Island require physical education in grades 1 through 12. However, all four of these states allow exemptions or waivers or substitutions of other activities.
- Only two states meet the recommended NASPE minute requirements for elementary schools of 150 minutes per week: Louisiana and New Jersey. Only one state meets the 225-minute recommendation for middle or junior high schools: Montana. Three states (Indiana, Montana, and South Carolina) and the District of Columbia meet the 225-minute recommendation for high school, but this may not be for all four years of high school.

In the same report, NASPE and AHA recommend that physical education become the cornerstone of a comprehensive school physical activity plan. Along with physical education, they encourage schools to develop a comprehensive approach to health and physical activity including recess, activity clubs, intramural sports, activity breaks, walking programs, health education, nutritional food choices, and faculty and staff wellness programs.

Individual schools often find it difficult to establish the policies needed for a comprehensive school wellness program inclusive of policies, practices, programs, and interventions. The reason is that comprehensive school wellness programs require resources and the inclusion and cooperation of administrators, teachers, school nutrition personnel, parents, and school health personnel across school levels to achieve real change. Effective comprehensive school wellness programs also require schools to make wellness a priority in a school climate that is primarily accountable for academic achievement.

State leaders can use their leverage to enforce policies that promote school wellness. State and local districts should

- create policy to increase physical education requirements that is backed with sufficient funding;
- staff the programs with a physical education specialist;
- require that new schools be built with adequate facilities for physical education and for extended physical activity programs, and develop a plan to add facilities to existing schools;
- provide support and funding for staff and teacher training to implement nutrition and physical activity initiatives;
- maintain an active district-level school health council with a school health coordinator to guide local schools in developing a school wellness plan; and
- build in accountability for enacting policies.

Schools also face a challenge in achieving stakeholder support. Participants and school personnel who are required to implement programs or are held accountable for results need to be brought in at the ground level. They need to be involved in the development of the plan and have an opportunity to provide input into the assessment process. Complete agreement of all stakeholders is often difficult, making the strategies used to gain support in a school wellness program critical.

Gaining Stakeholder Support

The success of a school wellness program depends on the involvement and support of several groups, including school leaders, school personnel, parents, students, and community members. School leaders include building leaders such as principals and assistant principals, as well as district-level leaders and school board members. School personnel who need to be involved are the teachers and all staff, including teaching assistants, custodial, food services, nurses, guidance counselors, and administrative assistants. Additional involvement may come from public health professionals, faculty at a nearby university, or local wellness advocates. The challenge is to gain the support and involvement of all groups to ensure success.

One strategic approach is to strive for collective efficacy, a belief that one's involvement can have a positive effect. In the case of school wellness policy, stakeholders may thrive on the belief that they can contribute to change and improve the health of children. Others may be more motivated by the potential of academic success. Still others will support an action or change only if they are supported in the process (i.e., teachers need to feel support from principals and principals from superintendents). With collective efficacy, individuals and groups of people are more willing to work toward a common goal. The challenge, as in any new initiative, is to discover the motivation and level of engagement of individuals or groups that are critical to successfully reaching the goals.

A research study (Parks, Solomon, & Lee, 2007) designed to measure teacher perceptions of the implementation of a school wellness plan provides a good example of stakeholders' motivation. Factors that influenced most teachers to be motivated and execute the plan to integrate more physical activity into the school day were primarily institutional:

- Encouragement from the principal, other teachers, the physical education specialist, and students
- Hearing success stories from other teachers
- Compatibility of integration with the teachers' present values and goals
- Inclusion of the plan in the school improvement plan where an improvement plan was required
- The feeling that the program's success was dependent on their effort

Another strategy toward gaining stakeholder support is to be knowledgeable of group member perceptions. As evidenced by an AFHK report in 2008, those in a position to be the most influential in the school wellness program are school administrators, and they are actually the least involved and perceived to be the least supportive. Action for Healthy Kids (2008) conducted research with 2400 stakeholders throughout the nation and found both commonalities and gaps in perceptions of effect. When asked who was in the best position to move a school wellness plan forward, respondents unanimously indicated school administrators. When asked who was the least supportive of school wellness programs, the response again was school administrators. Individuals involved in leadership roles tended to perceive that school wellness efforts were much more effective than did those more directly involved in the programs, such as teachers, parents, community, and food service personnel.

The following are selected questions and statistics on responses from the 2008 AFHK report:

- Do schools have effective wellness policies encouraging proper nutrition?

  - 72% of superintendents and 61% of principals, compared to 53% of food service professionals, responded positively.
- Do schools have effective wellness policies encouraging daily physical activity?
  - 68% of superintendents and 59% of principals, compared to 35% of physical education teachers, responded positively.
- Are schools implementing their wellness policies?
  - 77% of superintendents and 54% of principals responded positively, whereas 72% or more of physical education teachers and community health professionals responded *negatively*.
- Are schools monitoring implementation of school wellness policies and evaluating results?
  - 60% of superintendents believed they were, while 65% or more of all other respondents disagreed.
- Do schools engage wellness committees?
  - Two-thirds of the superintendents and half of the principals claimed that they did, while over 60% of all other respondents felt that most schools did not.
- Are parents supporting wellness efforts?
  - Over 70% of all respondents, including parents themselves, felt that parents did not do a good job of encouraging physical activity and healthy eating habits.
- Are schools educating parents on the need for more physical activity and nutritious eating habits?
  - The majority of all groups responding agreed that schools did not take opportunities to provide guidance to parents.

The Role of School Administrators and Teachers

In a school wellness program, all stakeholders play an important part; but the people who actually implement the program, administrators and teachers, must be in concert to decrease the perception gap and to achieve success. Administrators and teachers may not always be clear on their role in a school wellness initiative. The following lists suggest the roles of school administrators and teachers, respectively.

To ensure success of a school wellness program, school administrators should

The school wellness committee meets to develop and implement the schoolwide physical activity plan.

- make school wellness a priority and resource it accordingly;
- make school wellness a part of the school improvement plan, with a full assessment and reporting plan;
- appoint a physical activity director or coordinator (usually the physical education teacher);
- communicate success to the district office;
- communicate success to parents and the community;
- recognize efforts of teacher and student involvement; and
- provide adequate teacher training to implement the program.

To ensure success of a school wellness program, teachers should

- include health education in the curriculum;
- provide regular developmentally appropriate physical activity breaks in the day;
- agree to not use physical activity as punishment or remove children from physical activity as punishment;

- encourage children to be physically active and to eat healthily, and promote their successes;
- promote physical activity and healthy living through bulletin boards, posters, and other visuals;
- communicate to parents regarding how to guide children on nutrition and physical activity and ask them to be involved in school initiatives; and
- document required information for plan accountability.

Developing a School Wellness Plan

A school wellness plan is the foundation of the school wellness program and begins with the formation of a committee. The school wellness committee and the resulting plan should be a part of the school improvement program when schools are required to have one. The school improvement committee should provide an overview of the roles and responsibility of the school wellness committee before committee members are selected. As the committee is established, care should be taken to recruit a diverse group of individuals who have a vested interest in the program's success. Potential members include the following:

- Administrators
- Physical educators
- Health educators
- Dance teachers
- School counselors
- School nurses
- Several teachers representing different grade levels (elementary schools) or disciplines (secondary schools)
- Parents
- Students
- School food service managers
- District-level physical education coordinators
- District school meal program director
- A member of the district school health council
- Community members (stakeholders who can help facilitate the plan)
  - A member of the city or county recreation department
  - An expert on nutrition, physical education, or physical activity
  - A local university professor from the health or physical education department
  - Health care, social services, local health department representatives

After the committee is established, the process of developing a school wellness plan begins. The first step is to research existing policy; this is followed by a baseline assessment of the school practices currently in place. On the basis of this information, the committee will develop and implement an action plan and then build awareness and support among the stakeholders. Once the plan is implemented, some or all members of the committee will continue to serve in the role of monitoring, evaluating, and maintaining the plan.

Research and Assessment

The purpose of initial research is to gain an understanding of what needs to happen, to discover justification for changes, and to learn ways to initiate change. The best way for the committee to accomplish the research process is to divide into two subcommittees based on areas of interest or expertise: one for nutrition and another for physical education and physical activity. Table 2.1 suggests potential subcommittees. Once the subcommittees are organized, each group can elect a chairperson, determine research responsibilities, and establish a research completion date. The following are potential areas of inquiry regarding nutrition, physical education, and physical activity:

- What state and district laws, policies, or recommendations currently exist?
- How are policies shaped in the district?

TABLE 2.1

Subcommittees for the School Wellness Program

Nutrition	Physical education and physical activity
School food service manager	Administrator
District meal program director	Physical educator
School nurse	Dance teacher
Students	School counselor
Parents	Teachers
Health teacher	Parents
Administrator	Students
Member of the district school health council	Member of the city or county recreation department
Community stakeholder with expertise in nutrition	Community stakeholder with expertise in physical education or physical activity

- What federal or state regulations affect these policies?
- What recommendations exist from national governing agencies (e.g., NASPE, CDC)?
- What local organizations share interest?
- How does the health status of our state compare to that of others?
- What initiatives are in place within other schools in the district, state, or nation?
- What tools and technical advice are available for implementing action plans (e.g., AFHK, California LEAN [Leaders Encouraging Activity and Nutrition], Consolidated School Health Program, and CDC's Division of Adolescent and School Health [DASH])?

A critical part of developing a wellness plan is to establish a baseline assessment of what is currently happening in the school. This process includes determining existing strengths and deficiencies and verifying accountability to district and state policies. A preassessment will yield data to aid in school and community awareness and support and will provide justification for funding requests.

Several instruments are available for self-assessment that will be useful in the initial research process. One assessment tool, used in 46 states, is the School Health Index (SHI) developed as a part of the Consolidated School Health Program (CSHP). The SHI is both a self-assessment and a planning guide that is available free of cost from most state departments of education and the federal CDC Web site. The instrument is divided into eight modules structured around the CSHP. A committee may use the entire SHI or individual components. As with any model, the school wellness committee may choose to use other assessments or design their own. A sample committee-designed self-assessment is included in figure 2.1. The findings obtained from the baseline assessment will provide the information needed to begin an action plan.

Developing and Implementing the Action Plan

After completing an assessment of the current status, the committee is ready to develop and implement an action plan. With use of the ideas from this text, from the initial research inquiry, and from the baseline assessment, several steps will help in developing and implementing a plan for a school wellness program.

Step One: Create Short- and Long-Term Goals

The first step is to create short- and long-term goals. When writing goals, keep the following suggestions in mind:

Use the criteria for SMART goal setting:

a. **S**pecific goals should emphasize what you want to happen.

   i. What are you going to do and accomplish (e.g., develop, plan, build, schedule)?

   ii. Why is this important to do?

   iii. How are you going to do it?

   iv. Clearly define what you want to do and use specific language. For example, instead of setting a goal to increase physical activity in the classroom environment, set a goal for classroom teachers to schedule a 3- to 5-minute transition break between at least two content changes every day.

b. **M**easurable goals can be accomplished goals. If you cannot measure something, you cannot complete it. If you can measure progress, you can stay on track and reach your target dates. There can be short- and long-term measurements built into goals.

c. **A**ttainable goals are reachable goals and make it easier to stay committed. Write attainable goals that stretch you to the point of seeing a difference.

d. **R**ealistic goals are more likely to be accomplished. A realistic goal must be written based on where you are now and what is reasonable to accomplish in your situation. Set goals that can be attained, but with effort. Goals that are too high will set the stage for failure, while goals that are too low will send the message that you are not really determined to accomplish change.

e. **T**imely goals allow for a clear plan of action. The goal will typically not happen without a clear completion date and target to work toward. The time frame that you set must also be attainable and realistic.

Step Two: Prioritize Goals

The next step is to prioritize the goals. There are several options for prioritizing:

- Short-term and long-term items
- Easy-to-implement and difficult-to-implement items

FIGURE 2.1

Is Your School a Healthy and Physically Active Environment?

Take this survey to see.

Physical Education

Yes	No		
☐	☐	**1.**	Do your students have physical education a minimum of two days per week?
☐	☐	**2.**	Do your students have daily physical education (or 150 minutes a week) as recommended by NASPE and CDC?
☐	☐	**3.**	Does your school follow guidelines for the appropriate amount of class time in physical education (K-2: 30-minute periods; 3-5: 30- to 45-minute periods)?
☐	☐	**4.**	Does your school have adequate indoor and outdoor facilities to accommodate quality physical education a minimum of two days per week? Check all that apply:

_____ An indoor teaching station for each physical education class
_____ A paved area and grassy area for physical education
_____ A paved area and grassy area for recess separate from physical education

Yes	No		
☐	☐	**5.**	Does the physical education class have the same pupil/teacher ratio as a classroom?
☐	☐	**6.**	Are classroom teachers prohibited from keeping students out of physical education class as punishment for misbehavior or unfinished class work?

Recess

Yes	No		
☐	☐	**7.**	Are all students provided at least 20 minutes of unstructured daily recess?
☐	☐	**8.**	Are classroom teachers prohibited from keeping students out of recess as punishment for misbehavior or unfinished class work?
☐	☐	**9.**	Does the recess environment promote physical activity through the use of large apparatus (e.g., climbing equipment, swings, slides, basketball goals) and availability of play equipment (e.g., balls, ropes)?

Teacher-Led Initiatives

Yes	No		
☐	☐	**10.**	Do ALL classroom teachers provide opportunities for additional movement during the school day? Check all that apply:

_____ Energizers or transitional movement breaks
_____ Integrated movement during lessons
_____ Walking breaks
_____ Video- or teacher-led movement activities
_____ Other opportunities: _____

Yes	No		
☐	☐	**11.**	Do teachers promote physical activity through posters, bulletin boards, and other reading material?

Schoolwide Initiatives

Yes	No		
☐	☐	**12.**	Are there before- or after-school opportunities for physical activity? Check all that apply:

        _____ Walking clubs or jump rope clubs
        _____ Intramurals
        _____ Other opportunities: _____

Yes	No		
☐	☐	**13.**	Are there schoolwide physical activity opportunities during the day? Check all that apply:

        _____ Schoolwide walking program
        _____ Morning exercise videos
        _____ Teacher- or student-led exercise time
        _____ Other opportunities: _____

Yes	No		
☐	☐	**14.**	Are there special events that promote physical activity? Check all that apply:

        _____ Jump Rope for Heart
        _____ Field Day
        _____ Walk-to-school program
        _____ Diabetes Walk
        _____ Other opportunities: _____

Staff, Parent, Community Involvement

Yes	No		
☐	☐	**15.**	Are the administrators, faculty, and school staff offered a before- or after-school fitness program or discounts to local gyms?
☐	☐	**16.**	Does the school promote community-based physical activity programs? Check all that apply:

        _____ Posters or bulletin boards
        _____ Newsletters or brochures
        _____ E-mails to parents
        _____ Web site advertisement
        _____ Guest speakers
        _____ Local cable network
        _____ Other opportunities: _____

Yes	No		
☐	☐	**17.**	Is there communication with parents to encourage more healthy and active practices at home? Check all that apply:

        _____ Newsletters
        _____ E-mails
        _____ Web site advertisement
        _____ Other: _____

Yes	No		
☐	☐	**18.**	Are there evening or weekend school-sponsored activities to encourage healthy and active practices for the family? Check all that apply:

        _____ Family fitness night
        _____ Guest speakers at PTA/PTO meetings
        _____ Open gym time
        _____ Family walking clubs
        _____ Other opportunities: _____

(continued)

(continued)

Healthy Food Practices

Yes	No		
☐	☐	19.	Do the school lunches meet today's health and nutrition guidelines?
☐	☐	20.	Are healthy snacks and drinks the only options children can bring or be provided at school?
☐	☐	21.	Do students have at least 20 minutes to eat their meal after they have been served?
☐	☐	22.	Have vending machines or other modes of selling unhealthy snacks and beverages been eliminated from your school or replaced with only healthy options?
☐	☐	23.	Do classroom teachers teach health, safety, and responsible social behavior?

Support

☐	☐	24.	Are all teachers, staff, and administrators on board to make your school a healthy and physically active environment?
☐	☐	25.	Does your district office support nutrition, physical education, and physical activity initiatives?

How does your school add up?   Your total: _____

22-25 **Congratulations!** Your school is a model healthy and active school.

17-21 **Way to go!** Your school is very healthy and active. How can you become a model school?

12-16 Your school is fairly active. Set goals for immediate- and long-term improvement.

0-11 There are many ways to make your school more active. Start today!

Your strongest areas:

Your weakest areas:

Where can immediate change take place?

What requires a long-term plan of action?

- No-budget, low-budget, and high-budget items (high-budget items may include an additional goal of how to obtain funding)
- Items required by law (immediacy) or recommended by committee

Step Three: Develop a Separate Implementation Plan for Each Goal

Once goals are written, the logistics must be thoughtfully planned. A separate implementation plan will be needed for each goal, as the tasks and strategies will vary as well as the number of people involved. Each goal should include the following:

1. A description of the expected outcome
2. Specific action steps, procedures, or strategies to meet the outcome
3. A realistic time line for each goal or increment of a goal
4. A list of necessary resources to aid all participants
5. A plan to provide any necessary training
6. A list of potential barriers and solutions to overcome them
7. A plan of communication to build awareness and support
8. An evaluation plan

Building Awareness and Support for Your Plan

The way in which the plan is communicated will shape how it is viewed and accepted. Be sure to communicate with all stakeholders and identify those that are the most supportive. These individuals will help create acceptance among others. The success rate is higher when key audiences are enthusiastic about change and embrace the goals and action plan. The primary objective here is to publicize and gain acceptance from as many stakeholders as possible. Specific strategies may be necessary for different groups. Communication is ongoing and not simply an initial strategy to gain acceptance. Strategies for building awareness and support are intended to inform, maintain motivation, share progress, remind people of time lines, and celebrate accomplishments; they include the following:

- Strategically placing someone whom the intended audience respects in the role of communicating to each stakeholder group
- Being aware of how each group may be affected (both positively and negatively) and have a plan to alleviate concerns

- Using repetition and communicating through varied channels (e.g., oral communication, e-mail, letters, local cable channels, flyers, posters, person to person, Web sites, newsletters, radio)

Monitoring and Maintaining the School Wellness Program

An important part of the school wellness program—and one most often neglected—is a plan for how to monitor, evaluate, and maintain the program. This process allows schools to determine exactly what is working and what is not. The plan can then be revised and improved if necessary. Monitoring and evaluating also provide the opportunity to communicate progress and celebrate successes.

A good evaluation plan does not need to be extensive, but it does need to be thorough. All goals should be evaluated specifically in relation to the written outcomes in the original plan. Part of the original plan should include strategies to monitor and evaluate, as well as a decision on who will be in charge of implementing the process and who needs to be informed of the progress and outcome achievements.

Successful Ideas for a School Wellness Program

The school wellness program, though planned and designed for an individual school, can benefit from sharing the ideas of other schools and districts. As discussed in the previous section, the school wellness committee begins by assessing the present status of the school nutrition, physical activity, and physical education programs. The following are ideas in each of these areas that schools have used and that others may consider:

The School Nutrition Program

- Encourage students to bring healthy snacks to school and make healthy choices at lunch.
  - In grades K through 12, use stickers to promote healthy choices.
  - For grades K through 12, adopt marketing techniques to use in the school that promote healthy choices (e.g., signs, posters, Web site advertisement, school news commercials).
- Include food or beverage contracts with outside vendors for healthy choices only.
- Limit the times when snacks are available to students, and do not allow foods defined as having no nutritional value (e.g., sodas, sugary

Many schools are eliminating snack machines or contracting for only healthy snack options.

candy) or high-fat or high-sugar products with limited nutritional value (candy bars, potato chips, pastries, high-fructose fruit drinks).

■ Allow only fund-raisers that promote healthy practices (e.g., have a fun run instead of a candy sale).

■ Allow only student reward programs that promote healthy practices (e.g., have a treasure chest instead of candy treats; have a skating party instead of a pizza party; provide an extra recess period).

■ Provide healthy food at school events, sending a message to families that the school promotes healthy eating.

■ Implement a quality school meal program.
- Provide healthy, tasty, and appealing food and beverage choices.
- Provide a salad, soup, sandwich, and potato bar instead of a la carte items.
- Follow Recommended Daily Allowance nutritional standards for designated age groups.
- Allot adequate lunchtime for students to eat a healthy meal.
- Hire qualified food service staff and include ongoing professional development.
- Use locally grown foods or have a school garden.
- Involve students in planning menus or selecting foods and beverages to be served or sold.

■ Provide staff development to train teachers to implement health education in grades K through 12. The curriculum should guide students toward understanding
- proper food choices,
- the Food Pyramid (www.MyPyramid.gov and figure 2.2),
- how food provides energy input that transfers to productive physical and cognitive output, and
- how to adopt and maintain a healthy lifestyle.

The School Physical Education Program

■ Hire qualified and certified physical education specialists only.

■ Provide opportunities for physical education teachers to attend professional development specific to physical education.

■ Establish accountability within the physical education program.
- Use CDC's Physical Education Curriculum Analysis Tool (PECAT) to evaluate, create, or enhance the physical education curriculum.
- Use the national physical education assessment program (PE Metrics), the South Carolina Physical Education Assessment Program (SCPEAP), or other forms of student and program assessment. (*Note:* Health-related fitness testing should be a part of physical education assessment, but should never be the sole measurement of student achievement or teacher accountability.)
- Require physical education teachers to submit a yearly plan demonstrating a curriculum that meets national or state standards.
- Devote at least 50% of class time to instruction that incorporates moderate or vigorous physical activity.

Figure 2.2   MyPyramid.

- Establish a pupil/teacher ratio equivalent to that of other curricular areas.
- Allocate funding for adequate and developmentally appropriate equipment as well as an ongoing operational budget to achieve objectives of the physical education program.
- Allocate or investigate funding for adequate facilities indoors and outdoors to achieve objectives of the physical education program.
- Establish a plan and schedule to increase physical education time without jeopardizing quality of the program (e.g., maintain pupil/teacher ratio equivalent to that in other curricular areas, hire only qualified and certified physical education specialists). Ideally,
  - grades K through 2 should meet for 30 minutes daily,
  - grades 3 through 5 should meet for 30 minutes daily or for 45 minutes three to five times per week, and
  - grades 6 through 12 should meet for a total of 225 minutes per week.
- Minimize the time physical education facilities are used for other purposes during the school day (e.g., school assemblies, school pictures, lunchroom overflow).
- Include a policy that prohibits teachers from keeping students out of physical education class for punishment or makeup work.
- Include a policy that does not permit exemptions from physical education. Adaptations rather than exemptions should be made for students with special needs or on religious grounds.
- Recognize one physical education teacher as the school physical activity director and provide release time, additional pay, or both for fulfilling these responsibilities.
- Present an annual PTA or PTO program that highlights quality physical education.

The School Physical Activity Program

- Have a schoolwide sneakers-only policy so students are prepared for safe and quality physical activity experiences throughout the day.
- Require regularly scheduled daily recess periods in elementary schools.
- Establish a school policy disallowing teachers from prohibiting students from recess for punishment of inappropriate behavior or incomplete class work.

- Require regular physical activity breaks 3 to 10 minutes in length for every hour of seat work in grades K through 12.
- Provide intramural experiences and physical activity clubs before, during, and after school to encourage participation of all students. The experiences should include competitive and noncompetitive traditional (individual, small group, and team sports) and nontraditional (e.g., dance, yoga, martial arts, Pilates, gymnastics, skateboarding, roller skating, table tennis) activities. Involve students through interest surveys.
- Provide longer lunch periods and incorporate physical activity time before or after the meal.
- Start a school walking program incorporating an incentive component (e.g., documentation of miles, pedometer steps, walk across the state).
- Provide parent- or volunteer-supervised open gym time for grades 6 through 12 during the physical education teacher's lunch or planning period or during extended day and weekends.
- Allocate funding for adequate and developmentally appropriate playground equipment or outdoor fitness equipment: outdoor walking track; paved play area with basketball goals; volleyball court; space for Four Square and tetherball; and open field play space.
- Allocate funding for adequate and developmentally appropriate equipment for recess play in elementary school and for physical activity breaks in middle and high school (e.g., balls, jump ropes).
- Organize regular physical activity special events (e.g., walk-a-thon, dances, field days, Olympics day, bicycle safety, kite day, roller skating).
- Start a walk- and bike-to-school program.

The success of a school wellness program is dependent on the people involved. All individuals are important, but parents and others in the community can play an essential role in the successful implementation of the school wellness plan. The next two sections present ideas that have been used to educate and involve these two important groups of stakeholders.

Working With Parents

Parents typically need and want to be knowledgeable about school events. When new policies and

Schools should advertise community physical activity opportunities.

programs are implemented, parents need to be informed and encouraged to support and adhere to the requirements. Despite daily media coverage of the obesity epidemic, parents need to learn from valuable resources. The school is in a position to educate parents on the need for proper nutrition and physical activity for their children. Information can be disseminated in many ways, including these:

- Host a family night or Saturday event that focuses on physical activity and health for all ages (e.g., dances, kite flying, walk/run, sports, and health promotion booths).
- Hold seminars on nutrition and physical activity.
- Communicate through newsletters, Web sites, and e-mails about physical activity opportunities in the school and community. Provide weekly physical activity and nutritional tips.
- Engage the students in motivating family members to be more physically active and menu conscious.
- Highlight successful program initiatives to parents.
- Encourage nutrition and physical activity speakers to be used at PTA and PTO programs.

To guarantee support and success, parents need to be involved in the school wellness program. The involvement can take many forms:

- Encourage parents to support their children's participation in physical activity, to be involved in physical activity with the family, and to be physically active role models.
- Encourage parents to practice good nutritional habits at home and promote healthy choices when taking children to restaurants.
- Have a parent committee in charge of communication, promotions, and announcements regarding physical activity and nutrition. Include activity calendars.
- Have a parent committee in charge of walk- and bike-to-school initiatives.
- Encourage parents to help in supervising before-, during-, and after-school physical activity clubs, intramurals, recess, or events.
- Encourage parents to host a donation drive of slightly used or new physical activity equipment.
- Encourage parents to host a fund-raiser to build or renovate the outdoor play area.

Working With the Community

Communication is key to educating the community about what is happening in the school. These are ways to inform the community:

- Use Web sites, letters, local cable stations, and e-mails.
  - Involve students in communications to community members.
- Highlight successful program initiatives to the community.

Schools should involve the community in activities and programs to coordinate the school–community relationships that are critical to program success. Ideas to encourage community involvement include the following:

- Encourage community members to host a health fair.
- Encourage community members to host a summer camp fair publicizing opportunities for physical activity in the summer.
- Build or expand a partnership with local physical activity and wellness programs to coordinate and enhance opportunities available to children, faculty, and staff to be active outside of the school setting (e.g., YMCA, city recreation programs, and service clubs).
  - Build a reciprocal relationship with city or county recreation departments and negotiate fiscal arrangements to keep school and recreation facilities open for use.
  - Advertise community physical activity opportunities.
- Generate funding support from local businesses and industries.
- Invite guest speakers from the community who promote active and healthy lifestyles.
- Arrange a special rate for faculty and staff with local fitness and wellness centers.

Barriers and Common Struggles in Implementing School Wellness Programs

Most teachers and administrators with 15 or more years of experience have observed across their career span an obvious increase in the number of overweight children, an increase in the number of students diagnosed with behavior and learning disorders, and an increase in pressure to meet the required standardized test score minimums. Schools have either completely ignored or minimized health issues to focus on other priorities, and the consequences are evident.

The focus on standardized test scores and other school priorities that dominate school goals and time is the primary barrier to implementing school wellness programs. Other barriers include (1) lack of support from key stakeholders (i.e., school leaders, teachers, parents); (2) lack of student involvement or interest; (3) years of a failed school lunch program; (4) lack of funding and resources; and (5) lack of accountability and a solid evaluation system.

School Priorities

According to the Action for Healthy Kids (AFHK) report (2008), 63% of the stakeholders participating in the study declared that competition from other school priorities was the number one barrier to school wellness. This was followed by 54% reporting lack of time. The test score precedence has required teachers to spend more time on what has been labeled priority content (i.e., math, language arts, and science). In many districts, school leaders have elected to take time from or completely eliminate other "less important" content (e.g., health, physical education) or traditional school experiences (e.g., recess, intramurals, and lunchtime activity). However, there is no evidence supporting the conventional wisdom that narrowing the curriculum and eliminating other school experiences will help students succeed on standardized tests. Research does support the idea that the opposite approach will help the schools to reach academic goals.

The false dichotomy established between academic achievement and time spent in noncore subject areas of the curriculum can be averted through the establishment of a shared and supportive vision for a school wellness program at all policy levels.

- At the national level, the No Child Left Behind policy should include health and physical education, making them equal in importance to other academic areas.
- The Child Nutrition and WIC Reauthorization Act of 2004 requiring district-wide school wellness programs needs to include accountability.
- At the school level, wellness should be a part of the overall school improvement plan.

The school improvement plan should integrate health and more physical education time into the curriculum and provide additional physical activity opportunities. Implementing more physical education time within the school day is often an explicit struggle in a school wellness plan. While many suggestions were discussed in the previous section (e.g., facilities, pupil/teacher ratios, equipment, time recommendations), elementary school administrators often struggle with scheduling. When a school wellness committee develops the goal to include more physical education, they should provide suggestions for scheduling. One suggestion is to isolate physical education from the rotation of other special area classes (e.g., music, theater, art, and computer). A sample schedule is provided in chapter 3 to aid in development of this part of the school wellness plan.

Lack of Support From Key Stakeholders

Support and involvement from several groups of people are imperative if a school wellness program is to be adequately achieved. As identified in the AFHK report (2008), the perceptions of school leaders, teachers, and parents were that schools were not doing enough to implement healthy school practices. School leaders including principals, superintendents, and school board members face the challenge of meeting the demands of No Child Left Behind legislation as well as meeting tight budgets. With these worries and with what appears to be lack of time in the school day, school leaders find it difficult to justify time for nutrition concerns, physical education, and physical activity. While some school leaders may actually support a wellness program, these barriers prevent them from taking action.

Although teachers may support the idea that children need to be healthy and active, the focus on test scores controls their actions. Additionally, when new initiatives are brought to the attention of teachers, they generally take the form of a top-down mandate, leaving teachers with the feeling of "one more thing to do." Evidence supports the idea that teachers positively respond to initiatives supported by institutional factors such as feelings of ownership, support from the principal and other teachers, compatibility of integration with present values and goals, and the feeling of success dependency (Parks, Solomon, & Lee, 2007).

Other stakeholders perceived parents to show little or no support for school wellness programs (AFHK, 2008). Parents involved in the study clarified this opinion, and many testified that they did not do an adequate job of supporting sound nutrition and physical activity habits at school or home.

Lack of support from key stakeholders influences what become school priorities. These barriers

will remain unless those who are most influential are among the people most actively committed to school wellness. The following are recommendations for obtaining support from these individuals and groups:

- Enlightening all on the relationship of nutrition and physical activity to school attendance, academic success, children's ability to focus, and classroom behavior
- Building bottom-up support as opposed to top-down directives
- Setting simple and realistic short-term goals that can easily be obtained
- Celebrating the successes
- Inviting parents to be involved in specific activities or elements of the school wellness plan and showing appreciation for their contributions
- Building a relationship with parents that demonstrates mutual respect for the roles needed at home and at school to foster healthy and active lifestyles
- Acknowledging time constraints and competing priorities that administrators confront
- Acknowledging school leaders for effective programs and policies
- Engaging district leaders and school board members with the improved academic achievement outcome
- Acknowledging time constraints and competing priorities that teachers confront
- Valuing the input of teachers who are concerned with student gains—when teachers exert some control over decisions, school efficacy is strengthened

All stakeholders have a valuable contribution to make; but alliance among school leaders, teachers, and parents is critical to a school wellness program's success.

Lack of Student Involvement or Interest

Students are the intended beneficiaries of a school wellness program. However, the idea of increasing the health and well-being of students is not always positively received by students. While it is rare to find an elementary child who does not enjoy physical activity, motivating some middle and high school students may be a struggle.

A more difficult challenge is inspiring children and youth to eat nutritious food. Possible reasons are that we are educating a society in which most students frequent fast food restaurants, eat quick and nutritionally unbalanced meals from home, and have almost endless access to high-fat, high-carbohydrate snack foods. The idea of eating a nutritious meal with the intention of fueling the body has been replaced by intentions to satisfy cravings. The body, instead of being fueled for cognitive and physical activity, often reacts to foods and beverages with no or low nutritional value by achieving a lethargic state. The result is students who have little desire to be active and limited ability to concentrate.

In the AFHK report (2008), few respondents ranked students as being in a strong position to move school wellness forward. Beyond third grade, peer influence is often the strongest influence. Therefore, it would be instrumental to engage students in motivating peers and family members to be physically active and to eat healthy. Student groups have been powerful against smoking and alcohol and drug use. Many have taken a strong stance in pledging abstinence from sexual activity. There is no reason to believe that students cannot do the same to encourage active and healthy lifestyles.

Students empowered in school decisions are more likely to be supportive. The following are some suggestions for how to involve students and increase their interest level:

- Survey students to help plan physical activity options.
- Encourage the student government associations to become involved. Actively identify the students who can influence and promote change.
- Offer student club-sponsored intramurals or tournaments during lunch or extended day.
- Trust students to give valuable input on the school wellness committee.
- Allow students to identify problems and create solutions. Grant them ownership.
- Have students investigate the nutritional value of foods, and then have them help in identifying nutritious food that is tasty and appealing.

Failed School Meal Programs

Another barrier to overcome is the state of our school meal programs. Meals in most schools have evolved to high-fat or carbohydrate-loaded processed, prepared food items. On-site cooking is often just an unpacking and heating process. The primary reason for the failed school meal programs is budget cuts. School meal programs must show a financial profit or break even. The strategies most use to achieve this are eliminating staff and purchasing processed foods that would be appealing to their consumers: children. Nutritional guidelines have not been enforced, and an entire generation has been raised on hot dogs, hamburgers, pizza, processed chicken fingers, and French fries. School lunch and breakfast programs for low-income families were designed to guarantee a nutritious meal for individuals who may not have that opportunity at home. The sad fact is that despite the reduced or free meal, the food is providing little or no nutrition.

For systemic change, school districts are going to be forced to rethink funding and purchasing patterns of school meals and hiring practices of cafeteria staff. Schools must hire skilled staff to cook high-quality, tasty, nutritious meals. Staff will need to follow nutritional standards for all foods served at school including competitive foods (i.e, those marketed specifically to children and youth, vending machine items, beverages) Investigations into states or districts that have been successful in resurrecting failed meal programs may be the first step in this action plan. A publication titled *Making It Happen: School Nutrition Success Stories* (jointly sponsored by the U.S. Dairy Association, CDC, and the U.S. Department of Education, 2005) may prove to be a valuable resource for this change. This document recommends the following strategies for improving school nutrition:

- Establish nutrition standards for competitive foods.
- Influence food and beverage contracts.
- Make more healthful foods and beverages available.
- Adopt marketing techniques.
- Limit student access to competitive foods.
- Use fund-raising activities and rewards.

Lack of Funding and Resources

Lack of funding and resources was a primary barrier to school wellness identified by stakeholders in the 2008 AFHK report. Funding and resources are a challenge that most schools and districts share as they strive to make any school improvements.

Budget problems will continue to be a concern for schools. However, funds are often available through federally funded programs, industry, and other grants. Efforts should be made to reveal funding that supports critical school wellness initiatives. To aid in obtaining grants, a district office leader should take on the role of locating and writing grants for the schools. State departments of education can help by disseminating information to districts about state-supported initiatives. For example, 23 states have been funded by CDC's Division of Adolescent and School Health (DASH) to increase physical activity through the Coordinated School Health Programs. The program provides financial support and assistance to help

- implement effective physical activity and physical education policies, programs, curricula, and standards;
- provide professional development and technical assistance;
- implement strategies to reduce health disparities; and
- establish collaboration efforts with various stakeholders.

School wellness committee members may be able to brainstorm ideas for change or to research ideas from others; however, there is evidence that they are lacking resources that would provide them with the help to actually implement a plan. For example, if a school wanted to implement a bike- and walk-to-school program, the first action would be to determine the number of potential walkers and bikers within a mile of the school. Next, safety concerns such as the condition or existence of road shoulders and sidewalks would need to be investigated. A third part of the plan would be to investigate grants for funding. A Web-based search performed by a committee member would reveal the project called California LEAN, which provides information on establishing a program such as this.

Numerous organizations, such as the following, offer valuable detailed resource material to promote physical education and physical activity that districts can use:

- National Association for Sport and Physical Education
- National Association of State Boards of Education
- National School Boards Association
- Institute of Medicine
- United States Department of Health and Human Services
- Centers for Disease Control and Prevention
- Action for Healthy Kids
- California Project LEAN

In addition, a wealth of new resources are available, most of which can be found through a simple Web search. Use caution when searching for resources. For example, many quality programs and ideas are available at low or no cost. At the same time there are comparable programs that come with a high price tag. Furthermore, price does not correlate with appropriateness. Many programs are packaged to sell physical activity but encourage inappropriate practices such as limited activity and students placed on display. For more on how to identify activities that promote developmentally appropriate practices, see chapters 3 through 11 for the elementary program and chapters 12 through 16 for the secondary program.

Lack of Accountability and a Solid Evaluation System

The school wellness program is only as good as the evaluation system that assesses the quality of the program. Full implementation will occur only with program accountability. In the AFHK study, 42% of those responding stated that tracking and monitoring of policy implementation were nonexistent. With no systems in place to monitor or measure improvements, the planning and implementing process has no validity. A sure way to avoid collective efficacy is to ask stakeholders to spend countless hours researching, planning, and initiating the implementation of a wellness program only to fail to judge its effectiveness.

An ongoing accountability and evaluation system should be part of the planning and implementation process. States, districts, schools, and teachers should all be held accountable for implementation of policies and plans. Accountability systems can include incentives or punitive actions if necessary. Evaluation systems should be designed to assess the effectiveness of the policies and programs and follow up with adaptations. Goals should be celebrated as they are reached. The following are ideas for acknowledging success:

- A congratulations note from the principal or chair of the wellness committee
- School assemblies that recognize teacher, student, and parent success
- Rewarding the school wellness committee with a healthy banquet or another form of appreciation
- Notifying the district office of successes
- Using the school Web page, e-mails, local cable station, and newsletters to publicize accomplishments
- Using the local media to publicize accomplishments to the community

A school wellness program can be successful with support from all constituencies. A culture of physically active and healthy behaviors and attitudes on the part of students, faculty, staff, school leaders, families, and the community is the ultimate goal. While the obesity epidemic is a public problem, without a strong contribution from schools it is not likely to be reversed. A school mission statement should include educating young people to become healthy, productive citizens. Efforts to improve the nutrition level of school meals, eliminate unhealthy snacks, and increase physical education and physical activity are a part of this mission. Schools and districts across the country are stepping up to this challenge. Through outstanding leadership, effective strategies have been implemented. This book, along with other resources, can provide valuable knowledge to aid in the successful implementation of a school wellness program. School board members, district leaders, and school administrators must initiate and support change in order for students to lead physically active and healthy lives.

SUMMARY

1. Schools play a significant role in promoting healthy eating habits and physically active lifestyles.

2. The Child Nutrition and WIC Reauthorization Act of 2004 required all school districts involved in a federally funded meal program to establish a district wellness policy by the 2006-2007 school year. However, according to the 2008 AFHK report, only 54% of local school districts are actually meeting the minimum requirements.

3. A comprehensive approach to a school wellness plan involves state, districts, and schools uniting. Stakeholder support is instrumental to success at all three levels.

4. The school wellness committee is responsible for developing a school wellness plan. This committee can and should be part of the school improvement committee.

5. The process of developing a school wellness plan includes the following steps:
   - Researching existing policy
   - Conducting a baseline assessment of the current school practices
   - Developing and implementing an action plan
   - Building awareness and support on the part of stakeholders

6. Monitoring, evaluating, and maintaining the plan are an ongoing and critical part of the process that allows schools to revise the plan, communicate progress, and celebrate success.

7. The success of the school wellness program is dependent on all people involved, especially the following:
   - Administrative support is essential to achieve and maintain a successful school wellness program.
   - Teachers are instrumental in implementing the plan.
   - Parents need to be informed and encouraged to support the process.
   - Community leaders should be informed and involved in school initiatives.

8. Plans must include ideas to overcome barriers to success. Challenges reported by others include these:
   - Other school priorities and lack of time
   - Lack of support from key stakeholders
   - Lack of student involvement or interest
   - A failed school lunch program
   - Lack of funding and resources
   - Lack of accountability

9. A school culture of physically active and healthy behaviors and attitudes from all constituencies is the ultimate goal.

10. Without the support of school leaders to initiate and support change and hold others accountable, it is doubtful that we can reach the goal of healthy and active lifestyles for our students.

CHECKING YOUR UNDERSTANDING

1. What federal legislation and national initiatives have been instrumental in promoting change related to physical activity?

2. Why do national-level initiatives not always have a direct impact on schools?

3. According to the SHPPS, what percentage of districts include policies specific to elementary school recess?

4. With physical education as the cornerstone of the physical activity plan, name the eight other recommendations that NASPE and AHA have for a comprehensive approach to health and physical activity.

5. Provide a rationale for why stakeholder support is crucial to the success of a school wellness

plan. Name and describe one strategy for obtaining stakeholder support.

6. While all stakeholders play an important part, who is in the best position to move a school wellness program forward and why?

7. Explain the process of a school wellness plan once the school wellness committee is established.

8. What four options are there for prioritizing goals, and why might each be necessary?

9. Name four reasons why monitoring, maintaining, and evaluating the school wellness program are important.

10. Choose two potential barriers to implementing the school wellness program and establish an action plan to overcome each.

11. Reflecting back on your elementary years to the best of your ability, complete the sample survey in figure 2.1. What was your total score? List four strengths and four weaknesses. Select one of the weaknesses and using the information in this chapter, explain what immediate change could take place and what would be a long-term plan of action.

RESOURCES

A Portal to the Web Sites of a Number of Multi-Agency Health Initiatives and Activities of the U.S. Department of Health and Human Services and Other Federal Departments and Agencies
www.health.gov/default.asp

Action for Healthy Kids Wellness Policy Fundamentals
www.actionforhealthykids.org

Action for Healthy Kids: Wellness Tool
www.actionforhealthykids.org/wellnesstool/index.php

California Project LEAN: Policy in Action Training Package
www.californiaprojectlean.org

Center for Science in the Public Interest, Constructive Classroom Rewards: Promoting Good Habits While Protecting Children's Health
www.cspinet.org/nutritionpolicy/constructive_rewards.pdf

Changing the Scene: Improving the School Nutrition Environment
www.teamnutrition.usda.gov/resources/changing.html

Fit, Healthy, and Ready to Learn: A School Health Policy Guide
www.cdc.gov/healthyYouth/physicalactivity/promoting_health/pdfs/ppar_a17.pdf

My Pyramid
www.MyPyramid.gov

NASPE Guidelines for After-School Physical Activity and Sport Programs
www.aahperd.org/naspe

National Association of State Boards of Education Policies to Encourage Physical Activity
www.nasbe.org

National Center for Chronic Disease Prevention and Health Promotion: The Coordinated School Health Program
www.cdc.gov/HealthyYouth/CSHP/

National Center for Chronic Disease Prevention and Health Promotion: The School Health Index
https://apps.nccd.cdc.gov/shi/default.aspx

SMART Goal Setting
www.goal-setting-guide.com/smart-goals.html

South Carolina Physical Education Assessment Program (SCPEAP)
www.SCAHPERD.org

U.S. Department of Education. (2002). Public Law 107-110. The No Child Left Behind Act of 2001. Washington, DC: U.S. Government Printing Office.

U.S. Department of Health and Human Services, Centers for Disease Control and Prevention. *Addressing physical activity: Division of adolescent and school health (DASH)*. Available at www.cdc.gov/HealthyYouth/physicalActivity/pdf/Addressing_Phys_Activity.pdf.

REFERENCES

Action for Healthy Kids Special Report. (2008). *Progress or promises? What's working for and against healthy schools?* Available at www.actionforhealthykids.org/. Accessed December 2, 2008.

Healthy Schools for Healthy Kids [Report sponsored by the Robert Wood Johnson Foundation]. (2003). Available at www.rwjf.org/newsroom/product.jsp?id=15595/. Accessed December 3, 2008.

Institute of Medicine of the National Academies. (2004). *Preventing childhood obesity: Health in the balance.* Washington, DC: National Academies Press.

Lee, S.M., Burgeson, C.R., Fulton, J.E., & Spain, C.G. (2007). Physical education and physical activity: Results from the School Health Policies and Programs Study 2006. *Journal of School Health,* 77(8), p. 435-463.

Making It Happen: School Nutrition Success Stories. (2005). Available at www.fns.usda.gov/TN/Resources/makingithappen.html. Accessed December 4, 2008.

National Association for Sport and Physical Education. (2006). *Shape of the nation report: Status of physical education in the USA.* Reston, VA: Author.

National Association for Sport and Physical Education. (2008). *PE metrics: Assessing the national standards 1: Elementary.* Reston, VA; Author.

National Association of State Boards of Education. (2007). State Schools Health Policy Data Base. Available at www.nasbe.org/index.php/shs/health-policies-database. Accessed December 7, 2008.

Parks, M., Solomon, M., & Lee, A. (2007). Understanding classroom teacher's perceptions of integrating physical activity: A collective efficacy perspective. *Journal of Research in Childhood Education,* 21(3).

U.S. Department of Health and Human Services. (2001). *The surgeon general's call to action to prevent and decrease overweight and obesity.* Rockville, MD: U.S. Department of Health and Human Services, Public Health Service, Office of the Surgeon General.

U.S. Department of Health and Human Services. (2004). Section 204 of Public Law 108-265—June 30, 2004, Child Nutrition and WIC Reauthorization Act of 2004.

PART II

The Elementary Physical Activity Program

3

Quality Elementary Physical Education

OVERVIEW

The foundation of a good physical activity program is a good physical education program. It is the physical education program that has the major responsibility for giving students the skills, knowledge, and dispositions to lead a physically active lifestyle. Physical education programs educate people so that they have the skills and knowledge to be a participant and the dispositions that contribute to their wanting to be a participant. Although the major responsibility for designing and conducting a good physical education program will be given to the physical education teacher, it is important that administrators and classroom teachers know when they have a good program and when they do not. This chapter describes a good physical education program.

CHAPTER OUTCOMES

This chapter will help you

- identify the responsibilities of administrators to the physical education program,

- identify the responsibilities of the physical education teacher to the physical activity program,

- describe the contributions of a good physical education program to the cognitive and social-emotional development of children,

- identify the characteristics and goals of a good physical education program,

- understand the factors that affect the learning of motor skills,

- identify developmentally appropriate content for different grade levels, and

- describe how to organize and manage the physical education environment.

IN THIS CHAPTER

The bus arrives at the school entrance and children begin filing off. Ms. Reynolds, the physical education specialist, is on traffic duty this morning. She greets the children as they safely move from the bus to the building. As the children return the greeting, many eagerly ask, "What are we doing in PE today?"

This is a common question asked of elementary physical education teachers and, most likely, a question not asked of the classroom teacher about math, language arts, or other subjects. Is this an insult to the classroom teacher? No! The question illustrates the idea that children love to be physically active and that Ms. Reynolds is providing positive experiences for the children in her physical education class.

When you think back to your experiences in elementary physical education, what memories dominate your thoughts? Were your elementary experiences in physical education positive ones or negative ones? Do you remember your physical education teacher? Do you recall activities such as kickball, dodgeball, relays, or tag games? Do you remember gymnastics or tumbling activities or dances? Was fitness testing a part of your elemen-

tary physical education experience? Did you learn about the importance of physical fitness? Do you remember being taught skills and strategies when it came to game experiences? Do your elementary physical education memories match what is considered quality physical education today? Good physical education programs are positive experiences for students and prepare them for a lifetime of physical activity.

A quality physical education program provides children the opportunity to learn meaningful content with appropriate instruction (National Association for Sport and Physical Education [NASPE], 2003). Quality physical education today is standards based and is both developmentally and instructionally appropriate to the physical, cognitive, and social-emotional needs of children. The physical education curriculum is described in terms of long-term goals related to the K through 12 exit goals of a standards-based program and short-term student performance outcomes for each grade level. Good programs structure the learning environment to promote optimal experiences in order for the students to reach these goals.

Physical education programs are now designed to prepare students to be physically active outside of the physical education class and to give them the skills, knowledge, and dispositions they will need to be physically active for a lifetime. Today's physical education teacher must take on a leadership role to ensure that physical activity occurs at other times in the school day, as well as outside of the school day. The success of a quality physical education program is dependent upon district- and school-level administrative support for physical education as an integral part of the elementary school curriculum, as well as a willingness to hold teachers accountable for quality instruction.

The Role of the School Administration in the Physical Education Program

Position papers from NASPE (2003, 2008) recommend that school systems provide children the opportunity to learn through quality physical education. Specific recommendations for elementary school physical education include the following:

- Scheduling 150 minutes a week of instructional time in a developmentally and age-appropriate manner
- Hiring a qualified physical education specialist and holding teachers accountable for providing quality programs
- Allocating funds for adequate equipment and facilities

Sadly, few states and school systems provide financial support for these recommendations. Even more disheartening is that few administrators manage the issues that require little or no state funding, such as appropriate scheduling, allocating local or school funds for equipment (if classrooms have adequate equipment, so too should physical education), and holding teachers accountable for student learning. These practices have marginalized physical education over the years and have contributed to the obesity epidemic.

Scheduling Physical Education

There are many reasons children are not getting the amount of physical education each week that they should be. The amount of physical education a school provides is often constrained by the perception that increasing physical education time will reduce academic performance, by lack of personnel, by lack of facilities, and by a concern that increased physical education time will reduce the time allocated to other special areas (e.g., music, art, computer). Within these constraints, there are strategies that can be used to increase physical education time.

- Begin by buying into the philosophy that academic performance will improve with physical activity.
- While 150 minutes may not be an option for all school systems, most schools can schedule 90 minutes of physical education a week with a 1 to 400 teacher/student schoolwide ratio (see sample schedule in table 3.1).
- Students must be scheduled for class lengths that are age and developmentally appropriate (NASPE, 2008).
  - Grade K through 2 class periods should not exceed 30 minutes.
  - Grade 3 through 5 class periods should not exceed 45 minutes.
- The physical education schedule can be different from the other special area class schedules.
- Outdoor space can be used if weather is conducive, and cafeteria space or auditorium space can be shared. It may be valuable to raise funds for an indoor physical education facility. Outside community resources may share in the building expense in exchange for evening and weekend use.

Certified Quality Physical Education Teachers

While most states fund the employment of physical education specialists, many states do not provide funding for quality pupil/teacher ratios. A two- or three-day program of physical education (90 minutes per week) taught by a certified physical education teacher requires a teacher/pupil ratio of one certified physical education teacher for every 400 students in a school. The individual-class pupil/teacher ratio should be equivalent to that for the classroom. In some schools, physical education teachers are expected to teach two combined classes at one time. This practice is unsafe and not conducive to learning. Several states have taken legislative action against this practice.

A few states do not require the hiring of a certified physical education teacher. In lieu of funding a specialist, districts require the classroom teachers to provide a developmentally appropriate physical education program. Research on student learning

TABLE 3.1

Sample Schedule for 90 Minutes of Physical Education a Week (Three Classes per Grade Level) ⊙

Time	Monday	Tuesday	Wednesday	Thursday	Friday
8:00-8:30	K-A	K-B	K-A	K-B	K-A
8:30-9:00	K-B	K-C	1-A	K-C	K-C
9:00-9:30	1-B	1-A	1-B	1-B	1-A
9:30-10:00	1-C	2-A	1-C	1-C	2-A
10:00-10:30	Planning period	Planning period	Planning period	Planning period	Planning period
10:30-11:00	2-A	2-B	2-C	2-B	2-B
11:00-11:30	2-C	3-A	3-B	3-A	2-C
11:30-12:00	3-B	3-C	3-C	3-B	3-A
12:00-12:30	Lunch	Lunch	Lunch	Lunch	3-C
12:30-1:15	4-A	4-B	4-A	4-B	Lunch
1:15-2:00	4-C	5-A	5-B	4-C	5-A
2:00-2:45		5-C		5-C	5-B

Letters A, B, and C represent classes (e.g., first grade has 3 classes: 1-A, 1-B, and 1-C).

in physical education does not support using classroom teachers to teach physical education.

A competent administrator surrounds him- or herself with competent teachers, and the physical education teacher should be no exception. Efforts should be made to evaluate the physical education teacher and student learning in physical education on a regular basis and to document strengths and weaknesses. The physical education teacher should be required to present lesson plans and sample assessments to support the idea that learning is occurring. Because there are usually only one or two physical education teachers in an elementary school, it is important that physical education teachers be provided with opportunities to attend physical education workshops and conferences in order to continue to grow professionally.

Facilities and Equipment

Facilities are a concern as many schools, especially in the southern states, expect physical education to be taught outdoors year-round. An outdoor environment is ideal for teaching some skills, but an indoor facility is a must in order for quality programs to meet all of the curriculum goals. Indoor facilities should exist in every elementary school and should have adequate space and ceiling height (minimum 20 feet, or 6 meters) for the movement and activities of a physical education program.

A variety of sizes and kinds of physical education equipment is necessary for a quality program. The needs of the younger elementary student are different from those of the older student. Ideally, every child should have a ball when learning skills such as dribbling, tossing, and catching to self and throwing; and there should be a range of sizes that permit teachers to use smaller and lighter equipment for younger students. Without the appropriate amount of equipment, teachers have to resort to activities in which children are waiting turns. This is much like having only one pencil per four students in a classroom.

The increase in obesity of young children has made the support of physical education programs a national imperative. Despite limited funding, school district administrators will have to step up to the plate and support quality physical education by hiring and maintaining qualified teachers, by maintaining adequate class size and appropriate class time periods, and by allotting funds for adequate equipment and facilities.

The Role and Responsibilities of the Physical Education Teacher in the School Physical Activity Program

The NASPE (2003) recommends that children obtain a minimum of 60 minutes of physical activity in a day. It is not possible in most schools to provide the 60 minutes of daily physical activity for every student through the physical education program alone; this has led to development of the idea of having comprehensive school physical activity programs. Some students attend physical education one day a week; others attend two or three days; and a few have daily physical education. The physical educator is to provide maximum physical activity time within the class period, teach skills and activities that transfer into physical activity outside of physical education class, motivate children to be physically active, and take the role of physical activity director for the school. If students are to receive the amount of physical activity they need each day, other opportunities to be physically active within the school day must be provided. The physical education teacher has unique responsibilities in the school physical activity program to ensure that students are physically active within the physical education class. The physical education teacher also has the responsibility to help direct and guide opportunities for physical activity within the school outside the physical education class.

Provide Maximum Physical Activity Time Within the Class Period

Physical education class is just one avenue during a school day that provides the opportunity for physical activity. During the allotted class time it is recommended that children be moderately or vigorously active for at least half of the class period. Several factors can contribute to making this happen:

1. Effectively organize space, equipment, and students.

2. Provide adequate equipment that allows all children to be active at the same time (e.g., one ball per child).

3. Limit teacher talk or instruction time.

4. Plan practice opportunities that are structured for maximum participation (e.g., individual, partner, and small-group activities; nonelimination activities; activities that require no wait time).

5. Structure the class so that learning occurs while students are being physically active.

With maximum and quality activity time, children become more skilled, knowledgeable, and physically fit.

Teach Skills and Activities That Transfer Into Physical Activity Outside of Physical Education Class

Physical education programs have the responsibility to teach skills that students will need to participate in physical activity outside of the physical education class and skills they will need for a lifetime of physical activity. Skills learned in physical education class transfer to skills used in a child's play. From the kindergarten-age child playing tag, to the second grade child jumping rope, to the older child playing a game of kickball, the skilled child is more likely to participate in physical activity. If a child is confident in his or her skills, there is typically no hesitation to play; however, the low-skilled child, especially in the upper grades, is less inclined to take part in group activities for fear of failure and peer ridicule. Students need skills to be participants in physical activity.

Good physical education programs take the time to teach children activities they may do on their own. Examples of these are jump rope chants, nonelimination tag games, hopscotch, Four Square, tetherball, and basketball activities such as Horse and Around the World. Including these activities briefly in a physical education class and then encouraging children to play them on their own is likely to promote more physical activity on the playground and in their neighborhoods.

Motivate Children to Be Active

Another role of the physical educator is to encourage and motivate children to be active. There

Children get maximum activity when every child has a piece of equipment and does not have to wait a turn.

are many ways to do this, including promoting community activities, assigning physical activity homework or home fun, showing an interest in the out-of-class physically activity in which children participate, and leading by example.

Promoting Community Activities There are typically numerous activities in communities that promote physical activity, such as organized recreational sports, dance classes, gymnastics programs, and martial arts. A bulletin board in the gym, the school Web site, and regular announcements are simple ways to promote these opportunities. Brochures, Web sites, or newspaper announcements are available from most physical activity venues.

Homework and "Home Fun" While homework is often not a pleasant part of a child's evening, physical activity homework or *home fun* can be. Home fun may be practicing jump rope tricks with or without a jump rope; participating in simple exercises when commercials come on television; playing outside; walking the dog; talking a walk with a parent or guardian; participating in electronic games that specifically promote physical activity; or practicing manipulative skills such as throwing, kicking, and

striking. Physical education homework or home fun can be checked through an honor system by asking for a show of hands with young children and documenting on a physical activity calendar for older children. Sending a physical activity calendar home when children go on holiday or summer vacation is another way to encourage physically active lifestyles. Physical education teachers could ask the classroom teachers to send a physical activity calendar home with the summer reading list.

Praise for Participation A word of encouragement is a simple way to promote physical activity. Praising young students for play may sound somewhat strange to most of us; but for a generation that experiences limited physical activity, it may be necessary. Simply inquiring about student involvement in physical activity and praising students for that involvement carry weight with young children. To take this a step further, if a teacher shows up at a youth league sporting event or a dance recital, the child will be elated.

Leading by Example One final way to motivate children to be active is for the physical education teacher to lead by example. A physically active and fit physical education teacher is a positive influence. The physical education teacher should occasionally share with the students how physical activity fits into his or her life.

By maximizing physical activity time in physical education class, aiding students in transferring skills and activities to out-of-class play, and making efforts to motivate children to be physically active, the physical educator can greatly influence the daily physical activity needs of students.

Play a Leadership Role in the Development of the School Physical Activity Program

The increase in the number of overweight children and the decrease in physical activity time in school make for a national problem. Curtailing this national epidemic can be addressed at a local level, and the physical education teacher must be the "go-to" person to promote change in the schools. The physical education teacher is the physical activity expert in the building and should take on the role of physical activity director for the school. The responsibilities should include the following:

- Being an active member of the school wellness committee
  - Helping in the evaluation and planning process for the school
  - Actively learning about and promoting opportunities for physical activity in the community
- Serving as a resource person for classroom teachers
  - Informing classroom teachers about the need for and benefits of adding small bouts of physical activity to the school day
  - Providing resources and training to the classroom teachers
  - Aiding teachers in understanding and implementing appropriate practices for physical activity (see chapter 5)
  - Providing opportunities for the teachers to engage in physical activity before or after school
- Organizing schoolwide physical activity experiences
  - Planning schoolwide activities such as field day, fun runs, a walking program, and morning exercise breaks
  - Encouraging fund-raisers that promote physical activity (e.g., Jump Rope for Heart, Walk for Diabetes, St. Jude's Walk)
  - Planning before- and after-school clubs for activities such as jump rope, walking, dance, gymnastics, and intramural sports

Physical Education's Contribution to the Domains of Learning

Physical education is unique in that the goals and objectives of the program are addressed through three domains of learning: psychomotor, cognitive, and affective. In a typical lesson in the elementary classroom, the students are working predominantly, if not solely, in the cognitive domain. In physical education, the primary domain of learning is referred to as the *psychomotor* domain or learning through movement.

Psychomotor Domain

Psychomotor objectives in physical education include both the learning of motor skills and fitness outcomes. Standards 1 and 4 of the national standards for physical education (NASPE, 2004) address the psychomotor domain. Standard 3 directly addresses being physically active.

> Standard 1: Demonstrates competency in motor skills and movement patterns needed to perform a variety of physical activities.
>
> Standard 3: Participates regularly in physical activity.
>
> Standard 4: Achieves and maintains a health-enhancing level of physical fitness.

Cognitive Domain

The *cognitive* domain is also a part of a physical education lesson. The first stage in learning a motor skill is in fact cognitive (Fitts & Posner, 1967). Students must have a clear idea of what they are trying to do motorically. We often jokingly tell children that they cannot leave their head in the classroom, as they will need to think in physical education class. While the process of learning motor skills is heavily cognitive, there is also a knowledge base identified as important for children to learn at the elementary level. National standard 2 addresses the cognitive domain:

> Standard 2: Demonstrates understanding of movement concepts, principles, strategies, and tactics as they apply to the learning and performance of physical activities.

One purpose of this text is to aid classroom teachers and administrators in understanding that the reverse—learning through movement—can also happen. Learning through movement, in fact, enhances the cognitive process (see chapters 1 and 5) and, in turn, academic success.

Affective Domain

The third contribution of good physical education programs is to the *affective* domain. The affective domain addresses values, attitudes, feelings, and overall social development. National standards 5 and 6 address the affective domain.

> Standard 5: Exhibits responsible personal and social behavior that respects self and others in physical activity settings.

Because physical education provides an active and interactive environment, it is an arena that can help develop both personal and social skills that should be taught and enforced throughout the entire school day and continue into the home and community environment.

> Standard 6: Values physical activity for health, enjoyment, challenge, self-expression, and/or social interaction.

A lesson in physical education typically includes psychomotor, cognitive, and affective objectives. The following are sample objectives for a class of third graders who are ready to be challenged in their dribbling skills.

1. *Psychomotor:* The learner will be able to dribble a ball at jogging pace around the obstacle course without losing control of the ball more than once.

2. *Cognitive:* The learner will be able to identify the three cues for a controlled dribble around obstacles (medium level, change hands, and shield) when asked by the teacher.

3. *Affective:* The learner will be able to demonstrate acceptance of his or her role as a competent class citizen by quickly and effectively helping to build and later put away the obstacle dribble course.

Given that the major goal of physical education is to prepare students for a lifetime of physical activity, students should leave their physical education experiences valuing physical activity. Not all students enjoy the same activities. Programs that offer students the opportunity to engage in a wide variety of physical activities can help students find a lifelong interest in physical activity from among many choices. Good programs target values directly and teach to them.

Curriculum Scope and Sequence

A classroom teacher is responsible for teaching many subjects in elementary school, such as math, language arts, science, social studies, and health. Most states and districts have academic content standards (often aligned with national standards) for each subject area and specific grade-level student performance outcomes or exit goals. As discussed in the previous section, physical education also has a set of national standards that are used to design state and district standards. These are generally accompanied by suggested student performance outcomes for each grade level, sometimes called grade-level objectives (see figure 3.1).

While the elementary classroom teacher typically teaches one grade level, the physical education teacher teaches grades kindergarten through 5. In some situations prekindergarten or grade 6 is included. Although the classroom teacher must be aware of the scope and sequence of each content area across the grade levels (see sidebar on p. 60), the physical education teacher actually teaches students across all of the grade levels. The *scope* refers to the breadth and depth of the curriculum, while the *sequence* is the progression of content within a year and from year to year. The sidebar "Sample Performance Outcomes for Dribbling a Basketball" on page 58 demonstrates the skill of dribbling in basketball and illustrates how the content would progress across the grades. The dribbling example shows that a student would not be developmentally ready for an experience of playing a game of three-on-three basketball before learning the fundamental skills of dribbling. Asking a child to do so would be equivalent to asking a child to write a paragraph before he or she was capable of constructing a sentence.

The unique contribution of physical education to the elementary school curriculum is the development of the skills, knowledge, and dispositions to lead a physically active lifestyle. Understanding how motor skills develop is a critical skill that teachers need in order to make movement experiences developmentally appropriate.

FIGURE 3.1

The National Content Standards for Physical Education: Elementary School Grade-Level Emphases ⊙

Standard 1: Demonstrates competency in motor skills and movement patterns to perform a variety of physical activities.

Standard 1: Kindergarten, First, and Second Grade Emphases

- Demonstrate mature form in all locomotor patterns and the ability to vary and combine locomotor patterns with a smooth transition.
- Perform basic manipulative activities on the move (e.g., dribbling, collecting, catching, throwing, and striking).
- Adapt basic manipulative patterns to a partner.
- Demonstrate control in traveling and balance activities on a variety of body parts.
- Create expressive movement sequences with and without a defined rhythm.

Standard 1: Third and Fourth Grade Emphases

- Demonstrate mature form in selected manipulative patterns.
- Adapt a skill to dynamic and unpredictable environments.
- Acquire a few specialized sport skills.
- Combine movement skills in applied settings.

Standard 1: Fifth and Sixth Grade Emphases

- Demonstrate mature form in throwing, catching, and striking patterns.
- Combine manipulative patterns of specialized sport skills (e.g., dribble and shoot, dribble and pass, receive and pass).
- Demonstrate basic strategies for net and invasion games.
- Acquire the specialized patterns of one individualized and one lifetime activity.

Standard 2: Demonstrates understanding of movement concepts, principles, strategies, and tactics as they apply to the learning and performance of physical activities.

Standard 2: Kindergarten, First, and Second Grade Emphases

- Identify the critical elements of basic movement patterns (locomotor and manipulative skills).
- Use feedback to improve performance.
- Apply movement concepts to a variety of basic skills.
- Understand why people perform at different abilities and attribute those differences to practice and experience.

Standard 2: Third and Fourth Grade Emphases

- Use critical elements of a skill to improve performance and provide feedback to others.
- Apply simple learning and biomechanical principles in learning motor skills.

(continued)

(continued)

Standard 2: Fifth and Sixth Grade Emphases

- Identify and apply principles of practice and conditioning to improve performance.
- Use basic offense and defensive tactics of invasion and net activities in noncomplex settings.

Standard 3: Participates regularly in physical activity.

Standard 3: Kindergarten, First, and Second Grade Emphases

- Engage in moderate to vigorous activity outside of physical education class on a daily basis.
- Willingly participate in new activities.

Standard 3: Third and Fourth Grade Emphases

- Participate in organized activity and sport programs provided by the school and community.
- Identify an activity associated with each of the components of fitness.
- Monitor participation in physical activity for a period of time.
- Identify several vigorous activities that provide pleasure.

Standard 3: Fifth and Sixth Grade Emphases

- Identify community resources for participation in physical activity.
- Participate regularly in physical activity outside of the school.
- Monitor participation in physical activity and set reasonable goals for improvement.

Standard 4: Achieves and maintains a health-enhancing level of physical fitness.

Standard 4: Kindergarten, First, and Second Grade Emphases

- Recognize the physiological indicators of moderate to vigorous physical activity.
- Sustain a level of moderate to vigorous physical activity for at least five minutes.

Standard 4: Third and Fourth Grade Emphases

- Identify the components of health-related fitness and one activity related to the development of each of the components.
- Meet the health-related fitness standard as defined by Fitnessgram.
- Identify the benefits of participation in physical activity on a regular basis.

Standard 4: Fifth and Sixth Grade Emphases

- Meet the health-related fitness standard as defined by Fitnessgram.
- Identify personal strengths and weaknesses in fitness.
- Identify what can be done to improve each of the fitness components in terms of physical activities as well as exercises.

Standard 5: Exhibits responsible personal and social behavior that respects self and others in physical activity settings.

Standard 5: Kindergarten, First, and Second Grade Emphases

- Apply rules, procedures, and safe practices with little or no reinforcement.
- Follow directions.
- Support and work cooperatively with another on a task.
- Participate demonstrating consideration for others.

Standard 5: Third and Fourth Grade Emphases

- Work independently on a task without reinforcement.
- Work cooperatively and productively with a partner or small group.
- Willingly participate with others who may be different from oneself.

Standard 5: Fifth and Sixth Grade Emphases

- Work cooperatively and productively in competitive and cooperative settings.
- Utilize time productively to complete assigned tasks.
- Identify rules, procedures, and safe practices for a variety of activity settings.
- Work cooperatively with more and less skilled participants.
- Demonstrate support for others in practice and applied settings.
- Identify what one needs to practice, and practice it independently.

Standard 6: Values physical activity for health, enjoyment, challenge, self-expression, and/or social interaction.

Standard 6: Kindergarten, First, and Second Grade Emphases

- Willingly try new activities.
- Indicate that one enjoys an activity.
- Feel good about participation in physical activity.
- Use physical activity as a means of self-expression.

Standard 6: Third and Fourth Grade Emphases

- Choose a challenging activity and get better at it
- Identify the activities that are personally most enjoyable.
- Identify the relationship between success at an activity and enjoyment.
- Use physical activity as a means of self-expression.

Standard 6: Fifth and Sixth Grade Emphases

- Identify the benefits of different activities.
- Identify the activities that are personally most enjoyable.
- Seek challenges in physical activity.
- Use physical activity as a means of self-expression.

Sample Performance Outcomes for Dribbling a Basketball

- ■ Grade 5: By the end of the elementary years (grade 5), a student should be able to dribble an intermediate-size basketball the length of a basketball court while maintaining possession of the ball against a defensive player. A mature form of finger pad–only contact, ball at waist height, and eyes forward would be expected as well as various strategies to protect the ball from the defender. A fifth grade student should also be able to combine the skill of dribbling with other skills such as passing or shooting.

- ■ Grade 4: By the end of grade 4, a student should be able to dribble an intermediate-size basketball against a passive defender the length of a basketball court while varying the pathways, increasing and decreasing speed, shielding the ball, and changing hands.

- ■ Grade 3: By the end of grade 3, a student should be able to dribble an intermediate-size basketball in general space at a medium jogging speed using finger pads, keeping the ball at medium level, and demonstrating the ability to not look at the ball while dribbling. The third grade student should be able to change direction on signal, dribble in different pathways, and dribble around stationary objects. By the end of third grade the student should also be able to dribble with the nondominant hand while traveling at a slow jog without losing control.

- ■ Grade 2: By the end of grade 2, a student should be able to dribble a playground ball in general space (traveling through all of the activity space in the gym) at a slow jog without losing control. The student should contact the ball with the finger pads and keep the ball at medium level. The student should demonstrate the ability to avoid others while glancing at the ball only occasionally.

- ■ Grade 1: By the end of grade 1, a student should be able to dribble a playground ball in self-space with the dominant hand. The student should be able to demonstrate the skill using finger pads only and keeping the ball at medium (waist) level.

Factors That Affect the Development of Motor Skills

Motor skills are usually described in terms of fundamental or basic skills and specialized skills.
Fundamental skills are

- ▪ locomotor skills such as skipping and hopping;
- ▪ manipulative skills such as throwing, catching, and striking skills; and
- ▪ body management skills such as balance, rolling, and transferring weight.

Specialized skills are

- ▪ sport-specific activities such as dribbling a soccer ball, shooting a basketball, or performing a cartwheel; and
- ▪ leisure skills such as riding a bicycle, skateboarding, or in-line skating.

Because the development of specialized skills is dependent on the development of fundamental skills, a large part of the elementary physical education program is devoted to the development of fundamental skills. Examples of fundamental

skills and specialized skills are provided in table 3.2. The ability to perform motor skills is dependent on several factors including age, genetics, physical abilities, and motivation.

Age

Motor skill development is *age related*, meaning that there is a certain age when children are typically ready to learn specific motor skills. For example, most children are ready to learn how to skip and can skip by the end of kindergarten; however, all children cannot skip before exiting kindergarten. A first grade teacher could easily substitute the word "reading" for "skipping" and make the same statement. Development is *age related* but not *age dependent*.

Participation in the physical activities of our culture requires motor skills. Children learn motor skills through opportunities to participate in motor activities, formal instruction, and many practice opportunities. Children who are encouraged to participate in motor activities and have access to more formal instruction will have an advantage over those who do not. Developing enough skill to be a successful participant in many motor skills takes time. Motor skill patterns, particularly those

TABLE 3.2

Locomotor, Basic Manipulative, Body Management, and Sport-Specific Skills

Locomotor and body management skills	Fundamental and specialized skills
Fundamental locomotor skills: Walking Jogging Running Galloping Skipping Sliding Hopping Jumping Leaping *Body management skills*: Balancing Rolling Transferring weight from one body part to another Nonlocomotor actions (e.g., turning, twisting, rising-sinking, spinning)	*Fundamental manipulative skills*: Catching Throwing Kicking Volleying or striking with different body parts *Specialized skills:* Punting (soccer and football) Dribbling with feet (soccer) Dribbling with hands (basketball, team handball) Shooting a basketball Volleying (overhead and forearm pass) Striking with paddle or racket Striking with bat, hockey stick, or golf club
Sample combined skills: Run and leap Jump and hop (hopscotch) Slide and hop Jump, land, and roll	*Sample combined skills:* Dribble and pass with hands or feet Toss and strike with a racket or paddle Catch and shoot a basketball Catch and punt a soccer ball

fundamental patterns critical to all activities, progress from an immature stage to a mature stage. For example, a young child first jumps down, then forward, and then up. Children learn to strike a ball by striking a ball off a tee successfully before progressing to striking a ball gently tossed by a skilled thrower. Later, if instruction and participation opportunities continue, the student can eventually place-hit a pitched baseball or softball.

Genetics

Have you ever heard someone state that an individual was born a great athlete? Although we know that people do not come into the world as athletes, genetics does play a part in one's physical makeup and therefore one's tendencies toward excelling in particular activities. Height is an advantage in basketball; a large body frame is beneficial in many football positions; and successful distance runners typically have a small body frame. While it is unrealistic to expect every child to grow up to be a professional athlete or Olympic performer, it is not unrealistic to think that every child can acquire

a *participant level* of motor skills that will allow him or her to lead a physically active lifestyle. Having a participant level of skill means that a child can participate safely, independently, and with enough skill to make the activity enjoyable.

Physical Abilities

Physical abilities are related to the physical development of the child as well as his or her fitness level. How strong you are relative to your size, how flexible you are, and how much muscular and cardiovascular endurance you have affects your ability to perform physical skills. We call these health-related fitness components. There is also a set of skill-related fitness components that to some extent are linked to genetics, including balance, agility, power, speed, reaction time, and coordination. As an adult there are probably some components of skill-related fitness you have developed and others in which you have not reached your genetic potential. The important thing to remember is that health-related components can be developed and that skill-related factors are primarily critical factors only at an elite level of performance. With few exceptions, all children have the physical abilities to reach a participant level of ability in the curriculum of the physical education program. Good physical education programs do not ask students to do something they are not capable of doing successfully in the practice time allotted.

Motivation

Children who are motivated to be successful at motor skills will usually get better, and children who are better at motor skills are usually more motivated. Helping children be successful at motor skills is going to be a critical factor in their motivation to get better. If someone enjoys physical activity and wants to improve his or her skills, a high degree of motivation to improve will be a major factor in the degree to which the person is willing to practice and the quality of the practice.

It is the combination of developmental readiness, access to quality instruction, opportunities to practice, the level of health-related fitness, genetics, and the level of motivation that determines success in learning motor skills whether it be in sport, dance, gymnastics, cheerleading, or recreational activities such as biking, skating, and skateboarding. It is the physical education teacher's responsibility to plan a developmentally appropriate and age-related curriculum around these factors.

The goal of physical education programs in elementary schools should be developing skills.

Developmentally Appropriate and Age-Related Curriculum

To develop lifetime physical activity, a good teacher will plan and teach developmentally appropriate lessons that are age related. The curriculum will not be the same for kindergarten as for grade 5. A "one size fits all" curricular approach does not meet the physical, cognitive, and social developmental needs of all children in physical education, just as expecting children to read and comprehend at the same level is unrealistic in the classroom. An effective physical education teacher will teach age-related content and alter tasks, equipment, and the environment to meet the needs of each individual to ensure student success.

The curriculum (scope) that makes up a well-balanced elementary physical education program includes educational games, educational gymnastics, and educational dance. The foundation of these experiences is laid in grades K through 2 with the teaching of fundamental locomotor, manipulative, and body management skills and movement concepts. In the upper elementary grades, experiences include understanding and applying basic offensive and defensive game strategies, as well as sequencing movements and developing routines in gymnastics and dance. Physical fitness is part of the elementary program but is interwoven into all these experiences.

Motor skills in all of the content areas are developed over time, with different expectations for performance at different age levels. Table 3.3 provides an example of how locomotor, manipulative, and sport-specific skills are mapped across a two or three day a week physical education program. The map details the grade level at which the skills are introduced (I), the grade level at which continued practice is needed (C), and the grade level at which mastery is expected and should be assessed (M).

The Content Areas of the Elementary Physical Education Program

Locomotor skills

Manipulative skills

Body management skills

Educational games

Educational gymnastics

Educational dance

Physical fitness

TABLE 3.3

Sample Curriculum Map for the Locomotor, Manipulative, and Sport-Specific Skills in a Two- or Three-Day-a-Week Program

Skill	Pre-K-K	1st	2nd	3rd	4th	5th
LOCOMOTOR						
Locomotor skills, basic patterns	I	M				
Locomotor skills with flight	I	C	M			
Locomotor skills, combination movements		I	M			
MANIPULATIVE AND SPORT SPECIFIC						
Catching from skilled thrower or self-toss	I	C	M			
Catching various thrown objects while on the move			I	C	M	
Throwing underhand with accuracy	I	C	C	M		
Throwing overhand with force	I	C	C	C	M	
Throwing overhand with force and accuracy				I	C	M
Throwing and catching in dynamic situations			I	C	C	M
Kicking stationary ball with force for distance	I	C	C	M		
Kicking moving ball with force for distance		I	C	C	M	
Kicking moving ball for accuracy and distance				I	C	M
Punting a ball for height and accuracy			I	C	M	
Kicking and punting in dynamic situations				I	C	M
Dribbling a ball with hands or feet	I	C	C	C	M	
Dribbling a ball with hands or feet in dynamic situations				I	C	M
Volleying a ball as in Four Square			I	M		

(continued)

TABLE 3.3 *(continued)*

Skill	Pre-K–K	1st	2nd	3rd	4th	5th
Volleying a ball as in volleyball (underhand serve, forearm pass, and overhead volley)				I	C	M
Volleying in dynamic situations					I	C
Striking with paddles	I	C	C	C	M	
Striking with paddles in dynamic situations				I	C	M
Striking with a bat	I	C	C	C	M	
Striking with a bat in more dynamic situations				I	C	M
Striking with a hockey stick				I	M	
Striking with a hockey stick in more dynamic situations					I	C

I: introduced; C: continued practice experiences toward mastery; M: mastery expected.

Movement Concepts

Most elementary programs include as part of their physical education curriculum the movement concepts of Laban (see table 3.4). The original Laban framework (or adaptations of it) provides a "language" to describe movement, is taught as a primary focus in grades kindergarten through 2, and is used throughout the elementary years in each of the content areas to develop skilled movement. This language helps children to understand movement, describe their movements, and apply movements in varying contexts. The following are the movement concepts:

- Body awareness: the body and what the body does
- Space awareness: where the body moves
- Effort: how the body moves (the dynamics of movement)
- Relationships: with whom or what the body moves

Body Awareness: The Body and What the Body Does

Learning body awareness consists of developing an awareness of body parts and what they can do; exploring the movements that one's body can make, learning specific body shapes, and working with the concept of base of support.

Identifying Body Parts

Identifying body parts begins early in life. As toddlers develop language, they enjoy identifying objects and body parts. A common game for parents to play with their young child is *"What's this?"*: An adult points to an object or body part and the child calls it by name. With these early identifying experiences, children know most of the major body parts when they enter preschool. However, they are still learning more specific names of body parts as well as exploring what the body parts can do alone or in combination.

Sample task: One effective way for children to learn body parts is to match body parts with a partner in a fun activity called Busy Bee. The teacher calls out "elbow to elbow" and students touch elbows; he or she follows with "knee to knee," and then says "Busy Bee," at which point the children quickly find a new partner and stand back to back. The game continues with new body parts called. Children may also be asked to travel when Busy Bee is called and to emphasize the movement of different body parts in their movement (e.g., "Make your knees important in skipping").

TABLE 3.4

Movement Concepts

Body awareness *Actions of the body*	Space awareness *Where the body moves*	Effort *How the body moves*	Relationships *With what or whom the body moves*
Body shapes ■ Curved ■ Twisted ■ Narrow ■ Wide ■ Symmetrical ■ Asymmetrical Nonlocomotor ■ Swing ■ Sway ■ Twist ■ Turn ■ Bend/curl ■ Stretch ■ Sink ■ Push ■ Pull ■ Shake Locomotor ■ Walk ■ Hop ■ Jump ■ Slide ■ Gallop ■ Skip	Location ■ General space ■ Self-space Directions ■ Up/down ■ Forward/backward ■ Right/left ■ Clockwise/counterclockwise Levels ■ Low ■ Middle, medium ■ High Pathways ■ Straight ■ Curved ■ Zigzag Extensions ■ Large/small ■ Near/far	Speed, time ■ Fast ■ Slow Force ■ Strong ■ Light Flow ■ Bound ■ Free	Objects or others ■ Over/under ■ On/off ■ Near/far ■ In front of/behind/beside ■ Around/through Partners, small groups ■ Leading/following ■ Meeting/parting ■ Matching/mirroring

Adapted from Laban's movement framework.

Exploring the Movements the Body Can Make

The movements identified as nonlocomotor skills (e.g., bending, stretching, twisting) are taught through body awareness concepts. For example, children will learn to distinguish between twisting and turning motions or bending and stretching. They will learn to do these using different parts of the body to lead the actions.

Body Shapes and Base of Support

Body shapes are usually characterized in terms of wide, narrow, curled or round, and twisted. These concepts will later be used in specific activities in which the knowledge of body shapes is critical. For example, children will learn to make round, curled body shapes that will be vital in completing a cor-

rect forward or backward roll. They will learn to support themselves on different *bases of support* in educational gymnastics.

> *Sample task:* "Balance in a wide shape with two feet and two hands for your base of support; now balance on your right hand and right foot for a narrow base of support."

Body awareness incorporates learning the body parts and what the body parts can do exclusively as well as inclusively in the form of nonlocomotor movements (movements that don't take you anywhere) and stability. Through these experiences, the students gain a sense of body awareness and body management—concepts that are significant in dance, educational gymnastics, and game experiences.

Space Awareness: Where the Body Moves

Space awareness begins with teaching students the language of space. The concept of location is defined as *personal space* and *general space*. The concepts of *directions*, *levels*, *pathways*, and *extensions* describe movement through space of the body and its parts.

Personal and General Space

Children begin to learn about space through the concepts of *personal space* (understanding the movement possibilities an individual can perform in the immediate space or self-space) and *general space* (understanding the concept of surrounding). Space awareness is taught with the use of marks on the floor, carpet squares, or hoops to provide concrete examples of self-space. These props are typically removed within two or three lessons as the children gain a true understanding of their personal space in relation to others. General space is the term used to define all of the space in the activity area. When traveling in general space, children learn the concept of taking personal space with them. They travel throughout the activity area with a focus on not invading the space of others. Locomotor movements are typically used to teach this concept.

> *Sample task:* "Skip through general space as you take your personal space with you. Make sure you are never close enough to touch someone else and you are always looking for open spaces."

Learning to move without colliding with others is crucial to safe and effective movement experiences. Students learn to travel in general space first by focusing on where they are moving. They will later be expected to move without a direct focus.

Directions

The concept of *directions* provides the opportunity for children to experience forward, backward, sideways, up–down, clockwise, and counterclockwise movements.

> *Sample task:* "Gallop forward, and on the signal, change directions and gallop backward."

Pathways

Straight, curved, or zigzag patterns created through movement are the three *pathways*. Movement may be of the entire body through space or of its parts. It may also define the flight of an object moving in space.

> *Sample tasks:* "Use a zigzag pathway to avoid the defender while dribbling the basketball. Shoot the ball with a high curved arc from your hands to the goal."

Levels

High, medium, and low *levels* are taught as points of reference for body movements and for manipulation of objects.

> *Sample tasks:* "Dribble the ball at a medium level (waist high)." "When practicing your cartwheel, extend your legs to a high level."

Extensions

The concept of *extensions* is the final space awareness concept and is taught to aid the student in distinguishing between large and small movements of the body requiring full extension or flexed body parts.

> *Sample tasks:* "Swing the golf club using a large movement." "Now, putt the ball using a small movement." "Leap in the air with your arms extended away from the body." "Now, spin in a circle keeping the arms close to your body."

The concepts of space awareness are a necessity in physical education class, in the classroom, and in play for controlled body movements and safety. Space awareness concepts contribute to quality of movement that transfers into game play, dance or rhythmical experiences, and educational gymnastics.

Effort: How the Body Moves (The Dynamics of Movement)

To enhance the quality of movement, children need to understand the *effort concepts* of *time*, *force*, and *flow*. These concepts give movement its dynamic nature and distinguish skilled movement from unskilled movement.

Time

Time refers to quick (fast) and sustained (slow) speeds. Quick movement is "over in a flash," while sustained movement has an "ongoingness" about it. Children first learn about quick and sustained movement primarily through the concepts of fast and slow. Some children have jokingly been identified as having two speeds, fast and stop. Lack of understanding of the concept of time is why very young children do not pace themselves in aerobic activities. They typically go full speed and then tire quickly in need of a rest period. When you observe children in first grade playing tag, there are always quick bursts of movement and then a rest period. In the primary grades, children need to be introduced to the concept of time in the realm of fast/slow, accelerate/decelerate, quick/sustained, sudden/prolonged, and explosive/sustained movements.

This is most effectively done through contrasting movements (e.g., doing things at one speed and then at the contrasting speed). The option of including a medium-speed movement helps to extend the concept.

> *Sample tasks:* "Walk as slow as you can." "Now, walk as fast as you can." "Move quickly to a spot and when you get there, freeze and melt as slowly as you can to the floor."

Force

Force is another concept that is difficult for young children to comprehend. Have you ever been in line behind a family with young children playing miniature golf? Typically one parent is frustrated because a child hits the golf ball too hard. While manipulating a golf club is a difficult task for small children, comprehending how easy the stroke should be is even more of a challenge. The concept of force is taught through contrasting movements of hard/easy, strong/weak, heavy/light, and tight muscles/loose muscles.

> *Sample tasks:* "Travel using strong, heavy steps." "Now travel using light and delicate movement" or "Tighten all of the muscles in your body as if you were a statue." "Now, loosen your muscles and sink to the floor."

Flow

Flow is the third effort concept and is an intricate element in both dance and educational gymnastics movements. To teach this concept we contrast bound movement and free movement, for example jerky/smooth, rigid/relaxed, and choppy/continuous. The concept of flow is instrumental in helping students understand transitional moves.

> *Sample task:* "Make your body narrow and roll sideways as if you were a log rolling down a hill and kept getting caught on trees. Roll, pause, roll, pause, roll, and stop." "Now, repeat the task but pretend you are a log rolling smoothly down an open pathway."

Understanding the effort concepts of time, force, and flow will aid students in exploring new skills both on their own and in teaching and learning situations.

Relationships: With Whom or What the Body Moves

The concept of *relationships* includes relationships to *stationary or moving people* or to *objects* in varying movement experiences. Most activities in physical education class and play position a child to make meaning of the relationship he or she has with manipulative objects and large equipment and with others.

Relationships With People

Relationships with people can occur with one partner, within small groups, or between groups. Relationships with an individual include *leading/following, meeting/parting, mirroring, and matching.* Experiences with locomotor and nonlocomotor skills are usually used to teach these concepts.

> *Sample task:* "One partner is the leader and the other follows as you practice the different locomotor skills we have learned. Travel in different directions, pathways, and levels."

Moving in relation to a group of people can be cooperative or competitive. Problem solving may be part of the task. Experiences in groups of people are presented as children become socially and cognitively ready for these demands.

Relationships With an Object

Relationships with an object may include traveling over/under, onto/off, across, around, and through small apparatus or large apparatus or equipment. Using varied equipment and creating an obstacle course for children to move through is one way to teach these concepts. Some of the same concepts taught about relationships with objects may cross over into relationships with people. For example, some movement experiences require a child to go around, under, or even over another child.

Teaching relationship with objects also involves manipulating objects such as balls, rackets, and bats. Most children in kindergarten and first grade have not yet mastered manipulative skills. For this reason, work with the concept of relationships with objects continues from year to year as the children advance to a readiness level.

The movement concepts help the teacher to vary and extend the complexity of different movement experiences, thereby challenging the students. Initially lessons are designed with the learning objective solely on the movement concept. Later, learning the skill becomes the focus of the lesson, and the movement concepts are used to further develop and enhance the motor skills, as illustrated in the following lists.

Throwing

1. To self in personal space
2. With strong force against the wall
3. Quickly after the catch

4. So that a partner will catch the ball at medium level

5. To a partner moving to open space

6. In front of a moving partner

7. Over a net

Skipping

1. With small steps and big steps

2. In curvy and zigzag pathways

3. Fast and slow

4. Forward, backward, and sideways

The ability to understand these concepts and use these concepts across movement experiences will benefit children in numerous movement experiences in games and sports, dance, gymnastics, and everyday skills.

Locomotor Skills

Locomotor skills are sometimes referred to as traveling skills and are defined as a way in which the body moves from one place to another using the feet. Locomotor skills are developed in the K through 2 curriculum and are critical to the development of all other skills. Fifty percent of the ability to perform a manipulative skill such as hitting a tennis ball is related to the ability to position the feet appropriately for the action.

- *Fundamental locomotor skills:* walk, jog, run, gallop, skip, slide, hop, jump, and leap
- *Combined locomotor skills:* run and leap, jump and hop, slide and hop

Locomotor skills are developed using the movement concepts. A student skilled in jumping can jump emphasizing different body parts in the jump such as knees and arms (body awareness concepts); in different directions and pathways (space awareness concepts); softly or with great explosive force (effort concepts); and in relation to objects (over, onto) and people (relationship concepts).

By the end of grade 2, students should be able to combine skills into simple locomotor patterns and to vary the pattern using the movement concepts discussed in the previous section. Locomotor skills are combined in many games and in dance and educational gymnastics experiences in the early years. For example, students will transition from one locomotor pattern to another in simple dances, or approach a gymnastics bench using a locomotor skill of choice and then jump onto the bench (mounting). A second grade student is also beginning to apply locomotor skills with tactics such as faking and dodging when fleeing the "it" in a tag game.

In a good physical education program, you should be able to make these assumptions by the time the student enters the third grade:

- Fundamental locomotor skills will have been developed to a mature level.
- Students will be able to use the movement concepts previously discussed to vary those patterns.
- Students will be able to use locomotor and movement concepts skills in combination with each other.

Manipulative and Game Skills

Manipulative and game skills are primarily those skills used in the games and sports of our culture. Because children who are active are those who have the skills to be a participant in free play or organized sport, these skills are important to the development of the physically active lifestyle of the child. Manipulative and game skills include throwing, catching, striking, and kicking objects with and without implements and the ability to use the skills effectively in game and recreational play.

Expectations for the Primary Grade Child: Manipulative Skills

The primary grade child is introduced to fundamental manipulative skills such as throwing, catching, dribbling, and kicking (see table 3.3). Instruction and experiences in the primary grades provide opportunities for learning mature fundamental manipulative motor patterns and for practicing the basic skills in isolation. Expectations for second grade outcomes may include the following:

- Toss a ball to self and catch
- Throw using an underhand pattern
- Catch a ball thrown from a skilled thrower
- Kick a stationary ball for distance
- Dribble a ball with hands while traveling at a jogging pace
- Dribble a ball with feet while traveling at a jogging pace

While some 7- and 8-year-old children, through experiences in physical education or recreational play, may reach a mature level in a few manipulative skills, most will not be able to apply these skills in the context of full games and sports. In other words, it would be unrealistic to expect most 8-year-old children in a baseball-type game to catch a line drive or to throw with both force and accuracy.

Manipulative and games skills in the primary grades are developed with the movement concepts. The use of movement concepts helps the teacher develop versatility in movement skills. For example, primary grade students should be given experiences in dribbling a ball with the feet. The experience is enriched by having the students dribble in different pathways, at different speeds, and in relation to others and the size of the available space.

Expectations for the Upper Elementary Grades: Manipulative Skills

In the upper elementary grades (3-5), specialized and fundamental manipulative skills are first mastered in simple conditions and then combined before being used in more dynamic or complex game and sport activities. For example, teaching a soccer unit may involve the following progression:

- The student should be taught the specialized skills of dribbling, trapping and gaining control, passing, shooting for a goal, and punting.
- Skills in combination such as passing off a dribble or receiving a pass, gaining control of the ball, and shooting for a goal would follow.

- Small-sided games such as three versus two would be used to place the skills in a more dynamic or complex game-like environment.

Basic tactics and strategies used for offense and defense are incorporated as the students apply the skills in dynamic game-like situations. They are learned through practice in small groups.

Example: Several small areas are marked off, and children play a game of Keep Away in which three offensive players go against two defensive players. The object is for the offensive players to maintain possession of the ball using quick, short passes and moving to open space to receive a pass. On defense the object is to cut off the space and gain possession of the ball.

The final stage in the elementary game curriculum is modified small-group and small-sided play used to apply the skills, tactics, and strategies learned. Students are able to test their newly learned skills and knowledge.

Example: The teacher designs a game of four-against-four soccer. The field is divided into several small playing areas marked with cones for goals and other markers for boundaries. The goalie position is rotated on a regular basis.

These modifications allow for more practice of the skills, tactics, and strategies than a traditional

Upper elementary students learn offensive and defensive skills in small-sided games.

11-on-11 game in which some players rarely, if ever, touch the ball. (For more on game modifications, see chapter 7.)

It is important to note that these game experiences are not a step-by-step approach. Without the basic skills, children will not be successful in game play; however, through brief game-like experiences, the teacher is able to demonstrate to the students the need to continue practicing skills, tactics, and strategies. A few minutes of a modified game allows children a chance to apply the skills and to self-assess. It also gives the teacher an opportunity to assess the strengths and weaknesses of individuals and the class as a whole and to make decisions on continuing the content. This teaching strategy also serves as a motivator to the upper elementary–age child.

Sample expectations for fifth grade outcomes in the games area include the following:

- Throw demonstrating both force and accuracy.
- Hand and foot dribble and pass to a teammate while preventing an opponent from stealing the ball.
- Keep an object going with a partner in a cooperative paddle or racket striking activity.
- In a competitive paddle or racket striking activity, strike a ball to an open space where opponent is not positioned.

Educational Gymnastics

The focus of educational gymnastics is on control of the body, sometimes called body management. The purpose of educational gymnastics is to teach students how to manage and control the weight of their body. The content area of gymnastics is a critical part of the elementary program because of the emphasis on muscle-strengthening and bone-strengthening activity critical to normal physical development. The content of educational gymnastics normally includes

- weight support and balancing,
- traveling actions (rolling, step-like actions such as cartwheels and walking on hands, flight), and
- weight transfer (transferring body weight from one base of support to another).

Unlike traditional competitive gymnastics or tumbling activities, educational gymnastics is child centered or individualized. All students are not expected to do a task in the same way; instead the student is asked to work within a concept with more than one potential solution to increase body control through traveling, jumping and landing, balancing, rolling, and weight transfer experiences, as well as combinations of these skills. In tumbling or a traditional approach to gymnastics, students are instructed to attempt specific skills such as a headstand. In an educational gymnastics approach, students are asked to experiment with a variety of ways to accomplish a task; the response may not be a named skill. For example, if a student is given the task to balance such that three parts of the body are used as the base of support, there may be several potential responses:

- Two hands and one foot (with the front of the body facing up)
- Two hands and one foot (with the front of the body facing down)
- Two feet and one hand
- Two knees and one elbow
- Two hands and the head (tripod or headstand)

In educational gymnastics, students are expected to devise multiple ways to respond to a task. In traditional gymnastics, all would be expected to master only the tripod or headstand in the preceding list.

Traditional gymnastics requires a variety of expensive apparatus. In addition to the cost, the apparatus comes with many safety and liability issues that have discouraged many schools from including this level of gymnastics in the physical education program. Educational gymnastics requires some equipment but can be taught adequately with equipment such as mats, vaulting boxes, benches, and balance beams.

Primary Grades: Gymnastics Skills

In the primary grades, children learn the fundamental skills and concepts of gymnastics. They learn to balance on different parts of the body. They learn to move from one place to another using their feet, hands, hands and feet, rolling actions, and flight; and they learn to control the weight of the body as it moves from one position to another. Gymnastics movements are presented first as exploratory experiences and progress to refining quality in the skills (e.g., maintain stillness in a balance, stay round throughout a roll); combining the skills (e.g., create a balance at a low level and then roll, maintaining a narrow shape down the mat); and finally sequencing the skills (balance, roll, balance). Experiences occur on the floor, on mats, and on low equipment such as boxes, beams, and benches. These are sample expectations for second grade outcomes:

1. Balance on a variety of body parts demonstrating stillness.
2. Balance at different levels using extension of free body parts.
3. Balance in symmetrical and asymmetrical shapes demonstrating variety in use of free body parts.
4. Roll in different directions without hesitating or stopping.
5. Transfer weight from feet to hands momentarily.
6. Jump and land, and then roll, using a variety of jumps and rolls.
7. Travel in a variety of ways on a low beam or bench demonstrating dynamic balance.
8. Perform a simple balance, roll, balance sequence with two different balances.

Upper Elementary Grades: Gymnastics Skills

In the upper elementary grades, children need experiences that allow them to refine their skills and challenge themselves in the areas of balancing, traveling actions, and transferring weight. Students in the upper grades are expected to work with more difficult skills and sequences of skills with smooth transitions.

More experiences with inverted balances, balances on a narrow base of support, and balances on equipment allow for the challenge. Moving in and out of balanced positions and working with partner balance routines further extend the balance experiences. In the upper elementary grades, a variety of rolls should be mastered (i.e., shoulder roll, backward shoulder roll, forward roll, log roll) and combined with different balances. Transferring weight onto hands, with axial movements, with step-like actions, and on and off of equipment, is a valuable and enjoyable experience for this age group. The sequences should be more complex than in the younger years and include combinations of traveling, rolling, balancing, and transferring weight onto and off of equipment. The following are sample expectations for fifth grade outcomes:

1. Balance with control on a variety of objects (e.g., beams, boxes, benches).
2. Develop and refine a gymnastics sequence demonstrating smooth transitions.
3. Maintain stillness in a variety of inverted balances.

Body management and balance skills are critical to development.

4. Demonstrate a variety of rolling and weight transfer actions maintaining control.

5. Develop and refine a gymnastics sequence inclusive of contrasting movements (e.g., change in direction, speed, flow, levels, jumps, rolls).

Educational gymnastics provides valuable body management experiences that can actually enhance skills used in dance and sport, as well as management of the body for life skills. Just as in recreational sport, for the child who wishes to pursue more advanced or specific gymnastics experiences, there are opportunities in most communities.

Educational Dance Experiences

Dance experiences in the elementary school are usually considered in terms of three types: rhythmical experiences; creative experiences; and predesigned dances that are typically folk, line, or square dances. Rhythmical experiences are designed to help children become competent in recognizing and moving to a beat and tempo. Creative dance provides the opportunity for students to learn and apply movement concepts in an expressive way and to create new dances or modify existing dances. Creative dance can be done with or without music. Predesigned dances such as folk, line, and square dance provide opportunities to learn about various cultures or different historical time periods.

Primary Grades: Dance Experiences

Dance in the primary grades typically has a strong focus on creative movement and is invaluable in teaching the movement concepts. Simple singing dances are popular, as are predesigned dances that have simple formations and steps. Dances with few step patterns that are repetitive are the most appropriate for this age group. To teach steady beat, which is critical, the instructor has students move various body parts to the beat of clear rhythms and use different locomotor patterns to different beats. Sample expectations for second grade outcomes include the following:

1. Demonstrate mature locomotor patterns in simple combinations in time to the music.

2. Demonstrate mature locomotor patterns while performing simple predesigned dances.

3. Demonstrate an awareness of even and uneven rhythmical patterns in self-space and general space.

4. Create and demonstrate a variety of nonlocomotor movements (e.g., curling, twisting, bending, stretching, rising and sinking) in sequence and to music.

5. Create simple dances that express feelings, emotions, ideas, or actions.

Upper Elementary Grades: Dance Experiences

While the primary grade experiences focus on building a dance foundation, the students in the upper elementary grades are ready to apply the movement concepts to more complex creative dances that are guided by themes (e.g., spaghetti dance, zoo dance, dance to a poem, dance that contrasts the effort qualities of movement). They should also be able to perform more complex predesigned dances that are actual folk, square, and line dances and should have the opportunity to work in small groups and create dances from various steps taught in class. Sample expectations for fifth grade outcomes include the following:

1. Design and perform dance sequences that combine traveling with the movement qualities of time, space, force, and flow.

2. Design and perform dance sequences with repeatable patterns.

3. Demonstrate the ability to combine complex movement patterns in a partner relationship.

4. Demonstrate the ability to combine complex movement patterns with a group in various line, circle, and square formations.

Dance provides valuable movement experiences that can be used for a lifetime. Body awareness gained through dance experiences enhances gymnastics and sports. Just as in recreational sports and gymnastics, for the child who wishes to pursue more dance experiences, there are opportunities in most communities.

Organizing and Managing the Physical Education Learning Environment

Because children are moving, equipment is being manipulated, and space is often limited, the physical education classroom is a complex environment. A physical education teacher must organize space, equipment, and the students to promote a quality and efficient learning setting. While establishing routines for these organization elements is crucial, some routines are lesson or content specific and require careful consideration by the teacher in the planning process. (Organization and management specific to content are addressed in the relevant chapters.)

Organizing Space

Organizing space includes establishing areas for set routines, such as activity areas with clearly marked boundaries, a place where students go when they enter class, an area to sit for the lesson introduction, and a place to prepare to leave class. Other space considerations will be specific to the lesson and may involve making the best use of limited practice areas and the need to arrange groups or equipment for safety reasons.

Organizing Equipment

Small equipment should be placed in hoops or small containers and distributed on the perimeters of the activity area with multiple access points. Equipment that will be used later in the lesson or in other classes should be organized so as not to interfere with the ongoing activities while at the same time allowing access when needed. Efficient and easy access to equipment eliminates the problem of children waiting to obtain equipment and provides for more instructional time. A clear routine for retrieving and returning equipment should be in place.

Organizing Students

Pairing students with partners or organizing them into groups is a regular practice for physical education teachers. Most students will quickly respond to the task when requested to stand next to a partner. The teacher can organize children into partners or small groups by using colors, birthdays, or first initials or by having the children draw playing cards. It is in the best interest of the students for teachers to preorganize groups when small-group activities are planned or when students are likely to be left out if they choose their own partners or groups.

Organizing space, equipment, and students is just as important a part of a physical education or physical activity plan as the moving experiences, and a quality teacher takes time to plan these important management protocols. In doing so the teacher prevents discipline problems, increases physical activity time, and creates a positive social environment.

SUMMARY

1. Physical education is the foundation of a comprehensive school physical activity program.

2. Quality physical education is goal oriented, developmentally appropriate, and instructionally appropriate to the physical, cognitive, and social-emotional needs of children with a goal for students to be physically active for a lifetime.

3. Administrative actions are crucial to the success of physical education, an often marginalized subject. Administrators should provide appropriate scheduling, hire quality certified teachers and hold them accountable to state and national standards, and allot funds for adequate equipment and facilities.

4. As the foundation of the school physical activity program, the physical education teacher should provide maximum physical activity time within the class period, teach skills that transfer to out-of-class physical activity, motivate children to be physically active, and serve as a physical activity director for the school.

5. Physical education is unique in that the goals and objectives are addressed through three domains of learning: psychomotor, cognitive, and affective. The ultimate goal is to develop skills, knowledge, and dispositions so that students will lead a physically active lifestyle.

6. There is a scope and sequence within a grade and across all grades in elementary physical education. One-size-fits-all curriculums do not work.

7. Physical education curriculum content includes educational games, gymnastics, and dance experiences. The primary grades, which represent the foundation, focus on fundamental locomotor, manipulative, and body management skills. With a strong fundamental foundation, children in the upper elementary grades are ready to learn specialized skills needed in the three content areas. In elementary school, physical fitness is typically interwoven within the experiences rather than a separate entity.

8. Movement concepts become the language in the gym and enhance movement experiences. Movement concepts are learned in the primary grades but are used throughout the elementary experience. These include body awareness, space awareness, effort concepts, and relationships.

9. Basic offensive and defensive tactics and strategies become an important part of learning in the upper elementary years.

10. Physical education programs educate people so that they have the skills and knowledge to be a participant and the dispositions that contribute to a desire to participate in a variety of physical activities.

CHECKING YOUR UNDERSTANDING

1. Reflect on your elementary school experiences and respond to the questions at the beginning of the chapter.

2. What is the role of the school administrator in the physical education program? Why is this role important?

3. What specific responsibilities does the physical education teacher have in the school physical activity program?

4. Why is it important for physical education programs to have enough equipment so that each student has his or her own ball, rope, and so on?

5. List and define the three domains of learning in physical education and the national standards that support them.

6. Explain what is meant by the scope and sequence of a program.

7. List the four factors, beyond access to quality instruction and opportunities to practice, that may affect the development of motor skills.

8. Using the locomotor skill of skipping, write four tasks that demonstrate your understanding of how space awareness concepts can be used to enhance the skill.

9. List the fundamental manipulative skills and connect each with an example that may become more specialized in the later years. Example: Throwing as a fundamental skill may be used for shooting a basketball in the upper elementary grades.

10. Explain how the skill of kicking is advanced from grades K through 5. When are the specific kicking skills introduced? What grade levels continue to practice these skills? At what grade level is mastery expected?

11. What is meant by the statement that the physical education learning environment is a more complex environment than the regular classroom environment?

RESOURCES

National Association for Sport and Physical Education

www.aahperd.org/naspe

Web Sites Specific to Teaching Physical Education

www.pecentral.org
www.pelinks4u.org/

Graham, G., Holt-Hale, S., & Parker, M. (2009). *Children moving: A reflective approach for teaching physical education* (8th ed.). Mountain View, CA: Mayfield.

REFERENCES

Fitts, P.M., & Posner, M.I. (1967). *Human performance.* Belmont, CA: Brooks/Cole.

National Association for Sport and Physical Education. (2003). *What constitutes a quality physical education program?* Reston, VA: Author.

National Association for Sport and Physical Education. (2004). *Moving into the future: National standards for physical education* (2nd ed.). Reston, VA: Author.

National Association for Sport and Physical Education. (2008). *Comprehensive school physical activity program* [Position statement]. Reston, VA: Author.

The Elementary School Physical Activity Program

OVERVIEW

The purpose of this chapter is to provide an overview of an elementary school comprehensive physical activity program that will be useful for administrators and professionals contemplating developing a physical activity program at the elementary school level. While physical activity programs at the elementary school level can be as simple as a designated physical education time (chapter 3) and a required recess (chapter 6), schools should and will want to ensure that providing physical activity for students is an important part of their mission. Comprehensive physical activity programs at the elementary school level provide opportunities for students to be active in the physical education class (chapter 3), in the classroom (chapter 5), at recess (chapter 6), and before and after school (chapter 11). They also act to broker the participation of students in community events and community programs (chapter 10).

CHAPTER OUTCOMES

This chapter will help you

- identify the specific needs of the elementary school–aged child for physical activity and the types of activity appropriate for this age group;
- develop guidelines for what constitutes an appropriate school physical activity program for children;
- identify the role of the community in establishing opportunities for physical activity for school-aged youth;

- identify the components of a good school physical activity program;
- identify the responsibility for a school physical activity program; and
- design and maintain playgrounds and outdoor areas that are safe and appropriate for children.

IN THIS CHAPTER

Most adults will agree that children like to be active and need to be active. The idea of putting young children in a seat and asking them to be still for 5 hours a day presents difficulties for the children and for the adults they work with. What makes sitting still in school a real problem is that many children do not have the opportunity to be active when they leave school. They go home and for a variety of reasons are not allowed to go outside and just "play" as many previous generations of children have been able to do. We find them sitting in front of a TV or computer screen, relegated to indoor activities that do not encourage physical activity.

The recent emphasis on academic achievement in the school setting has negatively affected both the opportunities students have for physical education and other opportunities in the school day to participate in physical activity. This is in spite of the fact that all the available research clearly indicates that children who are healthy and who have opportunities for physical activity throughout the day will actually learn better and achieve more (see chapter 1).

The U.S. Department of Health and Human Services developed the Youth Media Campaign (YMC), a national initiative to encourage children aged 9 through 13 years to engage in and maintain high levels of regular physical activity (USDHHS, 2008). A report issued by this campaign indicated that 61.5% of children aged 9 through 13 years do not participate in any organized physical activity during their nonschool hours and that 22.6% do not engage in any free-time physical activity. The report issued by the Youth Media Campaign suggests that improving the levels of physical activity among this population will require innovative solutions on the part of schools, communities, and parents.

In response to the idea that children are not getting the amount of physical activity they need to lead healthy lives and develop in the way they should, policy makers at all levels have begun to realize that schools must assume some of this responsibility. While daily physical education programs would be an ideal solution to the problem, many states and school districts do not have the resources at this time to provide this much needed programming (see chapter 3). Many states have mandated at least 30 minutes of physical activity a day to occur at school through either physical education or other programs as part of a school physical activity program. Many other schools have made a commitment to develop comprehensive school physical activity programs.

The Need for Physical Activity for Elementary-Aged Children

Physical activity is critical to the health and development of children. Some of the scientifically proven benefits of physical activity for children identified by the USDHHS are as follows:

- Improved aerobic endurance
- Improved muscular strength

- Among healthy young people, possible favorable effect of physical activity and physical fitness on risk factors for cardiovascular disease (e.g., body mass index, blood lipid profiles, and resting blood pressure)
- Decreased blood pressure in adolescents with borderline hypertension
- Increased physical fitness in obese children
- Decreased degree of overweight among obese children
- Increased bone mass density among young people participating in weight-bearing exercise

The *2008 Physical Activity Guidelines for Americans* released by the USDHHS recommends that children (up to 12 years of age) receive 60 minutes (1 hour) or more each day of moderate- and vigorous-intensity physical activity. What is new in this edition of the guidelines in relation to previous recommendations is the idea that this activity should include aerobic activity as well as age-appropriate muscle- and bone-strengthening activities. These recommendations are summarized in the sidebar.

Bone-strengthening and muscle-strengthening activities remain especially important for children and young adolescents. Muscle-strengthening activities put stress on the muscles through increased work. Bone-strengthening activities are those that require children to bear weight and carry weight. They are important because the greatest gains in bone mass occur during the years just before and during puberty. In addition, the majority of peak bone mass is obtained by the end of adolescence. Children need opportunities to climb, hang, swing, tumble, and perform activities that require a lot of force production and strength to develop muscle and bone strength. Well-designed physical education programs and playgrounds with the appropriate equipment can facilitate this development.

Children's activity patterns are not those of adults. When left to play, children will alternate short bouts of strenuous activity with short periods of rest. These brief periods "count" toward the desired 60 minutes of moderate to vigorous physical activity. It is important to remember that the total amount of physical activity is more important for achieving health benefits than is any one component (frequency, intensity, or duration). That means that frequent opportunities throughout the day for short bouts of physical activity are sufficient if they add up to at least 60 minutes.

When given the opportunity, most children will naturally choose to run, hop, skip, jump, cartwheel, hang, climb, and swing in ways that promote muscle and bone strength and develop movement patterns and skills. Children don't need formal muscle-strengthening programs such as lifting weights or calisthenics. The recommended types of activities for children and definitions of the types of activities that children need are listed in the sidebar "Examples of Moderate- and Vigorous-Intensity Aerobic Physical Activities and Muscle- and Bone-Strengthening Activities for Children."

Summary of Physical Activity Guidelines for Young Children

Children should do 60 minutes (1 hour) or more of physical activity daily.

- **Aerobic:** Most of the 60 or more minutes a day should be either moderate- or vigorous-intensity aerobic physical activity, and should include vigorous-intensity physical activity at least three days a week.
- **Muscle strengthening:** As part of their 60 or more minutes of daily physical activity, children and adolescents should include muscle-strengthening physical activity on at least three days of the week.
- **Bone strengthening:** As part of their 60 or more minutes of daily physical activity, children and adolescents should include bone-strengthening physical activity on at least three days of the week.

It is important to encourage young people to participate in physical activities that are appropriate for their age, that are enjoyable, and that offer variety.

Department of Health and Human Services, *2008 Physical Activity Guidelines for Americans*

Examples of Moderate- and Vigorous-Intensity Aerobic Physical Activities and Muscle- and Bone-Strengthening Activities for Children

Aerobic Activities

Aerobic activities are those in which young people rhythmically move their large muscles. Running, hopping, skipping, jumping rope, swimming, dancing, and bicycling are all examples of aerobic activities. Aerobic activities increase cardiorespiratory fitness. Children often do activities in short bursts. Although technically these may not be aerobic activities, the term "aerobic" is used here to refer to activities that increase the heart rate.

Examples of Moderate-Intensity Aerobic Activities
- Throwing and catching with a partner
- Four Square
- Active recreation, such as hiking, skateboarding, in-line skating
- Bicycle riding
- Brisk walking
- Sports such as baseball, softball, or golf

Examples of Vigorous-Intensity Aerobic Activities
- Active games involving running and chasing, such as tag
- Bicycle riding
- Jumping rope
- Martial arts, such as karate
- Running
- Sports such as soccer, ice or field hockey, basketball, swimming, tennis

Bone-Strengthening Activities

Bone-strengthening activities produce force on the bones that promotes bone growth and strength. This force is commonly produced by impact with the ground. Running, jumping rope, basketball, tennis, hopscotch, and gymnastics are all examples of bone-strengthening activities. As these examples illustrate, bone-strengthening activities can also be aerobic and muscle strengthening.

Examples of Bone-Strengthening Activities
- Games such as hopscotch
- Gymnastics activities
- Hopping, skipping, jumping
- Jumping rope
- Running
- Sports such as basketball, volleyball, tennis

Muscle-Strengthening Activities

Muscle-strengthening activities make muscles do more work than usual during activities of daily life. This is called "overload," and it strengthens the muscles. Muscle-strengthening activities can be unstructured and part of play, for example when children play on playground equipment, climb trees, and play tug-of-war. Or these activities can be structured, for example in work with resistance bands.

Examples of Muscle-Strengthening Activities
- Games such as tug-of-war
- Gymnastics activities
- Rope or tree climbing
- Sit-ups (curl-ups or crunches)
- Swinging, hanging, climbing on bars or other playground equipment
- Carrying equipment such as mats or chairs

Children need weight-bearing activities to develop their skeletal and muscular systems.

A Word of Caution: Short-Term Versus Long-Term Effects

One of the dangers in looking at the short-term benefits of physical activity for health is that programs may see their role as providing exercise rather than physical activity for children. Providing exercise is easy; you just turn on a calisthenics video or convert recess into a boot camp experience. All of the research we have about how to interest children in becoming lifelong participants in physical activity suggests that these experiences are a big turn-off and in one sense do more harm than good. The physical activities that we provide for children need to be fun and enjoyable so that children will become participants in a lifetime of physical activity. Children do not find calisthenics or forced participation in vigorous physical activity either fun or enjoyable and are likely not to become participants if forced to exercise or to participate in activities not appropriate to their age group. Age-appropriate activities are identified in the sidebar "Examples of Moderate- and Vigorous-Intensity Aerobic Physical Activities and Muscle- and Bone-Strengthening Activities for Children" on page 76. Programs using only exercise as the criterion for programming may accomplish the short-term goal of providing more physical activity but are likely to fail in their long-term goal of encouraging students to be active for a lifetime.

The path to promoting physically active youth and adults begins with thinking through how to promote age-appropriate activity in youth. The recommendations of physical activity experts include the following:

■ *Provide time for both structured and unstructured physical activity during school and outside of school.* Children need time for active *play.* Play by its very nature should be freely entered into. Through recess, physical activity breaks, physical education classes, before- and after-school programs, and active time with family and friends, youth can learn about physical activity and spend time doing it.

■ *Provide children and adolescents with positive feedback and good role models. It has been said that if you do not practice what you teach, you are teaching something else.* Parents and teachers should model and encourage an active lifestyle for children. Programs that include opportunities for faculty and other adults to be participants (chapter 17) are likely not only to serve the adults but to set a great example for the students. Praise, rewards, and encouragement help children to be active.

■ *Withholding physical activity as punishment does not help children to be active.* Because children like to be participants in physical activity, it is often withheld as a punishment. It should not be. Conversely, requiring students to do physical activity such as push-ups or to run laps as punishment serves to discourage a physically active lifestyle.

■ *Help young people learn skills required to do physical activity independently and safely.* As appropriate to their age, youth need to understand how to regulate the intensity of activity, increase physical activity gradually over time, set goals, use protective gear and proper equipment, follow rules, and avoid injuries.

■ *Promote activities that set the basis for a lifetime of activity.* Children and adolescents should be exposed to a variety of activities, including active recreation, team sports, and individual sports. In this way, they can find activities they can do well and enjoy. Although the physical education program is responsible for teaching children skills needed for participation in sport and recreational activities, the physical education program should also teach children the skills and games they need in order to be participants in unstructured free play. Include exposure to activities that adults commonly do, such as jogging, bicycling, hiking, and swimming. Young people should have the opportunity to experience noncompetitive activities and activities that do not require above-average athletic skills.

What Is a Comprehensive Elementary School Physical Activity Program?

A comprehensive school physical activity program takes a systemic approach to the problem of increasing physical activity for children. The school program considers itself a partner in a total effort to increase the amount of physical activity that children get both in school and out of school. This means that school programs need to work cooperatively with community groups and parents. Systemic approaches are not quick fixes. Merely delegating the responsibility to provide physical activity to the physical education program, to a short recess a day, or to a 10-minute exercise DVD is unlikely to have the benefits that a more systemic approach to the problem would have. Schools have the potential to influence not only what students do while in their care but also what they do when they leave for the day. A systemic approach to the elementary school physical activity program makes the responsibility for providing physical activity an all-school function, not only to provide physical activity during the school day but also to assume some responsibility for what students do when they are not in school.

Comprehensive planning for physical activity in the school will take a multifaceted approach to providing opportunities for physical activity and make use of all opportunities in the school day to provide students with physical activity and to encourage physical activity outside of the school day. Comprehensive physical activity programs will include the following components:

■ Good physical education programs
■ Physical activity opportunities before, during, and after school
■ Daily recess
■ Activity breaks in the classroom and opportunities to learn academic content through movement
■ Collaboration with community programs and events
■ Parental participation

Figure 4.1 is a description of a comprehensive physical activity program in Oregon that has been very successful in winning the support of parents, students, and the administration as a result of the efforts of those involved. The various program functions are discussed in several chapters in this book and are reviewed briefly here.

Physical Education

In a perfect world, physical education would be required of all students every day. This is the recommendation of the National Association for Sport and Physical Education and physical activity guidelines for children (NASPE, 2008). Because most schools do not have the resources to offer physical education every day, schools must ensure that the physical education program is a good one and must look to other opportunities to provide students with the amount of physical activity they need on a daily basis.

A good physical education program should be conducted by a certified physical education teacher and should be designed to offer a curriculum to *educate* students for a physically active lifestyle. Good programs are standards based and provide students with the skills, knowledge, and values they need to lead a physically active life. As described in chapter 3, the physical education program is the foundation of a good physical activity program.

FIGURE 4.1

An Example of a Comprehensive School Physical Activity Program ⊙

The Physical Education Program at Independence Elementary School, Oregon

Students at IES receive 35 minutes of physical education three times per week. The curriculum is based on the national and state standards.

Before School

■ *Gym Rat Time.* On Monday and Wednesday, students have an opportunity to practice their circus arts skills (juggling balls, unicycling, stilts, pogo sticks, diabolos, flower sticks, juggling scarves, juggling rings, juggling clubs). Tuesday and Thursday focus on jump rope: individual, partner, long, and Double Dutch. Friday varies to include skills that students learned in physical education, Dance Revolution, basketball, and so on.

■ *Team (Together Everyone Achieves More) Time.* All students and staff meet in the gym every day when the bell rings to start school. Many parents join the activity. They do a dynamic warm-up routine, do a couple of dances, and close with a stretching and cool-down routine. This is followed by the Pledge of Allegiance, announcements, and an affirmation of cheer for the day. This gives students 100 minutes of physical activity a week and builds school "community." This is how Team Time works:

1. With the first morning bell, students meet in the gym at their assigned places. They are assigned by class to an area. This is so the teacher can come in to the gym, take attendance, do lunch count, and so on. Meg Greiner is already beginning the Team Time warm-up, so as soon as the students are in their assigned place and have checked their personal space, they start following Ms. Greiner.

2. In order to be sure that all the kids are safe and understand all the procedures, kindergarteners are assigned a fourth grade "buddy" to help them learn the routine. This provides an experienced model to follow.

3. The warm-up songs, which are usually fairly slow, call for cross-lateral movement and stretching.

4. The pace is picked up when the second song incorporates jumping patterns and more dynamic movements.

5. The third and fourth songs, sometimes led by students, call for previously learned dances (the students know more than 50 different dances).

6. The last song is much like the first song, paced more slowly to allow for cool-down and stretching.

7. The students have learned sign language (American Sign Language), so some days Ms. Greiner leads the class in a song with ASL.

8. After the cool-down, students are responsible for leading the flag salute.

9. Ms. Greiner follows the flag salute with any announcements.

10. Lastly, the students do their daily affirmations in order to set a positive tone for the day. Their affirmation is something like *"Learning rocks! Yes!"*

Lunchtime Programs (Third Through Fifth Grades)

At lunchtime, open gym time is supervised by the physical education teacher and playground aides. The focus of the activity changes with the week—for example, basketball, Capture the Flag, or circus arts.

Daily Recess

Recess is from 8:00 to 8:20 every day and for 20 minutes during lunchtime. Students are taught playground games during the first month of school. Parents helped to paint a "peaceful playground" template, and children are taught peaceful playground games. The school has utilized a "conflict manager" program that

(continued)

(continued)

the physical education teacher trains students for and supervises. These students can lead games and turn jump ropes. Other recesses are left to the discretion of the classroom teacher. Kindergarten students have several during the school day.

After School

Prime Time. Students can sign up for sports, dance, Road Runner Club, and circus arts.

Activity Breaks—Classroom Teachers

Many of the staff use Brain Gym exercises, especially the Hook-Up, Brain Buttons, and Cross Crawl, to activate and calm students, especially when they are standing in line.
Examples of classroom physical education opportunities:

- *Teacher 1:* I have a large pull-out ELD class, with mixed grades, right after recess. We start every class with 5 minutes of Team Time exercises, used as a transition to calm them down. We do two active exercises that cross the midline, and then do the Hook-Up (parts 1, 2, and 3) for our deep, slow breathing together to calm everyone down. I have different students lead the exercises every day, emphasizing a five-count breathe in and a five count breathe out to slow their heart rates down and get them calm for learning. This has helped us use the rest of our learning time much more efficiently, with less interruptions from behavior.

- *Teacher 2:* I am a fourth grade teacher. We do many chants that require rhythm and hand movements (clapping, snapping, signs, and so on); also, we move whenever the focus changes. We begin our focus and motivation in one place in the room, then move to another place for the guided practice, to still another place for direct instruction, and so on. Seating is always varied, and expectations for certain movements are always made clear. Lastly, we have a daily signal word—a word pertinent to our unit of study, along with a sign or movement that accompanies it. When we are getting ready for a transition, I give the directive, "When you hear the signal word, you will. . . ." Then I say the word and make the motion, and the students repeat it and make the motion before moving. This really focuses them, builds vocabulary, and clarifies expectations throughout the day.

- *Teacher 3:* We use the stage in the library to act out stories or important pieces of dialogue in a book. We do lots of drama games that fit our themes, especially with our book fair themes or the latest "library metaphor" (example of a library metaphor: librarian = captain, patrons = pirates, library = high seas, books = treasure, and so on). Then we do some drama around that and I dress in character. The one coming soon is librarian = cardiologist, library = heart of the school, books = life blood circulating through the school. We might do a round robin to look at biography or Caldecott or a book series. We do a Dr. Seuss book walk to music. We do a Dewey Decimal lineup; each student has a call number, and they put themselves in order.

Parental Participation

Each year the school hosts several events, including Circus Arts Night, Physical Education Nights, and Family Fiesta Night, with parents and children invited to play together. At the annual carnival, active carnival activities include a blow-up obstacle course, Dance Revolution, and the climbing wall.

All-School Events

Each spring the music teacher and physical education teacher conduct an annual "Move and Groove" program in which students showcase their skills. The physical education part starts off with children riding unicycles, followed by the pogo stickers and stilt walkers, followed by the wogglers (on a balance board sort of thing), followed by the jugglers with flower sticks, diabolos, balls, rings, and scarves. Then each class performs a specific dance and sings several songs. The conclusion is usually a large-group dance (all third, fourth, and fifth graders—around 200) and a sign language song.

Community Collaboration

The school collaborates with community programs and events. The gym is shared with the YMCA gymnastics programs. The students also have soccer, basketball, baseball, and cheerleading available through YMCA programs.

Physical Activity Opportunities Before, During, and After School

Before- and after-school programs are great ways to provide many students with opportunities for physical activity. Clubs such as walking clubs, intramurals, special events, and morning exercises that begin the school day are conducted successfully by many schools. These programs can be formal or informal and are discussed in chapters 5, 10, and 11. Most are conducted by both the physical education faculty and other faculty within the school as well as community and parent volunteers.

Recess

Recess is a critical part of the student's day, not only because it provides opportunities for physical activity but also because it provides opportunities for children to be children. Physical play helps children develop the confidence and social skills they need to be and feel successful. It is a critical part of their education. Schools have an obligation to provide adequate resources in terms of permanent and manipulative equipment for children and adequate, safe play spaces. Guidelines for planning and conducting recess are provided in chapter 6. Guidelines for establishing safe equipment and play spaces conclude this chapter.

Breaks in the Classroom and Movement Opportunities to Teach Academic Content

The 60 minutes of physical activity that children need during each day is cumulative. This means that it should not occur all at once or in long periods of sustained activity. Children spend most of their school day in the academic classroom. The classroom teacher can provide physical activity in a number of ways; these can take the form of short activity breaks as a transition between content areas, recess, and the use of physical activity to teach academic content. Movement is a great medium for learning, particularly for young children, and should be considered when instruction in academic content is being planned. Incorporating movement into the teaching of academic content, as well as the role of the classroom teacher in providing daily activity, is discussed in chapter 5.

Community Programs and Events

Government agencies, including schools, often work at cross purposes with each other and duplicate services. There are many well-intentioned programs in all our communities that have sought to deal with the lack of physical activity of both children and adults. Each operates separately for a variety of reasons, with separate facilities and programs targeting the same audience and essentially working with the same objectives. The efforts of each would be a great deal more successful if there were collaborative efforts sending one message with one voice. Schools need to be a part of that picture.

A major element of a systemic approach to developing a physical activity program is the establishment of relationships with the community. Many schools operate in isolation from what is happening around them. Communities provide many opportunities for physical activity for children, both through structured participation in sport teams (e.g., soccer, softball, tennis) and clubs (dance, fitness, walking), for example, and through special events such as marathons, walk your child to school programs, and special race days. In addition, the

A good physical activity program facilitates student participation in community activities.

health professionals in your community, as well as national professional and commercial organizations, are continuously sponsoring programs to encourage participation in physical activity. Schools need to become a part of these initiatives and can do so by collaborating with these organizations to involve school children and their families. Collaboration can be as simple as linking these opportunities to the school Web site or as elaborate as signing students up for participation and arranging transportation if needed so that students can participate. When collaboration takes place, everyone is a winner. When more people participate, they create a need for more opportunities.

Working With Parents

School physical activity programs should see their role as educating parents on the importance of providing physical activity opportunities for their children, facilitating those opportunities through school events that involve parents, and keeping parents informed on the opportunities being provided by the school and the community for students to be involved in physical activity. Schools will also want to involve parents as volunteers or paid workers for various parts of the program. Most schools have opportunities for physical education teachers to talk with parents at PTA or PTO meetings as well as special events. School Web sites with links to resources are a great way to keep parents informed and up to date on recommendations for physical activity for both students and parents.

The School Physical Activity Program: Who Is Responsible?

Administrators reading this chapter are probably thinking that they cannot add one more thing to the school's responsibilities. The role of the school has come a long way from the time when teaching students the three R's was their primary responsibility. When society has a problem, schools are asked to fix it. Schools today are being asked to fix the health issues connected with a population of physically inactive people. Because schools are compulsory and because they work with young children who are formulating habits that will likely remain with them as adults, schools must assume this responsibility. Although school administrators do have the ultimate responsibility for what goes on in their schools, they should not see the development of a physical activity program as their sole respon-

sibility. School wellness councils were mandated by the federal government (chapter 2) to play the major role in the establishment of school physical activity programs, and the physical activity program director (chapter 10) will play the major role in coordinating the program. Full, comprehensive programs will involve the following:

- The physical education teacher, most likely as the physical activity director
- Classroom teachers, trained to work with students in the classroom and at recess
- Parent and community volunteers to supervise aspects of the program

However, a program will be only as effective as the support it gets from the administration. With the health of an entire generation of students at stake, administrators will need to value the program and provide the resources and support needed to initiate and maintain it.

Designing and Maintaining Safe and Age-Appropriate Playgrounds and Outdoor Areas

A lot of the physical activity that children are provided in the school setting will take place out of doors in designated playgrounds, outdoor field space, or blacktop or concrete areas. Minimally each school should have a playground area and playground equipment for kindergarten that are separate from other facilities, a playground area with equipment for the upper grades, a blacktop or concrete area, and grassed field space.

Safety in playgrounds is the responsibility of the students who use them, the teachers who supervise them, and the administrators who design them and govern their use. While some of the information in this section appears also in the chapter on recess (chapter 6), it is provided here specifically for administrators. It is the administrator who has ultimate responsibility for the safety of children on the playground at a school. The liability issues associated with playgrounds have caused many schools to eliminate from the play area any play structures that could potentially result in a child being injured. While any physical activity can potentially result in injury to a child, the answer to the problem is not to prevent children from being active and doing the kinds of things that they need to do to develop physically, emotionally, and socially, but to design playgrounds with play structures that are safe for children, to maintain them, and to ensure that they are appropriately supervised during the school day.

The professional group that monitors and makes recommendations for playground safety is the National Program for Playground Safety (NPPS). The organization's online resources and comprehensive text, *S.A.F.E. Play Areas: Creation, Maintenance, and Renovation* (Thompson, Hudson, & Olsen, 2007), include checklists for school playground safety, links to Consumer Product Safety Commission Web sites, training materials for children, and recommendations for construction and maintenance of playgrounds.

The NPPS has identified four elements that make a playground safe:

- Supervision of children in play
- Age-appropriate equipment
- Fall surfacing for playground equipment
- Equipment and surfacing maintenance on a regular basis

Each of these "risk factors" contributes either positively or negatively to playground safety.

Today's playground structures for children are primarily what are called composite structures, meaning that the components are linked together to form one or two structures. Most components include play panels, track slides, steering wheels, climbing walls, arch climbers, balance beams, slides, parallel bars, cargo nets, and horizontal ladders. Each of these structures encourages students to hang, climb, swing, balance, and slide in ways that promote physical and motor development. These structures become more important with the new guidelines recommending that children engage in activities that promote muscular strength and bone density. The swings, seesaws, and merry-go-rounds that were characteristic of playgrounds of the past are declining in use.

Surfacing of Playgrounds

Children want to climb and need to climb. Equipment over 6 feet (1.8 meters) high doubles the rate of injury (Laforest et al., 2001). Suitable materials for landing include loose fill such as pea gravel, sand, and wood chips or fiber that is maintained at a depth of 12 inches (about 30 centimeters) in locations where children are likely to fall or jump. While many schools install the surfacing appropriately, they often do not maintain the depth of the surfacing

Mulch is a safe surface but needs to be replaced often to be maintained.

as the playground ages or place the surfacing where it is most needed. Adding surface depth needs to be a part of regular playground maintenance.

Supervision of Playgrounds

The best way to prevent accidents on playground equipment is to make sure that adults are present when children are on the equipment and that the adults are actively supervising the play. In order to do this they should be in a position to be able to see what children are doing. Since schools are often used by the public at times when schools are not open, many schools should have signs posted to indicate that adults should be present to supervise. Teaching children how to play safely on the playground will also reduce the number of poten-

tial accidents. The sidebar lists the "rules" children should be taught.

Age-Appropriate Design

When young children play on equipment designed for older children, or older children play on equipment designed for younger students, accidents can result. Many schools separate the playground equipment for kindergarten and the primary grades and separate the "recess" playground area from the areas used by physical education classes. Most composite structures are not appropriate for students above the third grade. Older students will need equipment they can use to participate in sports and games. Basketball areas, baseball diamonds, field space, a blacktop area marked off with games like Four Square and tetherball, and permanent fitness equipment (ladders, balance beams, and so on) are more appropriate for the older age groups. These areas are easy to maintain and are not likely to be abused when school is not in session.

Playground Maintenance

The school administrator is ultimately responsible for playground maintenance and will delegate the care of the playground to a district or school maintenance team. Schools will want to do careful planning for the playground facilities so that they are safe and more easily maintained. Many well-intentioned parent groups have constructed playgrounds for schools that are neither safe nor easy to maintain. Unless schools are willing to invest in composite surfaces, they will need to plan on regularly replacing the surfacing material as it wears away with weather and heavy use of equipment. Equipment needs to be inspected periodically for needed repairs or replacement. Someone needs to have this responsibility and must take the responsibility seriously.

SUMMARY

1. Children should have 60 minutes of physical activity a day including aerobic, muscle-strengthening, and bone-strengthening activities.

2. Children can accumulate the needed physical activity in short bouts.

3. Attempts to improve the physical activity of children should consider both the long-term and short-term effects of a program.

4. School physical activity programs should coordinate their efforts with community efforts.

Helping Children Play Safely on the Playground ⊙

Adults should

- make sure the playground is supervised,
- make sure the equipment is checked regularly and well maintained, and
- make sure there is soft surfacing underneath the equipment.

Rules for Children

- Play responsibly.
- Make sure an adult is present when you play.
- Tell an adult if playground equipment is broken, and do not play on it until it is fixed.
- Safety on swings: Sit down while you swing. Slow down before you get off of a swing. Do not walk near someone who is swinging. You could get hit if you walk too closely.
- Safety on climbers: Use both hands when you climb. Climb only on dry equipment. You could fall if it is wet.
- Safety on slides: Never climb up the front of the slide. Someone may slide down and hit you. It is safest to slide down with your feet first. Only one person should slide down at a time.
- Have FUN!

5. Comprehensive elementary school physical activity programs include a good physical education program, before- and after-school and lunchtime programs, recess, classroom breaks, and participation in community programs and events.

6. The school physical activity program is the responsibility of the entire school.

7. Playgrounds and outdoor areas for physical activity should minimally include both kindergarten and upper grade playground equipment, a blacktop or concrete area, and grassed field space.

8. Playground areas should have an appropriate surface, should be age appropriate, and should be well supervised and maintained.

CHECKING YOUR UNDERSTANDING

1. What are the health benefits to children of regular physical activity?

2. How should the 60 minutes of physical activity for children be distributed in types of activity?

3. Describe three activities that are aerobic, three that are muscle strengthening, and three that are bone strengthening.

4. Why should the physical activity program for children not be exercise and calisthenics?

5. What are the components of a comprehensive physical activity program?

6. Whose responsibility is the physical activity program?

7. What kinds of outdoor space for physical activity should a school have?

8. What are the four elements of a safe playground?

RESOURCES

CDC DASH Plan to Address Physical Activity, HHS
www.cdc.gov/HealthyYouth/physicalactivity/pdf/Addressing_Phys_Activity.pdf

CDC Division of Adolescent and School Health (DASH), HHS
www.cdc.gov/HealthyYouth/about/index.htm

Centers for Disease Control and Prevention (CDC), HHS
www.cdc.gov/physicalactivity

Dietary Guidelines for Americans 2005, HHS and U.S. Department of Agriculture (USDA)
www.health.gov/DietaryGuidelines

Eat Smart. Play Hard, USDA
www.fns.usda.gov/eatsmartplayhard

Healthfinder: A Guide to Reliable Health Information on Physical Activity and Other Topics; Health and Human Services (HHS)
www.healthfinder.gov

NIH Ways to Enhance Children's Activity and Nutrition (We Can!), HHS
www.nhlbi.nih.gov/health/public/heart/obesity/wecan

Office of Disease Prevention and Health Promotion, HHS
http://odphp.osophs.dhhs.gov

Office of the Surgeon General, Healthy Youth for a Healthy Future, HHS
www.surgeongeneral.gov/obesityprevention/index.html

Office on Women's Health, Powerful Bones. Powerful Girls; HHS
www.girlshealth.gov/bones

The President's Challenge
www.presidentschallenge.org

President's Council on Physical Fitness and Sports (PCPFS), HHS
www.fitness.gov

SmallStep Kids, HHS
www.smallstep.gov/kids/flash/index.html

REFERENCES

Laforest, S., Robitaille, Y., Lesage, D., & Dorval, D. (2001). Surface characteristics, equipment height, and the occurrence and severity of playground injuries. *Injury Prevention, 7,* 35-40.

National Association for Sport and Physical Education. (2008). *Comprehensive school physical activity program* [Position statement]. Reston, VA: Author.

Thompson, D., Hudson, S., & Olsen, H. (2007). *S.A.F.E. play areas: Creation, maintenance, and renovation.* Champaign, IL: Human Kinetics.

U.S. Department of Health and Human Services, Centers for Disease Control and Prevention. (2008). *Physical activity guidelines for Americans*. Available at www.health.gov/paguidelines. Accessed September 2009.

U.S. Department of Health and Human Services, National Center for Chronic Disease Prevention and Health Promotion Division of Nutrition. (2008). Division of nutrition, physical activity and obesity. Available at www.cdc.gov/nccdphp/dnpao/index.html. Accessed November 8, 2008.

5

The Role of the Classroom Teacher in Physical Activity Programs

OVERVIEW

As noted in earlier chapters, physical activity opportunities for children should occur in several short bouts totaling 60 minutes or more each day (National Association for Sport and Physical Education [NASPE], 2004). Given the fact that children are in school for one-half of their waking hours, physical activity opportunities need to happen during the school day. In the elementary school program, the classroom teacher is with the children almost the entire day. It will be the responsibility of the classroom teacher to provide opportunities for physical activity. This chapter explores the alternatives available to classroom teachers that will enable them to make sure students in their classrooms get at least 30 minutes of physical activity during the school day.

CHAPTER OUTCOMES

This chapter will help you

- discover ways to provide opportunities for physical activity,
- encourage and promote physically active lifestyles during and outside of the school day,
- recognize the importance of teaching and promoting quality health and nutritional habits,
- create or join a school wellness committee, and
- become a physically active role model to your students.

IN THIS CHAPTER

Physical education class time has been eliminated in some school districts and for others has been reduced to as little as one or two days a week. The primary reason is the push to give more time to academic achievement. The demand for more time in the classroom has not only decreased physical education time but also decreased or eliminated recess in many school districts.

The intentions to improve test scores, while legitimately motivated, have resulted in children sitting for unrealistic amounts of time with the expectation that they will stay focused. The result has been counterproductive, as academic performance actually decreases with less physical activity (Etnier & Sibley, 2003; Pate et. al., 2006; Pellegrini & Bohn, 2005; Sibley & Etnier, 2003; Tremblay, Inman, & Williams, 2000). In order to reverse this trend in elementary schools, classroom teachers must play a vital role in the school physical activity program.

Providing Opportunities for Physical Activity

The classroom teacher has a major responsibility to provide opportunities for daily physical activity. The demands on the elementary classroom teacher are many, and the pressures for student academic success rest on this one individual; however, providing opportunities for physical activity need not be a burden but can be an enjoyable part of the day. Teacher preparation for most of the ideas shared in this chapter is minimal; and the result is healthier, more focused, and better-behaved children (Bogden & Vega-Matos, 2000). There are multiple ways in which teachers can provide short bouts of physical activity, including these:

- Starting the day with activity
- Going for a walk
- Organizing and playing games
- Teaching simple dances
- Including a daily recess period
- Transitioning between classroom tasks with physical activity breaks
- Integrating physical activity into academics
- Interdisciplinary teaching with physical education

Start the Day With Activity

A routine of morning movement activities is a good way to start the school day. While some children have not been up for a long time, others have spent substantial time on a school bus or in a morning child care program. A little physical activity is just what both groups need to start a productive day. There are several options for morning activities:

- A school day opening led via television or a morning assembly
- DVDs or music that promotes or leads movement
- Teacher- or student-led routines

School days have traditionally started with morning announcements and the Pledge of Allegiance over an intercom system. Most schools have access to intraschool television viewing or large-screen projection systems and use this as an avenue to communicate to the student body. Schoolwide access provides an opportune way to lead students in morning activity. The schools that are using this approach follow the typical announcements and procedures by having students stand by their desk to participate in a morning movement routine. The child-oriented movement videos used in schools may be purchased from a reliable education source or created and videotaped by teachers or students in the school. However, in order to create their own videos, which are much more personable than commercial ones, students will need to learn the proper techniques for leading activities and for video recording.

Many schools incorporate a live news show each morning and follow by having the physical education teacher, a parent volunteer, or older students lead the student body in a morning movement routine. Still other schools have chosen the option of a morning assembly for announcements. These assemblies can easily incorporate movement experiences led by the physical education teacher, a classroom teacher, an administrator, or students. All faculty, staff, and children can participate in simple movements that can be conducted in self-space. Help for a successful morning assembly program incorporating physical activity is provided in chapter 4 (figure 4.1).

If the schoolwide approach is not appropriate, teachers can individually select DVDs or CD ROMs or download music from the Internet that directly leads the students in activities. Simple dances listed in chapter 8, as well as resources listed at the end of this chapter, will aid in the selection of appropriate material. Another option is teacher- or student-led activities. Exercises can be done with or without music; the teacher or student simply calls out the movements and leads the activity while facing the student body. Students in grades 2 and up might be encouraged to create a morning exercise routine as a group project and take turns with leadership responsibilities.

Whatever the manner of presentation, there are several factors to be taken into consideration when morning activities are planned. The activity should be

- time appropriate,
- enjoyable and varied,
- age related and developmentally appropriate, and
- appropriate to the available space.

Time Appropriateness

The recommended time range for a morning activity is between 5 and 15 minutes. This decision may be based on availability of time or the intensity of the activity. Ideally, you want the movement to be at a moderate to a high intensity level so as to briefly increase the child's heart rate. If some low-intensity activity is also mixed into the session, then the time allotted should be closer to 15 minutes.

Enjoyment and Variety

Enjoyment of the movement activity is an essential factor for motivation. An advantage of providing physical activity to elementary-age children is that most of them love to move. For the older elementary child, variety and up-to-date dance moves and music are often the motivators. Children at these ages also enjoy creating their own routines. As mentioned earlier, these can be prerecorded, or students can take the role of standing in front of the class and leading. Success in student-led activities is dependent upon cooperative and productive work sessions that result in a group-designed routine. The teacher may suggest basic dance steps or exercises for groups to use in designing a routine. Each group should then be given the opportunity to lead the class in the given routine for a couple of weeks. Repeating the same routine for a couple of weeks allows the students the opportunity to become familiar with the movements. Once they know the routine, the physical activity intensity level may increase because the concentration level decreases. A new routine every two weeks allows for variety and change in leadership roles.

Varying the activities is not as important for the primary grade child as it is for the upper elementary child. In fact, repetition is good for primary grade children. They enjoy reading a particular book or having it read to them until they have it memorized. They will watch the same movie over and over and become familiar with each scene. Young children also prefer familiarity in music and activities. As a teacher, you will be ready for a change long before the children are. Advice for the primary grade teacher is to find a favorite activity and make it part of the morning routine.

Age and Developmental Considerations

Given the age range and varying developmental levels of elementary children, the challenge is to find an activity that all children can do successfully. Movement routines for older children are not developmentally appropriate for the young child.

If the movements require a high level of coordination (e.g., push-ups, jumping jacks) or agility (quick changes in direction), they should be used only in the upper elementary grades. If older children are to gain the benefits of specific exercises, they should be taught the proper way to do them and provided options if they do not have the prerequisite skills or sufficient strength for success. For example, a child may perform a regular push-up or a modified push-up, in which the weight is on bent knees as opposed to toes tucked under. For the younger child, all movements should be simple to perform, relate to movements they know, and easy to follow. For example, young children may be asked to march in place like a soldier, flap their arms like a bird, or spin in a circle like a top.

Repetition of the same movement is helpful for all elementary children. One idea is to select four different movements, perform each for eight counts, and then repeat the sequence four times. Figure 5.1 lists dance movements that teachers or children may use in a routine, as well as sample routines that follow this format. They are organized by experience levels—beginning, intermediate, and advanced. Figure 5.2 includes exercises and sample routines appropriate for various grade levels (for more on fitness, see chapter 9).

The format of schoolwide morning activities can be altered to meet the needs of the various age groups. An option would be to show one video geared toward younger children before the announcements and another that is appropriate for older children after the announcements. Teachers can then tune in at the appropriate time. For schools that assemble in one location for morning announcements, the same approach can be used, or alternate days the movement activities can be used for K through 2 and grades 3 through 5. The grades not involved can be dismissed, allowing for more activity space. Another option is to have two assembly periods, one for each grade range.

FIGURE 5.1

Dance Steps for Creating Routines

The following steps are separated by level of difficulty: beginner, intermediate, and advanced. All steps listed can be performed to either four or eight beats of music. Usually a step to the right will be followed by that same step performed to the left (F = forward; B = backward; R = right; L = left).

Beginner

- March in place.
- Jump F, B with both feet.
- Heel, toe R, L (touch R heel out followed by R toe next to L foot, repeat L).
- Walk F, walk B.
- Sidestep (step R, step L beside, step R, touch L, reverse).
- Slide (step R, slide L together, step L, slide R together).
- Knees crisscross (touch knees and crisscross arms, reverse).
- Step touch (step R to side, touch L, reverse).
- High knees.

Sample routine:

1. March in place (R, L, R, L, R, L, R, L).
2. Heel, toe (RH, RT, LH, LT, RH, RT, LH, LT).
3. Walk F (R, L, R, L), walk B (R, L, R, L).
4. Slide step (step R, slide L together, step L, slide R together, repeat).
5. Repeat 1 through 4 (three more times).

Intermediate

- Grapevine (R, step behind with L, R, touch L, reverse).
- Turn, 2, 3, touch (turn clockwise to right, counterclockwise back).
- Coffee grinder (use R hand on floor and position legs out horizontally while turning in circle, reverse).
- Giddy-up (wave imaginary lasso in air while turning in place).
- Crisscross (jump up and land with wide feet, jump and cross, repeat with opposite foot crossing in front).
- Hamstring curls (step to side while pulling up inside leg and both arms from elbow down, reverse).
- Raise the roof (both hands above head pushing to ceiling).

Sample routine:

1. Grapevine (R, reverse L, and repeat).
2. Giddy-up (four counts and reverse).
3. Crisscross (eight counts).
4. Raise the roof (eight counts).
5. Repeat 1 through 4 (three more times).

Advanced

- Hip-hop R, L (hop on one foot and turn in place while pushing downward with both hands).
- Cabbage patch ("stir" with arms in front while transferring weight from one foot to other).
- Polka (hop, step, step, step).
- Schottische (step, step, step, hop).
- Triple step (two quick steps, one slow; goes 1 and 2; 3 and 4).
- Cha-cha-cha (step F, step B, triple step in place, step F, step B, triple step in place).

Sample routine:

1. Triple step (eight counts).
2. Cabbage patch (eight counts).
3. Cha-cha-cha (eight counts).
4. Hip-hop (eight counts).
5. Repeat 1 through 4 (three times).

Appropriateness to the Available Space

Decisions about what morning activities are appropriate are often based on space availability. The space may be the cafeteria, gym or multipurpose room, open space in a hallway or classroom, or simply the space beside a student's desk. For safety, children should have adequate space that they do not touch anyone or anything around them and are able to move a few steps in all directions without contacting desks, tables, or other objects. While some areas will be conducive to a variety of movements, others will greatly limit the activity. The teacher is responsible for making the area safe (i.e., moving furniture, allowing only self-space movement). There are many activities that can provide quality and enjoyable physical activity in a limited space, are both age and developmentally appropriate, and can be completed in 5 to 15 minutes.

FIGURE 5.2

Sample Exercises and Routines

The following sample exercises are arranged by grade level and intensity level. After each list is a sample routine that starts at a low intensity level, progresses to a moderate level, and then peaks at a high level. The routine then slowly decreases in intensity. A routine can last from 5 to 15 minutes. Teachers may create other routines using the sample exercises.

Grades K Through 2

- *High:* Jump, hop, march, jog, pretend to jump rope, and run (all in place).
- *Moderate:* Walk, climb, twist, spin, crab walk (walk on hands and feet with stomach facing up), bear walk (walk on hands and feet with bottom up), swimming arms, flapping arms.
- *Low:* Turn, sway, bend, stretch, reach.

Sample K through 2 routine:

1. Warm-up: Stretch your arms high to the sky and hold. Stretch one arm at a time and pretend to pick apples. After picking each apple, place it in a basket before picking one with the other hand. Reach toward the floor and pretend to pick flowers. After picking each flower, place in it a pretend vase and pick another with your other hand. Sway from side to side slowly as if the wind is blowing you.
2. Act as if you are climbing up a ladder. Have a seat and raise your feet as you spin in a circle. Walk like a crab forward four steps and back four steps. Stand and walk in place.
3. Speed up to a jog. Run as fast as you can. Pick up a pretend jump rope and jump on two feet. Continue, but now hop on one foot. Drop your rope and march in place.
4. Pretend you are swimming. Now slowly turn in a circle. Stop and bend over slowly, swaying your arms from side to side.

Grades 3 Through 5

- *High:* Run, jump, hop, scissor jump, jog, crisscross jump, jump turns, pretend to jump rope, jumping jacks, skip, jump kicks, ski jumps (side to side with feet together), bell jumps (forward and back with feet together)
- *Moderate:* Twist, high steps, cross crawls (touch elbow to opposite knee), jab punches, swim the backstroke, partner pass push-ups (face a partner, with both in push-up position, and pass a paper ball from hand to hand), partner curl-ups (toe to toe with partner, alternate doing a curl-up and handing a paper ball).
- *Low:* Side stretches, leg stretches, arm stretches, walk, march slowly, toe raises, alternate toe touches (slight bend in knees), deep breathing.

Sample grades 3 through 5 routine:

Suggestion: Have students do each movement to the count of 8 and repeat before going to the next movement.

1. Walk in place. March in place.
2. Add high steps to the march. Add your elbows and do cross crawls. Now stand in place and perform jab punches.
3. Jump in place. Scissor jump. Ski jump. Bell jump. Jump kicks.
4. Do the twist. Swim the backstroke. Face a partner in push-up position and hand the paper ball back and forth. Now, pass the ball doing a curl-up between each handoff.
5. End with leg stretches and then lie on your back and close your eyes, concentrating on deep breathing in and out.

Students can be active in limited classroom space.

Walking Breaks

A simple way to include physical activity in the school day is with a 10- to 15-minute walking break. A walk break provides a few minutes of sunlight and fresh air while simultaneously combining physical activity, social time, or academics or some combination of these. The only required equipment for walking is a pair of sneakers. Beneficial to students and teachers, walking is a quality physical activity that

- crosses all skill levels and can be adapted to meet various fitness levels,

- provides opportunities for children and teachers to socialize,

- provides an occasion to extend the learning environment to the outdoors, and

- contributes to academic success by helping students to be better able to focus on academic material.

Walking breaks offer an opportunity to provide physical activity to children in a noncompetitive environment. Children and teachers can benefit from walking regardless of their present fitness level. Noticeable improvements in cardiorespira-tory fitness will occur with walks as short as 10 to 15 minutes daily.

Taking time to go for a brief walk will provide much-needed social time for students to talk to one another and for teachers to talk to students. Peer social time is especially important for the upper elementary child, as peers are now an important part of their lives. As many schools limit talk time at lunch, recess becomes the only opportunity for freedom to converse with friends. Allowing a 10- to 15-minute walk-and-talk break can potentially result in more physical activity at recess time. Walk time before lunch may also encourage children to complete their meal since the need to socialize has already been met. Social time is also important for teachers. Two or more teachers may want to schedule walk time together.

A lesson can easily be extended to the outdoors by means of a walk. The outdoors provides ample opportunities to learn about many things such as weather, vegetation, insects, measurement, and geometric shapes. This can also be an opportune time for students to walk with a classmate while reviewing for a test or while practicing spelling words or multiplication tables. Walking field trips are another avenue of learning. These may include nature walks, neighborhood walks, community service walks (nearby senior citizen center or health care facility), walks to a local landmark, and walks in parks or historical battlefields.

Walking can provide many benefits to children and teachers. In addition to the fitness and social benefits, taking walk breaks can transfer to academic success. Walking can settle the highly active child or energize the lethargic child, allowing both to focus better when they return to the classroom. Children who are more focused learn better and are better behaved. Walking can also energize teachers, making them more relaxed, more receptive to the students, and possibly more creative.

Using Incentives

Teachers may choose to use motivational tactics when beginning a walking program. There are many tried-and-true options for motivating children:

- Choose a destination and accumulate class miles to reach the destination—for example, walk across your state.
- Add up miles to reach the distance of a marathon. Students can mark each mile on a score sheet or chart as they progress toward the 26-mile (42-kilometer) mark.
- Hand each child a Popsicle stick or section of a straw for every lap completed. The sticks or straws are then counted and added to an individual or class total.
- Name the walking event "caterpillar crawl" and have the children color a section of a caterpillar on a poster to graph their progress.
- Use pedometers to count steps taken. Set individual goals and have the children log steps each day.
- Keep a scrapbook or journal of walking field trips.
- Compete with other classes (within the school or at other schools) in terms of total class miles walked.
- Use walking games that are similar to traditional travel games (before electronic entertainment was placed in cars) to enliven the walk. For example, play I Spy or identification games with a theme such as a letter in the alphabet, colors, or shapes.

Be sure that candy and food treats are not used as incentives, as this does not promote healthy lifestyles. As walking becomes part of the daily routine, incentives are no longer necessary because the opportunity to go out and walk is enticing.

Teaching About Walking

Teachers may choose to take the opportunity to teach concepts directly related to walking. Walking for fitness is determined by the intensity level or pace of the walk. Most young children will want to walk very fast or ask if they can run, and they typically tire quickly. Opposite to the high-energy child is the lethargic child who has a tendency to move exceptionally slowly. A realistic goal to work toward is a moderate to high intensity level. The terms *slow, medium,* and *fast speed* or use of the names of animals—snail (slow), monkey (medium), or fox (fast)—helps children in making the distinction. You may start your class walks at a snail's pace with the idea of working toward the speed of the fast fox. Another option is to individualize the intensity level based on the present fitness or energy level of each student. Students choose to work at a low, moderate, or high intensity level to complete a particular course or number of laps, or maintain a moderate- to high-intensity pace and choose a different course or number of laps.

Children can be taught about how heart rate is affected by the intensity level of the walk. Young children will not measure their pulse accurately, but they can feel the obvious difference in the heart rate as the intensity increases. Upper elementary children can accurately take their heart rate as well as distinguish the change in heart rate after low-, medium-, and high-intensity walking. You will want to talk with the students about getting their heart rate up to a level that will help improve their health without asking them to conform to a target heart rate not recommended for this age group (see chapter 9).

Organizing and Playing Games

Children love games, and classroom teachers may choose to add physical activity to the day by organizing and playing a game with the children. While some games can be played in a classroom, they will elicit more physical activity outdoors or in a multipurpose room. There are many popular games that actually discourage movement (e.g., Duck, Duck, Goose; Red Rover; Heads Up, Seven Up), so teachers will need to select games that promote physical activity for all players or modify existing games to increase the physical activity level. Chapter 7 presents more detail on selecting games, and the

CD-ROM provided with this text offers examples of quality games that promote physical activity.

A common choice for play in preschool and the primary grades is the use of activity centers or stations. Centers that promote active play can be organized outdoors or in a multipurpose room. The idea is to allow a few minutes of play at one center (3 to 5 minutes) before giving a signal to change to another. Task cards with pictures and brief directions can be used to promote the activity. Sample task cards are shown in figure 5.3. Ideas for center play for the younger children include the following:

- Tossing and catching with scoops
- Jumping rope
- Target throw
- Hopscotch
- Hula hoop play

Activity centers for the upper elementary child may include common playground games or activities that promote practice of skills learned in physical education class. Typically the older children need at least 10 minutes participating in a center; their attention span is longer, and the activities are conducive to longer play. These are some ideas:

- Four Square
- Basketball games such as Around the World or Horse
- Tetherball
- Jump rope (short, long, or Double Dutch)
- Chinese jump rope or jump band activities
- Frisbee throwing
- Horseshoes
- Small-sided games (three versus three) of soccer, touch football, or Ultimate Frisbee

FIGURE 5.3   SAMPLE TASK CARDS FOR GRADES K THROUGH 2

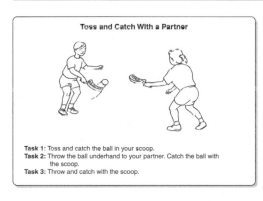

Toss and Catch With a Partner

Task 1: Toss and catch the ball in your scoop.
Task 2: Throw the ball underhand to your partner. Catch the ball with the scoop.
Task 3: Throw and catch with the scoop.

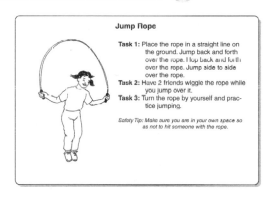

Jump Rope

Task 1: Place the rope in a straight line on the ground. Jump back and forth over the rope. Hop back and forth over the rope. Jump side to side over the rope.
Task 2: Have 2 friends wiggle the rope while you jump over it.
Task 3: Turn the rope by yourself and practice jumping.

Safety Tip: Make sure you are in your own space so as not to hit someone with the rope.

Target Throw

Task 1: Stand behind the first line and throw the beanbags at the target.
Task 2: Stand behind the second line and throw at the target.
Task 3: Stand behind the third line and throw at the target.

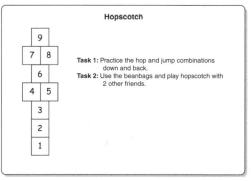

Hopscotch

Task 1: Practice the hop and jump combinations down and back.
Task 2: Use the beanbags and play hopscotch with 2 other friends.

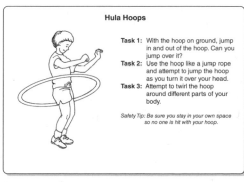

Hula Hoops

Task 1: With the hoop on ground, jump in and out of the hoop. Can you jump over it?
Task 2: Use the hoop like a jump rope and attempt to jump the hoop as you turn it over your head.
Task 3: Attempt to twirl the hoop around different parts of your body.

Safety Tip: Be sure you stay in your own space so no one is hit with your hoop.

Fourth grade students actively involved in playground centers.

Activity centers can be organized in which children rotate from one area to another on the teacher's signals. Younger children should participate in all of the centers, while older children may be allowed to choose play stations and on a signal make a second choice. Popular activities may have to be controlled for numbers and a fair selection system created. Children should be expected to arrange all equipment as they found it before moving to the next center, or collect the equipment at the end of the activity if another class is not going to use it. A sample center rotation is shown in figure 5.4.

Teacher-led games or activity centers need not be daily occurences; a teacher or group of teachers may want to make this a special weekly event. Game play can be a great way for teachers to reward students. The teacher may elect to join in the games, thus modeling the intended outcome of being physically active into adulthood.

Teaching Simple Dances

Dancing has always been a favorite activity for young children, and its popularity has increased with musicals and television shows that highlight dance (e.g., *High School Musical, Hannah Montana,* and *Dancing with the Stars*). The more dance expe-

riences children have, the more likely they are to use dance as a source of physical activity as adults.

Many dances are available that are simple to teach children and that can be taught in limited space. Students can practice dances they learned in their physical education class, or the classroom teacher can teach students a new dance. A classroom teacher does not have to be a skilled dancer to give children these experiences. Chapter 8 provides sample dances for specific grade levels, resources for finding dances, and hints for teaching dance. A multipurpose room, the cafeteria (outside of scheduled lunchtime), the center of a classroom with all desks moved to the side, or outdoors will provide the space needed for most dances. Once the children have learned a dance, it becomes a quick and easy way to add moderate to vigorous physical activity to the day.

Recess

An important part of every child's day is recess. Recess is defined as an *unstructured* break time during the school day that allows kids to engage in physical activity and practice life skills like negotiation, cooperation, problem solving, and conflict resolution. Recess is in itself a learning experience.

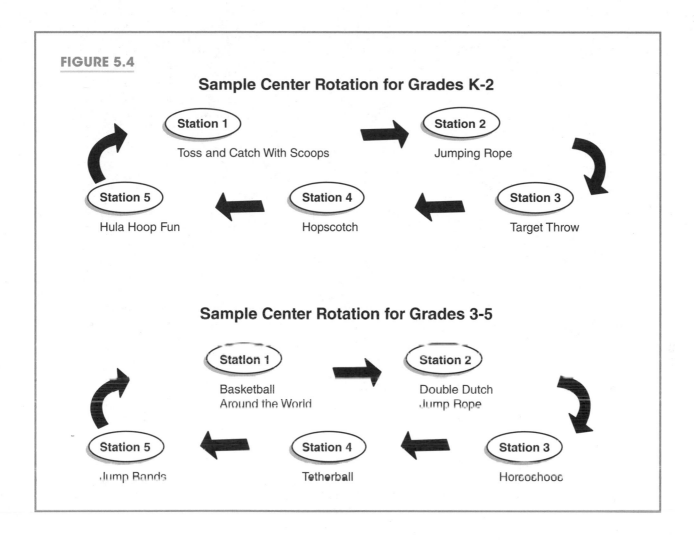

FIGURE 5.4

Sample Center Rotation for Grades K-2

Station 1 — Toss and Catch With Scoops
Station 2 — Jumping Rope
Station 3 — Target Throw
Station 4 — Hopscotch
Station 5 — Hula Hoop Fun

Sample Center Rotation for Grades 3-5

Station 1 — Basketball Around the World
Station 2 — Double Dutch Jump Rope
Station 3 — Horseshoes
Station 4 — Tetherball
Station 5 — Jump Bands

The role of the classroom teacher at recess is simply to supervise for safe play. For many children, recess is the only unstructured part of their day, as many attend highly structured after-school day care programs.

For primary grade children, teachers should incorporate daily recess periods that are approximately 15 to 20 minutes in length. Ideally, a recess break for young children should occur once in the morning and then again in the afternoon. Upper elementary–age children benefit from one longer recess period (approximately 30 minutes), as they need time to organize the specific activities they choose to play.

Children should be encouraged to be physically active during recess. As mentioned earlier in the chapter, class walks promoting social time can potentially increase physical activity and decrease standing time at recess. The play environment should be constructed to elicit movement (e.g.,

climbing apparatus, open field space), and manipulative items (e.g., balls, ropes) should be brought out for recess to enhance and encourage activity. Chapter 6 in this text is devoted to designing appropriate recess opportunities for children.

Transitional Physical Activity Breaks

Quick transitional physical activity breaks can be provided when a class is changing from one subject matter to another (e.g., language arts to math). Sometimes referred to as energizers or moving breaks, these activities are easy to organize and require very little space and time. The students can stand beside their desks or tables and participate in activity for 3 to 5 minutes. Once the students become accustomed to activity breaks, they become more efficient at moving from class work to activity and back to class work. A sample activity is presented in figure 5.5. Additional activities are presented on the

CD-ROM. The purpose of the transitional physical activity break can be determined by the teacher and may serve to

- refocus the brain,
- energize the lethargic child and release vitality in the high-energy child,
- refocus the body from sitting, and
- close a lesson or open a new one with an *active* review.

Breaking up academic content is far more productive than content overload. Primary-age children should be involved in movement at least once every 30 minutes. Upper elementary–age students should have one movement break for every hour of seat work. It has been found that Asian countries such as Japan and Taiwan have longer school days yet more productive learning. Researchers have theorized that the productivity level is related to the idea that these schools space their content with regular movement breaks (Stevenson & Lee, 1990). Scientifically speaking, short movement breaks can stimulate the release of adrenaline and dopamine, increasing energy levels as well as improving storage and retrieval of information (Jensen, 2000). The same movement that gives an energy boost to a lethargic child can provide an avenue of release for the highly energetic individual. This energy boost or release can help the brain to refocus and prepare for additional information.

FIGURE 5.5

Sample Transitional Activity (Grades 2-8)

Name of activity: 12 Days of Fitness

Organization: Students standing beside desks

Equipment: Visual for each day

Directions: The teacher leads the students through the 12 Days of Fitness by building upon each day. If time is limited, you can start with day 12 and count down. Have children sing along to the tune of "The Twelve Days of Christmas." The song begins with "On the first day of fitness my coach told me to do . . . a stork standing very, very still." It then continues day by day.

1st day: A stork standing very, very still (Stand on one foot with opposite foot against knee and arms extended outward.)

2nd day: Two side stretches (With one hand on hip, bend on the same side and stretch opposite arm across head in a "C" shape. Take second stretch the other direction.)

3rd day: Three muscle poses (Bend arm and flex bicep alternating arms.)

4th day: Four jumping jacks (Jump into a wide shape while simultaneously extending arms above the head in a wide shape.)

5th day: Five hula hoops (Pretend to turn a hula hoop around your waist slowly five times. Sing it slowly like the "five golden rings" in 12 Days of Christmas.)

6th day: Six front kicks (Alternate kicking legs in front of body.)

7th day: Seven jab punches (Alternate punching fists in front of body.)

8th day: Eight jogs in place (Alternate jog steps in place.)

9th day: Nine jumping ropes (Pretend to turn a rope and jump.)

10th day: Ten knee lifts (Alternate lifting the foot and raising knees up.)

11th day: Eleven scissor kicks (Alternate jumping and landing with right foot in front and left in back, and then left in front and right in back.)

12th day: Twelve raise the roofs (Bend arms at elbows and turn palms facing the ceiling. Extend arms toward ceiling as if "raising the roof.")

Prolonged sitting has a negative effect on the body. Sitting contributes to lower back problems, poor eyesight, poor breathing, and overall body fatigue. Adults in sedentary jobs have more of these physical ailments than do their counterparts working in physically demanding jobs. Children are no different, and short bouts of movement can counteract the negative effect of sitting.

Finally, specific content can be added to an energizing movement break, which will then serve as a review time. A sample math review activity might be to jog in place while counting by twos or reciting multiplication tables. Children can review spelling words by spelling a word aloud and jumping in place when a vowel is used. Additional examples are on the CD-ROM provided with this text, as well as in many of the resources listed at the end of the chapter.

Integrating Physical Activity Into Academics

The traditional classroom environment involves primarily auditory and visual modes of delivery. However, educators are aware that children do not all learn in the same way and that most need multimodal learning experiences inclusive of auditory, visual, and kinesthetic or tactile modes. It has been said that learners retain

- 10% of what they read;
- 20% of what they hear;
- 30% of what they see;
- 50% of what they hear and see at the same time;
- 70% of what they hear, see, and say; and
- 90% of what they hear, see, say, and DO (Fauth, 1990, p. 160).

As standardized test scores continue to decline, the missing link may be a decrease in or absence of physical activity in the school day. Movement is a perfect medium for learning. This does not suggest that every lesson should integrate movement, or even that one lesson a day should. What we do suggest is that integrating movement into the occasional lesson will be an effective tool to enhance learning as well as an opportunity for physical activity. Additional effects may include an increase in enthusiasm toward learning and a more positive overall learning environment.

As mentioned in the previous section, the purpose of transitional movement is to provide a quick physical activity break. If desired, the movement can be used to review academic content. Physical activity integrated into academic areas, on the other hand, is designed to meet at least one of the lesson objectives. For example, an objective for a lesson on geometric shapes may be for the students to identify the number of sides and the formation of seven different geometric shapes: triangle, square, rectangle, pentagon, hexagon, heptagon, and octagon. The students can be divided into small groups and asked to use their bodies and make as many of each shape

Using physical activity to make shapes is fun and reinforces academic content.

as possible using the number of people in the group. Another option is to provide each group with a ball of yarn and ask them to make the shape by working cooperatively and forming the yarn into the shape. Physically making the shapes enhances the learning process with the body mass.

Movement experiences are not meant to replace the traditional methods a classroom teacher uses to teach. Instead, they should be used in conjunction with these methods to enhance the learning experience. When children use their bodies as a learning tool, they will better understand a concept and retain the information longer. When academic learning experiences are combined with related physical activity, learning is more likely to occur.

Figures 5.6 through 5.9 provide ideas to incorporate physical activity into math, language arts, social studies, and science lessons, respectively. Addi-

---

FIGURE 5.6

Sample Math Activity 💿

Name of activity: Alligator Power

Concepts:

- Compare whole numbers, fractions, or decimals using symbols (>, <, =).
- Distinguish between the "greater than" (>) and the "less than" (<) symbols.

Organization: Students stand by desk facing the board.

Equipment: Chalkboard, whiteboard, large flash cards, or electronic display.

Directions:

- The teacher writes two numbers on the board.
- In response, the students turn their bodies toward the greater number and spread their arms into a wide shape (this shape imitates the ">" and the alligator "mouth").
- When the teacher confirms the correct answer, the students pretend to eat the number by making a quick snap with the arms (clapping hands together and back apart one time).
- The students then face the board and await the next problem.
- If the numbers are equal, the students jump once and raise their arms straight above their head.

Content modifications:

Use problems instead of individual numbers (e.g., have 2 + 3 and 3 + 4 written on the board).
Alter the problems to meet grade-level content (e.g., addition, subtraction, multiplication, division, fractions, or decimals).

tional ideas can be found in the included CD-ROM and through resources provided at the end of this chapter. For all activities, it is important that the classroom teacher modify either the content or the physical activity to meet grade-level standards (district, state, and/or national) and lesson objectives.

For example, Alligator Power (figure 5.6 on p. 100) is an excellent activity to aid in the learning of the concepts of greater than, less than, or equal to. The activity works well for individual numbers, addition, subtraction, multiplication, division, fractions, and decimals.

FIGURE 5.7

Sample Language Arts Activity

Name of Activity: Act or Link

Concept: Distinguish between action and linking verbs.

Organization:

- Move desks and chairs to create an open space in the middle of the room.
- Students form a large circle in the open area.

Equipment: Chalkboard, whiteboard, or electronic display and a list of sentences. Each sentence should include one action verb or one linking verb that is underlined. The action words should express actions that can take place in self-space such as jump, run, hop, and shake.

Activity:

- The teacher reads or shows (or both reads and shows) one of several written sentences.
- While standing in the circle, the students respond accordingly:
  - If the underlined or emphasized word in the sentence is an *action verb*, the students do the action. For example, in the sentence "Jane jumped up high," "jumped" is an action verb so the students jump in place until the teacher says "freeze" (approximately 10 seconds).
  - If the underlined or emphasized word in the sentence is a *linking verb,* all students quickly link arms. For example in the sentence "The dog is sick," the verb is a linking verb so the students link arms until the teacher says "release."

Content modifications:

- If the students are ready for compound sentences, use a timer and have them change the movement when the timer sounds. For example, if the sentence is "Linda ran outside to play while Joe was content to keep reading," they run in place for 10 seconds and then quickly link arms.

FIGURE 5.8

Sample Social Studies Activity

Name of activity: Travel our State

Concepts: Places and regions in your home state.

Organization: Students stand by desk or in an open area of the room.

Equipment:

- A travel plan created by the teacher that emphasizes different landmarks and tourist attractions.
- A large map of the state, divided into regions.

Directions:

- Using South Carolina for our example, the teacher reads each statement and allows the students to imitate the movement for about 10 to 15 seconds before reading the next one.
    - Run up the steps to the capitol building in Columbia.
    - Ride the waves on your new surfboard at the beach near Charleston.
    - Raise your hands in the air as you soar down a roller coaster in Myrtle Beach.
    - Hike to the top of Table Rock in Travelers Rest.
    - Catch a fish in Lake Jocassee.
    - Swim across Lake Hartwell.
    - Paddle your canoe in Lake Murray.
    - Ride your bicycle on the back roads from Spartanburg to Charleston.
    - Slam dunk a basketball at the Bi-Lo Center in Greenville.
    - Kick a field goal at Williams-Bryce Stadium in Columbia.
    - Stretch high like a giraffe at the Greenville Zoo.
    - Climb to the top of the Peach in Gaffney.
    - Drive a racecar at Darlington Raceway.
    - Swing your golf club on one of the many golf courses in Hilton Head.
    - Walk through the fields of cotton in Orangeburg.
    - Run in the race across the Cooper River Bridge in Charleston.
    - Tiptoe through the old battlefields in Cowpens.
    - Trudge or march through the wetlands in Edisto.

Content modifications:

- After traveling the state, the students could work in groups and place each movement in the correct region. A large map highlighting each region should be posted in the room. The South Carolina example would include the Blue Ridge Mountains, Piedmont, Coastal Plains, Costal Zone, and Sand Hills. Have each location from the travel experience printed on an index card. A student from each group draws a card. The group decides on the location by region and places the card in the correct region. If the class agrees with the group decision, the movement can be repeated.

FIGURE 5.9

Sample Science Activity

Name of activity: What Does It Matter?

Concepts: Properties of matter and changes they undergo.

Organization:

- Move desks to the side of the room, leaving an open space in the middle of the room, or use an outdoor space.
- Children are scattered in their own personal space.

Equipment: Music or none.

Directions:

- *Gas:* We are going to move like we are atoms in a gas state. How do you think they would move? Right, they would move very spaced out from one another. They would be light and free flowing. Now, I'm going to put on some music and I would like all of you to move around the area as if you were an atom in a gas state.

- *Liquid:* Now we are going to move like atoms in a liquid state. How do you think the movement of the liquid state will be different from the gas state? Correct, the atoms in a liquid are closer than in a gas state and cannot move as freely as gas atoms. We talked about how atoms in liquid state flow. To demonstrate this flow and limited freedom, everyone is to get in groups of three to five in a line one behind the other. Now place your hands on the shoulders of the person in front of you. I am going to turn on music and I would like the leader to lead the class around the room in a curvy pathway. Be careful not to touch the other liquids. (When the music stops, change leaders and continue.)

- *Solid:* Next we are going to move like atoms in a solid state. The atoms in a solid state are so close together that they can hardly move at all. The atoms in a solid are also in a set arrangement or pattern and cannot move from their spot. I would like everyone to get back to back with another group, actually touching the group behind you and standing shoulder to shoulder with your group. (Demonstrate with two groups, if necessary.) When the music starts, pretend that your feet are glued to the floor. You are only allowed to make small swaying movements with your bodies. Remember, an atom in a solid cannot move from its spot, so neither can you.

- *Assess:* Now that we know how atoms look and move in the three states of matter, I am going to test your knowledge. We are going to spread out again and start in our personal space. I will call out "solid," "liquid," or "gas" and you, as a class, will have to work together to show me how the atoms would act in the state of matter that I call out.

Content modifications:

- Once students can differentiate between a solid, liquid, and gas and can identify specific examples, they are ready for a challenge.
- Have the students demonstrate the appropriate movement when you call out an example, such as water, helium, chair, vapor, blood, ice, or rock.

Interdisciplinary Teaching

Interdisciplinary teaching, an educational process encouraged in many school districts, combines one or more concepts from different subject areas to help students interrelate knowledge. In this process all subject areas represented are equally important; the key to success is the interrelationship built between the subjects. The following are benefits of interdisciplinary teaching:

- Learning experiences are more meaningful, enjoyable, and rewarding.
- Different learning styles are addressed.
- Learning is transferred from one subject to another.
- Additional practice in multiple content areas occurs.

An interdisciplinary curriculum can expand across all content areas in a school. In this chapter we will focus on the interrelationship between physical education content and the content areas addressed in a single classroom setting. Note that the term physical education is used instead of physical activity as in the previous section. In this section the discussion focuses on the subject matter content of physical education, and not just physical activity as in the previous section. Physical education content and all subject areas can interrelate with one another. For the purposes of this chapter we will address primarily the role of the classroom teacher in interdisciplinary practice, rather than the reciprocated act of interdisciplinary teaching by the physical education teacher.

Fogarty (1991) provided 10 models for integrating curriculum. The continuum addressed possibilities within a single discipline, across several disciplines, and within or across learners. Purcell-Cone and colleagues (2009) adapted and decreased the continuum to three models that progress from simple to complex. The three models—connected, shared, and partnership—represent a guide to interdisciplinary teaching. Teachers may develop a learning experience that requires overlap and adaptations of the models (see figure 5.10).

The *connected* model can be achieved by one teacher and involves making connections between one subject area and physical education. The classroom teacher may use physical education content to provide clarity to a concept, to make it more interesting to the children, or to review content previously learned in physical education class while connecting it to new content in the classroom (Purcell-Cone et al., 2009). The classroom teacher must know the content from both subjects. The following is an example of content in a connected math lesson.

Connected Model: Measuring the Distance of a Jump

- The lesson focus is on different forms of measurement in math.
- The integration is with jumping for distance, a skill learned in physical education.
- The children will jump as far as they can and measure the distance jumped. They will repeat the jump three times.

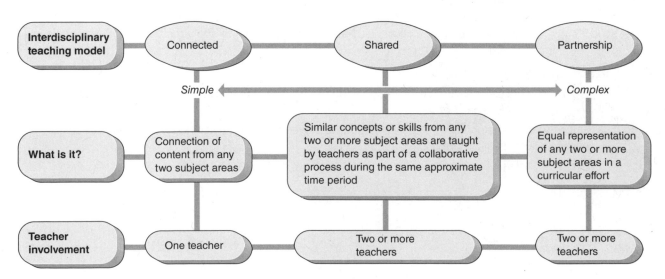

Figure 5.10   A comparison of the connected, shared, and partnership interdisciplinary teaching models.

- The jump will include cues from the teacher encouraging the students to bend their knees and swing their arms back and then, on take-off, swing the arms forward to increase their distance.
- For the math, a partner will measure the jumps using both metric and standard measurements, record the distance, and average the three jumps.

The *shared* model requires that teachers share in establishing the interrelationships between concepts, topics, or skills in two or more subject areas. It is most beneficial if the classroom teacher and physical education teacher teach the shared content on the same day. For this approach, the classroom teacher does not have to be as well informed about the physical education content. However, crucial to the success of the shared model is that teachers take the time to collaborate. The shared model is an excellent way for students to understand that concepts, topics, and skills can be applied across subject areas. The following is an example of content used in teaching the shared skills of rhythm and rhyme.

Shared Model: Teaching Rhythm and Rhyme

- The classroom teacher is teaching the use of rhyme in poetry and instructs the students to read the poetry with a clear and steady rhythm.
- The physical education teacher is having the students develop jump rope routines and teaching students to jump with a clear and steady rhythm.
- The two teachers can share in helping the students make a connection between rhythm in poetry and rhythm in rope jumping.

The third model, the *partnership* model, involves a team of teachers working together to focus on one theme. The concepts, topics, and skills across the subject areas are intermingled. Just as in the shared model, an individual teacher does not have to be familiar with all the subject areas, but communication and considerable planning time are required for success. This model might be used by a grade level of teachers and include all related arts classes and the physical education teacher. It is not uncommon for this model to be used schoolwide and to include parents and the community. An example is a multicultural theme, with the students learning about the history, customs, games, dance, clothing, and art of a culture. The following is an example of the use of a partnership model.

Partnership Model: Teaching History

- All of the teachers in the school who teach fifth grade have been asked to focus on westward expansion.
- The fifth grade is studying the history of the early American settlers in social studies, studying the music of this time period with the music teacher, and drawing pictures of the trip west in art.
- The physical education teacher will teach square dancing as an important part of the culture of that time and will also have students create a dance of an episode involving covered wagons.

The simplest and most commonly used of the three interdisciplinary models is the *connected* model, as it involves only one teacher and two subject areas. State standards-based instruction has made the connected model easier for teachers to use since expectations for all content areas and for students of each grade level are identified and easily accessed on the Internet. Relating physical education content to another subject area requires that the teacher have a true understanding of both content areas. It is recommended that teachers consult with the physical education teacher or a reliable written resource to ensure accuracy of the information. The following are potential connections between various content areas and physical education:

Social Studies

- Dances, games, and sports from different cultures
- A movement sequence created to depict actions related to family life, early settlers, or industrial trade, for example

Science

- Using Newton's laws of motion to understand how to increase and decrease force production in ball skills
- Balancing on different body parts to learn the bones and muscles
- Learning about weather patterns and cloud formations through the movement concepts of shapes, force, and flow
- Creating a movement sequence to depict actions related to the growth of a plant from a seed, life cycles, space, and the structure of matter

A map permanently drawn on the playground encourages integration of physical activity and social studies.

Math

- Using pedometers to accumulate steps during a day and then taking the information to measure and graph distance
- Estimation combined with physical challenges—for example, how many crab walks will it take you to get from point A to point B?
- Connecting body shapes used in balances to geometry

Language Arts

- Using literature that promotes movement and having children act out the movements (see chapter 8 for sample books)
- Writing a story and then creating a dance that tells the story
- Creating movement sequences that use action verbs and then altering the sequences by adding adverbs
- Creating a dance from a poem

Specific samples of lessons can be found on the CD-ROM included with this book and in various resources listed at the end of the chapter.

Physical Activity as a Routine

The examples just presented include many ways to incorporate physical activity into the school day. When teachers make a small change in their daily routine to include physical activity, the students reap the benefits. Activity does not have to be strenuous. It is best done in several short bouts throughout the day and should occur on a regular basis. Table 5.1 includes a sample third grade daily schedule that incorporates these ideas.

Administrators and teachers often have concerns about adding physical activity to the school day. One concern may be that too much is being asked of a classroom teacher who has many other daily responsibilities. Some teachers and administrators may still have reservations, concerned that physical activity time will take valuable time from academic time. Teachers who are comfortable with a highly structured classroom environment may experience discomfort with the thought of too much movement in the classroom. They may fear that students are out of control or that following physical activity the students will take too long to settle down. The intention of this chapter is not to add to these

TABLE 5.1

Sample Third Grade Schedule Incorporating Physical Activity Into Each Day

Happy Valley Elementary School: Third Grade Daily Schedule

	Monday	Tuesday	Wednesday	Thursday	Friday
7:55-8:10	Announcements and movement time	Announcements and movement time	Announcements and movement time	Announcements and movement time	Announcements and movement time
8:10-9:40	Language arts (LA)	Language arts	Language arts	Language arts	Language arts with movement integrated
9:00-9:05	Energizer within LA	Energizer within LA	Energizer within LA	Energizer within LA	
9:40-9:50	Rest room and water break	Rest room and water break	Rest room and water break	Rest room and water break	Rest room and water break
9:50-10:30	Math	Math with movement integrated	Math	Math	Math
10:30-11:00	Physical education	Music	Art	Physical education	Computer, media
11:00-11:35	Science with movement integrated	Science	Science	Science	Science
11:35-11:45	Walk and talk time	Walk and talk time	Walk and talk time	Walk and talk time	Walk and talk time
11:50-12:20	Lunch	Lunch	Lunch	Lunch	Lunch
12:20-12:50	Social studies	Social studies	Social studies with movement integrated	Social studies	Social studies
12:50-1:20	Recess	Recess	Recess	Recess	Recess
1:20-1:30	Rest room and water break	Rest room and water break	Rest room and water break	Rest room and water break	Rest room and water break
1:30-2:00	Health	Health	Health	Health with movement integrated	Health
2:00-2:20	Creative writing, silent reading	Creative writing, silent reading	Creative writing, silent reading	Creative writing, silent reading	Creative writing, silent reading

Result: Smart, healthy, happy children at Happy Valley Elementary School.

concerns but to challenge them. Every teacher can make a change in the daily routine by adding recess (for every child) and transitional movement activities to the day. Neither of these takes lengthy preparation time on the part of the teacher. As teachers experience firsthand the benefits of providing physical activity, they can try out other ideas from this chapter. The result will be a more relaxed and productive learning environment. Students will be more motivated; their attitudes about school will be positive; and learning will be enhanced while behavior problems will decrease. Long-term effects may include an increase in standardized test scores and a decrease in absenteeism.

Promoting Physically Active Lifestyles

The main goal of a quality physical education program is for children to engage in lifelong physical activity. The child who is physically active will establish habits that may continue into adulthood. In this chapter we have provided a variety of ideas for how classroom teachers can incorporate physical activity into the school day. However, simply providing the opportunities cannot guarantee active children. A responsibility that all teachers have is to encourage children to be physically active. Teachers can promote active lifestyles in several specific ways:

- By reinforcing student participation
- By supporting physical education
- By making physical activity a positive experience
- By never using the elimination of physical activity as punishment
- By involving parents and the community

Reinforcing Student Participation

Elementary-age children welcome praise and attention from teachers. Good teachers have a genuine interest in what their students do and take time to inquire about the students' interests and the activities in which they are involved. For a teacher to ask about what physical activity the students participated in over the weekend, or what activity programs the children are taking part in after school (e.g., dance, sports, self-defense classes), is both gratifying and motivating to a young child. This process can be as simple as using share time to discuss these activities or documenting activities as a group.

Older children may be asked to document their personal physical activity by using an activity calendar, journaling, writing a story, or illustrating an activity. Another popular method is through a daily log. Children can be encouraged to write down what they do in their free time, with the goal for physically active play time to outweigh sedentary electronic play time.

Teachers may choose to assign a "home fun" assignment in addition to or in conjunction with homework. Encourage students to stand and jog in place using punching arms during television commercials. As another option, when practicing spelling words, children can make the shapes of the letters with their body. These options will make homework more enjoyable as well as including kinesthetic movement to aid in the learning process.

Reinforcement of physical activity following recess will help to encourage the less active child. This may happen indirectly when the teacher compliments the children who are active. In some cases, teachers may have to be more direct: They can help the inactive child join in with others, help the child identify ideas about what he or she can play at recess, or encourage others to invite the student to play with them.

Supporting Physical Education

An additional way to encourage children to be active is to show an interest in what they are learning in physical education. When the students return from physical education class, inquire about what they learned. Communicate with the physical education teacher, and connect physical education content with subject matter in the classroom. Just being knowledgeable and showing an interest is motivational to students.

Another way to support the physical education program is to show respect for the role that physical education plays in educating the child. Physical education in some schools is a marginalized subject and not viewed as essential to a child's education. (For more information on quality physical education, see chapter 3.) Some teachers have been guilty of keeping children from physical education class for academic remediation or because the child has not completed his or her work for the day. This practice is no more acceptable than taking a child from math class because he or she needs remedial work in physical education.

Making Physical Activity a Positive Experience

When children come into the world, movement is their mode of exploration. Crawling and walking are childhood milestones. As a child begins to run, a smile demonstrates the excitement of this newfound movement. Children's enthusiasm for moving and being active should not be destroyed when they enter school. As educators we need to ensure that movement is a positive experience throughout elementary schools so that children will continue being physically active as youth and later as adults.

Specific chapters in this book address appropriate practices to use in dance, in games, and at recess. These same practices carry over into any classroom activity. A teacher should select activities that place all children in an active and success-oriented role. Activities that shame students in front of their peers for their physical or cognitive deficiencies have no merit and can possibly have a lasting negative effect (e.g., Duck, Duck, Goose; spelling bees). Another inappropriate practice common in schools is to use exercise as punishment. On the one hand we want children to enjoy movement and to yearn to be physically active, but then we tell them to run laps for misbehaving. Finally, teachers should be sure to present opportunities for physical activity in a positive way. The more motivated the teacher is about the benefits and joy of physical activity, the more motivated the students will be. Table 5.2 includes appropriate practices for classroom teachers to follow in physical activity and inappropriate practices to avoid.

TABLE 5.2

Appropriate Practices for Physical Activity in the Elementary School Environment

Appropriate Practice	Inappropriate Practice
ACTIVE AND MAXIMUM PARTICIPATION FOR EVERY CHILD	
▪ All children are involved in activities that allow them to remain moderately to vigorously active for the majority of the activity time. ▪ More than one game is occurring in order to allow more participation (e.g., a number of kickball games are going on at recess that have no more than eight players per team). ▪ Playground equipment or play equipment (e.g., balls, jump ropes) is sufficient and available. ▪ All children participate in scheduled physical activity time.	▪ Planned activities do little to encourage moderate or vigorous activity. ▪ Children are waiting in line, exposed to only a few "turns," or eliminated through the rules of play. ▪ Games are played that are dominated by only the highly skilled, aggressive player, leaving others inactive. ▪ Games are played that are unsafe physically, psychologically, or in both ways (e.g., dodgeball, Red Rover). ▪ Lack of playground or play equipment limits play. ▪ Children are denied physical activity as a punishment for misbehavior or for not completing classroom assignments or homework.
APPROPRIATE EQUIPMENT AND PLAY SPACE	
▪ Playground apparatus is matched to the size, confidence, and skill level of the child to encourage use. ▪ Separate playgrounds are designated based on grade level (i.e., one for grades K-2 and one for grades 3-5). ▪ A designated field space and paved area marked for physical activity are available for recess (e.g., Four Square courts, tetherball, outdoor volleyball standards, hopscotch, basketball goals). ▪ Play equipment such as balls and jump ropes are matched to the size and skill level of the child to encourage use.	▪ Limited or no playground equipment is available to encourage active play. ▪ No field or paved spaced is available to encourage a variety of play opportunities. ▪ Either no play equipment is available or it is limited (e.g., only one jump rope and one ball). ▪ If play equipment is available, it is adult sized, thus not allowing success and potentially being intimidating or unsafe for children.

(continued)

TABLE 5.2 *(continued)*

Appropriate Practice	Inappropriate Practice
FORMING GROUPS, TEAMS, AND PARTNERS	
▪ Groups, teams, and partners are formed in ways that preserve the dignity and self-respect of every child. For example, teachers preselect the groups, teams, or partners using knowledge of children's skills and social relations in ways that will facilitate fair participation in the activity. Other ideas include color of clothing, birthdays, and seating arrangement. ▪ The teacher varies ways to organize groups, teams, and partners that will encourage children to play with and accept all members of the group. ▪ Teams are changed daily to promote the chance for all to be on a winning team.	▪ "Captains" are chosen to publicly select one child at a time, exposing some children to ridicule and embarrassment. To be chosen last makes the public statement that you are not very good, that others do not want you, and that you will not be valued on the team. ▪ Teams or groupings do not allow for diversity (e.g., gender, skill level). ▪ Teams are allowed to be the same day after day, promoting the dominance of one team over the other.
GENDER-DIRECTED ACTIVITIES	
▪ Boys and girls have equal access to activities and are encouraged, supported, and socialized toward successful achievement in all aspects of physical activity. ▪ Teachers use gender-neutral language and provide leadership opportunities equally.	▪ Teachers encourage students to participate in gender-specific traditional roles (e.g., boys in aggressive play and girls in traditional feminine roles such as cheering or rope jumping). ▪ Girls receive limited opportunities for leadership roles. Teacher language and actions are gender biased, and comparisons between boys and girls are made.
RULES GOVERNING GAME PLAY	
▪ Teachers select, design, and modify games to maximize participation and to meet the developmental level of the children. ▪ Teachers modify the rules, regulations, equipment, and playing space to match the varying abilities of the children.	▪ Official adult rules of team sports or equipment are used, resulting in low rates of success and enjoyment for children. ▪ Games and activities are used that are above the cognitive or physical developmental level of the younger elementary–age child (e.g., kickball for grades K and 1).
COMPETITION	
▪ Activities emphasize self-improvement, participation, fair play, and cooperation instead of just winning the game. ▪ Children are given choices on cooperative or competitive play. While one child finds enjoyment in competition, another may not. For example, children are allowed to choose between playing a game in which the score is kept or one that is just for practice. ▪ Fair play or sportsmanship is encouraged through such ideas as shaking hands and making positive comments to opponents. ▪ Put-downs are never allowed.	▪ Winners and losers are the main focus of activities. ▪ Teachers compare the winners to the losers. ▪ Teachers use rewards and punishments for winning and losing in class and playground activities. ▪ Put-downs are ignored and a sense of fair play is not encouraged.

Appropriate Practice	Inappropriate Practice
FITNESS AND THE USE OF FITNESS ACTIVITIES AS PUNISHMENT	
■ All elementary children are taught the benefits of exercise. ■ Children are taught that physical fitness occurs through increased physical activity opportunities. ■ Upper elementary children (grades 3-6) are taught correct procedures for exercise and the different exercise categories (i.e., flexibility, cardiorespiratory, muscle strength, and muscle endurance). ■ Fitness activities are geared toward children. For example, instead of doing push-ups as a means to gain muscular strength and endurance, children should be encouraged to climb on the playground equipment, swing, imitate how animals travel, or practice cartwheels in the grass. ■ Physical activities and exercises are designed to be motivating and enjoyable, thereby promoting attitudes toward lifetime physical fitness.	■ Primary grade students are asked to perform standard calisthenics. ■ Upper grade students perform standard calisthenics with no specific purpose in mind or correct technique instruction. ■ Children are bored as the same exercises are used daily, eliminating the motivation factor of enjoying movement (e.g., teachers use only jumping jacks when there are many ways to make jumping fun and interesting). ■ Exercise is used as punishment for misbehavior or lack of participation (e.g., running laps or doing push-ups), thereby turning children off to exercise as opposed to encouraging fitness for a lifetime.

Eliminating Physical Activity as Punishment

Finding negative consequences for inappropriate behavior is a challenge in the public schools today, and a common practice is to take away what children like the most. For most teachers, reducing or removing recess is the number one choice for punishing children who misbehave or do not complete schoolwork. The children who need physical activity the most, enabling them to stay focused in the classroom or behave appropriately in class, are the ones who are typically punished. This practice has not been proven effective, as often the same children are missing recess. While there are limited techniques available to teachers to discipline children, taking away an opportunity to be physically active is one that may prove counterproductive.

Other options for punishment may include isolating the individual within the class or during lunchtime. In some cases, working with the child and parents for a plan to change behaviors can be productive. Building in reward systems as increments of the required school work are completed or when evidence of appropriate behavior is presented is a positive and typically effective method. Encourage the child to earn the right to

- sit with a special friend at lunch or eat lunch with the teacher,

- have extra art or computer time when work is completed,
- walk with the teacher during class walking breaks,
- lead the class during morning movement time or during an energizer, or
- take care of the class pet.

Some teachers have been successful by rewarding students with an *extra* play time at the end of the day or at the end of the week. Children can earn extra minutes for good behavior, or minutes can be removed for inappropriate behavior. The minutes can be charted for individuals or for the class. Teachers who have tried this approach concede that having other opportunities for physical activity throughout the day has actually helped students who had typically had to sit out from recess. These students are more focused in class and complete their work. Rarely do children miss out on the extra play time, and the incentive typically increases the play time. Many teachers share that they are now choosing physical activity as a reward instead of more sedentary activities such as viewing a movie or having computer game time.

Involving Parents and the Community

The promotion of physically active lifestyles extends beyond the classroom and becomes the role of the

Children waiting in lines will limit the amount of physical activity.

parent or guardian. In many communities, parents involve their children in structured physical activity such as sport teams; cheerleading; or classes in dance, gymnastics, or self-defense. Other parents may choose not to place their children in organized activities or may not be able to afford the expenses of some programs. There are inexpensive or free organized activities in most communities. Many churches and recreation facilities offer gym and field space for play. Parks and recreation facilities are also including walking trails in many neighborhoods. The teacher can help in promoting community activities by working with the physical activity director of the school (usually the physical education teacher), posting information in the classroom, sending a newsletter home, and reinforcing students who do participate.

Play in neighborhood parks and the backyard does not cost money. Parents and teachers need to encourage children to get out and play when they are at home and reinforce the students who do. The reasons many parents give for not allowing children to play freely outside include safety issues. If safety is a concern, neighborhood parents can spend at least an hour of social time outside with each other while the children play. Many communities are building play areas in neighborhoods; and some are surrounded by walking paths, allowing adults to walk and visit while the children play. Encourage families to take an evening walk before or after dinner. This is a great time for the parents and children to spend quality time together.

Another reason children do not play outside is the enticement of electronic, sedentary play indoors. The electronic stimulus can and should be limited by parents. Teachers may want to send the following suggestions home to parents:

- Compare the amount of screen time and physical activity time your family is getting.
- Set limits on daily screen time (the recommendation is 30 minutes for preschool children, not exceeding 2 hours for older children).
- Require children to log screen time.
- Locate the electronic media in a family room. Do not allow televisions, gaming systems, and computers in the child's room. Not only does this physically isolate family members and decrease interaction; children with these devices in their room spend an average of

1.5 hours more on screen time than children without them. Some of this time may be when parents assume that the child is sleeping.

- Make mealtime family time by turning off the television. Family meals are a good opportunity to talk to one another.
- Encourage other alternatives for spending time, such as playing outside, learning a hobby, or just being active with family and friends.
- Parents need to set a good example.

Teachers need to increase student awareness of a wide variety of activities that may be available in the community. Pictures, posters, and books in the classroom that promote activities such as hiking, cycling, skateboarding, martial arts, dance, gymnastics, and sport will help to motivate students to seek what might be an attractive activity option. One final way to promote physical activity is to invite guest speakers who will talk to children about the benefits of healthy, active lifestyles.

Promoting Quality Health and Nutritional Habits

In conjunction with increased physical activity, proper health and nutritional habits are essential in preventing and combating childhood obesity. Most states have curriculum standards and expectations for classroom teachers to teach health. Now, more than ever in the United States, the schools play a crucial role in educating children and parents on proper health and nutritional habits. Health and nutrition concepts can be taught as separate subject matter or integrated into other content areas such as science or language arts. Students can be taught about the following health habits:

- Nutritional choices
  - Determining the nutritional values of food
  - Reading labels on food products
  - Planning healthy, nutritionally balanced meals
  - Making good snack choices
  - Journaling daily food intake and analyzing habits
  - Relating food intake to energy output (physical activity)
- Harmful substances to avoid (e.g., drugs, nicotine)
- Prevention of injuries (e.g., bicycle safety, using crosswalks)
- Positive solutions for dealing with stress and maintaining emotional wellness

Teachers can also aid in the promotion of quality health and nutrition by assessing the quality of food served in the school cafeteria. If the school lunch program does not meet nutritional standards, the school wellness committee (see chapter 2) should address this issue and propose changes to the program. This process may require action at the district level. District level action may not occur unless several schools take a position on the nutritional rights of children.

One final recommendation for promoting healthy and nutritional habits is for teachers to avoid using unhealthy products such as candy for rewards. When there is a reason to celebrate, there are many ways to use healthy and tasty food choices. It is easy to remedy the practice of allowing unhealthful choices by having a no-junk-food policy in the school. This type of policy has been successful in many schools in which a recommended snack list is sent home to parents, candy "treats" are banned, birthday parties are celebrated with popcorn instead of cupcakes, soda and snack machines are eliminated from the building, and fund-raisers promote selling of products other than candy.

Working With the School Wellness Committee

As mentioned in previous chapters, school wellness committees are becoming prevalent in many school systems. Due to national legislation, coordinated school health programs, or district or state requirements, many schools are taking a proactive approach in an effort to improve the overall school community. Teachers may be appointed to these committees (see chapter 2), or the school administrator may ask for volunteers. If you are employed in a school that does not have a school wellness committee, you may choose to initiate this process.

Being a Physically Active and Healthy Role Model

Classroom teachers can significantly influence a child's present activity behaviors both during and outside of school by providing opportunities for children to be physically active. However, a teacher's influence surpasses the movement opportunities he or she provides.

As children grow into their own identities, there are adults in their life whom they emulate. Given this reality, the actions and behaviors of teachers are very influential. A teacher who is physically active can have great impact. By simply joining the students in the physical activity opportunities shared in this chapter, a teacher demonstrates the importance of physical activity. With the exception of recess (the time children need to be free of adult decision making), all activities in this chapter are conducive to teacher participation. Keep a pair of sneakers at school, and join your students in the fun.

Living a physically active lifestyle is part of teaching it. Teachers should share their personal interest in physical activity with students by informing them of their own fitness or recreational experiences. Suggestions for teachers to increase personal activity time outside of the school day include the following: (1) Add a 20- to 45-minute walk to your day; (2) learn to play tennis, golf, or another recreational sport; (3) join a fitness club and start a workout program; or (4) start a before- or after-school teacher fitness club (see chapter 17 for more information). Just as for children, the key to making physical activity and physical fitness a part of everyday life for an adult is to find something enjoyable. For more information on physical fitness, see chapter 16.

A teacher's physically active actions, healthy appearance, and overall attitude about physical activity will positively influence children to adopt and maintain an active lifestyle. Beyond being a role model, teachers who are physically active may be less stressed, be more productive, be more creative, have more energy, and have a better self-concept. Finally, a healthy and active faculty and staff will have reduced absenteeism.

SUMMARY

1. In the academic push to increase standardized test scores, children are being asked to sit and stay focused for unrealistic amounts of time. The reality is that academic performance actually decreases with less physical activity.

2. Classroom teachers are vital to reaching the goal to encourage and promote physical activity in the school day.

3. There are multiple ways to incorporate physical activity into the school day that involve very little preparation time and do not impose added demands on the classroom teacher.

4. Physical activity integrated within a lesson or between content areas actually helps students to retain information and refocus.

5. A scheduled daily recess period and walking break can rejuvenate students and teachers.

6. Teachers can promote physically active lifestyles by reinforcing student participation in physi-

cal activity, supporting the physical education program, making physical activity opportunities positive experiences, never eliminating students from physical activity as punishment, and involving parents and the community in physical activity promotion.

7. Teachers should inquire about the school wellness plan for the school and district.

8. A physically active and healthy classroom teacher speaks volumes to children.

CHECKING YOUR UNDERSTANDING

1. In addition to recess, what are five other ways classroom teachers can provide opportunities for physical activity in the school day?

2. Starting the day with activity is a great way to get the students ready for the school day. What four factors need to be taken into consideration and why?

3. How can a walking break provide an opportunity to extend academics to the outdoors? How does walking transfer to academic success when the students return to the classroom?

4. Why do upper grade elementary children benefit more from one longer period of recess as opposed to two shorter ones as suggested for the primary grades?

5. In addition to increasing physical activity, name four reasons why a classroom teacher would use transitional activity breaks.

6. In addition to increasing physical activity, name two reasons why a teacher would integrate physical activity into a lesson.

7. Describe how you and the physical education teacher would initiate and carry out a lesson using the shared model of interdisciplinary teaching.

8. When physical activity becomes a part of the daily routine, what are five potential short-term effects and two potential long-term effects?

9. List three reasons why children should not be punished by having recess or other forms of physical activity taken away. Provide three ideas for options that teachers may use instead.

10. List five health or nutritional concepts that need to be taught to children in elementary school.

11. Do you consider yourself a physically active and healthy role model for your students? If not, how could you change this?

RESOURCES

Active and Healthy Schools

www.activeandhealthyschools.com

Energizers

Free downloads of great energizer ideas can be obtained at www.ncpe4me.com/energizers.html

National Association for Sport and Physical Education: Integrating Physical Activity Into the Complete School Day

www.aapherd.org/naspe

National Coalition for Promoting Physical Activity 2005 Resource List

www.ncppa.org

Hannaford, C. (1995). *Smart moves: Why learning is not all in your head.* Alexander, NC: Great Ocean.

Helion, J.G., & Fry, F.F. (2003). *Interdisciplinary teaching through games and activities.* Dubuque, IA: Kendall/Hunt.

Jensen, E. (2000). *Learning with the body in mind: The scientific basis for energizers, movement, play, games and physical education.* Thousand Oaks, CA: Corwin Press.

Purcell-Cone, T., Werner, P., Cone, S.L., & Woods, A.M. (2009). *Interdisciplinary teaching through physical education* (2nd ed.).Champaign, IL: Human Kinetics.

Sutherland, C. (2006). *No gym? No problem! Physical activities for tight spaces.* Champaign, IL: Human Kinetics.

REFERENCES

Bogden, J.F., & Vega-Matos, C.A. (2000). *Fit, healthy, and ready to learn: A school health policy guide. Part I: Physical activity, healthy eating, and tobacco use prevention.* Alexandria, VA: National Association of State Boards of Education.

Etnier, J.L., & Sibley, B.A. (2003). The relationship between physical activity and cognition in children: A meta-analysis. *Pediatric Exercise Science,* 14(3), 243-256.

Fauth, B. (1990). Linking the visual arts with drama, movement, and dance for the young child. In W.J. Stinson (Ed.), *Moving and learning for the young child* (pp. 159-187). Reston, VA: American Alliance for Health, Physical Education, Recreation and Dance.

Fogarty, R. (1991). Ten ways to integrate curriculum. *Educational Leadership* (October), 61-65.

Jensen, E. (2000). *Learning with the body in mind: The scientific basis for energizers, movement, play, games and physical education.* Thousand Oaks, CA: Corwin Press.

National Association for Sport and Physical Education. (2000). *Appropriate practices for elementary school physical education.* Reston, VA: Author.

National Association for Sport and Physical Education. (2004). *Physical activity for children: A statement of guidelines for children ages 5-12* (2nd ed.). Reston, VA: Author.

Pate, R.R., Davis, M.G., Robins, T.N., Stone, E.J., McKenzie, T.L., & Young, J.C. (2006). Promoting physical activity in children and youth: A leadership role for schools. *Circulation: Journal of the American Heart Association,* 114, 1214-1224.

Pellegrini, A.D., & Bohn, C.M. (2005). The role of recess in children's cognitive performance and school adjustment. *Educational Researcher,* 34(1), 13-19.

Purcell-Cone, T., Werner, P., Cone, S.L., & Woods, A.M. (2009). *Interdisciplinary teaching through physical education* (2nd. Ed.). Champaign, IL: Human Kinetics.

Sibley, B.A., & Etnier, J.L. (2003). The relationship between physical activity and cognition in children: A meta-analysis. *Pediatric Exercise Science,* 15(3), 243-256.

Stevenson, H.W., & Lee, S.Y. (1990). Contexts of achievement. *Monographs of the Society for Research in Child Development* (Serial no. 221), 55(1-2).

Tremblay, M.S., Inman, J.W., & Williams, J.D. (2000). The relationship between physical activity, self-esteem, and academic achievement in 12 year old children. *Pediatric Exercise Science,* 12(3), 312-323.

6

Recess

OVERVIEW

Recess is a *break in the elementary school day in which children are allowed time for active, free play.* Due to increased pressure to improve standardized test scores and concern for student safety, recess may be slowly disappearing from the elementary school day. Recess is an essential component of the elementary education experience and most worthy of rescuing. This chapter describes the benefits of recess and provides the reader with ideas to make recess a physically active time.

CHAPTER OUTCOMES

This chapter will help you

- define recess;
- identify the benefits of recess;
- identify ways to engage children in physical activity during recess;
- describe the role of the playground supervisor;
- teach children games they can play and organize during recess; and
- manage, organize, and equip the playground for a physically active recess.

IN THIS CHAPTER

Recess provides an *unstructured* break that gives children *discretionary time* to engage in physical activity. Recess should not be substituted for an instructional program in physical education, and physical education should not replace recess. Recess and physical education are both critical components of the elementary school program, yet they serve distinct purposes. Recess is child-directed free play. Physical education is a teacher-directed instructional program.

Schools vary in the length and number of recess periods given children and the facilities available. Recess usually occurs outdoors in a designated area or playground. Recess may be held in the classroom, a multipurpose room, or another inside area during inclement weather. Recess plays an important role in a comprehensive school physical activity program and can provide a portion of the activity that a child needs every day to maintain health.

Contributions of Recess

With all of the attention being focused on the health benefits of physical activity, what is sometimes ignored is the role that recess plays in the physical, social, and cognitive development of the child. The following sections describe those benefits.

Physical Benefits of Recess

Childhood health problems associated with inactivity are on the rise in the United States. The percentage of children who are overweight has more than tripled since 1980. Children have been increasingly diagnosed with conditions we typically associate with adulthood, such as high cholesterol, high blood pressure, or other signs of heart disease. These health risks can be significantly reduced with increased amounts of physical activity.

As noted in previous chapters, school-aged children and youth should participate in at least 60 minutes of moderate to vigorous physical activity each day (National Association for Sport and Physical Education [NASPE], 2004a). Active participation in a regularly scheduled recess can make a significant contribution toward meeting the 60-minute guideline. Research has shown that children who do not get the physical activity they need during the school day do not for the most part make up for it after school (Dale, Corbin, & Dale, 2000). Opportunities to engage in physical activity, such as recess, may help to alleviate some of the health problems associated with physical inactivity. Recess provides the opportunity for sheer physical activity and practice of fundamental motor skills. Children run, chase, dodge to avoid being tagged, skip, jump, hop, kick, catch, and throw.

Contributions of Recess to Social Development

Many important life skills are learned on the playground. Free play allows children the opportunity to practice life skills, such as cooperation, taking turns, following rules, sharing, communication and negotiation, problem solving, and conflict resolution (National Association for Sport and Physical Education [NASPE], 2006). Decision-making and negotiating skills develop as children decide how to form teams, who kicks first, if a ball is fair or foul, if the runner is safe or out, who turns the rope, and how many misses the jumper gets. Children practice negotiating when bargaining for their team to kick first or when establishing rules for play. They learn to share and take turns. They develop and practice problem-solving skills and conflict resolution when one team calls a ball fair and the other calls it foul, or when some say the runner is safe while others say he or she is out.

Contributions of Recess to Cognitive Development

Children learn through play. Free play allows children the opportunity to be creative and to use their imagination. Through play, children try different roles and see the world through the eyes of others. On the playground a child may become the captain of a ship, a cook, a dragon slayer, or a stagecoach driver.

Recess has been referred to as the "fourth R"— the first three being reading, 'riting, and 'rithmetic. Recess is recognized alongside of these core subject areas due to the important role it plays in enhancing the learning of subject matter. Mounting evidence confirms the critical role that physical activity plays in cognitive functioning (Castelli et al., 2007; Jensen, 1998; Ratey, 2008; Hillman, Erickson, & Kramer, 2008; Hillman et al., 2006). The brain needs downtime to recycle chemicals crucial for long-term memory formation (Jensen, 1998). Breaks are also essential for attention and alertness. Not only do fit and healthy children learn more and perform better, but physical activity itself significantly influences the learning process.

Student Management

Management of student behavior is a major problem for many teachers. Keeping children focused on academic work for hours at a time is not an easy task. Providing recess opportunities for students

Children need unstructured time to develop social skills.

Recess Is at Risk

There is a trend among many public school districts in the United States to eliminate recess in elementary schools. Advocates of eliminating recess contend that school time would be better spent in academics. The increased pressure for schools to demonstrate student academic achievement in an ever more demanding curriculum has been largely responsible for this perspective. Others cite the playground injuries that result in lawsuits brought against the school.

The National Association for the Education of Young Children (NAEYC, 1998) suggests that school administrators consider the benefits of outdoor play before eliminating recess from their curriculum:

1. Play is an active form of learning that unites the mind, body, and spirit. Until at least the age of 9, children's learning occurs best when the whole self is involved.

2. Play reduces the tension that often comes with having to achieve or needing to learn. In play, adults do not interfere and children relax.

3. Children express and work out emotional aspects of everyday experiences through unstructured play.

4. Children permitted to play freely with peers develop skills for seeing things through another person's point of view—cooperating, helping, sharing, and solving problems.

5. The development of children's perceptual abilities may suffer when so much of their experience is through television, computers, books, worksheets, and media that require only two senses. The senses of smell, touch, and taste, and the sense of motion through space, are powerful modes of learning.

6. Children who are less restricted in their access to the outdoors gain competence in moving through the larger world. Developmentally, they should gain the ability to navigate their immediate environs (in safety) and lay the foundation for the courage that will enable them eventually to lead their own lives.

actually facilitates classroom management. After the initial calming of students upon return to the classroom, teachers will find that students are on task and less fidgety (Jarrett et al., 1998). This is especially true for hyperactive students. Because recess is an essential part of the school day, it should not be used as a privilege but rather be a right. It is of utmost importance that all students have a recess. Teachers need to find ways to discourage undesirable classroom behavior (e.g., not finishing classroom work, not turning in homework) other than denying students their recess time.

Recommendations of Policy Groups for Recess

Numerous organizations, including the National Association for the Education of Young Children (NAEYC, 1998), the United States Department of Health and Human Services and the United States Department of Education (USDHHS & USDE, 2000), and the American Association for the Child's Right to Play (IPA/USA, n.d.), support recess as an essential component of a child's physical, social, and academic development. Many organizations including the National Association of Early Childhood Specialists in State Departments of Education (NAECS-SDE) (2002) and NASPE (2006) have also prepared position statements regarding concerns and recommendations for recess. These groups have reached the following consensus:

- All elementary school children should engage in at least one daily 20-minute period of recess.

- Recess should not replace physical education classes. Physical education provides a sequential instructional program with opportunities for children to learn and develop motor skills, movement concepts, and physical fitness. Recess allows unstructured opportunities for children to use skills and to engage in physical activity.

- Schools should provide supervised daily recess for children in prekindergarten through grades 5 or 6. Recess should not be scheduled back to back with physical education classes.

- Recess should not be viewed as a reward but as an essential educational support component for all children. Students should therefore not be denied recess as a means of punishment or to make up class work.

- Adequate and safe spaces and facilities should be provided so that all students can be physically active at the same time. Outdoor spaces should be used whenever the weather allows.

- Developmentally appropriate equipment should be provided for children to engage in enjoyable physical activity.

- Physical education and classroom teachers should teach children positive social skills for use during recess.

- Adults should intervene only when a child's physical or emotional health is at risk. Activities should be child directed.

- Safety rules should be taught and reinforced. Bullying and aggressive behavior must not be allowed.

- Recess should be supervised by qualified adults to ensure that the recess experience is productive, safe, and enjoyable. Adults should check equipment and facilities regularly for safety.

Encouraging Active Play

One of the problems with the idea of recess as a nonstructured activity is that if given the opportunity and the choice, not all children will choose to engage in moderate to vigorous activity. Some children will sit off to the side and watch others or talk to friends during recess. It is important for the teacher in charge of recess to encourage active play. There are several ways to ensure that all students are physically active during recess:

- Make sure that every child has an equipment option.

- Help an inactive child find a partner to play with.

- Help an inactive child find an activity he or she likes to do.

- Teach children games they can organize themselves.

- Provide a variety of play choices through the availability of large and small equipment (i.e., plenty of balls, hoops, ropes, and so on).

- Reinforce those who are active.

Scheduling Recess

Administrators are faced with the task of scheduling all classes in the school for recess. It would be ideal for schools to have enough space so that each classroom teacher could decide when it would be best for their class to go out to recess every day. Most schools do not have the outdoor facilities to support this policy. It would not be appropriate to have large numbers of classes, particularly those of different ages, in limited space at the same time. This means that schedules have to be determined for recess that involve factors related to the appropriate amount of time needed for an age level, the lunch schedule, and the physical education schedule.

Time Students in the primary grades can profit from 15- to 20-minute recess periods twice a day. One longer recess (25-30 minutes) is more appropriate for the intermediate grades.

Lunch It is as common for recess to be scheduled after lunch as it is for language arts to be scheduled at the beginning of the school day. There is now cause to reconsider this 100-year-old tradition. Experts today say that recess should be scheduled before rather than after lunch. Research indicates that when recess is scheduled before lunch, students consume significantly more food and nutrients (Bergman et al., 2004; Getlinger et al., 1996). The Montana Team Nutrition Program developed guidelines and resources (www.opi.state.mt.us/schoolfood/recessBL.html) following the Recess Before Lunch Pilot Project (www.opi.mt.gov/pdf/schoolfood/rbl/RBLPilot.pdf). Montana schools reported that scheduling recess before lunch had these results:

- Student behavior on the playground, in the cafeteria, and in the classroom improved.

- Students wasted less food and drank more milk, leading to increased nutrient intake.

- The cafeteria atmosphere improved.

- Children were more settled and ready to learn upon returning to the classroom.

To view more school success stories for implementing a recess-before-lunch policy, visit www.educationworld.com/a_admin/admin/admin389.shtml.

The Physical Education Schedule Another consideration for scheduling recess is the physical education schedule. In an effort to provide students with opportunities for physical activity throughout the school day, recess and physical education should not be scheduled back to back. When students go from recess directly to physical education or vice versa, this creates a large block of physical activity time, often leaving the remaining part of the school day free of physical activity. Much like hours of sedentary time, large blocks of physical activity time can be counterproductive, leaving students too physically tired to reap the full benefits of the later physical activity. For example, when students leave recess and go directly to physical education class, they are often too hot and tired to participate fully. It is also necessary to schedule recess in an area that does not interfere with physical education classes being conducted outdoors.

Teaching Children Playground Games

The quality of recess is enhanced when children can direct and organize their own activities. Child-directed games and activities result in increased physical activity time, decreased behavior problems due to boredom, and increased opportunity for developing cooperative skills. Many children will want to play the games and sports they have learned in their physical education program during recess or after school. Classroom teachers, physical education teachers, and playground supervisors will also want to teach children low organized games for this purpose. Low organized games are simple games that children can organize and set up themselves.

Children will often organize their own small-sided game.

Children today are not as familiar with the traditional playground games enjoyed by earlier generations. There is a need to teach children traditional games, as well as other low organized games, so they will have more options when making physical activity choices (see chapter 7 for more on games). Figure 6.1 presents a few traditional playground games. Variations of these games and additional playground games may be found on the accompanying CD-ROM.

Equipment for Recess

If children are to be physically active during recess, adequate and age-appropriate equipment should be available (see sidebar on p. 125). Classroom teachers may have a bag of recess equipment stored in their classroom for their class to use during recess, or the school may have a locker or storage space reserved for housing recess equipment. In the latter situation, children would retrieve the desired equipment on their way to recess and return it to the locker or designated storage area at the end of recess. Whether equipment is stored in the classroom or a community locker, one or two students should be assigned the responsibility of taking out and returning equipment for the week. Teach students to take responsibility for keeping track of the equipment and always returning it to the storage area. Equipment left on the playground may not be there the next time students want to use it.

Designating Play Areas

Identifying play areas for specific games or types of play serves to decrease bullying and increase physical activity as students enter these areas and engage in an activity. When a play area is designated for particular activity, supervisors should permit students only engaged in the activity to be in that area. A play area may be designated for jump rope activities, kicking games, basketball, or tag games. Boundaries for play areas may be marked using orange traffic cones. Signs may be posted identifying the activity for the specified area.

FIGURE 6.1

Traditional Playground Games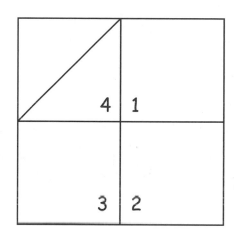

Four Square

The court consists of four equal-sized squares. The size of the court can range from 8 by 8 feet (2.4 by 2.4 meters) for younger players to 16 by 16 feet (about 5 by 5 meters) for upper elementary players. Squares are labeled 1, 2, 3, and 4. A diagonal line is sometimes drawn across square 4 to mark it as the server's square.

Each player stands in one of the four squares. The server, in square 4, starts the game by bouncing the ball once behind the serving line, and with an open hand strikes the ball into one of the other squares. The player receiving the serve must let it bounce once before hitting it into another square. Play continues until a fault has been committed by one of the four players.

Faults include

- stepping over the line while serving,
- hitting the ball out of bounds,
- hitting a line with the ball,
- failing to return a hit made to your square, and
- using an overhand throw or hitting the ball with a fist.

When the game has four players, the player who committed the fault moves to square 1 and the others rotate to fill in the empty squares. For example, if the server, 4, commits the fault, he or she moves to square 1, 1 moves to 2, 2 moves to 3, and 3 becomes the new server. After each fault, everyone moves up a square to eventually become the server.

If the game has more than four players, the one who commits a fault leaves the court and joins the line of players waiting to get in the game. The player in the front of the line moves to square 1, and the other players move up a square.

Hopscotch

The first player in line throws a marker into box 1. The player then hops on one foot to the end of the court, hopping over the square that contains the marker. This same player, once in the last box, turns and hops back again. He stops at the second box, picks up the marker from the first box, and hops out.

A player who successfully complete her first turn without any faults proceeds to throwing the marker inside box 2 and so forth. Players should take turns, always starting where they left off, until someone has successfully navigated all the spaces.

Wherever there are two boxes side by side, a player can land with one foot in each block. Single boxes are hopped on one foot.

(continued)

(continued)

A player forfeits a turn and must return to the back of the line when a fault is committed. Faults include

- failure to throw the marker so that it is completely inside the intended box,
- stepping on a line,
- hopping into the box that contains the marker, and
- using hands to support oneself while picking up a marker.

The first player to complete the course successfully wins the game.

Kickball

Players form two teams. One team lines up to kick and the other team assumes fielding positions (as in softball). The game is played similarly to softball and with the following rules:

1. The ball is rolled by the pitcher to the kicker. After the kick, the kicker runs the bases as in softball.

2. The fielding team can put the kicker out by catching a fly ball, tagging a runner who is between bases, or forcing the runner out by getting the ball to a base before the runner gets there.

3. No leading off or base stealing by the base runners is allowed.

4. There are unlimited outs. Teams switch places after everyone on the kicking team has kicked. One point is scored each time the kicker safely returns home.

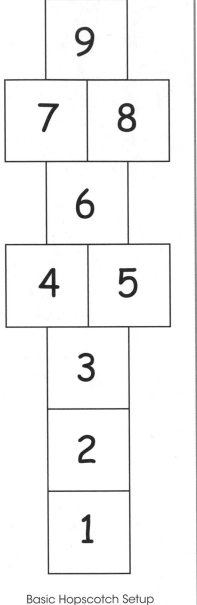

Basic Hopscotch Setup

Change activities from time to time to allow for variety. Having designated areas for specific types of play also helps playground supervisors to monitor playground behavior.

Play areas should also be designated for use by a particular age group. Playground structures are designed for the intended use of specific age groups. The preschool, primary, and intermediate grade levels should each have their own large-equipment areas with equipment specifically designed for their age group. Equipment designed for younger children is dangerous when used by older students and vice versa. Separate play areas for the different age groups should be made available, and children should be allowed to play only on equipment that is developmentally appropriate.

Grade-Appropriate Equipment for Recess

Equipment for Grades K Through 2 That Should Be Included

- Rubber 13-inch (33-centimeter) playground balls
- Rubber 10-inch (25-centimeter) playground balls
- Rubber size 3 soccer balls
- Rubber bases
- Removable flag belts
- Plastic scoops with balls
- Nubby balls
- Spider balls
- Bean bags
- Hoops
- Cones
- Foxtails

Equipment for Grades 3 Through 5 That Should Be Included

- Rubber 8.5-inch (21-centimeter) playground balls
- Rubber size 4 and 5 soccer balls
- Rubber size 6 (junior) footballs
- Removable flag belts
- Short jump ropes
- Long jump ropes
- Ankle ring ball hops
- Jump bands
- Rubber base set
- Vinyl cones (to designate play areas)
- Rubber size 5 and 6 basketballs
- Sidewalk chalk (to mark blacktop area)
- Chinese jump ropes
- Hoops
- Rubber horseshoes
- Bocce
- Badminton set
- Batting tees
- Foam bats
- Wiffle balls
- Foam juggling rings

Supervising the Playground

"Seventy percent of all school injuries occur during recess or physical education. A review of injury data has revealed that lack of proper supervision is considered a 'contributing factor in playground injuries over 40% of the time'" (Bossenmeyer, 2009). Supervision of the playground requires

- policies for active supervision,
- establishing rules for appropriate behavior, and
- managing student behavior in positive ways.

Active Supervision

Adult supervision is essential to keep children safe during play. Approximately 40% of the injuries that occur on playgrounds are due to inadequate supervision. Adults responsible for supervising the playground should know how children play. Knowing how children of different ages play will help guide the observations of supervisors. They will know what to look for as they watch the children they are responsible for.

Early primary children play with a partner or in small groups, often running and chasing one another. As children get older they enjoy playing in larger-group activities that they can organize themselves. All children enjoy climbing on and hanging from playground apparatus such as climbing ladders, monkey bars, and jungle gyms. Supervision of these areas is easily focused since these structures are stationary. Upper elementary grade children are not as physically active as they enjoy time for social interaction through team games or talking with friends.

Teachers should *actively* supervise the playground. Active supervision means that supervisors should not sit or stand and talk to other adults but should move around the playground and visually scan areas of play. Students on the playground should sense that the supervisor sees what they are doing. Through proximity control, or moving near children who are playing, your mere presence can often disrupt or defuse a potential altercation.

Playground supervisors may be parents, volunteers, hired staff, or the classroom teacher. However, the quality of supervision depends on the supervisor's knowledge of safe play behavior. The National Program for Playground Safety recommends that all supervisors understand the basics of playground safety and monitor as follows:

- Check for broken equipment and make sure children do not play on it.

- Remove unsafe modifications, such as ropes tied to equipment, before allowing children to play.
- Check for properly maintained protective surfacing.
- Make sure children wear sneakers.
- Watch for and stop dangerous horseplay, for example when children throw protective surfacing materials or jump from playground equipment such as swings or from great heights.
- Watch for and keep children from wandering away from the play area.

Establishing Playground Rules

Students often spend time on the playground under different sets of rules or in some case with no rules at all. Students may be on the playground before school, during recess, after school, or during after-school programs and are expected to abide by guidelines for playground behavior established for these different program areas. This inconsistency in expectations for behavior sends mixed messages to children and leads to confusion regarding playground rules. It is important for students to have one set of rules to follow whenever they are on the playground, whether this is before school, during recess, or after school. Schoolwide playground rules would help in providing consistency in expectations for playground behavior. The establishment of schoolwide playground rules could be the charge of the school physical activity committee (see chapter 10), the school physical activity director, or a faculty committee.

Once rules are established, they should be taught to all students, posted at all school exits leading to the playground, posted on the playground, and enforced by all individuals who supervise students on the playground. Personnel in all school programs that use the playground, before- and after-school programs, and recess must understand the rules as they were intended and enforce the rules when supervising students on the playground.

Based on the needs of a school, the following are playground rules that may be established to address particular areas of concern:

- Stay inside the playground area (make sure that the meaning of "area" is clear to both students and supervisors).
- No climbing, jumping, or playing on top of fences.

Be Aware of Drawstrings on Clothing

Drawstrings on jackets can become snagged on playground equipment, on school bus handrails or doors, and on escalators or other mechanical equipment. Incidents of snagged drawstrings or toggles have resulted in injuries and even deaths.

- Use playground equipment for its proper purposes only.
- Report accidents to the playground supervisor.
- Be courteous and considerate of others.
- Respect the rights of others.
- Do not leave the playground without permission.
- Share equipment and space.
- Leave things like rocks, dirt, and pinecones on the ground.
- Standing on or jumping from climbing equipment is not allowed.
- Touch football and kicking games are to be played on the playing field.
- Basketball and jump rope are to be played on the blacktop.
- Do not interfere with another class activity or physical education class using the facilities.

Teaching Appropriate Student Behavior

One of the six national standards for physical education (NASPE, 2004b) identifies a physically educated person as one who exhibits responsible personal and social behavior that respects self and others in physical activity settings. Physical education teachers provide learning experiences designed to promote student achievement of this affective standard in much the same way as they do for psychomotor and cognitive outcomes. Successful performance in physical activity settings, whether in the gym, on a playing field, on a court, or on the playground, requires not only motor skills for game play but also the personal and social skills needed for performing those skills while interacting with others. These self-initiated personal and social behaviors include taking turns, sharing equipment, adhering to safe practices, following rules and procedures, taking responsibility for one's own actions without blaming others, encouraging others and refraining

from put-downs, using cooperative skills, playing within the rules of a game, showing self-control, and resolving interpersonal conflicts.

Personal and social behavior must be taught. Because children are active and engaged with each other during recess, recess provides a perfect opportunity to teach appropriate behavior. Teaching involves clearly communicating expectations for performance and holding students accountable for their behavior.

During recess, playground supervisors often hear reports of unfair play, name calling, or other irresponsible behaviors and then upon investigation hear students blaming others. Hellison (2003) has identified strategies for using the physical activity setting to help young people take more responsibility for themselves and the well-being of others. One can use Hellison's model of five levels of responsibility in teaching responsible behavior to students and defining for them just exactly what responsibility means and what they are to take responsibility for. These levels of responsibility are useful for schools to establish, communicate, and reinforce on the playground as well as in the classroom. When all teachers share the same expectations and communicate in the same language with each other and with students, efforts to increase levels of student responsibility are more effective.

Level IV, Caring Students at Level IV, in addition to respecting others, participating, and being self-directed, are motivated to extend their sense of responsibility beyond themselves by cooperating, giving support, showing concern, and helping.

Level III, Self-Direction Students at Level III not only show respect and participation but also are able to work without direct supervision. They can identify their own needs and begin to plan and carry out their physical education programs.

Level II, Participation Students at Level II not only show at least minimal respect for others but also willingly play, accept challenges, practice motor skills, and train for fitness under the teacher's supervision.

Level I, Respect Students at Level I may not participate in daily activities or show much mastery or improvement, but they are able to control their behavior enough that they don't interfere with the other students' right to learn or the teacher's right to teach. They do this without much prompting by the teacher and without constant supervision.

Level Zero, Irresponsibility Students who operate at Level Zero make excuses, blame others for their behavior, and deny personal responsibility for what they do or fail to do.

Hellison developed four general strategies for putting the five levels into practice:

- *Awareness.* Students are made aware of the levels through teacher explanation and student discussions.

- *Experience.* Students actually experience the levels by respecting others or trying to give support to others.

- *Sharing and problem solving.* Student sharing or problem-solving sessions are conducted to address problems that arise. Decision-making and problem-solving experiences giving students choices are used when problems arise at each of the levels. For instance, a problem involving name calling may present itself.

- *Self-reflection.* This is time set aside for students to reflect on their behaviors in relation to the levels. Students may identify their actual level of performance and perhaps the level they intend to put into practice the next day.

Using Hellison's model, students are taught who they are and how their actions are based on the choices that they make. Students are asked repeatedly to think about the level of responsibility they have chosen and to make adjustments accordingly. The ultimate goal is to send the message to students that they are responsible for deciding for themselves what to value and whether what they are doing is working for them.

Hellison's levels of responsibility have been adapted for use in the classroom (see figure 6.2) and the playground. Hinson (2001) has adapted the levels of responsibility by reducing the five

---

What's Your Level?

Level 0: Irresponsibility

Home: Blaming brothers or sisters for problems

Playground: Calling other students names

Classroom: Talking to friends when teacher is giving instructions

Physical education: Pushing and shoving others when selecting equipment

Level 1: Self-control

Home: Keeping oneself from hitting brother when really mad at him

Playground: Standing and watching others play

Classroom: Waiting until an appropriate time to talk with friends

Physical education: Practicing, but not all the time

Level 2: Involvement

Home: Helping to clean up supper dishes

Playground: Playing with others

Classroom: Listening and doing class work

Physical education: Trying new things without complaining and saying, "I can't"

Level 3: Self-responsibility

Home: Cleaning room without being asked

Playground: Returning equipment during recess

Classroom: Doing a science project that is not a part of any assignment

Physical education: Undertaking to learn a new skill through resources outside the physical education class

Level 4: Caring

Home: Helping take care of a pet or younger child

Playground: Asking others (not just friends) to join in play

Classroom: Helping another student with a math problem

Physical education: Willingly working with anyone in the class

Figure 6.2　Hellison's levels of responsibility.

levels to three categories of behaviors: unacceptable, acceptable, and outstanding (see table 6.1). Identified under each level are characteristics of a person acting at that particular level as they relate to recess and the playground. In implementing the levels, teachers do not tell students how to act but rather teach self-responsibility by holding students responsible for choosing their level of involvement.

Handling Playground Conflict

Because playgrounds are interactive settings where children are largely left to play without adult interference, there are likely to be conflicts that they will need to learn how to resolve. The following are examples of some of the more common decisions students will need to make that can lead to conflict:

- Who gets to kick first?
- Who gets to be the roller?
- Who jumps next?
- Was the kick foul or fair?
- Who is on what team?

In teaching students responsibility by holding them responsible for their behavior, one must also provide them with some tools for success. Classroom teachers and physical education teachers must teach students how to make decisions and resolve conflicts that may arise during physical activity settings. Teach students the hand game Rock! Paper! Scissors! for use in deciding "Who gets to . . ." (see sidebar).

In resolving differences during game play that are due to different perceptions of an event, such as a kick called foul by some and fair by others, or a pitch called a strike by one team and a ball by the other team, teach students that a "do over" is appropriate. In a "do over," the action in dispute (e.g., the kick or the pitch) is performed again; in these examples the student is allowed another kick or pitch.

Playground Bullying

Most of us can recall the scenario in which a classroom bully behaves aggressively toward or harasses weaker students. However, not all aggressive behavior is bullying. Bullying is repeated physical, verbal, or psychological attacks or intimidation with intent to harm. A student is being bullied when he or she is repeatedly hurt or victimized by negative behaviors of one or more others.

Children today are not as constructive in play as in the past and do not know how to organize and play many traditional playground games. This leads to idle time on the playground when bullying is most likely to occur. It is important that students have the resources (e.g., space, equipment, dispositions [values], and knowledge) needed for active participation in games and activities when on the playground.

Newer research on bullying suggests that bullying does not usually occur in the presence of adults but rather when adults are not aware of what is happening. In view of this, one strategy to prevent bullying is to incorporate quality supervision practices (Bossenmeyer, 2008). Established programs like those offered by www.Peacefulplaygrounds.com or http://stopbullyingnow.hrsa.gov/ were designed to prevent bullying by working with supervision strategies as well as with all students as preventive measures.

According to Bossenmeyer of Peaceful Playgrounds (2008), there are four rules that schools should adopt regarding bullying:

1. Do not bully.
2. Help others when you see bullying occur (step in or get help from an adult).

TABLE 6.1

Levels of Responsible Behavior on the Playground

Unacceptable	Acceptable	Outstanding
Not following directions	Following directions	Being self-responsible
Not participating	Participating	Cooperating with others
Arguing	Taking care of equipment	Returning equipment
Hitting or pushing	Respecting others	Helping others
Being out of control	Being under control	Acting as a role model

Rock! Paper! Scissors!

Both players count aloud to three or say the name of the game (e.g., "Rock! Paper! Scissors!"), each time raising one hand in a fist and swinging it down on the count. On the third count (after saying "three" or "scissors"), the players form one of these shapes with their hand:

- Rock, represented by a fist.
- Paper, represented by an open hand, with the fingers together.
- Scissors, represented by the index and middle fingers extended and separated.

The objective is to select a gesture that defeats the opponent's. Outcomes are determined as follows:

Rock breaks scissors; rock wins.
Paper covers rock; paper wins.
Scissors cut paper; scissors wins.

If both players choose the same gesture, the game is tied and is played again.

3. Include others (invite students to be a part of games and activities).
4. Tell an adult at home or at school if you experience bullying.

SUMMARY

1. Recess is a break in a child's school day that provides unstructured time for active, free play.

2. Recess provides an opportunity for children to engage in physical activity and to develop and refine fundamental motor skills.

3. During recess, children develop important life skills such as cooperation; taking turns; following rules; and problem-solving, decision-making, and negotiating skills.

4. Through creative and imaginative play, children try on different roles and see the world through the eyes of others.

5. Experts recommend that all students engage in at least one daily 20-minute recess period.

6. Ensure that all students are physically active during recess.

Children can solve problems on their own when provided with the necessary tools.

7. When scheduling recess, consider students' lunch and physical education schedule. Recess should be scheduled before, rather than after, lunch and not back to back with physical education.

8. Teach children simple games that they can organize and direct on their own during recess.

9. Effective playground supervisors know how children play, are active in their supervising, and use proximity control.

10. Establishment and enforcement of school-wide playground rules provide consistency in communicating expectations to students about playground behavior.

11. Play areas should be designated for different activities and age groups.

12. Children can be taught responsible behavior and how to make good choices.

CHECKING YOUR UNDERSTANDING

1. What is recess?

2. Describe the physical, social, and cognitive benefits of recess.

3. What recommendations and concerns do policy groups have regarding recess?

4. What steps can be taken to ensure that all students are physically active during recess?

5. Identify three guidelines or considerations for scheduling recess.

6. Describe characteristics of an effective playground supervisor.

7. Identify five rules for students to follow during recess.

8. What can you do to promote responsible behavior on the playground?

9. Describe Hellison's model for teaching personal and social responsibility.

RESOURCES

International Play Association
www.ipausa.org

National Safe Kids Campaign
www.safekids.org

National Program for Playground Safety
www.playgroundsafety.org

Peaceful Playgrounds
www.peacefulplaygrounds.com

Stop Bullying Now
http://stopbullyingnow.hrsa.gov/kids/

Bailey, G. (2001). *The ultimate playground & recess game book.* Vancouver, WA: Educators Press.

Bailey, G. (2007). *Recess success!* Vancouver, WA: Educators Press.

Hellison, D. (2003). *Teaching responsibility through physical activity* (2nd ed.). Champaign, IL: Human Kinetics.

Hinson, C. (2001). *6-Steps to a trouble-free playground.* Wilmington, DE: PE Publishing.

Hinson, C. (2001). *Games kids should play at recess* (2nd ed.). Wilmington, DE: PE Publishing.

REFERENCES

Bergman, E.A., Buergel, N.S., Englund, T.F., & Femrite, A.(2004). The relationship of meal and recess schedules to plate waste in elementary schools. *Journal of Child Nutrition and Management, 28*(2).

Bossenmeyer, M. (2008). Why bullying programs succeed or fail. Available at www.peacefulplaygrounds.com/why-bullying-programs-succeed-or-fail.htm.

Bossenmeyer, M. (2009). Playground liability: Accident or injury. Available at www.peacefulplaygrounds.com/playground-liability-accident-or-injury.htm.

Castelli, D.M., Hillman, C.H., Buch, S.M., & Erwin, H.E. (2007). Physical fitness and academic achievement in third- and fifth-grade students. *Journal of Sport and Exercise Psychology, 29,* 239-252.

Dale, D., Corbin, C.B., & Dale, K.S. (2000). Restricting opportunities to be active during school time: Do children compensate by increasing physical activity levels after school? *Research Quarterly for Exercise and Sport, 71*(3), 240-248.

Getlinger, M., Laughlin, C., Bell, E., Akre, C., & Arjmandi, B. (1996). Food waste is reduced when elementary-school children have recess before lunch. *Journal of the American Dietetic Association, 96,* 906-908.

Hellison, D. (2003). *Teaching responsibility through physical activity* (2nd ed.). Champaign, IL: Human Kinetics.

Hillman, C.H., Erickson, K.I., & Kramer, A.F. (2008). Be smart, exercise your heart: Exercise effects on brain and cognition. *Nature Reviews Neuroscience, 9,* 58-65.

Hillman, C.H., Motl, R.W., Pontifex, M.B., Posthuma, D., Stubbe, J.H., Boomsma, D.I., & de Geus, E.J.C. (2006). Physical activity and cognitive function in a cross-section of younger and older community-dwelling individuals. *Health Psychology, 25,* 678-687.

Hinson, C. (2001). *Games kids should play at recess* (2nd ed.). Wilmington, DE: PE Publishing.

IPA/USA and American Association for the Child's Right to Play. (n.d.). *The case for elementary recess.* Available at www.ipausa.org/recesshandbook.htm.

Jarrett, O.S., & Maxwell, D.M. (2000). What research says about the need for recess. In R. Clements (Ed.), *Elementary school recess: selected readings, games, and activities for teachers and parents* (pp. 12-23). Lake Charles, LA: American Press.

Jarrett, O.S., Maxwell, D.M., Dickerson, C., Hoge, P., Davies, G., & Yetley, A. (1998). The impact of recess on classroom behavior: Group effects and individual differences. *Journal of Educational Research, 92*(2), 121-126.

Jensen, E. (1998). *Teaching with the brain in mind.* Alexandria, VA: Association for Supervision and Curriculum Development.

National Association of Early Childhood Specialists in State Departments of Education. (2002). *Recess and the importance of play: A position statement on young children and recess* [Online]. Available at www.naecs-sde.org/policy.

National Association for the Education of Young Children. (1998). *The value of school recess and outdoor play.* www.naeyc.org/ece/1998/08.asp.

National Association for Sport and Physical Education (2004a). *Physical activity for children: A statement of guidelines for children ages 5-12.* (2nd ed.). Reston, VA: NASPE.

National Association for Sport and Physical Education. (2004b). *Moving into the future: National standards for physical education* (2nd ed.). Reston, VA; NASPE.

National Association for Sport and Physical Education (2006). *Recess for elementary school students: A position paper from the National Association for Sport and Physical Education.* Reston, VA: NASPE.

National Program for Playground Safety, School of Health, Physical Education & Leisure Services, University of Northern Iowa. www.uni.edu/playground.

Ratey J. (2008). *Spark: The revolutionary new science of exercise and the brain.* New York: Little, Brown and Co.

United States Department of Health and Human Services & United States Department of Education (2000). *Promoting better health for young people through physical activity and sports.* Washington, DC: USDHSS & USDE.

7

Games in the Elementary School

OVERVIEW

Children derive a lot of their physical activity from playing games, which makes games an important part of any school physical activity program. This chapter includes a brief overview of the place of games in both the physical education program and the physical activity program of a school. The focus is on selecting and teaching low organization games and on modifying games to be used in the physical activity program of a school.

CHAPTER OUTCOMES

This chapter will help you

- understand how games are used in the elementary school;
- select games to be used as part of the physical activity program that require limited organization, are safe, promote moderate to vigorous physical activity, and are developmentally appropriate and enjoyable for the elementary-age child;
- modify games that do not meet these criteria;
- encourage children to create games; and
- organize and conduct games with your class.

IN THIS CHAPTER

A game is a structured activity that is intended to be played for amusement and involves a goal to accomplish. The purpose and design of a game vary in complexity depending on the age group for which it is designed. Some games promote physical activity while others are more sedentary. Playing games has always been a valuable part of our culture. Active games that are carefully chosen and conducted as an educational experience have the potential to make a valuable contribution to the growth and development of children physically, cognitively, and socially. Through games, children learn how to interact with each other in socially acceptable ways in both cooperative and competitive settings. They learn how to make decisions, follow directions, and solve problems. Appropriate game experiences provide an opportunity for children to test their skills and to have fun. Conversely, inappropriate game experiences have the potential to contribute in a negative way to a child's development.

Some games promote more physical activity than others. The level of physical activity in a game varies on a continuum of inactive to highly active. Most of you probably have good memories of experiences in games such as Kick the Can, Capture the Flag, Four Square, hopscotch, hide-and-seek, or child versions of sports. Some children today will have these same memories, but for countless others this will not be the case. Some children in today's society are not active and do not play freely outdoors for a variety of reasons, including these:

- Parents or guardians work late, placing children home alone or in day care.
- Neighborhoods are perceived as unsafe.
- The lure of electronic games overrides the desire to play outdoors.
- Children do not know traditional games.

The school day may be the only opportunity for many children to play outdoor games and learn to play games that promote moderate to vigorous physical activity.

Games in Physical Education Class

Games on the playground, whether teacher led or child initiated, provide opportunities for physical activity, social development, and the sheer joy of play. Games used for a physical education class have a different intent. The physical education program has a more specific focus and is designed to develop psychomotor skills and objectives associated with the cognitive and affective domains of learning related to developing a physically active lifestyle. The physical education program should give students the skills they need to be active participants in games and should prepare them to organize games they will want to play when they leave the elementary school.

Psychomotor Game Skills

The role of the elementary physical educator is to teach the motor skills needed for students to be competent in a variety of physical activities. While some elementary-aged children will later excel in athletics, the physical education program is designed to develop participants in physical games and activities at a recreational level of competency. If you have a clear idea of what to expect students of a particular age to be able to do, and if you understand what the physical education program is trying to do, you can make better game choices in the physical activity program.

Becoming a competent game player begins in the early elementary grades as a child masters locomotor skills and is introduced to manipulative skills. In the upper elementary grades, additional instruction and practice are designed to help students achieve and maintain a mature pattern of the manipulative skills in isolation (e.g., throwing a ball) and in combination (e.g., catching a ball and throwing quickly to a base). Students also learn to vary patterns according to the requirements of the game (e.g., speed, force, direction, and trajectory) and to begin to apply skills in various games and modified versions of sports.

Cognitive Learning in Games

In the physical education program, students develop an understanding of movement concepts as they relate to games and establish a beginning level of game knowledge. That is, they begin to understand and learn how to apply basic tactics, strategies, and rules to score, to gain possession, and to maintain possession of objects. These concepts are presented using small-sided game situations like one versus one and two versus one. The learning of the more complex tactics, strategies, and rules continues in the middle school years.

Affective Learning Through Game Skills

Games open up unlimited avenues to teach toward the affective domain in physical education. Games have the potential to promote the development of social skills and to teach the importance of fair play. They allow children an opportunity to express excitement, to gain personal satisfaction, to work toward a goal, and to begin to value the benefits of physical activity. Teaching games provides children the opportunity to

- work to achieve a goal,
- work together to meet a common goal,
- be successful as a team,
- learn about winning and losing, and
- learn to accept differences in others.

These skills are not developed through participation alone. A teacher must target desired behaviors and design learning experiences to promote their development. The physical education teacher must plan for the development of affective objectives and design an environment to encourage these objectives. Games can develop both desirable behaviors such as leadership and cooperation and undesirable behaviors such as cheating and inappropriate aggressive behavior; the role of the teacher is thus critical in ensuring that games are used to develop positive and not negative behavior. The teacher will want to discourage negative behaviors while recognizing and encouraging positive behaviors, as these involve skills that cross over into all aspects of daily life.

Game experiences in physical education class are designed to help children become competent and confident game players. The idea is that children will apply the knowledge, skills, and values learned in physical education class to recreational play. To encourage specific game play out of class, physical education teachers may teach the children a game they can play independently, have them play it briefly, and encourage them to continue play on their own time. For example, Four Square is a playground game played by many children outside of physical education class (see chapter 6 for game description). It requires that the children be able to use an underhand volley to strike a ball in a very controlled manner. The physical education teacher may teach the skill of the underhand volley or strike used in the game to second graders. In third grade, she reviews the skill and continues to teach the tactics and strategies needed for successful offensive and defensive play. The children are then taught the rules of the game and allowed to play it during the last few minutes of a class period. With the level of skill competency reached in class, the students will feel confident to take part in this popular game at recess. Children who are competent and feel confident are more likely to develop and maintain a physically active lifestyle.

Low Organization Games for the Physical Activity Program

Games in the physical activity program of a school will primarily be *low organization games* rather than games designed to practice specific motor skills as in physical education. Low organization games are those that most of you played on the playground or outside with your friends as a child, such as Red Light Green Light, Jump the Creek, Kick the Can, hide-and-seek, stickball, and kickball. Low organization games require minimal setup and teaching time. Time, space, and equipment are often factors when classroom teachers or other adults are trying to identify appropriate games for children. Low organization games are usually the games of choice.

Many low organization games have been played for decades but are not desirable. In order to ensure that the games we teach children in school and allow children to play in school are good ones, we have established the following criteria for their selection:

- *Enjoyment:* The game should be fun and should be one that students want to continue to play.
- *Maximum participation:* The game should provide continuous physical activity for every child.
- *Physical and emotional safety:* The game should not put children in physical danger or be psychologically threatening to them.
- *Developmental appropriateness:* Games should be age appropriate and should not require physical, social, or cognitive skills that the child has not acquired.

The remainder of this section will help you to select quality games using specified criteria and to modify games that do not meet the criteria.

Games such as Duck, Duck, Goose minimize the opportunity for physical activity.

Enjoyment of Games

Games, by nature, are enjoyable to most children and adults. When children play without supervision or imposed rules, they find ways to make games fun. For example, a baseball game played by youngsters while the older sibling plays "the real game" might include a paper cup smashed into a ball shape, convenient objects as bases (fence post, corner of the concession stand, sticks, or rocks), and their hand as the "bat." The rules are kept simple and are based on the number of players. If there are not enough players, the term "ghost man" is used to replace a runner and bring in a batter. No adult is involved, and the young players are having fun.

Children should enjoy playing games led by teachers and should be able to find success in playing the game. Games that eliminate players, are dominated by the highly skilled, are physically threatening, or require skills that a child does not have are not fun for many children. Children who do not find success and enjoyment in physical activities are likely to become nonparticipants in physical activity. While not every child will obtain the same degree of enjoyment from any given game, teachers need to make the effort to create positive game experiences. Table 7.1 includes examples of negative situations found in many game experiences, followed by positive solutions.

There are many games described in this book (and accompanying CD-ROM), as well as other books and Web sites, that will bring joy to children. *The Physical Best Activity Guide: Elementary Level* (2005), put out by the National Association for Sport and Physical Education (NASPE), is a great source of activities and games that will promote health-related fitness. When a game is thoughtfully selected to meet the needs of all students, the experience will be positive and enjoyable.

Maximum Participation

Probably the most common problem with low organizational games is that many do not promote a moderate or vigorous level of physical activity. The reason may be that they are organized in a format that limits participation or that they are designed to eliminate players from participation as the game progresses. Games need to be selected or modified to maximize participation.

Organizational Format

There are traditional games that have been played for years and quite a few new ones that may be

Games in the Elementary School ■ **137**

TABLE 7.1

Positive Solutions for Negative Game Experiences

Negative game experiences	Positive solutions
Games are dominated by the highly skilled players. Some players criticize lesser-skilled students. Lesser-skilled students are told that it is their fault the team lost.	**1.** Modify the rules and skills involved to allow success for all. **2.** Require cooperative team play by encouraging working together. **3.** If necessary, use punitive actions against students who, through their dominance, keep others from playing.
Games are selected that are too difficult or too easy for children.	**1.** Search for games that are listed for the age or developmental level of the children playing. **2.** Do not mix an extreme age range of children together in a game. A safe range is two years. **3.** Modify the game if the children are not successful or are bored.
The game design eliminates children from playing, placing them on the sidelines for most of the game.	**1.** Do not use elimination games. **2.** If elimination games are played, there is a quick way to come back into the game that requires cooperation from a teammate or involves a short time period (e.g., count to 10).
Children are targets as in kickball and dodgeball. Fear becomes a part of the game.	**1.** Do not use games in which objects are thrown at children. **2.** Modify the rules so the targets are objects, not people.
Children are placed in situations in which they have to be chosen in order to participate in the game (e.g., Duck, Duck, Goose; Heads Up, Seven Up).	**1.** Do not have games in which only the more popular or the slower children are chosen. Some children will do nothing but sit during the game, and the result is low self-esteem. **2.** Modify the game or do not use it.
Teams are chosen by captains calling names one by one.	**1.** Teachers organize the teams in advance of play to save children from this dreadful experience and to preserve play time. **2.** Use colors of shirts, desk arrangements, or other ideas such as drawing a card to create the teams.

popular because they are easy to organize rather than because of the physical activity they provide. In these games children are typically in a large circle, or in opposing lines, or in a large group (half the class opposing the other half), or in a line waiting a turn. Games that fall into these categories include Duck, Duck, Goose; Steal the Bacon; and relay races. Figure 7.1 depicts these formations and highlights the number of children active at one time. These examples and many other games played in the same organizational formats typically have children wait-

ing their turn for an unrealistic time period. In some cases children may not get an opportunity to be an active participant at all. Games that use a scattered formation (e.g., Team Tails and Team Bowling in figure 7.2) or a small-group formation (e.g., Keep Away and three-on-two soccer in small grid areas in figure 7.3) are examples of low organized games that maximize physical activity. While the term "low organization game" implies that little time will be spent in organizing the game, physical activity should not be minimized.

Sample Games in Formations That Do NOT Promote Physical Activity ⊙

Note: For each game, the only physically active players are designated in larger font.

Steal the Bacon

Steal the Bacon is a common game that places *one team in a formation facing the other*. Each student is given a number. When the child's number is called, he runs to the middle and tries to steal the "bacon" and return before the opposing student does the same. In this example, number 5 has been called. After number 5 has had a turn, he has to watch until all of the other numbers are called and then, depending on time, will be called again.

Team A		Team B
①		①
②		②
③		③
④		④
⑤	⚽	⑤
⑥		⑥
⑦		⑦
⑧		⑧
⑨		⑨
⑩		⑩
⑪		⑪
⑫		⑫

Duck, Duck, Goose

Duck, Duck, Goose is a common *circle formation* game played in preschools and early primary grades. The enjoyment of this game is in the anticipation of being chosen as the *goose* (G) by one student (the "it") who walks around and touches heads, calling "duck" over and over until she decides to touch one head and say "goose." The student chosen as the goose chases the "it," trying to catch her before she returns to the spot vacated by the goose. If the "it" is caught by the goose, she has to go to the mush pot in the middle of the circle. The disappointing, inactive aspect of the game is that players are always or almost always called a duck. The ducks watch while the goose gets to run after the "it."

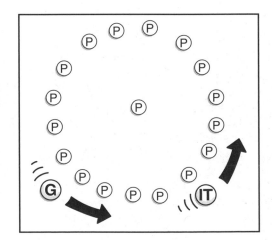

Relay Games

Relay formation is a common way to have children race one team against another. While relays are easy to use and require very little organization and equipment, the diagram depicts how little physical activity actually occurs. In this situation, five students are active while 25 are watching and waiting a turn.

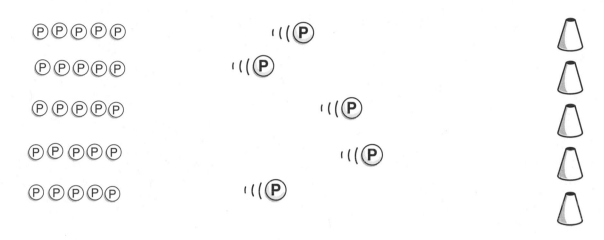

FIGURE 7.2

Sample Games in a Scattered Formation That DO Promote Physical Activity

Team Tails

Team Tails is played with students scattered and attempting to pull the tails of the players on the opposing team. Players on one team have a red flag in the back of their pants and those on the other team have yellow. The object of the game is to pull the flags from the opposing players. Once a flag is pulled, it is dropped on the ground. A player whose flag is pulled must go to jail. Another teammate rescues him by bringing the tail to jail. Players exit jail in the order in which they came in, and the opposing team is not allowed to have a jail guard. In this game, children rarely stay in jail for more than a minute; for some this is a needed rest, as the game is fast action.

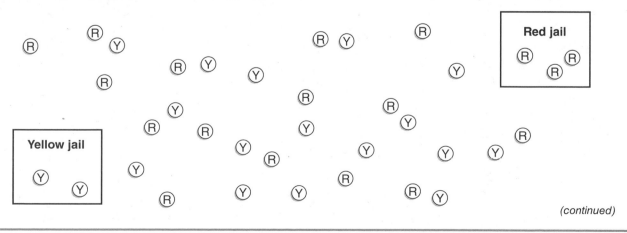

(continued)

(continued)

Team Bowling

Team Bowling is played with students divided into two teams and scattered on opposite sides of the playing area. Bowling pins are placed on the end lines of each team, and a no play zone is marked in front of each pin area. There is one playground or high-density foam ball per two players. The object is to roll the ball and knock down the opposing team's pins. No throwing or kicking is allowed. Opponents may gather the ball with their hands or feet on defense. All children are actively involved offensively or defensively.

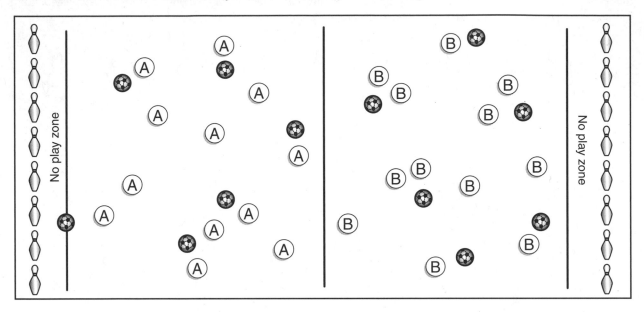

FIGURE 7.3

Sample Games in a Small-Group Formation That DO Promote Physical Activity

Keep Away

Keep Away is best played in a scattered formation in which all players can move, with the exception of the one in possession of the ball. The game can be played using any size ball or disc (which players throw) or a soccer ball (which they pass). The object of the game is for the offensive players (O) to maintain possession of the ball while the defensive players (D) try to gain possession. A turnover results in the teams changing roles, with the last offensive player to touch the ball remaining on offense. In the illustration, several games are occurring at the same time.

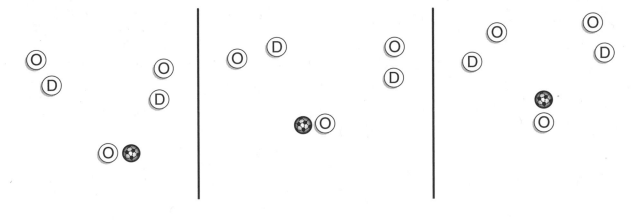

Three-on-Three Soccer

Three-on-three soccer can be played using a large field space set up in a grid formation. It is a great way to have all children actively involved in a modified version of this popular sport. A fourth player can be added to each team as a goalie if desired. However, that position should be rotated on a regular basis.

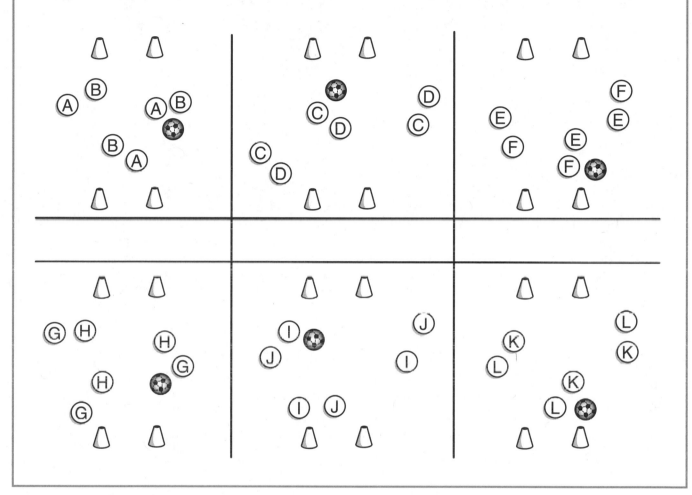

Elimination of Players

The elimination of players is another culprit that deprives children of maximum participation in games. Several versions of tag and popular games like Simon Says and Musical Chairs use this protocol. Often the very children who need the most physical activity spend the game time sitting and watching. They are usually the first to be eliminated. These games can usually be modified through giving the eliminated player a different role, making a rule that allows that player to come back into the game quickly, or changing the purpose of the game. Examples of simple modifications to each of these games are shown in the sidebar, "Modifying Games to Abolish Elimination."

As discussed earlier in this chapter, games are played for various reasons. However, given the limited physical activity that children attain daily, every opportunity should be provided to allow for maximum participation. Games in which children are waiting turns, are primarily stationary, or are eliminated will not provide adequate physical activity.

Modifying Games to Abolish Elimination

Freeze Tag

In a simple game of Freeze Tag, players are tagged and must freeze.

- The winner of the game is the last player tagged.
- As players are tagged, they are to sit to the side and watch for the remainder of the game.

A simple way to change the game is to play Freeze and Defrost Tag.

- The game involves two "taggers," denoted by yellow flags in their hand, and four defrosters denoted by red flags.
- If someone is tagged, the defrosters have the responsibility of "melting" them back into the game with a simple touch of the red flag.
- A tagger can freeze a defroster, which requires the defrosters to unfreeze each other quickly. Stop the game if all defrosters are frozen, and choose new freezers and defrosters.

Simon Says

In the game of Simon Says, players follow the leader in doing an action that the leader tells them to do using the phrase "Simon says." They are eliminated if they do an action that the leader tells them to do but without saying "Simon says." For example, if the leader says "Simon says jump in place," players are expected to jump in place. If the leader says "Skip in place," any student who skips is eliminated and sits for the remainder of the game. In a modified version, the class is divided into two teams. Instead of being eliminated, players just change teams. The challenge is for the players to stay on the same team or to change teams as few times as possible.

Musical Chairs

The game Musical Chairs is typically set up with as many chairs as there are students, minus one. Chairs are arranged facing alternate directions.

- When the music starts, the students travel around the chairs.
- When the music stops, children try to quickly sit in a chair.
- The child that did not find a chair is eliminated and sits out the rest of the game.

For this modified version, the setup is the same, or hula hoops can be used in place of chairs.

- When the music starts, the students travel around the chairs or hoops using the locomotor skills called by the teacher (e.g., walk, skip, gallop).
- When the music stops, all sit in a chair or stand in a hoop. If there is not a free chair or hoop, one student shares.
- This continues until the entire class has to share one chair or one hoop. At this point, for safety reasons, it is best to say that all have to have one body part touching the chair or in the hoop.

Factors That Affect the Selection of Appropriate and Safe Experiences for Children

Children have a right to be safe when playing a game. When you are choosing and conducting game experiences for children, you need to consider many factors that will make the experience both positive and safe:

- The skill and developmental level of the children
- An appropriate space for play
- Active supervision
- Safe behavior of the participants
- Safe equipment
- Emotional safety

Choosing Games at an Appropriate Developmental Level

The selection of a game should be based on the developmental level of the child. Development varies within and across age groups in regard to skill, cognition, and social levels. The teacher selecting a game must take the following into consideration: (1) Children are not miniature adults, so games and sports in the adult form are not appropriate for elementary children; and (2) games appropriate for an upper elementary grade child are much different from those designed for the primary grade child. To aid in the selection of developmentally appropriate games, the discussion that follows provides information about the typical skill, cognitive, and social levels of children across grades.

Skill Level

The range of skill level increases as children progress through elementary school. Skill level can be influenced by a combination of physical abilities, physical development, and experiences. While there are obvious differences in physical development across grades, children in the same grade are typically more similar to one another than to children of different grade levels, with some exceptions. Children have different experiences outside of the school day that play a major role in the development of skill. For example, participants on recreational soccer teams will potentially be more advanced than those who are not.

A teacher should make every effort to have children of similar abilities and age involved in game play. Whenever possible, the age range should not go beyond two years. Beyond two years, the difference in developmental level and skill may be too great and thus jeopardize the potential for success and the safety of the younger, less skilled children.

A teacher should select games that meet the skill level of the students. For example, Red Light, Green Light is a game that would not meet the skill level or interests of a 10-year-old child, just as a game of kickball is too complex for the 6-year-old. Attempting games that are developmentally inappropriate for the child may be unsafe. While Red Light, Green Light may cause boredom among older children, it probably would not cause a safety issue. Kickball for 6-year-olds, on the other hand, could. Most children at age 6 do not have the tracking abilities, motor skill, or space awareness to catch a high-flying ball. Two children attempting to make the catch could easily have a serious collision. Additionally, many 6-year-old children do not yet have a mature kicking pattern that permits them to run and kick a rolling

ball. The result for some will be a kick, a miss, and a fall on their back. Therefore, it is imperative that teachers search for games that fit the developmental and skill levels of the participants. While many sources label games by age or grade level, do not assume that the source is reliable. If you attempt the game and it appears to not match the needs of the students, modify it or select another game. Several appropriate age-level games are provided on the CD-ROM included with this book. The following are general guidelines for skill characteristics of elementary children that will aid in selecting developmentally appropriate games.

Pre-K to Grade 1

- Children at this age are typically highly energetic.
- They tire easily and then recover quickly.
- Large muscles are more developed than the small muscles.
- Development of hand–eye coordination is just beginning.
- The children are rhythmically inclined.
- They have not fully developed all locomotor skills (e.g., leaping) and most combination patterns (e.g., adding a change of direction to a slide step, combining a run and jump).

This age group benefits more from simple tag games, rhythmical games, parachute games, and games that promote the practice of locomotor skills and basic manipulative patterns involving hoops, beanbags, and a variety of balls. Rotating children through stations or centers encourages opportunities for manipulative skill practice with limited equipment.

Grades 2 and 3

- Eye–hand and eye–foot coordination are progressing.
- Locomotor skills are developed.
- Manipulative skills may be mature for many students.
- Reaction time is still slow.

Children in grades 2 and 3 still benefit from tag games, rhythmical activities, and parachute activities. They are ready to play simple games that involve object manipulation (balls, beanbags, and so on). Grade 3 children are ready to be introduced to modified sport-specific small-sided games. Modifications will need to be made to account for the fact that they are not at the mature stage in most manipulative skills and that their reaction time is still slow.

Children in grades 2 and 3 benefit from tag games.

Grades 4 and 5

- Manipulative skills for most have reached the mature stage when performed in simple conditions.
- Coordination has improved, and visual acuity and tracking are as in an adult.
- Reaction time has improved.
- The range of skill level increases due to varied experiences.

Most children in grades 4 and 5 are ready to test their skills in more advanced tag games and games that both involve object manipulation and require accuracy. They have more interest in sport-related games, and most children at these ages enjoy a challenge.

The Role of Cognitive Development in the Selection of Games

With reference to Piaget's stages of cognitive development (Piaget, 1972), children in grade pre-K through grade 1 are not yet logical thinkers since they are in the preoperational intelligence stage. Children age 7 to 11 are in the concrete operational intelligence stage. They begin to think logically and can learn basic tactics and strategies of game play

and do simple problem-solving tasks. While logical thinking begins with most children in the early part of grade 2, for some it may begin toward the later part of the year.

How children play tag illustrates their level of logical thinking. Children in grade pre-K through grade 1 will simply run and scream to avoid the chasers. Although they can be taught space awareness, they do not start using tag game strategies until second grade. These strategies may include faking, watching for the chasers before making a move, and using others as an aid or a screen to avoid being tagged.

It is at about age 12 when most students are ready for complex strategies and a higher level of problem solving in games. The following cognitive characteristics of children will aid teachers in selecting developmentally appropriate games.

Pre-K to Grade 1

- Children at this age have a short attention span.
- They are curious learners.
- They are creative and imaginative.
- They are imitative.

Due to their short attention span, it is often best to plan more than one game with this age group. After a few minutes, they are ready for a new adventure. Select games that provide the opportunity to mimic movements of animals; copy the actions of the teacher; or encourage exploratory movements both with and without manipulative skills. Simple tag games are enjoyed by children of this age. The tag games should involve several obviously indicated (e.g., pinnies, balls, flags) chasers and the idea of freezing when tagged, with all others having the role of freeing the tagged players. These children are not yet ready for tag games involving teamwork.

Grades 2 and 3

- The children's attention span has increased dramatically.
- They enjoy challenging themselves.
- Perceptions of skills are typically higher than actual skill level.
- Logic abilities allow for strategies in simple games.

This age group wants and needs to be challenged through self-testing types of games. These are best played either alone or with a partner or in small groups. Activities may include, for example, practice in dribbling a ball, a game of catch with a partner, or a game of three-against-two Keep Away within a group. Tag games should be complex enough to allow use of basic strategy. Modified sport-related games for grade 3 add the cognitive challenge that this age group needs to experience.

Grades 4 and 5

- The children are able to make simple plans for success in a game.
- They desire the challenge of basic problem solving and game strategy.
- They want to learn the rules of games.
- They have some knowledge of sports and want to relate this to their game play.
- They may have problems separating the idea of how adult sports are played from how a teacher structures a low organized game or why a teacher uses small-sided game play.

Children in the upper elementary grades are capable of learning and applying strategies to games but must balance their cognitive level with their skill level. They want to learn the rules of the game and hold to them. They may question a teacher's knowledge as they compare it with their own knowledge of adult or recreational sport. They also enjoy challenging peers with their sport knowledge.

The Role of Social Development in the Selection of Games

The playing of low organized games is in itself a social event. However, there is a large range of social maturity in the elementary school. While an older elementary school child yearns for the peer interaction that games can provide, the younger child is concerned only with self. Young children are learning to share; and older children know that without cooperation, competition will not work. In this section we look at characteristics of children related to social growth that will aid in selecting developmentally appropriate games.

Pre-K to Grade 1

- At this age children are egocentric.
- They seek adult attention.
- They do not understand or accept defeat.
- They can be rough in their play.
- They have unrealistic perceptions of their own ability.
- They can begin to work with a partner in a limited cooperative manner.

Children in these early years are self-centered. During play of any kind, they vie for attention and will direct the teacher, "Watch me, watch me!" Setting up a game environment that allows self-testing stations or centers allows the child to focus on self but in a shared environment. Games played with children of this age should not include competition, as they do not understand or accept losing and may not understand the concept of winning. Team games and relays do not meet the social or emotional needs of this age group and should not be used. While rough play is a social characteristic of this age group, attempts need to be made to help children understand the safety factor involved. Young children have to be taught in tag games that the idea is to touch gently, not literally capture the opponent. The children typically perceive their abilities to be higher than they actually are, and there is no gain in telling them otherwise. In their eyes if they are bouncing and catching a basketball, they are a basketball player.

Grades 2 and 3

- The children can work independently, with a partner or small group.
- They are gradually moving toward peer-centered behavior but show no real evidence of group loyalty.
- They are able to understand and follow simple rules.
- They do not lose graciously, but are making the transition in that direction.

Children in grades 2 and 3 are socially in a transition stage. They need to be provided game experiences that have simple rules, which they will make every attempt to follow. Because they are becoming more peer centered, this is a good time to incorporate the need for cooperation in games. Tag games that require a cooperative effort to "free" individuals are popular with this age group, as are simple challenges that require cooperation like parachute games, keep-it-going games, and collective scoring games (e.g., "See how many balls your small group can toss into the box"). Children by the end of grade 2 are making the transition into handling competitive situations. However, intervention is required to teach them to win graciously and lose with dignity. The best way to do this is to have students end the game with a handshake or a high five along with words of encouragement (e.g., "good game"), to not make a big deal of the win–loss aspect of the game, and to not allow put-downs.

Grades 4 and 5

- Most children have little interest in playing with the opposite gender.
- Competitive urge increases.
- The child seeks peer group approval.
- The child accepts self-responsibility.
- Leadership abilities are evident in some.
- The child desires to excel in physical activity.
- The child respects rules, yet questions them.

Children in the upper elementary grades enjoy team activities but work better on teams with a small number of players. Some are very competitive while others prefer a more cooperative experience. Select games that are both cooperative and competitive, and give children a choice on whether or not they want to keep score. Competition is a valuable experience when all the participants have an equal chance of winning. When the same students always win and the same students always lose, it is not a valuable experience. The teacher can control this by making sure that the skills required are appropriate for all the students and that the teams are equal.

While most students in this age group handle competition well, the teacher must take care that winning and losing do not go beyond the moment. The sidebar "Ideas for Deemphasizing Winning and Losing" includes ideas on how to draw attention away from winning and losing. Some children at this age are highly competitive and have a tendency to place pressure on teammates and even blame individuals if the team loses. The individual on the receiving end begins to have negative feelings of self-worth and potentially toward playing games. The prevention of this behavior is the responsibility of the teacher.

The need for rules is understood and respected, but it is not unusual for this age group to question rules. An explanation may be necessary to help them understand that adherence promotes fair play for all. When modifying games, it is a good idea to allow the children input in deciding the rules. This will confer more ownership of the rules.

Boys and girls are still similar in skill at this level, but societal issues begin to separate them. The role of the teacher is to prevent the focus on gender by dividing teams equally by gender. You do not want to play boys against girls or to label games as being for only boys or only girls. Explanation and experiences need to be provided to teach children of this age that cooperation with all team members is necessary for success in games.

Ideas for Deemphasizing Winning and Losing

1. While there is nothing wrong with announcing the winning team, do not call out the score on a regular basis during game play or overemphasize the score at the end of the game.

2. If you feel a need, congratulate the winners for the victory and the losing team for a well-played game. Generally, there is no need for teacher interaction as the game comes to a close other than to require the two teams to shake hands and express a sense of fair play.

3. Do not reward the winning team with ribbons, trophies, posting of the team name, or any other form of external reward. The intrinsic joy of play and thrill of victory should suffice.

4. Be sure to organize new teams each day with the intention of having equally skilled teams.

5. The discussion of the game should stay on the playing field and not filter into the classroom. Bragging rights should not exist, nor should discussion be allowed about the factors contributing to the loss.

Selecting the Playing Area

The selection of the playing area and supervision of that playing area are primary safety factors in the selection of games. There may be quality games that simply cannot be played because adequate and safe game space is not available.

When organizing a game for play, the teacher must take into account what type of playing area is most appropriate and the safety of the area. Many games are best played in a field space with grass, while others work better on a paved area. Games that promote running or potential contact with another player, such as kickball, soccer, and tag, are best played on grass—a better surface for breaking a potential fall. Games that have little or no chance of physical contact such as Four Square, Around the World, or jump rope games can be safely and effectively played on a paved area.

Whatever the location, the teacher leading the game should survey the playing area for broken glass, dangerous holes, or obstacles that may interfere with play such as protruding playground equipment, trees, and fences. If the game is a good one, children will be moving fast and should not be in a position where they can run into an obstacle and get hurt. Broken glass should be removed; holes should be avoided by placement of a marker over them or relocation of the game; and boundaries should be well defined (use cones if necessary) to prevent children from encountering potential injuries from other protruding objects. If indoors, investigate the location of tables, chairs, desks, or other equipment that may be a safety hindrance to the game.

Several tag type-games have children running from one end of a playing area to the opposite end. A common error that teachers make is having children run from one wall to another. A wall or another obstacle such as a fence should never be the stopping point. The "end" line should allow plenty of space (minimum of 10 feet, or 3 meters) for decreasing speed and provide stopping time before someone gets to the wall or fence.

A final thought about play space safety concerns the road and traffic. Whenever possible, games should not be played near a street or parking area. However, if the game must be located near the street or a parking area, clear rules should be established about how the ball is retrieved. For young children, a good practice is for only adults to retrieve the ball. Older children can request permission while the adult supervises the retrieval.

Active Supervision

Teachers who are supervising children playing games will need to play an active role to maintain a safe environment. Teachers should be standing or moving so that they are in a position to observe all children at all times. A standard practice for this is called *back to the wall*, which basically means that the teacher should not have his or her back to the children at any time. Another good rule of thumb is to trust your intuition. While observing play, a teacher who senses that students are not following the rules that would maintain safe play needs to stop the game and make clear the expectations for safe play.

The way in which a teacher manages a game can determine how safe it is. Good game management involves the following:

- A clear signal should be established that requires students to immediately stop play and listen to the teacher. This should be used at the end of play time but also in the event that an unforeseen incident occurs, requiring the students' immediate attention.
- Clear safety procedures should be taught to students and reinforced throughout the year; these include avoiding collisions, staying in control, not throwing balls at others, and staying within assigned boundaries.
- The following game-specific safety protocols should be taught and enforced throughout the year:
  - If a game involves striking with a bat or racket, it should be made clear to students that this implement is not to be used when another person is within close proximity and should be laid down and not thrown down after a successful hit.
  - Students must call "mine" if they are attempting to catch a ball in a game such as kickball or a version of softball.
  - They must make sure that others are clear of the target area if they are throwing at an object.
  - They must avoid blocking the pathway of a runner in games involving fast running (e.g., kickball, tag, and racing).
  - They are to tag gently instead of pushing in a tag game.
  - They should play flag or touch football only, with no tackling allowed.

Part of teaching and supervising game play is holding children accountable for their safety and the safety of others. Children need to be taught to be responsible for safe play and always to move in control. Children can be taught safe practice in games. Young children move fast without a great awareness of space or each other, which can lead to collisions with others and obstacles. Space awareness is a skill that should be taught in physical education and reinforced by the classroom teacher in games. Children as young as pre-kindergarten age can move safely in a large area if taught. Teach children that when they travel in open spaces they should be aware of others so as not to bump or crash into people. Encourage them to use all of the space and not travel in bunches. They should not be allowed to move out of control.

Many games that children enjoy playing are a form of tag. Tag games are popular among this age group but can be unsafe unless children understand the concepts of space awareness and demonstrate the ability to use the concepts in their movements. Simple one-on-one tag games can help teach them to chase one person while watching out for others. Avoid traditional games such as Crows and Cranes (one team chases another team back to their "line") or Brownies and Fairies that encourage children to run in close proximity of each other.

Safe Equipment

The safety of the equipment is the responsibility of the teacher. The physical education teacher should be a good resource to help in the selection of equipment, but each teacher is responsible for evaluating the condition of the equipment. Over the last couple of decades, equipment has changed to better meet the needs of children and to allow for safer play. Equipment is lighter, sized for different-aged students, and made of materials that are less likely to cause injury. There are foam-coated balls of all sizes and foam-coated bats, golf clubs, and hockey sticks. There are softballs that are light and safe, called Ragballs and Incrediballs. Volleyball trainers have been designed that are larger and lighter weight; and basketballs, soccer balls, and tennis rackets are now available to meet the needs of the child at different stages in development. This equipment should be available and used not only because it is safer, but also because children can be more successful using it.

Intent of the Game

There are many games that are simply unsafe and therefore should not be played in situations in which children are forced to participate. According to Williams (1992), some of the most widely played games are the most likely to turn children off to physical activity because of the feelings associated with them. For many players exclusion, embarrassment, and feelings of shame are common when children are forced to play these games for what was intended to be a fun activity break. Williams (1992, 1994, 1996) created a Physical Education Hall of Shame in which to place several well-known games and practices. Probably the worst offenders in the Hall are games or practices that have the potential to place an individual into an unsafe situation either physically or emotionally. Games that are unsafe are inappropriate in physical education class and in any school physical activity environment.

Accidents happen when a child slips or falls or runs into another child. These are accidents that one would try to prevent but would hardly hold the teacher responsible for. When the teacher fails to look at the potential danger of each game or to teach children to play the game safely, the teacher

is responsible. When the teacher selects a game that deliberately puts the child at risk, the teacher is responsible. Many games fall into this category.

At the top of the list of games that put children in physical danger is any form of dodgeball. While dodgeball is popular with some and despised by others, the problem basically comes down to the fact that children should not be forced by an adult to be a target for other children. The NASPE summarized the physical education profession's opposition to this game in a 2006 position paper. The document focused primarily on safety and should be adhered to by all who are selecting games for children to play.

Another game that is a major problem from a safety perspective is Red Rover. This game has been around for years, and that in itself is difficult to understand. Children are asked to run as fast as they can through the tightly clasped arms of students on the other team. Usually the weaker student is chosen as the "break-through point." Two potential results are an injury when a child is clotheslined by two outstretched arms and a broken arm that was previously interlocked with another child. When selecting games for children, we must measure the intent of the game against the value and safety of the game. Often the intent of the game is good, and the game can be played safely with proper safety management.

Emotional Safety

Safety in game play is about not only physical safety, but also emotional safety. Positive play experiences can boost the self-esteem of children, and negative play experiences can damage their self-worth. The good news is that the negative experiences can be prevented by the teacher. Practices that need to be avoided to protect the emotional safety of children include the following:

- Conducting games that place students on display
- Having team captains pick teams
- Allowing children to be cruel and to put others down

Placing Students on Display

Games should be conducted such that all or most children are active at one time and never become an audience to watch a few or only one perform. Physical activity, unlike a lot of classroom work, is a public experience. Everyone knows how you are performing, when you succeed, and when you fail. While the higher-skilled student may relish the attention, the lower-skilled student is often humiliated. Many games and activities place students on display, and several made the Hall of Shame discussed earlier. Included in this list are Duck, Duck, Goose; Steal the Bacon; and any game that promotes child-against-child competition with most of the class watching. A few games are even more degrading in that they add a "mush pot" to draw more attention to the "loser." It would be comparable if classroom teachers asked all students who failed the test to stand. These games should not be played or should be modified to promote a positive experience for all skill levels.

A common activity that places children on display is a relay race. While relays are a quick and easy way to organize students and have races, often the lowest-skilled child on a team goes last. The whole class is watching, and this student is often put in a position of failure in front of his or her peers. There is little joy in the experience for this child. For relays to be acceptable, the following criteria should be met:

- The activities should not have a specific skill focus, thereby placing children on an equal playing field (e.g., beach ball carry, sack race, balloon pop).
- The order of the team members should change (i.e., after each race the first person goes to the end of the line).
- The number of players on a team should be four or less to increase active time.
- No put-downs should be allowed, only words of support.
- After every couple of activities, a few players should change (i.e., the first and last person in line on each team move to the team on their right).

Picking Teams

There are a variety of ways to group children for play without isolating and shaming them. When handled inappropriately, the way a team is picked can emotionally scar a child. There should never be captains choosing teams. This is a very humiliating experience for those children chosen last or even close to last. The feeling of not being wanted cannot be avoided in this situation. There are many other effective and emotionally safe ways teachers can divide students into teams, including randomly dividing them by birthdays, color of clothing, and even the draw of a card. If a classroom uses grouping such as rows or work groups, the teachers can use those groupings in a variety of ways. Whatever the choice of grouping, every attempt should be made to have a fair mix of skill and gender. Selecting teams should also be a preplanned, efficient process so as not to take away from game time. For more on this concept, see the discussion of players in "Organizing and Conducting Games" later in the chapter.

Put-Down Behavior

Name calling and belittling others take away from the joy of play. Game experiences are often not fun for children because of the negative interactions they have with other children. The old saying "Children are cruel" in reality should be "Children are only as cruel as adults allow them to be." At no point should children be allowed to put down others. Name calling and poking fun have no positive effects. School personnel are responsible for stopping bullying before it ever gets out of hand. A quality teacher or adult leader in any game situation will stop this behavior immediately and use punitive actions if necessary. On the positive side, if children show obvious caring actions, they should be complimented accordingly. The physical and emotional safety of self and others can be taught through both direct and indirect actions. Children need to know that school is safe in every sense of the word.

Modifying Games

There are many great games that meet the criteria discussed in this chapter. However, as you search Web sites and books, you will find many games that promote very limited movement, support one or more inappropriate practices, or are unsafe. Using the information discussed in this chapter, you should recognize and be apprehensive when you come across games involving inappropriate and unsafe practices. You should either continue your search and find another game or modify the inappropriate parts of the game. Most often the aspect that needs to be modified is an inadequate level of physical activity.

Modifying Games to Increase Physical Activity

The following are game modifications designed to increase the level of physical activity:

- Change the organizational format.
- Alter rules that stop the flow of the game.
- Add or modify equipment.
- Increase or decrease the playing space.

Organizational Format

Earlier we considered formations and groupings that are not conducive to promoting physical activity, including relays, one line against another, large-circle games, and other large-group games in which only a few students are active. Changing these formations or groupings can increase physical activity. Reducing the number of players in a game by increasing the number of games in progress (e.g., not one circle but three or four circles) promotes more activity and motor skill practice. This change allows for better cooperation, as it is easier to work together as a team in small groups than with an entire class. Instead of traditional kickball, in which half the class plays against the other half, simply have two games occurring at the same time, reducing the playing size to six against six. More children are active and there is less waiting turns to kick.

Changing the Rules

Too many or too few rules have the potential to stop the flow of a game. Altering the rules can increase activity and add to both the participation and enjoyment levels. If you have ever watched a youth league basketball game, you know that calling an infraction on every walk would stop the flow of the game. For this reason, most youth-level

Increasing the number of taggers increases cooperation.

referees are taught to simply inform the young child to dribble. Rules of low organization games need to be as simple and as few as possible so as to keep the game active.

Adding Equipment

Inadequate or limited equipment can restrict physical activity. As mentioned earlier, a variety of equipment is now available that is appropriate in size and texture for children. Adult-sized equipment is not only unsafe but also takes away from quality play. Limiting the amount of equipment in a game also limits quality play. If only one ball is available for an entire class, it is difficult to allow maximum participation. Many games call for one ball but can be modified to include more. One example is Newcomb, a traditional game in which two teams throw a ball over the net to each other. In this game, a point is scored if the other team misses the ball and it hits the floor within the boundaries. Adding two balls to the game or adding two balls and placing a sheet over the net are equipment changes that make the game much more exciting and involve more players. Adding two or more balls would require the use of foam-covered balls.

Size of the Playing Field

The size of the playing field can restrict movement or detract from the game. If the space is not large enough, physical activity can be limited. However, if the space is too large, the difficulty of the game may increase to the point of eliminating some children from moderate or vigorous activity. For example, if a fifth grade teacher is organizing a few small-sided games of flag football for a class, the boundaries should be reduced to allow for maximum scoring and for the number of teams. As opposed to a 100-by 53-yard (91- by 48-meter) regulation field, two or three 30- by 15-yard (27- by 14-meter) fields would be more realistic.

A popular game, Hot Potato, is typically played in one large circle. The object of the game is when the music starts to pass an object such as a beanbag around the circle and try to stay in the game as you eliminate other players. Players are eliminated and made to sit in the mush pot if they get caught with the beanbag when the music stops. Hot Potato has been modified in figure 7.4 to demonstrate how to change the organizational format, alter the rules, add equipment, and increase the playing space to provide maximum participation and appropriate practices.

FIGURE 7.4

Example of Changing
a Popular Game (Hot Potato)

Hot Potato is typically played in one large circle. The object is to pass an item such as a beanbag around the circle and try to stay in the game as you eliminate other players. Players are eliminated and made to sit in the *mush pot* if they get caught with the beanbag when the music stops. The following scenario illustrates possible modifications to this game.

- We have 24 students in our class and will change the formation from one large circle to four small circles.

- For equipment, we had one beanbag, and now we need four. Or, we can place two beanbags in each circle, in which case we will need eight.

- We want to increase our space to allow for some rule changes we are going to make. Each circle should be a minimum of 30 feet (9 meters) from all others. Each player within the circle must be 10 feet (3 meters) from the player on either side.

- We are going to make this game active and improve the flow with some rule changes.
  - When the music starts, those with the beanbags use an underhand toss and advance the beanbags clockwise.
  - At any time the teacher can announce "reverse," and the tosses are to go counterclockwise.
  - When the music stops, the teacher calls out a locomotor movement (e.g., jog, skip, gallop). The person with the beanbag (or the person who last touched the beanbag) must take the beanbag with him and travel clockwise to the next circle using the called locomotor movement as his mode of travel. The children remaining in the circle are to do the movement in place.
  - When the music restarts, the children stop the locomotor movement and the game begins again.

For this new version, the objective is for players to see how few times they have to change circles while practicing good underhand throws. The name of the new game is "Hottest Potato."

Process of Modifying Games

Modifying a game is a process that begins with analyzing the existing game. The analysis leads to decision making for changes. Next, the game is played and evaluated. This is the step-by-step process:

1. Analyze the game (see questions in figure 7.5).

2. Brainstorm new ideas with another teacher or with students to determine how to make the game better.

3. Write the new version and review it.

4. Play it with your class.

5. Evaluate it, and if it is a good game, play it again. If it is not, you have two choices: redesign it or trash it.

Using the questions in figure 7.5, the traditional game of Squirrel in the Trees is analyzed to demonstrate how the process works. The original game, the analysis and brainstorm process, the new game, and the evaluation follow. Use the questions to help you analyze a game. Keep in mind that you do not have to address all of the subquestions. They are simply suggestions to promote thought. The figure on the CD-ROM takes you through the process of modifying Squirrel in the Trees.

FIGURE 7.5

Analysis Questions for Modifying Games

Grade Level

Is this game appropriate for the grade level I teach? Do the children have the physical, cognitive, and social skills needed to play?

Purpose

What is the purpose of this game?

1. For physical activity?
2. To practice skills or strategies? If so, what skills or strategies?
3. To teach cooperation?

Physical Activity

Does the game promote moderate to vigorous physical activity?

1. Should I reduce or increase the number of players on a team?
2. Should I reduce or increase the number of teams?
3. Should I reduce or increase the movement of players?
4. Should I change the organizational pattern?
5. Is there any other way I can make the children more active?

Rules

Do the rules stop the flow of the game?

1. Are there rules that should be omitted because they restrict the flow of the game?
2. Are there rules that should be added to enhance opportunities?
3. Is there any other reason a rule should change?
4. Are there any safety concerns that warrant a rule change?

Equipment and Playing Area

Are the equipment and playing area appropriate for the game?

1. Do we need larger or smaller equipment?
2. Do we need lighter equipment?
3. Should we add equipment?
4. Should we reduce the amount of equipment?
5. Should I reduce the playing area?
6. Should I increase the playing area?
7. What surface should this game be played on?

Squirrel in the Trees

Equipment: None

Formation: Scattered in groups of three

Purpose: Agility and chasing, fleeing, and dodging (psychomotor objective), cooperation (affective objective)

Arrange class in groups of three scattered about the playing area. Two players join hands to form a "hollow tree," and the third player, the squirrel, stands in the middle. One to three extra children are standing outside of the trees. On a signal from the teacher, all the squirrels try to find new trees and different squirrels are left out. After four turns, have children return to their original positions and change the roles of squirrels and foxes.

Analysis Questions: An Overview of the Analysis Process

■ *Grade level:* As described, this game is designed for preschool to grade 1. I would like to make it simple enough for grades K through 3 yet challenging enough that grades 2 and 3 would enjoy it because of strategies they could potentially bring into the game.

■ *Purpose:* What is the purpose of this game? While the need for cooperation and the ability to make quick moves are evident in this game, there is not much else. I think bringing in more of a tag game aspect would increase the use of chasing, fleeing, and dodging skills and strategies. I still want to find a way to keep the cooperation element, though. I could do this by finding a way to have participants free players who are tagged.

■ *Physical activity:* Does the game promote moderate or vigorous physical activity? This game has limited participation in that only one-third of the students are moving at one time and then only for a few seconds. I need to find a way to increase the movement of the players. I do not like the organization of the small groups and think I might turn it into more of a tag game with players moving in general space. The children need to be more active.

■ *Rules:* Do the rules stop the flow of the game? This game really does not have time to flow. Each round is over so quickly. I want to add more to the game to enhance not only the flow, but also the fun. Safety will be a concern as always in tag games, but safety elements are easily addressed and taught to children through our space awareness concepts. I think a story line will help make the game fun and challenging. I am trying to think of other connections with squirrels and how they play and function in real life.

■ *Equipment and playing area:* Are the equipment and playing area appropriate for the game? No equipment is needed for the original game, and very little space is used. My new game will bring in some equipment, and I would like to enlarge the playing area to increase the movement. The game should then go from low physical activity to moderate or high levels. While my new version of Squirrel in the Trees will be safe in a gym, I think outside in a field area would be best.

Squirrels Go Nuts

Created by Tina J. Hall

Additional modifications by the students at Granbery Elementary School, Nashville, Tennessee

Student formation: Scattered (outdoors is best, but a gym is okay)

Equipment:

Five or six cones (trees) scattered in playing area

Three hula hoops (foxholes) on one end of playing area

(continued)

(continued)

Three or four long jump ropes (fence) on other end of playing area

Eight to 10 small (baseball or softball size) balls (nuts) on far side of "fenced area"

Two or three pinnies or tag shirts for the foxes to wear

Purpose: This is a great warm-up or instant activity, as well as an activity for working on space awareness and dodging, fleeing, and chasing skills, tactics, and strategies. The psychomotor objective would focus on these skills; the cognitive objective would bring in the simple strategies; and the affective objective would focus on helping get others back in the game.

Play: On the "go" signal, the foxes (two or three) try to tag as many squirrels (all other players) as they can. If tagged, a squirrel goes into a foxhole. The other squirrels may rescue the "caught" squirrels by going over the "fence" into the "field of nuts," picking up a nut, and taking it to the captured squirrel. Upon receiving the nut and thanking his rescuer, the squirrel pretends to eat it for energy and escapes from the foxhole. The nut is returned to the field, and the squirrel is back in the game. (My students added a "free walk back" for when a squirrel returns a nut. Holding the nut up in the air as the squirrel runs or walks back demonstrates this.) The squirrel bringing the nut to the captured squirrel must dodge the foxes in hopes of freeing a "friend." (In some classes, the children have to be encouraged to rescue others. The children should be told that when a nut is brought to a foxhole, it should be given to the squirrel that has been in the foxhole the longest.) If a squirrel is tagged while taking a nut to rescue a friend, she must return the nut to the field before going into a foxhole. The trees (cones) may be used by any squirrel for a safe base. However, only one squirrel can be on a tree at a time. If a second squirrel gets to a tree, the squirrel on it must leave. On the signal to stop, all nuts are returned, all squirrels are free, and new foxes are picked. Game play is usually only about 3 minutes before new foxes are chosen.

Evaluation (to be completed after the game is played): The children helped me to make the game better, and we included these changes. One problem was that occasionally a child tended to stay on a tree too long. When this was an issue, we decided to make a 10-second rule. A fox could not stand there and count, but the teacher or a child helper (injured or sick child) could say the child's name and how many seconds he or she had left. The other problem is making sure that no child stays in a foxhole more than a few seconds. This might mean having more nuts, encouraging more students to rescue, making sure that people are leaving in the order they came in—or not having really fast foxes!

This game has been a favorite of the young children and provides an opportunity for moderate to vigorous activity depending on the role of the individual player. Children can improve the skills of chasing, fleeing, and dodging through this experience. The tactics and strategies of the game develop as the children mature cognitively. The affective aspect is great, especially when the teacher makes it clear before the game starts that helping others is an objective and teaches toward this objective during and after every game.

Modifying some games can be time-consuming while others can be modified quickly. Working with other teachers on the process only makes it better. Children are also very good at this process. Be open to allowing them input on the games you are modifying or to making this a class assignment. The teacher should continue to analyze the game as the children are playing. After playing the game, the children are the best critics. When searching for low organized games, be sure to select games with a critical eye, using the information you have learned in this chapter, and modify them if necessary.

Child-Designed Games

The previous section focused on modification of games by the teacher, yet suggested the involvement of children in improving the game. Another type of game play situates the child as the creator. This is an experience that many of us grew up with in our neighborhood and possibly an experience that some children still have today. As a school experience, the benefits have to do with both the cognitive and affective domains of learning. From a cognitive perspective, the child is involved in the process of problem solving, creating, and designing. The affective domain is addressed as the child must work with others in the planning and play experience and must learn to accept the different opinions of others. Child-designed games are best when children are at the age and maturity level that enables them to work well with others.

The best approach for child-designed games is to have the children create the game and then play the game. During the process of creating the game, you should have the children determine the following:

- The purpose of the game
- The equipment and boundaries
- The rules
  - What are the players allowed to do?
  - What are the players not allowed to do?
- The penalties
  - What happens if a player breaks a rule? What happens if a player is out of the boundaries?

Once the children have designed the game and played it a for few minutes, they will need to stop and assess the quality of their game. If necessary, changes should be made before they continue playing. The teacher should allow students to conduct this process and should intervene only for safety reasons or for not treating others with respect. The playing of the game should lead the children to see what is going well and what is not. However, if a group has had ample time for assessing the game but appears to be "stuck," the following probing questions may aid the process:

- Is there a problem with any of your rules?
- Are your boundaries too small or too large?
- Is the equipment appropriate?
- Is it too easy or too hard to score?

If a teacher wants to extend the learning process, he or she may require the students to name the game, write the rules and a description of the game, draw a diagram indicating the organization of the game, and finally teach the game to another group of children.

A negative aspect of having children create games is that it is a time-consuming process and that for part of the process there is limited or no physical activity. A teacher must plan for and accept this as the advantages outweigh the disadvantages. Following are suggestions for making game creation a positive learning experience:

- Group size should be six or less.
- Provide some structure by identifying equipment, space, or the skill or game type that must be used:
  - Your team may elect to use any of the equipment (beanbags, balls, hoops, ropes, flags, cones).
  - Your playing area is marked off by poly spots or cones. You can use all or part of that area, but you may not go beyond that space.
  - The skills of throwing and catching must be used in the game.
  - Your game must be an invasion-type game that includes both offense and defense.
- Require that everyone be physically active during most or all of the game time. If there is a fairly inactive position, there needs to be a plan for rotation out of that position.
- Set a time limit for game design before students must put the game into action.
- Allow the students to make the game either cooperative or competitive.

Giving students the opportunity to design their own games is not just a matter of telling the students "Here is some equipment, go make up a game." It is a teacher-guided process. Some classes will be slow with the process while others will take to it immediately. Do not be surprised if the game they "invent" is very close to another game or sport. With multiple opportunities, children will improve in game creation. Who knows, the next "classic" game may come from your class.

Organizing and Conducting Games

Taking your class outside to play a game is a process that has to be planned as with any lesson taught in the classroom. In other words, there has to be a "game plan." Much of the organization for games can be done in the classroom before students go outside. The game plan has to take into account the following:

- Players
- Equipment and playing area
- Game description, rules, and demonstration
- Conducting the game

Players

When planning for players, you must take into account the number of players needed to ensure adequate participation time. The number of players will then help determine how many groups or teams are needed. The formation of the players and teams has to be established, as well as how they will be organized within that formation. Do not forget the recommendation of having several small-group games instead of one large group in team games. This practice promotes more physical activity, provides more practice of motor skills, and allows a better opportunity for cooperation.

There are many strategies for grouping students. Figure 7.6 includes several suggestions for grouping students with partners, in small groups, or in teams. Often a game requires even numbers but the makeup of the class that day is uneven. In reality, most activities work fine with uneven numbers. If the game your class is playing does not work with uneven numbers, have a rotation method such that students wait their turn for no more than 3 minutes. While waiting to enter the game, the extra player can practice one or more skills needed for the game.

Another factor to take into consideration is designing game experiences so that all children have an opportunity to win. The following strategies may be helpful:

- Group students homogenously by skill level. If several games are occurring at the same time, children can compete against other students of the same playing ability.
- Group students heterogeneously with the intent of making the skill levels as equally dispersed as possible. After a game is played, if one team is dominating or another appears to be at a huge disadvantage, change a few team members.
- Give students a choice of competition level. Those who are highly competitive may choose one playing area; those who are noncompetitive can choose another area; and those who are somewhere in between on the competitive continuum can play in a third area.

Equipment and Playing Area

Planning for equipment includes deciding what kind of equipment is available for use, what will be the safest, and what kind will allow the most success for the students playing (match their size, strength, and skill level). Following that decision, teachers should create a list that answers these questions:

- How much of each piece of equipment is needed for the game?
- What equipment is needed to define boundaries (e.g., cones, markers)?
- How will team members be identified (e.g., pinnies, armbands, flags, strips of material)?

Additional equipment concerns are to determine how to get the equipment to the play area, organize the area quickly, and return the equipment. A suggestion is to assign a few students as game helpers (this can change every week). They will be responsible for obtaining and returning equipment and organizing it for use. For the upper elementary grades, game helpers can go out to the play area a few minutes early and prepare the play area.

Game Description, Rules, and Demonstration

The game description should be concise, the rules kept to a minimum, and any areas of confusion demonstrated in the environment in which it will be played. Be familiar with the rules and be clear on how the game is played. The rules should be kept to a minimum with only essential information. If more rules need to be added later, you can stop the game and make the additions.

Conducting the Game

Once the students have been sent out to play, the teacher's role is to supervise and evaluate the game by walking the perimeter of the play area. Begin by observing for safety and for student understanding of the game rules and description. If play appears safe and the students understand the game, the teacher role now changes to observing and evaluating both the quality of the game and the play of the students. The game can be analyzed to determine if there is a need to make more modifications. It may be necessary to stop play and make changes to any rule that appears to impede the flow of the game. Be aware of the fatigue level and interest level of the students, and change the groups or the game as needed.

A final thought about game play is to not overplay a game. A successful game will be more in demand if it is stopped while it is still being enjoyed. A common practice is to find one game and play it on a regular basis. While some games are worth revisiting, remember that variety adds spice to life.

Additional Game Opportunities

The ideas discussed thus far have related primarily to games played outdoors that have the main objective of physical activity. There are situations in which inclement weather or time does not permit a quality outdoor game experience. In these cases there are games that can be played indoors. Games

FIGURE 7.6

Grouping Children for Game Play

Partner Ideas

It is important for students to work with a variety of others. The following are ideas for having students form partners.

- For times when a student does not have a partner, have a strategy for finding one quickly. One idea is to have a "lost and found" department where students go if they do not have a partner. If someone else does not have a partner, she will meet him there. If an individual goes to the lost and found and no one joins him, he may join two others, making a team of three.

- Give students instructions for a "shake hands review" as in the following example (students are learning the state capitals). This will ensure that each student has four different partners for the week.
  - Find a partner and shake hands with them. One will tell the capital of North Carolina and the other the capital of Oklahoma.
  - Find a different partner and give them a high five. One will tell the capital of South Carolina and the other the capital of Texas.
  - Find your handshake partner again and shake.
  - Find a new partner and give them a low five. One will tell the capital of Alabama and the other the capital of Wisconsin.
  - Greet your high five partner again. Now, your handshake partner.
  - Find a new partner and give them a knuckle tap. One will tell the capital of Arkansas and the other the capital of Michigan.
  - Now, find your low five partner. Visit your handshake partner again. Where is your high five partner? Now, return to your knuckle tap partner. That is your partner for today.

- These are other instructions you can give students when you want them to form partners:
  - Find someone you have not worked with this week.
  - Find someone that has two of the same letters in their last name as you do.
  - Find someone who has the same number of letters in their first name as you do.
  - Find someone the same height as you.

- If the students are grouped by rows, squads, or tables, have them work with a partner from that group and next time have them work with someone else from the group.

Small Groups

If the numbers do not work, simply change a few students.

- Four groups
  - Seasons of birthday (fall, winter, spring, summer)
  - Combining birthday months (e.g., January to March, April to June, July to September, October to December)
  - Deck of cards (hearts, spades, diamonds, clubs)
- Allow students to form groups by calling out the size of the group and giving them only 5 seconds to accomplish the grouping task.
- Make index cards with all the students' names. Shuffle and separate the cards into the number of groups needed.
- If you know your students, group them ahead of time as part of your game plan.
- Find a partner. One of you is the color blue and the other is red. You have 5 seconds to decide. (Red team and blue team)
- Find a partner. One sit and one stay standing. (Sit team and stand team)
- Have everyone stand and cross their arms. Those with the right arm on top are one team, and those with the left on top are the other.

may also be used in the elementary school to fulfill other objectives, including teaching cooperative skills and enhancing academics.

Indoor Games

When indoor games are played, often physical activity is at a minimum. That does not always have to be the case. However, be careful not to jeopardize the safety of the students by promoting movement in small spaces that are not conducive to this type of activity. It may be necessary to move desks and other obstructions in the room and to select equipment that is better for indoors, such as balloons, beach balls, yarn balls, or paper balls. When selecting indoor games, adhere to as many of the practices discussed in this chapter as possible. Figure 7.7 includes two examples of games that can be played in limited indoor areas. More examples are available on the CD-ROM.

Cooperative Games

When there is a need or desire to help children learn cooperation skills, many game experiences can contribute to this objective. Some games that can be played indoors or out were designed to enhance cooperation. Many cooperative games also promote a moderate to vigorous physical activity level. When selecting cooperative games, you should make every attempt to achieve both goals. Figure 7.8 includes two examples of cooperative games. More examples are available on the CD-ROM.

Games to Enhance Academics

Games are an excellent opportunity for enhancing academics. Movement aids in the retention process, provides a different avenue for learning, and is enjoyable to children. Games can be used in all academic subjects. For example, in social studies when

---

FIGURE 7.7

Indoor, Limited-Space Games

Who's the Leader?

Grade level: Second grade and up.

Room formation: All desks aside, opening space in the middle of the floor; or all desks in the center with the perimeter of the room used for the circle.

Player formation: One big circle.

Equipment: None.

Purpose: To guess the leader of the movement activities.

Description:

- Two students are asked to leave the room while the teacher selects a leader.
- The leader starts some type of movement that all can do in self-space (e.g., jump, jog, arm flaps). The movements should range from low to high intensity.
- Once the movement starts, the two students are asked to return. The returning students are trying to guess who the leader is. Each guesser gets one chance or 1 minute to determine who the leader is.
- The leader must change the movement often and try to by sly about it.
- When the game is over, two more players are asked to leave the room, and a new leader is selected.
- Hint: The teacher will need to demonstrate how to be a good and sneaky leader, and also tell the students doing the movements that they have to help by looking at everyone and never staring at the leader.

Perfect 100: Catch It If You Can

Grade level: Kindergarten through grade 5 (with scoring adaptations and less challenge for grades K-1).

Room formation: Desks aside, allowing for self-space of each player.

Player formation: Scattered in self-space.

Equipment: One beanbag, small ball, or paper wad ball per player.

Purpose: To practice and challenge the players in various catching skills.

Description: Each student starts the game with a perfect 100 and is trying to maintain that score as he tries the various challenges. A description of each activity and a blank space next to it should be given to each student for a score sheet. At the end of the game, the students add their scores. The skills get progressively more difficult. All tosses must be underhand, and height of the toss should be above the head but not past three-fourths of the distance to the ceiling.

Have students throw the object (K-2 children use a beanbag, older children a small ball or paper wad) and catch it according to the following instructions:

- 10 times: Catch at a medium level (waist level).
- 10 times: Catch at a low level (below knees).
- 10 times: Catch at a high level (above head).
- 10 times: Toss from right to left hand, with the toss above your head.
- 10 times: Catch with dominant hand only.
- 10 times: Catch with nondominant hand only.
- 5 times: Jump and catch above your head.
- 5 times: Clap hands once after the toss and before the catch.
- 5 times: Clap hands once and thighs once before catching.
- 5 times: Turn around once and catch.
- 2 times: Toss from in front of your body but catch behind your back.
- 3 times: Position dominant arm at about a 45-degree angle or slightly more with elbow facing forward. Raise your hand toward your ear as you balance a beanbag or a penny on your elbow. Lower the elbow quickly and try to catch the object with the same hand.
- 10 times: With a partner, stand five giant steps apart and toss and catch.
- 5 times: One partner spins, and during the spin the other partner tosses the ball. At the completion of the spin, try to catch the ball. Switch roles.

Score:

Perfect 100: The pros will be calling you soon!

90-99: Wow, you are a superstar!

80-89: Great job! What are those challenges you still need to work on?

79 or below: Keep on working—practice can make perfect in this game.

FIGURE 7.8

Cooperative Games

Beanbag Freeze

Grade level: K through 2.

Student formation: Scattered in self-space.

Equipment: One beanbag per child and music (optional).

Purpose: To *help* others return to play and to travel in different locomotor patterns while balancing a beanbag on the head.

Description: Players place a beanbag on their head and walk around the playing area.

- If the beanbag falls off the head, the player must freeze.
- Another player, while maintaining balance of the beanbag, attempts to free the frozen player by picking up the dropped beanbag and placing it on that individual's head. This helping action places the player back in the game.
- If the beanbag falls off the helper's head, she too must freeze. The result may be several people frozen and in need of help all in one place.
- The teacher may need to point out frozen players that need help.
- Challenges: Change the locomotor skill or direction of travel.

Process questions:

- How many of you helped someone today?
- How did you feel when someone helped you?
- How did you feel when you helped someone?

Pass the Hoop

Grade level: Grades 3 through 5.

Player formation: Several circles of six to eight players.

Equipment: Two hula hoops per circle.

Purpose: To *work together* to pass the hoop around the circle without breaking the circle.

Description: Players all join hands. Two of the players disconnect hands, the hoop is placed over one arm, and the two reconnect their hands.

- On the signal "go," the players pass the hoop around the circle without dropping hands. They are successful when the hoop returns to the start.
- After one successful attempt, ask them to strategize a way to accomplish the task more quickly and then try it again.
- Challenges: (1) Time the game and then repeat, with the challenge to beat the previous time. (2) Add the second hoop, and have one hoop go clockwise and the other counterclockwise. The challenge occurs when the two hoops meet.

Process questions:

- What strategy worked best for your group to be successful?
- If you, as an individual, were struggling, did someone help? How?
- How does taking time to communicate help with games like this?

children are learning about other countries, games from those countries or the region can be played. Brief games during academic time help children to stay focused and less fidgety. Chapter 5 includes sample games and activities devoted to integrating movement with academics.

SUMMARY

1. Active games that are carefully selected can contribute to the physical, cognitive, and social growth of children.

2. The school day may be the only time some children have the opportunity to play physically active games.

3. Games in physical education have a more specific purpose than games played on the playground.

4. Low organization games are great for classroom teachers to use because they require minimal setup and teaching time.

5. Games selected for play should provide enjoyment and maximum participation, be physically and emotionally safe, and be developmentally appropriate for the age level of children playing.

6. There are many games that do not promote physical activity. Careful selection or game modifications will be necessary to ensure that the students are participating at a moderate to high intensity level.

7. Safety first is a valuable adage to follow when one is selecting, organizing, and directing games.

8. It is important to understand where children typically are developmentally when selecting, organizing, and directing games. This includes skill level, cognitive level, and social level.

9. Teachers can modify games to increase physical activity by doing one or more of the following: (a) changing the organizational format, (b) altering the rules, (c) adding or modifying equipment, or (d) changing the size of the play space.

10. Child-designed games involve a process of design, play, evaluate and alter, and play again. Certain limitations and guidelines are provided by the teacher.

11. A well-planned game takes into account organization of players, equipment, and playing area; a decision about how the game will be presented; and a decision about how to best supervise the game play.

CHECKING YOUR UNDERSTANDING

1. How can games contribute to the growth and development of children?

2. What were your favorite games growing up? Why?

3. While many of us spent a good bit of our childhood playing outdoors, what are reasons some children rarely play outdoors today?

4. Describe how the purpose of games in physical education class is different from that for games played on the playground.

5. Share a negative experience you remember from playing games as a child. How about a positive experience?

6. What five safety questions should a teacher ask when selecting, organizing, or directing a game?

7. Choose a grade level and determine the expected developmental level of the children at this level from a physical, cognitive, and social perspective.

8. Find two games from a Web site or a book and, using the questions in figure 7.5, analyze and modify the games.

9. Design a game plan for one of the games you chose for question 8.

RESOURCES

Belka, D.E. (1994). *Teaching children games: Becoming a master teacher.* Champaign, IL: Human Kinetics.

Horowitz, G.L. (2009). *International games: Building skills through multicultural play.* Champaign, IL: Human Kinetics.

National Association for Sport and Physical Education. (2005). *The physical best activity guide: Elementary level.* Champaign, IL: Human Kinetics.

Orlick, T. (2006). *Cooperative games and sports: Joyful activities for everyone* (2nd ed.). Champaign, IL: Human Kinetics.

Sutherland, C. (2006). *No gym? No problem! Physical activities for tight spaces.* Champaign, IL: Human Kinetics.

Web Sites for Games

www.afterschoolpa.com/base.html
www.gameskidsplay.net

REFERENCES

National Association for Sport and Physical Education. (2005). *The physical best activity guide: Elementary level.* Champaign, IL: Human Kinetics.

National Association for Sport and Physical Education. (2006). *Position on dodgeball in physical education. A position paper from the National Association for Sport and Physical Education.* Available at www.aahperd.org/NASPE/pdf_files/pos_papers/dodgeball.pdf.

Piaget, J. (1972). *The psychology of the child.* New York: Basic Books.

Williams, N.F. (1992). The physical education hall of shame. *Journal of Physical Education, Recreation and Dance* (August), 57-60.

Williams, N.F. (1994). The physical education hall of shame II. *Journal of Physical Education, Recreation and Dance* (February), 17-20.

Williams, N.F. (1996). The physical education hall of shame III: Inappropriate teaching practices. *Journal of Physical Education, Recreation and Dance* (August), 57-60.

8

Teaching Dance and Rhythms

OVERVIEW

Dance and rhythmic activities provide enjoyable avenues for physical activity for children. Children have an opportunity to practice and refine nonlocomotor and locomotor skills combined in a variety of ways. Dance experiences for children include folk, line, and creative dance. Creative movement experiences may integrate children's literature, poems, action words, social studies, or science concepts. Opportunities to simultaneously move and learn provide children with rich movement experiences. If you do not think of yourself as a dancer, think of yourself as a beginner and learn with your students. This chapter provides you with information that will be useful for teaching dances.

CHAPTER OUTCOMES

This chapter will help you

- read and understand directions for dances,
- identify dances appropriate for beginners,
- identify guidelines to follow when teaching a folk or a line dance,
- integrate grade-level curriculum into creative movement experiences, and
- handle management issues that arise when teaching dance and rhythms.

IN THIS CHAPTER

People of all ages enjoy the benefits of dancing, from the toddler bouncing and stamping with music, to adolescents performing the Electric Slide at a school dance, to seniors learning the two-step at the community center. Moving to music is an enjoyable physical activity for all ages. Dance and rhythmic activities provide pleasure as well as health benefits and an opportunity for social interaction. Unlike many other individual, dual, or game-like activities, dance also offers an opportunity for self-expression.

Young children have been entertained through singing games and rhythmic activities for centuries. Since the 1700s, children have been amused by the rhythmic beat of hand claps and gestures such as those for "Patty Cake, Patty Cake." Still today, children enjoy making an arch while singing "London Bridge" and then lowering at the song's end to "catch" someone. Nursery rhymes have long provided early rhythmic experiences for young children.

Whether the activity is moving to music using hand gestures or performing a folk dance, the purpose of dance and rhythmic activities remains the same: moving in rhythm. Dance and rhythmic activities contribute to the goals of the elementary physical activity program and can provide opportunities for children to be physically active within the physical education program of a school. Through such experiences, children can develop motor skills, express and communicate feelings, and develop imagination and creativity. They also have the opportunity to learn the skills they need to be physically active in a movement form that is important to our culture. The elementary physical education curriculum should give students a variety of dance experiences including folk, line, and creative dance. The following describes what is appropriate and inappropriate practice for children's dance in the physical education program.

■ **Appropriate practice.** The teacher includes a variety of rhythmical, expressive, creative, and culturally enriching dance experiences designed with the children's physical, cultural, emotional, emotional, and social abilities in mind.

■ **Inappropriate practice.** The teacher does not teach dance, or teaches dance to students with no sequencing or progression.

All dance movements are composed of locomotor or nonlocomotor movements (or both) performed using different qualities of body, space, effort, and relationships with objects or other dancers (the BSER framework [body awareness, space awareness, effort, relationships]; see table 8.1). Actions of the body are varied through changes in where, how, and with what or whom the body moves. Examples

Nursery Rhymes

Patty cake, Patty cake, baker's man,
Bake me a cake as fast as you can;
Roll it, pat it, mark it with a B,
Put it in the oven for baby and me.

London Bridge is falling down,
Falling down, falling down.
London Bridge is falling down,
My fair lady.

Ring around the rosie
A pocket full of posies;
Ashes! Ashes!
We all fall down.

are quickly sliding clockwise with a partner or twisting in self-space while changing levels.

The ways in which movement concepts (BSER) are combined determine the characteristics of a folk, line, or creative dance. Sometimes dances are categorized by relationships and are referred to as partner dances, square dances, circle dances, or line dances. All types of dances are composed of some combination of motor skills and movement concepts. See chapter 3 for more on movement concepts.

Folk Dance

A folk dance is characteristic of the people of a land and their culture. The climate of a land or country is often reflected in the tempo of the music or dance steps. Folk dances from colder regions may require quick steps and high levels of energy as opposed to dances from tropical regions. A folk dance may also tell a story of a historical event. Props used in a dance may reflect a natural resource in a country.

Bamboo poles are used in Tinikling, the national dance of the Philippines. Bamboo grows abundantly throughout the Philippines and is used for food, housing, and furniture. Tinikling represents the culture of people living in this archipelagic country.

Children learn about a culture through folk dance when characteristics of the land and its people are included and explicitly taught as part of the movement experience. Through folk dancing children have not only an opportunity to learn about people of other times and countries, but also an opportunity to practice and combine locomotor skills and gestures to music.

There are many folk dances that are developmentally appropriate for the elementary school child. Simple folk dances are appropriate for young children, and moderately difficult to more difficult dances are suited for upper elementary grades. Several folk dances that are widely used with elementary-aged students are identified in the sidebar.

TABLE 8.1
Movement Concepts

| Body awareness
Actions of the body | Space awareness
Where the body moves | Effort
How the body moves | Relationships
With what or whom the body moves |
|---|---|---|---|
| Body shapes
■ Curved
■ Twisted
■ Narrow
■ Wide
■ Symmetrical
■ Asymmetrical
Nonlocomotor
■ Swing
■ Sway
■ Twist
■ Turn
■ Bend/curl
■ Stretch
■ Sink
■ Push
■ Pull
■ Shake
Locomotor
■ Walk
■ Hop
■ Jump
■ Slide
■ Gallop
■ Skip | Location
■ General space
■ Self-space
Directions
■ Up/down
■ Forward/backward
■ Right/left
■ Clockwise/counterclockwise
Levels
■ Low
■ Middle, medium
■ High
Pathways
■ Straight
■ Curved
■ Zigzag
Extensions
■ Large/small
■ Near/far | Speed, time
■ Fast
■ Slow
Force
■ Strong
■ Light
Flow
■ Bound
■ Free | Objects or others
■ Over/under
■ On/off
■ Near/far
■ In front of/behind/beside
■ Around/through
Partners/small groups
■ Leading/following
■ Meeting/parting
■ Matching/mirroring |

Popular Elementary Folk Dances

First and Second Grades

Chimes of Dunkirk—Belgium
Patty Cake Polka—America
La Raspa—Mexico
Seven Jumps—Denmark
Captain Jinks—America

Third Through Fifth Grades

Virginia Reel—America
Troika—Russia
Red River Valley Square—America
Tinikling—Philippines

Reading and Understanding the Directions for Dances

Sometimes learning a dance from the directions can be an overwhelming experience for a beginning teacher. It need not be. The process involves these steps:

- Getting to know the dance or activity, the formation of the dance, and the steps that are used in the dance
- Identifying the beat of the music and rhythmic qualities of the music
- Putting the steps to the music
- Practicing the steps until the transitions between movements are smooth
- Placing the dance into the organizational pattern of the dance (e.g., partners, circle)

The first step in planning a dance or rhythmic experience is getting to know the dance or activity. This is accomplished through careful study of the instructions for the dance or rhythmic activity you plan to lead. Many current resources for teaching dance provide a description of the dance, the formation, counts and steps, and variations. Often the majority of the dance terms relevant to the dance are explained within the instructions. Other terms may be found in the glossary that is included with most resources. The glossary is helpful for identifying formations, steps, and figures.

The formation of a dance refers to the relationships of the dancers. Common dance formations include circle, double circles, square, single line, double lines, and scattered (see figure 8.1). Folk dances and social dances are often performed in

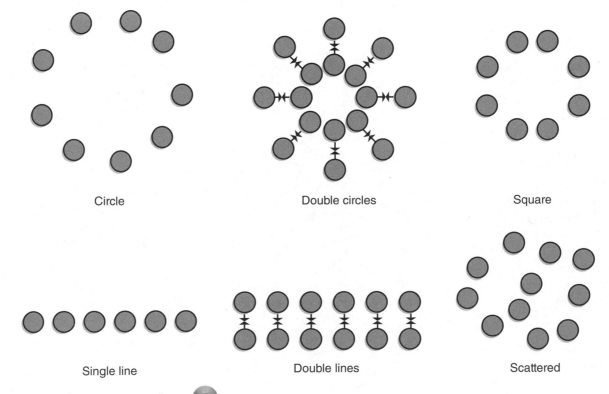

Circle   Double circles   Square

Single line   Double lines   Scattered

Figure 8.1   Dance formations.

these formations. Steps and figures common to these dances are described in the sidebar "Common Dance Steps."

After studying the formation and steps, become familiar with the music of the dance or activity. Find the beat of the music and become familiar with the rhythm and the pattern of the tune. Step patterns for dances are usually given with the time signature of the music. The time signature of the music (e.g., 4/4, 3/4, 2/4) indicates how many beats are in a musical measure. A 4/4 time signature means that there are four beats to every measure; a 3/4 time signature means that there are three beats to every measure, and so on. For dances appropriate for elementary children, usually a step or action is assigned to each beat. Most children's dances are performed in 2/4 or 4/4 time, and the directions will indicate what to do on each beat. Often the actions of a measure are repeated (e.g., slide four steps to the right, slide four steps to the left).

Try putting the steps to the music. Practice the steps until transitions are smooth between figures and parts of the dance. In dance there is an action for each count of a measure, so you need to be ready for the next measure after completing the previous one. Next, practice your instructions and cues for the dance with the music. Practice the dance with a partner or a small group before leading a full group.

Two very popular dances for children are the Patty Cake Polka, an American dance, and La Raspa from Mexico. The directions for these dances follow. You will notice that the description of the actions of the dance is followed by a set of cues that you will use in your teaching. La Raspa, like many dances, has a chorus; the action described in the chorus is usually repeated after different figures of the dance. A figure of a dance is a sequence of actions that go together to form a pattern (e.g., do-si-do with your partner in four counts or four slides to the left followed by four slides to the right). The music for the Patty Cake Polka is 2/4 time, which means that there are two quarter notes or two beats for each measure. Two beats to each measure usually means that there will be two steps to each measure. In the Patty Cake Polka example it means that on the first beat the dancer touches his or her heel and on the second beat touches the toe. The directions are then converted by the teacher into cues. Music with a 2/4 time signature is commonly used for polkas and marches. The La Raspa dance has a faster *tempo* but about the same level of difficulty. The music for La Raspa is 3/4 time, which means that there are

---

Common Dance Steps

bleking—Have feet together; then hop on the right foot, extending the left foot diagonally with the heel touching the floor (count 1), and hop on the left foot, extending the right foot diagonally with the heel touching the floor (count 2); may be repeated (cues: right, left).

do-si-do—Partners face each other and walk forward toward each other four steps, passing right shoulders, until they are standing back to back. Next, without turning, they take one step sideward to the right and then walk backward four steps, passing left shoulders, to place. Arms may be crossed in front of the dancer's chest.

elbow turn—Partners lock elbows and walk around in a circle back to where they started. Elbow turns may be done with the right or left elbow.

grapevine—Cross right foot over in front of the left foot (count 1); step to left on left foot (count 2); cross right foot behind left foot (count 3); step to left on left foot (count 4) (cues: right, left, right, left; or right over, left, right back, left; count: 1, 2, 3, 4). Step may be done to the left or the right.

heel and toe—Touch heel of one foot to the floor forward (count 1), then touch the toe of the same foot to the floor backward (count 2). Variation: Touch heel of one foot diagonally forward, hopping very slightly on the other foot (count 1). The toe of the same foot is then touched to the floor across the other foot and close to the instep, again with hopping on the other foot (count 2).

sashay—A slide step in which the body is in the air most of the time. The weight is lifted off the lead foot with a low spring and is carried over to the trailing foot; for an instant both feet are off the floor at the same time.

schottische—Step forward on the right foot (count 1); close with the left foot, putting weight on left foot (count 2); step forward again on the right foot (count 3); hop on the right foot and swing the left forward (count 4); repeat, starting with the left foot forward, close with the right foot, and so on (cue: step, close step, hop; count: 1, 2, 3, 4). The schottische can be done forward or sideways.

stamp—Strike the floor forcibly with the foot.

three beats to every measure. See if you can follow the directions to teach yourself the dance.

Patty Cake Polka 🔘

Formation

Double circle of partners

Action

1. Partners join hands. Both extend the counterclockwise foot forward and touch heel to floor (inside partner left foot, outside partner right foot). They bring same foot back, touching toe to floor beside other foot.

Repeat.

2. Four slide steps counterclockwise around circle.

3. Repeat 1 and 2 in clockwise direction with clockwise foot (inside partner right foot, outside partner left foot).

4. Clap right hand with partner three times, clap left hand with partner three times, clap both hands with partner three times, clap own thighs three times.

5. Link right elbow and skip once around in place (eight counts).

Cues

1. Heel, toe

   Heel, toe

2. Slide, slide, slide, slide

3. Heel, toe

   Heel, toe

   Slide, slide, slide, slide

4. Clap right, right, right

   Clap left, left, left

   Clap both, both, both

   Clap knees, knees, knees

5. Skip and turn

To make the action progressive, the inside partner moves from the turn on to the next outside partner on his or her left.

La Raspa

Formation

Either free formation with couples around the room, or couples in a double circle facing each other

Action

■ Chorus. Partners face each other and join both hands. Both hop on left foot, extend right foot forward, and touch heel to the floor. Both hop on right foot, extend left foot forward, and touch heel to the floor; both hop on left foot, extend right foot forward, and touch heel to the floor, then hold. Continuing, they hop on right, extend left, hop on left, extend right, hop on right, extend left, and hold. They repeat this entire action three times.

■ Figure 1. If in a circle, partners join inside hands and two-step counterclockwise around the circle (16 counts). If partners are dancing as couples, they take a closed dance position to do a two-step turn.

■ Chorus.

■ Figure 2. Partners stand right side to right side and join hands with arms outstretched. They skip around in place clockwise for eight counts. They reverse directions, left side to left side, and skip eight steps in counterclockwise direction.

■ Chorus.

■ Figure 3. Dancers clap own hands once, link right elbows, and turn partners clockwise eight counts. They clap own hands again, hook left elbows, and turn eight counts counterclockwise.

■ Repeat.

■ Chorus.

Summary

Chorus

Right-left-right-hold

Left-right-left-hold

Right-left-right-hold

Left-right-left-hold

Right-left-right-hold

Left-right-left-hold

Right-left-right-hold

Left-right-left-hold

Figure 1:

Two-step turn

Chorus

Figure 2:

Right shoulder turn, left shoulder turn

Chorus

Figure 2:

Clap, right elbows, swing; clap, left elbows, swing

Chorus

Partners practice the bleking step before performing the La Raspa dance in circle formation.

Selecting Folk Dances

When selecting folk dances for beginners, consider music with a strong beat and eight-count phrases (e.g., slide to the left [1, 2, 3, 4] followed by slide to the right [1, 2, 3, 4]). Dances in which there is lots of repetition of movements are also appropriate for beginners. Repetition of movement phrases may be offered throughout a dance (e.g., Patty Cake Polka) or in the chorus of the dance (e.g., La Raspa). Also consider the steps and formation of the dance. Select dances with basic locomotor movements, such as walk, slide, or skip, along with simple steps such as toe touches and stamps for beginners. Many dances for young children also include gestures in place (e.g., clap, clap, clap). Dances performed in scattered formation, in single circles, or longways sets are also appropriate for beginners. See table 8.2 for simple folk dances. The CD-ROM includes instructions for these dances.

Teaching a Folk Dance

Teachers must first know the dance they are going to teach and should have practiced it with music.

The sidebar presents some recommendations for teaching a structured folk dance.

■ *Demonstration.* Let students see the dance performed to the music. Demonstrate the dance by showing a video, either a commercial one or a recorded performance of another class. If a video is not available, perform the dance yourself.

■ *Begin with the music.* The initial step in teaching a dance is to have the children listen to the music of the dance. Then have them clap or tap their foot to the beat of the music. Once the children can identify the beat, have them move about by walking or stepping to the beat. Then add clapping as they step or march to the beat of the music while traveling throughout general space.

■ *Have students learn the dance independently.* After students have successfully demonstrated an awareness of the beat of the music, it is time to teach the steps of the dance in scattered formation. It is best to have students first learn the steps to the dance independently in scattered formation, even if the dance is to be performed in a formation, such as a circle, or with a partner.

■ *Break down the steps into small sections.* Start by demonstrating the first steps of the dance, no more than the first eight counts, without the music. Then, have the children perform these steps, first without the music and then with music. Next, demonstrate the second eight counts of the dance and have the children practice these moves without the music. Then have the children do the first steps (part A) along with the second eight counts (part B). Then have students do part A and part B to music. Continue adding on parts in this fashion until the children do the complete dance. Don't assume that doing a part just once is enough for students to have learned that part. They will need to do each part several times before they feel comfortable moving on to another part of the dance.

■ *Add the formation and partners if appropriate.* Once the steps are learned independently, the child is ready to move into a formation or to dance with a partner. When students are ready to dance with a partner, it is not important that boys dance with girls. What is of utmost importance to ensure a fun and enjoyable movement experience is that every child select a friend or a partner that he or she would enjoy dancing with. Most often, children prefer same-gender dance partners. Dancing with a partner of the same gender is developmentally appropriate for children.

TABLE 8.2

Elementary Folk Dances

Dance	Origin	Formation	Basic steps
DANCES FOR K THROUGH 2			
Bingo	American	Single circle	Walking, grand right and left
Chimes of Dunkirk	Belgian	Double circle	Skipping
Circassian Circle	English	Single circle	Walking, skipping
Seven Jumps	Danish	Single circle	Step-hop
Shoemaker's Dance	Danish	Double circle	Skipping, heel-toe
DANCES FOR GRADES 3 THROUGH 5			
Big Circle Square Dance	American	Double circle	Shuffle
D'Hammerschmieds G'selln	German	Two couples	Step-hop
Korobushka	Russian	Double circle	Schottische
Mayim! Mayim!	Israeli	Single circle	Grapevine
Virginia Reel	American	Longways set	Walk, skip, do-si-do

With use of the teaching progression just explained, you would teach the folk dance Patty Cake Polka by giving the following instructions:

1. Today we are going to learn a dance called the Patty Cake Polka. It is an American folk dance. So it is an old dance that boys and girls have enjoyed for many, many years. Today you will have fun doing the Patty Cake Polka. This is what the Patty Cake Polka looks like. (Show a video of the dance being performed or perform the dance yourself.)

2. Listen to the music that I am going to play. I want you to listen for the beat of the music. Once you think you hear the beat, clap your hands to the beat. Now stand up and march in place to the beat of the music. Let's travel through general space marching to the beat of the music. You can clap your hands while you are marching if you would like.

3. Find a spot facing me where you have space to move and you can see my feet. I will show you the first step of the dance. With weight on the left foot, put the right heel out, touch the toe, right heel out, touch the toe. Try that with me, heel, toe, heel, toe. Next are four slide steps. With weight still on the left foot, move the right foot to the side and slide, slide, slide, slide. Let's try that together, slide, slide, slide, slide. We will start with the beginning heel-toes and add the slides. Ready, heel, toe, heel, toe, slide, slide, slide, slide.

(If you are going to face the children, it is important for you to use the foot on the opposite side of the foot you want them to use and to tell them you are doing so, since a few children in the group will figure out that you are using the "wrong" foot. This procedure is called mirroring.)

4. Now we are ready to put that to music. The dance does not start at the same time the music starts. There is a little bit of music that is an introduction; then we start with the heel-toes. I will play the music and I want you to listen for an introduction. See if you can hear it and decide when the heel-toe would start.

5. With the music, heel, toe, heel, toe, slide, slide, slide, slide.

6. Now, we are going to do the same thing but to the left. With weight on the right foot, put the left heel out, touch the toe, left heel out, touch the toe. Try that with me, heel, toe, heel, toe. Next are the four slide steps. With weight still on the right foot, move the left foot to the side and slide, slide, slide, slide. Let's try that together, slide, slide, slide, slide. We will start with the beginning heel-toes and add the slides. Ready, heel, toe, heel, toe, slide, slide, slide, slide.

7. Let's start from the very beginning, ready, heel, toe, heel, toe, slide, slide, slide, slide, heel, toe, heel, toe, slide, slide, slide, slide. Did you end up in the

same spot that you started in? Yes, you should have if you took the same-size slides to the right and then back to the left.

8. Let's do that much with music (with music playing).

> Heel, toe, heel, toe
>
> Slide, slide, slide, slide
>
> Heel, toe, heel, toe
>
> Slide, slide, slide, slide

9. Now we are ready to learn part two. Bring your right hand across your body, palm facing out, like you are clapping someone's hand three times in a row. Ready, right, right, right. Now bring the left hand across for three claps. Left, left, left. Now, bring both hands up for three claps; both, both, both. Now pat your hand on your thighs three times. Knees, knees, knees. Let's add all of this to the first part. Ready, from the beginning (without music):

> Heel, toe, heel, toe
>
> Slide, slide, slide, slide
>
> Heel, toe, heel, toe
>
> Slide, slide, slide, slide
>
> Clap right, right, right
>
> Clap left, left, left
>
> Clap both, both, both
>
> Clap knees, knees, knees

Now let's try it with the music. (Repeat the preceding steps with the music.)

10. When I say "go" I want you to go stand in front of a friend that you can work with and be a good partner to while learning the steps to the dance. Go.

Stand facing your partner, and reaching forward, hold your partner's hands. (Partnerships are in scatter formation.) Decide with your partner which foot you are going to start with. Once you make that decision, show me by putting the heel of that foot forward. (Look for one partner's left foot and the other partner's right foot to be forward.) Now, let's try the steps we have learned so far with a partner, ready:

> Heel, toe, heel, toe
>
> Slide, slide, slide, slide
>
> Heel, toe, heel, toe
>
> Slide, slide, slide, slide
>
> Clap right, right, right
>
> Clap left, left, left
>
> Clap both, both, both
>
> Clap knees, knees, knees

Now let's try it with the music. (Repeat preceding steps with the music.)

11. Now for the last part of the dance. Just watch while I demonstrate; then I will give you a chance to try it with your partner. The last part is an elbow turn. Link right elbows with your partner and skip once around in place for eight counts. Like this, skip, 2, 3, 4, 5, 6, 7, 8, and you should be right back where you started from. Let's try it, ready, skip, 2, 3, 4, 5, 6, 7, 8. Did you end up where you started from? Let's try it again and this time try to time it so that you end up right back where you started from in eight counts. Ready, skip, 2, 3, 4, 5, 6, 7, 8. Now let's put all the parts together. From the beginning (without music):

> Heel, toe, heel, toe
>
> Slide, slide, slide, slide
>
> Heel, toe, heel, toe
>
> Slide, slide, slide, slide
>
> Clap right, right, right
>
> Clap left, left, left
>
> Clap both, both, both
>
> Clap knees, knees, knees
>
> Skip, 2, 3, 4, 5, 6, 7, 8

Now let's try it with the music. (Repeat preceding steps with the music.)

12. Now once you and your partner finish the eight-count turn, be ready to start with the heel and toe again; then we will keep repeating the steps. Let's try it. (Do the preceding steps with music; repeat several times.)

13. Now let's try the Patty Cake Polka as a circle dance. When I say "go" I want one partner to go stand with their heels on the outside of the circle you see on the floor and stand so that you are facing out. Go. (Make sure students are facing out and evenly spaced around the circle.) This time when I say "go," I need for the partner that is not standing on the circle to go stand facing their partner that is on the circle. Go. Pretend that our circle is a large clock. In which direction would the hands on the clock move? Yes, that direction is called clockwise. Stand in the middle of the circle and use your arm to indicate a clockwise direction. The other direction is called counterclockwise. Put the heel of the counterclockwise foot forward (inside partner left foot, outside partner right foot). That is also the direction that we all will be moving in when we do the slides. Why is it important that everyone move in the same counterclockwise direction? Yes, so we won't run over someone. Why is it important that

we all take the same size-slide steps? Yes, so we can return to the spot that we started in without running into others. And so we can keep our circle round. Now we are ready to do the Patty Cake Polka in a circle with music. *(Do all steps with music.)*

Children enjoy performing new skills they have learned. Once children learn a dance, they enjoy performing it time and time again. This provides an opportunity for them to practice their motor skills and to refine or improve upon their performance. During performances, remind children that movements should be "dancelike"; like a dancer, they should be light on their feet.

Self-Designed Folk Dances

Once children have learned a folk dance, they can be asked to vary it by adding their own step patterns and organizations to the music, either individually, with partners, or with a small group. For example, after students have learned the Patty Cake Polka, ask them to replace the eight-count elbow turn with their own eight-count move. Students can also design their own dances by selecting and combining steps. A good guideline to follow is to have students select movements to be done within eight-count phrases. Then have students design a 32-count dance that is repeatable. Options within this framework include, but are not be limited to, two different steps performed for 16 counts each or four different steps performed for eight counts each.

Students may design their dances individually, with a partner, or in a small group. Working with a partner or in a small group gives students a chance to develop and practice cooperation by successfully working with others to accomplish a task. Working cooperatively with others by sharing ideas, considering the ideas of others, and collaborating to tackle a project or to solve a problem enhances the development of responsible personal and social behavior in a physical activity setting. As discussed in earlier chapters, responsible personal and social behavior is one of the six qualities of a physically educated person as identified by the national standards for physical education (National Association for Sport and Physical Education [NASPE], 2004).

Children enjoy performing the steps to music.

Guidelines for Teaching Folk Dance

1. If possible, show the children the whole dance or the steps of the dance to music (demonstration or DVD).

2. Let the students hear the music early.

3. Sometimes it is helpful to use a drum or another instrument and clap hands, snap fingers, tap thighs, or step to the beat to teach the rhythm of the dance.

4. Early in a child's dance experience, choose dances that do not specify starting on a specific foot (R, L) or having a boy–girl partner relationship (choose a friend).

5. Choose dances with strong underlying beats and distinct musical phrases that occur in sets of 8 or 16 beats.

6. Even if the dance is done with a partner or in a group formation (or both), teach any new steps first without a partner or any formation.

7. Use one-word cues to help students formulate their step patterns and sequence.

8. Call cues for directional or pattern changes one or two counts ahead to help students anticipate what comes next in the dance.

9. Teach the dance in the pace or time in which it will be performed. Slowing the speed early will only cause the learners to relearn the step later at a faster pace.

10. In dances with more than one part, teach using a progressive part method: A, B; then A + B; then C; then A + B + C; and so on.

11. For beginners, each part of the dance needs to be highly repetitive.

Using Dance Resources

Several resources are available for providing folk dance experiences for children. Some resources include actual verbal calls along with the music, as well as a music-only version. Other folk dance materials may include a video of dancers performing the dance. Consult the physical education teacher or physical activity director of the school for suggestions and recommendations. For resources, see the end of the chapter. Many dances are included on the CD-ROM.

Line Dancing

How many times have you seen the Electric Slide provide opportunity for physical activity? From third grade throughout adulthood, line dancing provides physical activity at many school and community events. The repetition of movements done with simple changes in direction make line dances simple to perform and therefore fun for all ages.

Line dances are composed of basic locomotor and gesture-like or axial movements done to the beat of a particular song or contemporary music. There is no partner; everyone is moving together.

Line dances are taught in much the same way as folk dances: Using a progressive part method, teach part A; then do part A with music; then teach part B; then do parts A and B with music; teach part C; then do parts A, B, and C with music.

The Electric Slide is a four-wall line dance. A line dance typically involves designated dance movements performed facing one direction and then repeated following a quarter turn. The line dance continues as the same dance movements are repeated facing different directions—first facing forward, then to the left, then facing the back of the room, then the other side of the room, then facing forward again. The dance is done facing all four walls. It was choreographed to the international hit song "Electric Boogie" by Marcia Griffiths but can be done with a variety of alternative contemporary music. The Macarena is also a four-wall line dance. "La Macarena" is a song by Los del Rio.

The Macarena

Right arm out, left arm out, right palm up, left palm up

1. Right arm goes out palm down, lift left heel, drop right heel.

2. Left hand goes out palm down, lift right heel, drop left heel.

3. Turn right palm up, lift left heel, drop right heel.

4. Turn left palm up, lift right heel, drop left heel.

Fold right arm, fold left arm, hand to right ear, hand to left ear

5. Place right hand on left shoulder, lift left heel, drop right heel.

6. Place left hand on right shoulder, lift right heel, drop left heel.

7. Place right hand to right back of ear, lift left heel, drop right heel.

8. Place left hand to left back of ear, lift right heel, drop left heel.

Right to left hip, left to right hip, right to right hip, left to left hip

9. Place right hand on left hip, lift left heel, drop right heel.

10. Place left hand on right hip, lift right heel, drop left heel.

11. Place right hand on right hip, lift left heel, drop right heel.

12. Place left hand on left hip, lift left heel, drop right heel.

Roll, roll, roll, turn

13. Roll hips with hand on hips.

14. Roll hips with hand on hips.

15. Roll hips with hand on hips.

16. With small jump, turn 1/4 turn to right.

Repeat.

Getting Creative With Line Dances

Line dancing can provide a creative movement experience. Using this basic four-wall framework of dance movements and quarter turns, students can create their own line dance.

1. Have students select one to several movements. (See the sidebar "Line Dance Steps or Moves" for suggested moves.) For example, select one movement to be performed for eight counts, or four movements to be performed for 32 counts (eight counts each move). Two moves could be performed for 16 counts each. There are numerous options.

2. At the end of the 32 counts, a quarter turn to the left is made. After the quarter turn, the steps are repeated facing the new direction; students

Line Dance Steps or Moves

Walk	Toe touches
Jump	Step kicks
Hop	Knee lifts
Skip	Grapevines
Slide	Bleking step
March	Schottische
Jumping jacks	Cha-cha
Lunges	

repeat the moves and turn again. Students are now facing the back of the room. They repeat the movement and turns until the music ends.

3. A sample creative line dance:

Step touch—eight counts

Jumping jacks—eight counts

Grapevine—16 counts

Quarter turn

Repeat

4. Let students make suggestions or select their own music.

Creative Dance

Creative dance experiences give children an opportunity to make decisions regarding where and how the body moves. When participating in creative dance, children design their own dance by sequencing movements and using selected qualities of effort, time, and relationships rather than performing a dance created by others as in folk and line dancing. Creative movement gives children an opportunity to express feelings, thoughts, and ideas through movement.

Although one can teach creative dance working directly with the movement concepts (e.g., contrasting slow and quick, rising and sinking actions, moving slow and strong to a space and heavy and light to the floor; see chapter 3), most classroom teachers will want to use a stimulus for children to draw upon to create the movement experience. A stimulus may be something as simple as a balloon. Children could explore the shape of the balloon and how it changes as it inflates, deflates, or bursts. They may explore the way the balloon travels when released and propelled by the exiting air. Numerous options are available for use as a stimulus: magnets, popcorn popping, spaghetti boiling, a thunderstorm, a children's book. Children's literature, poems, and action words may also be used to prompt creative movement expression.

Using Children's Literature to Stimulate Sequences in Creative Movement

Children's literature provides an excellent stimulus for creative dance as well as a way to integrate language arts into the physical activity program. There may be a book that your students especially like or one that you think will help teach or reinforce a particular subject (see the sidebar "Suggested Children's Literature Appropriate for Dance"). Having students dance the story is a fun way to reinforce learning or for them to express themselves through movement.

1. Look for books with themes or action words that could be used to develop a lesson on creative dance.
2. Select words and phrases directly from the book and arrange them on a chart similar to the one in figure 8.2.

Children can be asked to express themselves through movement.

The Tiny Seed by Eric Carle

High in the air

Strong wind

Tiny, small

Flies higher

Flying very low

Wind pushes

Fall gently down

Settle down

Snow falls

Rain falls

Grow round and full

Burst open

Grow up toward the sun

Growing fast

Taller and taller

Giant flower

Petals drop

Sail along

Wind blows harder

Sways and bends

Shakes the flower

Quickly sail far away

Strong wind	Settle down	Burst open	Growing fast	Sways and bends	Shakes	Quickly sail
fast, direct	slow, gentle	sudden, explode	direct, fast, extend	back and forth, slow, to and fro, bent	indirect, sudden	fast, smooth

Figure 8.2 Phrase chart.

3. Once all of the words and phrases are listed, explore the movement qualities (fast/slow; heavy/light; direct/indirect) of each of the words you will use.

4. Organize the words into a logical movement sequence that has a beginning, middle, and end.

5. Movement sequences vary from three to seven parts, depending on the age of the child. There are many action words and phrases to choose from. Narrow those chosen to a manageable number so that children can remember and practice the sequence, and give them time to practice.

6. Have students share their sequence with the class (asking half the class at a time to do this prevents students from having to perform alone and saves time).

Allow children to explore and interpret the phrases that either you or the students themselves have selected. They should explore many phrases before selecting those to be used in the sequence. When deciding on movements for the sequence, be sure to select phrases that elicit movements with contrasting actions, perhaps a gently flowing movement and a quick explosive movement. Be sure to build the sequence by adding one part at a time. Have children practice transitioning from the beginning movement to the middle movement. Children should practice for quality movement actions as they perform each movement and transition from one to the next. They should practice their sequence so that it is repeatable; they should remember their sequence so that they are practicing the same movements each time. Figure 8.3 presents a movement lesson using Eric Carle's *The Tiny Seed.* Another movement lesson using *Elephants Aloft* is included on the CD-ROM.

Suggested Children's Literature Appropriate for Dance

In the Small, Small Pond by Denise Fleming

In the Tall, Tall Grass by Denise Fleming

Where Once There Was a Wood by Denise Fleming

Elephants Aloft by Kathi Apelt

Straight Line Wonder by Mem Fox

The Tiny Seed by Eric Carle

Swimmy by Leo Lionni

Action Words

Action words are an excellent stimulus for creative movement expression. Whether from a list of words (figure 8.4) or from within short stories or poems, action words inspire creative movement while integrating language arts into the physical activity program. Movement is a natural way for children to explore and demonstrate understanding.

The following activity demonstrates the way in which a list of action words can be used to inspire creative movement:

Creative Movement Inspired by Action Words

Objectives

By the end of this lesson, every child will be able to do the following:

1. Use movement to express images elicited by action words

2. Explore concepts of space by moving in different directions, levels, pathways

3. Contrast effort actions of time (fast/slow), force (heavy/light), and flow (smooth/jerky)

4. Develop a simple sequence of three to five action words that expressively interprets the selected words

Equipment

List of action words (figure 8.4)

Action word cards (put each action word or contrasting action on a large card so that children can see the word or phrase spelled out and you can hold a card up to change the action)

Organization

Children scattered throughout general space

Activities, Teacher Cues, and Content Development

■ *Set induction:* Begin the class by gathering the students around you and asking them if they can think of a single word that describes the way something moves. Guide students in naming some action words and then describing the movement qualities elicited by these words. For example, is the movement (time) fast or slow, (force) heavy or light, (flow) smooth or jerky, (space) straight or flexible?

■ *Individual activities:* At this point, have the students scattered throughout general space. Show the

FIGURE 8.3

Sample Movement Lesson Using The Tiny Seed

Objectives

By the end of this lesson, every child will be able to do the following:

1. Interpret action word phrases through appropriate nonlocomotor and locomotor actions and movement qualities.
2. Demonstrate smooth transitions between nonlocomotor and locomotor movements.
3. Contrast effort actions of time (fast/slow), force (heavy/light), and flow (jerky/smooth).
4. Develop a simple sequence with a beginning, middle, and ending that appropriately and expressively interprets selected action words and phrases.

Equipment

Hand drum

Carle, E. (1987). *The Tiny Seed*. New York, NY: Simon & Schuster Books for Young Readers.

Organization

Children scattered throughout general space.

Activities, Teacher Cues, and Content Development:

Set Induction

Begin the class by gathering the students around you and introducing them to the children's book, *The Tiny Seed*. The book is about the journey of a seed that is carried aloft by the autumn wind and faces many obstacles and hazards before blooming into a summertime flower. Students will explore the movements described in action phrases throughout the story.

Individual Activities

Have the students scattered throughout general space. Have students make a tiny shape with their bodies at a very low level. Then "grow" from the tiny shape into a very tall shape. Do this slowly—one body part at a time. Give students 10 drum beats to grow into the tallest shape. Make the tall shape sway and bend. Continue to have students explore a variety of action phrases from the story.

Creating a Sequence

Having had the students explore a variety of action phrases, it is now time to build a sequence. Start with a tiny shape; then move into a tall shape that gently sways and bends in the wind. For the middle part of the sequence, students demonstrate the action phrases of *strong wind, flying very low,* and then *flies higher*. The end of the sequence may include a *settle down* then *grow towards the sun* and *burst open*. Have students create their own sequence with a beginning, middle, and end using 3 to 5 contrasting action phrases from the story.

Closure and Assessment

Encourage students to practice their sequence several times and do it the same way each time. Make it look polished. Then in small groups or with a partner, have them take turns showing their sequence. Those observing the sequence could have a checklist to check for held shapes (three seconds), 3 to 5 contrasting travels, and actions that are expressive and appropriate.

FIGURE 8.4

Action Words

Traveling Actions

run	slither
skip	hop
creep	gallop
rush	dart
flee	

Turning Actions

spin	whirl
twirl	whip
swivel	

Contracting Actions

shrink	shrivel
close	narrow

Rising Actions

lift	rise
climb	heave

Vibratory Actions

shiver	shake
quiver	tremble
wobble	vibrate
patter	shudder

Stopping Actions

freeze	hold
perch	grip
anchor	pause
settle	

Expanding Actions

grow	reach
release	open
spread	

Jumping Actions

leap	hurl
toss	bound
prance	bounce
soar	fly

Percussive Actions

stamp	punch
explode	pound
patter	

Sinking Actions

collapse	sink
lower	drip
fall	

word "prance." Ask students to identify something that might prance. They may answer "a horse." Through questioning, identify movement qualities by asking questions such as "Is the prance fast or slow?" "Heavy or light?" "Smooth or jerky?" Ask students to demonstrate "prance." Ask them to change pathways when prancing, then levels.

Ask students to identify something that might "settle." They may answer "a leaf." Through questioning, identify movement qualities through such questions as "So is 'settle' fast or slow?" "Heavy or light?" "Is the movement direct or indirect?" Ask students to demonstrate "settle." Have students begin with a prance and then settle.

Use this same general process to explore several other action words:

a. Display and identify the action word.

b. Ask students to think of something that _____.

c. "How would you describe the movement in terms of time? Is the movement fast or slow? Sudden or sustained?"

d. "How would you describe the movement in terms of force? Is the movement heavy or light?"

e. "How would you describe the movement in terms of flow? Is the movement smooth or jerky?"

f. "Is the movement direct or flexible?"

g. Students demonstrate the movement elicited by

_____.

h. If the movement is more static or nonlocomotor, then combine it with a locomotor movement, transitioning from one action to the next.

■ *Creating a sequence:* Having explored a variety of action words with contrasting movement qualities, it is now time to build a sequence. Select three to five action word cards for the sequence. Select contrasting movements, some locomotor, some nonlocomotor. For example, begin with "prance." Then add "settle," encouraging a smooth transition; then add "dart." Finally, finish with "shrink." Cues for the sequence could be PRANCE – SETTLE – DART – SHRINK. Allow students to develop their own unique sequence based on three to five action word cards they have chosen. Challenge them to select contrasting actions. Students should also select and sequence some locomotor and some nonlocomotor actions individually.

■ *Closure and assessment:* Encourage students to practice their sequence several times. While they are practicing, have them focus on effort qualities of time, force, and flow. Students should practice long enough that they can repeat the sequence by doing it the same way each time, can make it look polished. Then in small groups or with a partner, have them take turns showing their sequence. Those observing the sequence could have a checklist to help them observe for moving under control, using at least one locomotor and one nonlocomotor movement, and using contrasting actions that are expressive and appropriate.

Coordinating Dances to Enhance Grade-Level Curriculum

Dance selections can be coordinated to go along with the curriculum of a grade level. Folk dances can be selected from an era that is being studied as part of the social studies curriculum. For example, when children are studying colonial times, the Virginia Reel or Patty Cake Polka may be used to further demonstrate and convey social life in the colonies. If the grade-level curriculum requires study of a particular country, dances native to that country should be selected. When students are learning about Europe, integrate the folk dance Chimes of Dunkirk; when they are learning about Mexico, teach La Raspa.

Creative movement experiences can also be coordinated with curricular topics in science. Creative movement can be used to illustrate how a seed grows and develops into a plant or to demonstrate a thunderstorm. Movement experiences may be created and performed by individual students, in partnerships, or in small groups. A group movement experience may recreate the movement of water through the water cycle.

Creative dance and movement experiences may also be coordinated with the language arts curriculum. As previously described, children's books, poetry, or single action words may be used as a stimulus for creative movement expression. Published stories and poems can be used, as can stories or poems written by the children as part of a creative writing unit. Children enjoy seeing their favorite stories and poems come to life.

Handling the Management Issues Related to Dance

There are management issues specific to the teaching of dance. These issues are different from the management concerns that arise in the classroom or in other physical activity settings. Teachers who are new to teaching dance may not have experience dealing with problems that may come up when getting students into formations, when students are unwilling to "dance," when organizing students into partnerships, and when teaching with music; and they may not have experience demonstrating dance steps.

Getting Students Into a Formation

Getting students into formations such as a circle or double circle can sometimes be a challenge in itself. Once students have learned the dance in a scattered formation, it is time to progress to the intended formation of the dance. Forming a single large circle is a difficult task for early elementary-level students, especially if there is no visual aid or point of reference available. Use existing gym floor markings or create marks using floor tape or poly spots to provide a visual guide. For example, when getting students into circle formation, have them stand in a spot on the center circle of the basketball court and take a giant step backward. If a center circle is not available, use floor tape to mark a broken circle of the desired size on the floor. Once students are in the desired formation, instruct them to look around and see how round the circle is and to also notice the size of the circle. Challenge students to maintain the shape of the circle while performing the dance. At the end of the dance, have students examine their formation and compare it to the original one. Discuss how the beginning formation changed and what needs to happen in order to maintain the beginning shape during performance of the dance (e.g., not drifting to the center of the circle, maintaining even space between dancers, everyone taking the same-size steps). Also point out to students that if they take three steps into the circle and then three steps back, they should be returning to the original spot. This same concept applies to moving to the side.

Children are often asked to hold hands in the process of forming a closed circle. A frequent result is that some students get their hands and arms pulled to the extent that they lose their balance and fall down. Instruct students to always let go when they feel their hand being pulled.

For formation of a double circle, first use one partner from each partnership and have these students form a single circle. Once they have formed the single circle, have them turn in place so that they are now facing out rather than facing the center. Next, have their partners join them by standing in front of them, facing them. The second partner is now standing facing the direction of the center of the circle and is also forming the outer circle.

Hesitant Learners

Teachers sometimes have students who are unwilling or hesitant to try an activity. When it comes to dance, some students may have preconceived notions about dance and their ability to perform a dance. They may be reluctant to participate. The following approaches are helpful for encouraging unwilling or reluctant students:

■ Consider replacing the word "dance" with a different word. Rather than telling students they will be learning a dance, tell them they will be learning and participating in a "rhythmic activity" or simply "moving to music." Once students discover that they can move in rhythm to music and that moving to music can be fun, tell them that what they have been doing is in fact called "dancing."

■ Introduce the dance or rhythmic activity with sincere enthusiasm. A student's attitude toward an activity is influenced by the manner in which the activity is presented. Students are more likely to join an activity that can be viewed as fun and inviting.

■ Provide a positive atmosphere. Encourage students to try the dance moves, and acknowledge their efforts. Communicate your confidence in their ability to perform the movements by letting them know that in fact they already know how to do the moves (such as step, slide, skip, turn); now they will be combining the moves in different ways and putting them to music.

■ Talk with students about the experience. Ask them what they enjoyed or what went well, what parts were challenging, or what part they would like to change the next time.

■ Students should be made to feel comfortable and successful. Help them capture the spirit of the dance, which is found in the fun and joyous fellowship shared in doing the dance.

■ Begin teaching dances that you know almost all students really enjoy and can learn easily.

Choosing a Partner

Many folk and social dances require dancing with a partner. The intent of most partner dances is for the dance to be performed with mixed-gender partnerships, with dance instruction referring to the gentleman's position or the lady's position. In the elementary school setting, mixed-gender partnerships are not necessary and should not be required. Simply ask students to select a friend they would like to dance with to be their partner. If students select a partner of the same gender, which they

most likely will do, that is acceptable as well as age appropriate. It is also important that students have an opportunity to work with different peers in a physical activity setting. So provide opportunities for them to work with different partners. You can accomplish this by simply asking students to "select someone to be your partner that you have not been partners with." This can occur at the beginning of a lesson or at any time throughout the lesson.

Given that the majority of elementary-level students will be dancing with same-gender partners, it is inappropriate to refer to their roles as the "gentleman's" and "lady's" or "boy's" and "girl's." Referring to the positions as "inside" and "outside" partner can also become confusing for students. Consider using colored jerseys or vests called pinnies to designate the different positions. Use one color for all the partners on the right and a second color for all partners on the left. Then you can refer to these positions by color rather than by gender role.

Teaching With Music

Most dance and rhythmic experiences include music. CD players, iPods, and other portable devices are used for playing music. Many CD players have a remote that allows the instructor to operate them from the center of the room without running back and forth; iPods can be plugged into most speaker systems. Another feature available on CD players is variable speed control, which allows the instructor to adjust the tempo, or rate of speed, of the music to meet the needs of the students. The CD player or other playback hardware should be placed on a stand to avoid jarring from stamping feet and for easy access.

When teaching with music, it is important to give cues for the upcoming dance steps a couple of beats before they are to occur. For example in the Patty Cake Polka, students do an elbow turn for eight counts and then do a heel, toe, heel, toe. So the cues for the heel, toe should be given on counts 7 and 8 of the elbow turn.

Use of Demonstrations

When teaching a dance step, it is important to demonstrate how to perform the step. Demonstrations should effectively communicate the direction in which to travel or the side of the body used in performing the step. When demonstrating a dance movement, teachers must decide whether to stand facing the group or with their back to the group. When facing the group, the movement should be mirrored. For example, if the movement calls for three slides to the right, the teacher will use the verbal cues for traveling right but will be sliding to the left; this will result in movement in the same direction as the students in the group. When the teacher demonstrates with his or her back turned toward the class, students can match the movements demonstrated. A disadvantage to having the back turned to the class is that the teacher is not able to see how students are performing the step. However, when demonstrating a line dance, this may be the appropriate choice given the turns that are performed and the resulting changes in the direction students will be facing while performing the steps. When providing demonstrations for individual students, you should be positioned beside the student.

SUMMARY

1. Dance and rhythmic activities provide opportunities for students to be physically active, interact with others, develop and refine motor skills, and express and communicate feelings.

2. Dance movements are composed of locomotor or nonlocomotor movements (or both) combined with movement concepts.

3. Teaching folk dances provides students with the opportunity to move to music as well as learn about different cultures.

4. When teaching dance to beginners, select dances with simple steps, repetition of movements, and music with a strong beat.

5. The following are guidelines for teaching a dance:
   - Practice and know the dance you are going to teach.
   - Demonstrate the dance for students.
   - Let students hear and become familiar with the music.
   - Have students learn steps independently before adding a partner.
   - Break the dance into small parts. Teach one part and practice it; then teach the next part, practice it, and add it to the previously learned part.

6. Line dances have a four-wall framework in which repeated dance movements followed by a quarter turn allow the dancer to eventually face all four walls or directions while performing the dance.

7. Creative dance experiences provide opportunities for children to explore concepts; design sequences; and express feelings, thoughts, and ideas through movement.

8. Children's books, stories, and action words provide stimuli for creative dance experiences and opportunity to integrate language arts into the physical activity program.

9. Dance and rhythmic activities should be positive, enjoyable experiences for children.

10. When teaching dance, remember these guidelines:
    - Use a physical reference such as floor markings when getting students into a formation.
    - Allow students to choose a friend to be a partner and to work with many different partners.
    - Call cues for movements a few beats ahead of when the movements are to occur.
    - Use demonstrations effectively.
    - Introduce activities with sincere enthusiasm and provide a positive atmosphere.

CHECKING YOUR UNDERSTANDING

1. Identify and describe three forms of dance appropriate for elementary school physical education and physical activity programs.

2. What does a time signature of 3/4 indicate?

3. What criteria should be used when selecting dances for beginners?

4. Describe the progression of tasks or steps used when teaching a folk dance.

5. What guidelines should a teacher follow when teaching a dance?

6. Describe how children's literature can be used as a stimulus for a creative movement experience.

7. Identify three common dance formations and describe how to get children into each formation.

8. Identify common management issues that arise when teaching dance and explain how they should be handled.

RESOURCES

Lloyd Shaw Foundation
www.lloydshaw.org

New England Dancing Masters
www.dancingmasters.com

The Electric Slide: The Basic Choreography
www.the-electricslidedance.com

Line Dance Video
www.youtube.com/groups_videos?name=linedancers

Bennett, J., & Riemer, P. (2006). *Rhythmic activities and dance* (2nd ed.). Champaign, IL: Human Kinetics.

Cone, T., & Cone, S. (2006). *Teaching children dance* (2nd ed.). Champaign, IL: Human Kinetics.

Cone, T.P., Werner, P.H., & Cone, S.L. (2009). *Interdisciplinary elementary physical education* (2nd. ed.). Champaign, IL: Human Kinetics.

Hipps, H.H., & Chappell, W.E. (1970). *World of fun: Around the world in folk dance.* Oklahoma City: Melody House. (CD-ROMs and manual of instructions)

Lane, C. (1998). *Multicultural folk dance: Treasure chest.* Champaign, IL: Human Kinetics. (Includes videos, music, and instructional guides)

Mehrhof, J., & Parris, P. (2002). *And the beat goes on: Rhythmic activities for k-8.* Emporia, KS: Mirror.

Overby, L.Y., Post, B.C., & Newman, D. (2005). *Interdisciplinary learning through dance.* Champaign, IL: Human Kinetics.

Purcell, T.M. (1994). *Teaching children dance: Becoming a master teacher.* Champaign, IL: Human Kinetics.

Weikart, P.S. (1989). *Teaching movement and dance: A sequential approach to rhythmic movement* (3rd ed.). Ypsilanti, MI: High/Scope Press.

Weikart, P.S. (1997). *Teaching folk dance: Successful steps.* Ypsilanti, MI: High/Scope Press.

REFERENCE

National Association for Sport and Physical Education (2004). *Moving into the future: National standards for physical education* (2nd ed.). Reston, VA; NASPE

9

Fitness for the Elementary School Child

OVERVIEW

There are two approaches to developing fitness, an exercise and a physical activity orientation. An exercise approach to fitness uses calisthenics, exercises, and jogging kinds of activities that have as their sole purpose the development of fitness. A physical activity approach to fitness encourages participants to attain fitness through enjoyable activities. Experts recommend a physical activity approach for elementary-aged students. Fitness for children should focus on participation in physical activity rather than strenuous exercise. Fitness experiences can have a lasting effect on children's attitudes toward participating in physical activity. Physical activities that are fun will motivate children to seek further opportunities to be physically active. Repetitious exercises and fitness testing that seemingly serve no purpose discourage future engagement in physical activity. These ideas are completely developed in the Physical Best program put out by the National Association for Sport and Physical Education (2005). The purpose of this chapter is to help the classroom teacher understand the components of fitness, understand how it is developed, and choose and conduct activities that will promote fitness.

CHAPTER OUTCOMES

This chapter will help you

- define health-related fitness,
- describe two approaches to fitness and identify the approach to fitness that should be taken in the elementary school,
- identify and describe the components of health-related fitness,
- identify and describe basic principles of fitness training,
- describe the lifetime activity orientation to fitness,

- identify several guidelines to follow when fitness testing,
- plan and implement a variety of activities that can improve the physical fitness of children, and
- support fit kids as a classroom teacher.

IN THIS CHAPTER

Physical fitness is a process maintained through a physically active lifestyle that begins in childhood. Rope jumping, climbing on playground equipment, and active game play are daily opportunities for physical activity that become part of a child's active lifestyle. The percentage of children and adolescents who are obese has tripled since the 1970s. There are many diseases and health risks associated with obesity. Not only does obesity increase the risk of diabetes and heart disease, but it also affects one's joints, breathing, sleep, mood, and self-esteem. The impact of obesity completely encompasses a person's quality of life. The increase in childhood obesity is distressing and becomes even more so when coupled with the fact that obese children have a 70% chance of becoming obese adults.

Obesity is a result of excess energy consumption (caloric intake) and insufficient energy expenditure (calories burned), the latter of which directly relates to the amount of physical activity and exercise one gets. Energy expenditure through daily physical

Fitness is developed through participation in physical activities that are fun for children.

activity and exercise is key to weight control. Fortunately obesity is both reversible and preventable. Physical activity can help treat and prevent obesity.

What Is Physical Fitness?

What is physical fitness? Physical fitness is a set of attributes that people have or achieve that relates to the ability to perform physical activity (Morrow et al., 2005). There are two types of physical fitness, skill-related physical fitness and health-related physical fitness. *Skill-related physical fitness* includes agility, speed, power, balance, reaction time, and coordination. These components are important to performance in certain sports but are not absolutely necessary for maintaining health. Most skill-related fitness variables are strongly associated with genetic makeup. *Health-related fitness* is the level of fitness needed to carry on daily routines and be free of disease associated with a sedentary lifestyle.

The emphasis on fitness testing in the school program has changed from a skill-related emphasis to a health-related emphasis. In the 1970s, a high level of skill and fitness was needed to achieve positive results on commonly used fitness tests. Fitness scores were based on norm-referenced standards. The fitness tests used in today's schools (mostly Fitnessgram) place emphasis on health-related fitness and are criterion based rather than norm based. High levels of fitness are not needed to reap the benefits for good health, so the criterion for getting into the "Healthy Fitness Zone" is achievable by most if not all children. With regular and moderate physical activity, all children can obtain sufficient health benefits as indicated by criterion-referenced health-related fitness testing. This chapter focuses on the components of health-related fitness.

In developing health-related fitness, children should participate in activities designed to help them understand health-related fitness components and value the contribution they make to a healthy lifestyle. The goal of fitness development for elementary school children is participation in physical activity leading to fitness. If children are physically active at things they like to do, then they will become fit and will maintain their fitness over time. This orientation is known as the *lifetime activity* orientation. Encouraging children to achieve all the components of fitness through a range of physical activity is important.

Health-related fitness consists of components of physical fitness that have a relationship with good health (American College of Sports Medicine, 1998). While skill-related fitness is linked to health-related fitness, you do not need to be skilled to do well on the components of health-related fitness. Health-related fitness has five components:

- Aerobic capacity (or cardiorespiratory fitness)
- Body composition
- Flexibility
- Muscular strength
- Muscular endurance

The types of activities that develop each of these components are listed in table 9.1.

Aerobic Capacity

Aerobic capacity is also known as cardiorespiratory fitness. *Cardiorespiratory fitness* refers to the ability of the heart, blood vessels, and lungs to supply the body with oxygen and nutrients during extended periods of moderate to vigorous physical activity.

TABLE 9.1

Activities Related to Improving Fitness Components

Health-related fitness component	Activity
Cardiorespiratory endurance	Brisk walking, jogging, running, jumping jacks, PACER
Muscular strength	Push-up, curl-up, chin-up
Muscular endurance	Push-up, curl-up, chin-up
Body composition	Brisk walking, jogging, running, jumping jacks, PACER
Flexibility	Static stretches: hamstring stretch, straddle stretch, sit-and-twist

Aerobic capacity has been associated with reduced risk of cardiovascular disease, high blood pressure, colon cancer, diabetes, obesity, and other health problems in adults (U.S. Department of Health and Human Services, 1996). Aerobic capacity is therefore the most important area of fitness for children. Jogging, swimming, rope jumping, dribbling a soccer ball, playing tag games, riding a bike, and skating are examples of activities that get the heart working and build cardiorespiratory fitness.

Body Composition

Body composition refers to the ratio of body fat to lean body tissue. Physical activity plays an important role in controlling body weight by promoting calorie consumption and fat loss. Body weight includes fat, bones, muscle, and vital organs. *Overweight* indicates too much body weight for a given height and frame size. *Obesity* refers to an excessive amount of body fat that is associated with increased risk of serious and often fatal diseases. A person can be overweight without being obese.

When more calories are consumed than expended, weight is gained. When more calories are expended than taken in, weight is lost. Cardiorespiratory activities performed for a longer duration help burn calories and improve body composition. *Body composition* in children is achieved through reducing the caloric intake but more importantly through participating in those activities that are largely cardiorespiratory, such as jogging, running, jumping rope, playing tag games, and other activities that sustain moderate to vigorous effort over time.

Flexibility

Flexibility refers to the range of motion that can be achieved at a joint through any particular movement. Flexibility is joint specific, meaning that you can be flexible in some joints and not in others. You could be flexible in the shoulders but not in the hips. It is important to be flexible enough to have full range of motion at a joint. Flexibility is needed for good posture and is an important part of injury prevention. Fitness experts talk about two kinds of flexibility:

■ *Dynamic flexibility* is the ability to perform movements over the full range of motion in the joint (e.g., swinging a bat, twisting from side to side, or kicking an imaginary ball). Dynamic flexibility depends to some extent on static flexibility but also on factors such as strength, coordination, and resistance to movement.

■ *Static flexibility* refers to the ability to assume and maintain (hold) a position at one point in the range of motion of that joint (e.g., toe touch). Static flexibility depends on the structure of the joint; tightness of muscles, tendons, and ligaments; and tolerance of the individual for a stretched muscle.

Flexibility programs cannot change the structure of a joint. What they do is increase the elasticity and length of muscle and the connective tissue. Stretching activities that increase the length of muscles, tendons, and ligaments help develop and maintain flexibility. See figure 9.1 for stretching exercises. Flexibility is improved best when the muscle is warm from activity and when the stretch is applied slowly and gradually. What you don't want to do is sudden and hard stretches, which can lead to injury. Many people continue to use ballistic stretching, which is a forceful and "bouncy" movement like rapid toe touches. Ballistic stretches can cause injury and are not recommended. A flexibility training program should use the following types of stretching:

■ *Dynamic stretching:* Move the joint through its full range of motion in a functional movement in an exaggerated but controlled manner (e.g., lunge walk using exaggerated size of step and slow controlled movement). This type of stretching is useful for warming up and cooling down.

■ *Static stretching:* Stretch a muscle and hold for 15 to 30 seconds. Stretch to the point that you feel a "pull," but not pain. This method is most recommended for increasing flexibility of a joint.

The most acceptable type of stretching to improve flexibility with younger children is static stretching. Flexibility can be increased by holding a stretch for 30 seconds or by holding a stretch for 8 to 10 seconds, easing off, and repeating three times. Flexibility is achieved for children through activities such as dancing, gymnastics, stunts, and tumbling and through activities that increase the range of motion of a joint.

Muscular Strength and Endurance

Muscular strength and endurance are two separate but interrelated components of health-related fitness. *Muscular strength* is the capacity of a muscle to exert force against a resistance. Upper body and abdominal strength are required for correct posture

Over back Cross chest Sit-and-reach Sit-and-twist

Crossover hang Calf stretch Butterfly Hang time

Straddle stretch Pelican

High 10 Side lean Number 4 Snake

Knee hug Stride

Figure 9.1 Flexibility exercises.

Children respond better to fun activities that are challenging than they do to exercises.

and a well-functioning back. *Muscular endurance* is the capacity of the muscle to continue to perform for an extended period of time. Good muscular endurance allows muscles to work for lengthy periods without fatigue. Physical activities that involve leg and arm movements for an extended period of time require muscular endurance.

Muscular strength is developed in children primarily through those activities that require the child to bear weight; use force; or use the weight of the body as in climbing, skating, tumbling, lifting, striking, throwing, and kicking. Muscular endurance is developed in children when they continue to do these activities for long enough periods of time to "make the muscle tired."

Exercise Principles for Developing Fitness

Children or adults who are physically active will benefit further by increasing the amount (e.g., frequency, intensity, and duration) of physical activity. To maintain or build upon physical fitness gained through physical activity, the following basic principles of training can be applied:

- Overload
- Specificity of exercise
- Progression
- Regularity
- Individuality

Overload   The overload principle refers to the fact that you must do a little more work than you are accustomed to doing to become more fit. The acronym FITT tells you how:

Frequency: how many times you exercise per week
Intensity: how hard you exercise
Time: how long you exercise
Type (specificity): what type of exercise you perform

Specificity of Exercise   To develop an aspect of fitness, do things that focus on that ability. If you want to develop cardiorespiratory endurance, you must do activities that develop that fitness component. If you want to develop flexibility in your leg muscles, flexibility exercises that develop a different part of the body will not do it. This is also true for sport-related activities. For example, children must do some prolonged running to develop the cardiorespiratory endurance and muscular strength and endurance in the muscle groups associated with running to be able to run longer distances. To become better at swimming, you must develop the fitness components specific to that activity and the demands of that activity in order to be a physically stronger swimmer.

Progression   The increase in frequency, intensity, and time should be gradual to prevent soreness and injury. The body needs time to adapt to increased demands. Children should understand that improvements in fitness take place over time and that the process is gradual. For example, children will need to sit-and-reach (hamstring stretch) on a regular basis for several weeks before improvements in flexibility will be achieved.

Regularity   The idea of regularity is basically the "use it or lose it" principle. Any gains in fitness are quickly lost, particularly cardiorespiratory endurance (within a month), when you stop exercising. Regular participation in physical activity is essential for children to develop and maintain appropriate levels of health-related fitness.

Individuality   The principle of individuality states that we are all different. We all have a different starting point in terms of fitness level, and we all have a different potential for both the rate and degree of change possible. Fitness goals should therefore be *personalized,* and children should have lots of opportunities to choose between activities and participate in a wide variety of different activities.

Harmful Exercises and Safe Alternatives

Some stretches and exercises traditionally used by those conducting exercise sessions are potentially harmful and may cause injury. Exercises that are considered risky and should be avoided are shown in figure 9.2, along with safe alternatives.

Approaching Fitness Positively

To encourage lifelong physical activity, fitness activities must be positive experiences for children. It is easier to make the experiences positive if personal goals are set and children are reinforced for improvement and not necessarily their fitness score. Fitness activities should leave every child feeling competent and confident. Obviously, embarrassing, boring, criticizing, or shaming children will turn them off and reduce the likelihood of their continued participation in physical activities. It is of utmost importance that fitness activities provide enjoyable and meaningful experiences for children. When praise, encouragement, and a variety of activities are offered, children will be motivated to seek physical activity on their own. Table 9.2 includes appropriate and inappropriate practices regarding physical fitness.

Health-Related Fitness Testing

Fitness tests are currently used by some states as program assessment and to track fitness levels of students, but the primary purpose of testing fitness is to give students and teachers feedback on students' health-related fitness levels and to help students set personal fitness goals. What you don't want to do is test to see where students are in their fitness levels and then do nothing with the data

to improve student fitness levels. Many programs use fitness tests as a self-testing activity that allows students to track their improvement over time.

There are several youth fitness test batteries now available to provide an overall assessment of physical fitness. Two youth fitness test batteries are the President's Challenge and Fitnessgram. The President's Challenge test is norm referenced, which means that a student's score is based on where he or she stands in relation to all other students who took the test. The Fitnessgram is criterion referenced, which means that if a student meets or does not meet a criterion he or she gets the same score regardless of other scores on the test. In a criterion-referenced test you could potentially have every student pass (or every student fail).

Fitnessgram

Fitnessgram offers a complete battery of health-related fitness tests that are scored using criterion-referenced standards. It is used for evaluating the five components of health-related fitness: aerobic capacity (cardiorespiratory fitness), muscular strength, muscular endurance, flexibility, and body composition. It is easy to use and comes with software that allows teachers and schools to easily produce reports and download data. The following tests are part of the Fitnessgram battery.

1. Aerobic capacity: Select from the PACER (a 20-meter progressive shuttle run), a one-mile walk or run, or a walk test.

2. Muscle strength, endurance, and flexibility: Use a curl-up test (abdominal endurance), trunk lift (trunk extensor strength and flexibility), push-up, pull-up, flexed arm hang or modified pull-up (upper body strength), sit-and-reach (back and hamstring flexibility), and shoulder stretch (shoulder flexibility).

3. Body composition: Select from a skinfold test to measure percentage of body fat (measurements at the triceps and calf) or body mass index (calculated from height and weight).

Each Fitnessgram item identifies a minimal level necessary to achieve health in that component, which places the student in the Healthy Fitness Zone. For example, for a 10-year-old boy, the Healthy Fitness Zone for push-ups is 7 to 20 push-ups (see table 9.3). The 10-year-old boy would need to do at least seven push-ups to move into the Healthy Fitness Zone in muscular strength. For practical reasons, when the test is administered, students stop at 20 even if they can do more than that.

FIGURE 9.2

Harmful Exercises

Safe Alternatives

Double Leg Lift

This causes the back to arch and puts pressure on the spine.

Reverse Curl

This helps strengthen lower abdominal muscles without excessive stretch on lower back. Lift the knees to chest, raising hips off the floor, but do not let the knees go past the shoulders. Return to starting position and repeat.

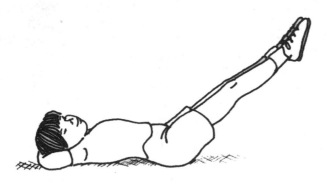

Straight Leg Sit-Up With Hands Behind the Head

This causes excessive stress on the spine and lower back. It causes pulling and hyperflexion on the neck.

Bent Knee Sit-Up

This helps strengthen abdominal muscles. Cross arms over chest with hands on shoulders; tighten up abdominal muscles and rise up to touch elbows to thighs. Then return to starting position and repeat.

Curl-Ups

This helps strengthen abdominal muscles. Put fingers on the side of the head to support the neck; tighten up abdominal muscles; lift shoulders and hold for 6 or more seconds. Then relax to starting position.

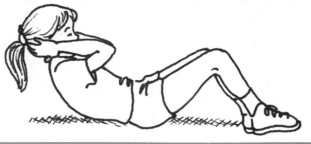

Harmful Exercises

Deep Knee Bend

This causes hyperflexion, stretching, and stress to the knee joint.

Standing Toe Touch With Straight Legs

This causes stretching of the ligaments and joint capsule of the knee.

Safe Alternatives

Forward Lunge

To stretch the quadricep, hip, and thigh muscles, take a step forward with the right foot, touching left knee to floor. Knees should be bent no further than 90 degrees. Repeat with the other foot.

Toe Touch With Slightly Bent Knees

This stretches the hamstring muscles and avoids straining the knee ligaments.

(continued)

(continued)

| **Harmful Exercises** | **Safe Alternatives** |

Neck Circles

Tipping the head backward during any exercise can pinch arteries and nerves in the neck and put pressure on the discs.

Neck Stretch

Instead of tipping the head back, stretch the neck muscles by dropping the head forward and slowly moving it in a half circle to the right and then left.

Donkey Kick

Hyperextension and arching of the lower back results when foot position is higher than the buttocks.

Knee-to-Nose Touch

To strengthen the buttocks muscles, keep the back straight with the leg in line with the back; keep head straight and in line with the back. Focus eyes at the floor.

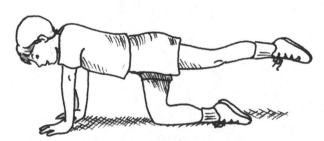

Harmful Exercises

Ballistic Bar Stretch

This is potentially harmful to the knee joint when the extended leg is raised 90 degrees or more and the trunk is bent over the leg.

Hurdler's Stretch

This puts the knee in a rotated position, which can cause excess stretching of the ligaments and damage to the cartilage.

Safe Alternatives

Back-Saver Toe Touch

To stretch the hamstrings, sit with one foot against the wall or extended out with one knee bent. Clasp hands behind the back and bend forward, keeping lower back as straight as possible.

Hamstring Stretch

To stretch the hamstring and calf muscles, lie on the back with knees bent. Raise one leg and grasp toes while pulling on back of thigh. Push heel toward ceiling and hold. Repeat with the other leg.

TABLE 9.2

Appropriate Practices for Physical Fitness in the Elementary School Environment

Appropriate practice	Inappropriate practice
EXERCISE AND THE USE OF EXERCISE AS PUNISHMENT	
▪ In their physical education class, elementary school children are taught the purpose of exercise, health-related fitness components, correct procedures for exercise, and the different exercise categories—stretching, strength, and so on—used to develop each component of fitness. They experience a variety of exercises within each type, which provides them with the knowledge and ability to select exercises to match the purpose. Children are taught the difference between correct and counterproductive exercise, enabling them to be wise consumers of fitness information and decreasing the likelihood of engaging in potentially harmful exercise. ▪ Exercises (e.g., curl-ups, push-ups) are taught as positive physical activity learning experiences but are not a primary part of elementary physical education.	▪ Children perform standard calisthenics routinely with no specific purpose in mind and without following safe, appropriate techniques. ▪ Exercises are used that compromise body alignment and place unnecessary stress on the joints and muscles (e.g., deep knee bends, ballistic stretches, standing toe touches). ▪ The time or number of repetitions for any individual exercise is insufficient to provide a warm-up or affect the designated muscle group(s). ▪ Exercise (running or push-ups, and so on) is used as a punishment for misbehavior or lack of participation.
DEVELOPING HEALTH-RELATED FITNESS	
▪ Children participate in activities that are designed to help them understand the concepts of health-related fitness and to value the contributions they make to a healthy lifestyle. Activity-based fitness is emphasized rather than fitness through formal exercises or calisthenics. ▪ Fitness is presented as a positive experience in which students feel socially and emotionally comfortable, able to overcome challenges on a personal level. The joy of participation in health-enhancing activity leading to lifetime fitness is the goal of fitness development in elementary school physical education.	▪ The teacher requires participation in group fitness activities but does not help students understand the reasons for fitness development. The process of fitness development is not monitored, and guidance for setting personal goals and strategies for goal attainment is not provided. ▪ All children are required to do the same fitness activities regardless of their fitness levels. ▪ Teachers do not teach students the difference between health-related and skill-related fitness. ▪ Calisthenics or mass exercise is *the* avenue for fitness development.

TABLE 9.3

Healthy Fitness Zone Scores

Age	PACER (no. of laps)		Curl-up (no. completed)		Push-up (no. completed)		Back-saver sit-and-reach* (inches)		Body mass index	
BOYS										
8	Participation		6	20	5	13	8		20	15.1
9	Lap count not recommended		9	24	6	15	8		20	13.7
10	23	61	12	24	7	20	8		21	14.0
GIRLS										
8	Participation		6	20	5	13	9		22	16.2
9	Lap count not recommended		9	22	6	15	9		23	13.5
10	7	41	12	26	7	15	9		23.5	13.7

*Test scored pass/fail; must reach this distance to pass.

Fitnessgram computer software includes a reporting system for students and parents. Students with favorable scores (i.e., those in the Healthy Fitness Zone) receive congratulatory feedback and reminders to maintain physical activity levels. Students with scores in the "Needs Improvement" category receive prescriptive feedback about how to improve their scores. See figure 9.3 for a sample Fitnessgram report.

The President's Challenge Test

The President's Challenge offers several different programs including the Physical Fitness Test and the Health Fitness Test. The Physical Fitness Test assesses a student's basic level of physical fitness in five events: curl-ups or partial curl-ups, shuttle run, endurance run/walk, pull-ups or right angle push-ups, and V-sit or sit-and-reach. The Health Fitness Test is used to assess a healthy level of fitness in each of five events: partial curl-up, one-mile run/walk, V-sit (or sit-and-reach), right angle push-up (or pull-up), and body mass index.

Guidelines for Fitness Testing

Rather than emphasize a child's fitness score, it is more important to emphasize regular participation in physical activity.

- Fitness experiences should always be fun and enjoyable for children.
- Fitness assessment should be part of an ongoing process intended to help children understand and improve and maintain their fitness.
- Fitness results should be shared privately with children and their parents for developing personal goals for maintaining and increasing a health-enhancing level of fitness.
- Children should be rewarded for progress, and one child's scores should not be compared to those of another.
- Fitness tests should not be administered for the purpose of recognizing children to receive awards but rather to reinforce the establishment of physical activity behaviors that will lead to lifetime fitness.

The examples in table 9.4 of inappropriate and appropriate practice in regard to fitness testing should clarify the role of fitness testing in the elementary school.

Appropriate Fitness Activities for Children

For children, fitness is a process developed and maintained through enjoyable physical activities. Children should begin to identify favorite activities that become part of their physically active lifestyle. Jumping rope, climbing on playground equipment, or riding a bike provides daily bouts of physical activity that serve to develop and/or maintain fitness. The games chapter (chapter 7) in this book and on the CD-ROM for the book include games and activities that will promote physical activity in children. The Physical Best (2005) program also provides an excellent source of activities that will engage students in physical activity and promote fitness. To increase fitness levels through activity, you will want to choose activities that do the following:

- Engage the student in vigorous activity like running. Select tag games, scavenger hunts, activities that require jumping, and small-sided team games like soccer and basketball.
- Develop muscular strength and endurance. For upper body strength, choose weight-bearing activities like climbing, hanging, and swinging or parachute fitness activities.
- Develop flexibility. Choose activities that take the joint through a full range of motion. Examples are striking, kicking, gymnastics, climbing, and swinging activities.

Physical education will include a full range of fitness activities as part of a comprehensive program. What follows are several activities that the classroom teacher can use to promote and enhance physical fitness.

Rope Jumping for Fitness and Fun

Rope jumping is an excellent physical activity for improving cardiorespiratory fitness, muscle strength, and muscle endurance. Because it is an aerobic activity, it can help with body composition as well. Additional benefits include increased coordination and rhythm. Trying out new rope turning and jumping skills also provides opportunity for personal challenge. The minimal cost and space requirements of rope jumping increase the likelihood of continued participation throughout adulthood as part of a physically active lifestyle.

Rope jumping activities may be individual or may be performed with a partner or in a small

FITNESS**GRAM**®

Felicia Fitness
Grade: 6   Age: 13

Your scores on 4 of 6 test items were in or above the Healthy Fitness Zone. Scoring in the Healthy Fitness Zone will help you look and feel better. Keep up the good work!

Instructor: Sally Smith

	Date	Height	Weight
Current:	11/14/04	5' 1"	105 lbs

AEROBIC CAPACITY

	Needs Improvement	Healthy Fitness Zone

The PACER
Current: 34

VO2Max
VO2max is based on your aerobic test item score. It indicates your ability to perform activity such as running, cycling, or strenuous activities and sports at a high level. Healthy Fitness Zone begins at 36.
Current: 44

MUSCLE STRENGTH, ENDURANCE, & FLEXIBILITY

(Abdominal) Curl-Up
Current: 23

(Trunk Extension) Trunk Lift
Current: 8

(Upper Body) Push-Up
Current: 5

(Flexibility) Back-Saver Sit and Reach R, L
Current: 11.00, 10.00

BODY COMPOSITION

Percent Body Fat

Healthy Fitness Zone	Needs Improvement

Very Low
Current: 25.74

Being too lean or too heavy may be a sign of (or lead to) health problems.

ACTIVITY

On how many of the past 7 days did you participate in physical activity for a total of 30-60 minutes, or more, over the course of the day?

On how many of the past 7 days did you do exercises to strengthen or tone your muscles?

On how many of the past 7 days did you do exercises to loosen up or relax your muscles?

Number of Days

MESSAGES

Your aerobic capacity score is in the Healthy Fitness Zone. To maintain fitness, you should be active most days of the week. Try to play active games, sports, or other activities you enjoy a total of 60 minutes each day.

Felicia, your body composition is in the Healthy Fitness Zone. To maintain this level, it is important to do physical activity most days. You should also eat a healthy diet.

Your abdominal strength is in the Healthy Fitness Zone. To maintain your fitness, do curl-ups or other abdominal exercises 3 to 5 days each week.

Your flexibility is in the Healthy Fitness Zone. Maintain your fitness by stretching slowly 3 or 4 days each week, holding the stretch 20-30 seconds.

You can improve your trunk extension by doing repeated trunk lifts in a slow, controlled manner. Do these exercises 3 to 5 days each week.

To improve your upper-body strength, do modified push-ups, push-ups, and climbing activities. Do these exercises 2 to 3 days each week.

Healthy Fitness Zone for 13 year-old girls
  The PACER = 23 - 51 laps
  Curl-Up = 18 - 32 repetitions
  Trunk Lift = 9 - 12 inches
  Push-Up = 7 - 15 repetitions
  Back-Saver Sit and Reach =
    At least 10 inches on R & L
  Percent Body Fat = 13.00 - 32.00 %

To be healthy and fit it is important to do some physical activity almost every day. Aerobic exercise is good for your heart and body composition. Strength and flexibility exercises are good for your muscles and joints.

Figure 9.3   Sample Fitnessgram computer report.

TABLE 9.4

Appropriate Practices for Physical Fitness Testing in the Elementary School Environment

Appropriate practice	Inappropriate practice
■ Teachers use fitness assessment as part of the ongoing process of helping children understand, enjoy, and improve or maintain their physical fitness and well-being. ■ Test results are shared privately with children and their parents as a tool for developing personal goals and strategies for maintaining and increasing the respective fitness parameters. ■ As part of an ongoing program of physical education, children are physically prepared in each fitness component so that they can safely complete the assessments. (Assessment packages, such as Fitnessgram, provide a scientifically based fitness assessment, while educational materials such as those of Physical Best are essential for providing the scientific and health-related background necessary for comprehensive fitness education for effectively implementing health-related fitness education.)	■ Teachers administer physical fitness tests once or twice each year for the purpose of identifying children to receive awards or to meet a requirement of the school district or state department. ■ Children complete physical fitness test batteries without understanding why they are performing the tests or the relationship to their activity level and individual goals. Results are interpreted based on comparison to norms rather than in terms of how they apply to children's future health and well-being. ■ Individual scores are publicly posted, comparisons are made between student scores, or grades are based on fitness scores. ■ Children are required to take fitness tests without adequate conditioning.

group. Appropriate rope jumping activities for primary children should involve a stationary rope placed on the floor in either a straight line or a shape. Many primary-level children cannot jump a self-turned rope; however, by third grade all children who have had some rope jumping experiences should be able to jump a self-turned rope continuously. All children enjoy jumping long ropes that are turned by others.

Activities for rope jumping are grouped into three categories: (1) movements guided by rope patterns, (2) long-rope jumping, and (3) short-rope jumping.

Movements Guided by Rope Patterns

When the jump rope is placed on the floor, many of the activities involve jumping, hopping, or moving from one end of the rope to the other or moving in and out of a shape. When jumping, children should take off on two feet and land on two feet; when hopping, they should take off from one foot and land on one foot. Remind children to always land on their feet. Some children find enjoyment in landing or sliding on their knees. This should be discouraged for safety reasons and in an effort to encourage quality movement.

Ask children to place their rope on the floor in a straight line away from others. There should be

ample space for moving around the rope. The following are instructions that you can give:

1. Stand at one end of your rope. See if you can jump to the other end of your rope.

2. See how many jumps it takes to get back to the other end of your rope.

3. This time swing your arms and see how far you can jump, trying to jump the full length of the rope.

4. Jump back to the other end taking as few jumps as possible.

5. This time jump from one side of the rope to the other while traveling to the other end.

6. This time jog around your rope.

7. Stand at one end of your rope; now hop to the other end.

8. Now arrange your rope in a shape different from a straight line, perhaps a circle or a square.

9. Jump across the shape.

10. Hop into the shape and hop out.

11. Arrange your rope into a letter of the alphabet.

12. Stand at the bottom of the letter and jump across it.

Long-Rope Jumping

Beginning jumpers enjoy long ropes because they do not have to focus on turning the rope in addition to jumping. Long ropes should be heavy enough to keep the rhythm; beaded ropes constructed of heavy plastic sections are recommended. Long ropes should be 9 to 14 feet (2.7 to 4.3 meters) in length depending upon the age and skill of the jumper. The longer the rope, the more difficult it is to turn.

Children should be taught correct technique for turning a long rope. The rope should be held at waist level in front of the body. When turning the rope the elbow should be kept close to the body and the rope turned using the forearm. The rope should barely touch the floor at the bottom of each turn.

Children enjoy running in or entering the long rope while the rope is being turned. Entering on the side where the rope is moving toward the jumper after reaching its peak is known as entering the front door. A back door entry is from the side where the rope is moving away from the jumper. Entering a turning rope is easiest from an angle. To enter, a jumper stands by the turner and moves to the center of the rope. See figure 9.4 for long-rope activities.

Short-Rope Jumping

After children gain the rhythmical jumping skills required for long-rope jumping, they are usually ready to progress to short-rope jumping. Much like long-rope jumping, short-rope jumping provides fitness and skill benefits. Short-rope jumping plays a significant role in conditioning.

The length of the rope is dependent on the height of the jumper. The rope should be long enough that the handles reach the armpits or slightly higher on a person who is standing on the center of the rope.

FIGURE 9.4

Long-Rope Activities

The following long-rope activities are arranged in order of difficulty, beginning with less difficult activities and progressing to more challenging tasks:

1. Snake in the Grass. Turners hold the rope low to the ground and wiggle the rope back and forth on the floor. Jumpers try to jump over the rope without touching it.

2. Ocean Waves. Turners move their arms up and down, making waves in the rope. Jumpers try to jump over the rope without touching it as it moves.

3. The jumper stands between the turners near the center of the rope with back facing the rope. The turners use three pendulum swings, then turn the rope over the jumper's head and continue turning until the jumper misses.

4. Long-rope jump: The jumper stands at the center of the rope. Turners turn the rope overhead of the jumper. The jumper, keeping feet together and landing on the balls of the feet, jumps the rope each time it passes under the feet.

5. The jumper runs through the turning rope by entering front door and following the rope through without jumping.

6. The jumper enters the front door of a turning rope, jumps once, and then exits.

7. Front door tasks, done after the jumper runs in the front door:
   - Jump the letters in first name, then exit.
   - Jump the letters in last name, then exit.
   - Jump the letters of the alphabet, then exit.
   - Hop on one foot four times, then the other foot four times, then exit.
   - Jump four quarter-turns in one direction, then exit.
   - Dribble a basketball while jumping.

8. Back door entry: Turners turn the rope away from the incoming jumper. The incoming jumper stands near the right shoulder of the left rope turner. The jumper watches the rope closely as it hits the

ground and swings away from them. When the rope is at the top, the jumper runs through the "open window," exiting near the right turner's right shoulder.

9. Back door—jump—exit: Jumper does a back door entry, jumps the rope once, and then exits by the right turner's right shoulder. Then he or she reenters back door near right turner's left shoulder. Jumpers repeat this figure-eight pattern four times. They can take turns doing this pattern four times.

10. Children play school by jumping a number of times to pass a grade level. To pass kindergarten, the jumper must run through the front door of the turning rope. To pass first grade, the jumper enters the turning rope, jumps one time, and runs out. The game progresses as jumpers take the same number of jumps as the grade level.

11. When children can jump continuously, they enjoy simple counting chants such as the following:
    - Tick tock, tick tock.
    - What's the time on the clock?
    - It's one, two, three (up to 12 midnight).
    - I like milk, I like tea,
    - How many boys (girls) are wild about me?
    - One, two, three (and so on).
    - Hippity hop to the butcher shop,
    - How many times before I stop?
    - One, two, three (and so on).
    - Nathan, Nathan (student's name) at the gate,
    - Eating cherries from a plate.
    - How many cherries did he (she) eat?
    - One, two, three (and so on).

12. Hot Pepper: Turners begin by slowly turning the rope toward the jumper. The jumper enters front door and jumps the rope. The turners progressively turn the rope faster and faster. The following are sample Hot Pepper chants:
    - Mabel, Mabel (student's name), set the table.
    - Bring the plates if you are able.
    - Don't forget the salt and
    - Red hot pepper!
    - (On the words "Red hot pepper," the rope is turned as fast as possible.)
    - Ice cream, ginger ale, soda water, pop.
    - You get ready 'cause we're gonna turn hot!

13. Partner stunts: Turners turn the rope front door. Two jumpers, or partners, start in the middle together. Partners explore different ways of jumping together:
    - Jump facing each other and holding hands
    - Jump side by side holding hands
    - Jump-turn away from each other
    - Invent a partner stunt

14. Once children can perform stunts, they enjoy performing them to stunt chants such as the following:
    - Teddy Bear, Teddy Bear, turn around.
    - Teddy Bear, Teddy Bear, touch the ground.
    - Teddy Bear, Teddy Bear, show your shoe.
    - Teddy Bear, Teddy Bear, jump-turn too.
    - Teddy Bear, Teddy Bear, go upstairs.
    - Teddy Bear, Teddy Bear, say your prayers.
    - Teddy Bear, Teddy Bear, turn out the light.
    - Teddy Bear, Teddy Bear, say good night.

Generally, primary-level children need 7-foot (2.1-meter) ropes, with a few 6- and 8-foot (1.8- and 2.4-meter) lengths available. Children in grades 3 through 5 need a mixture of 7- and 8-foot rope lengths.

Good posture is essential in rope jumping. See figure 9.5 for instructions on how to turn a short rope. The body should be in good alignment, with the head up and eyes looking straight ahead. The jump is made with the body in an erect position. While turning the rope, the elbows should be kept close to the sides of the body, and the wrists should be used to supply the force to turn the rope. Many children mistakenly lift the arm in effort to get the rope overhead rather than making small circles with the wrists. Soft landings should be made on the balls of the feet, with the knees slightly bent to absorb force. See figure 9.6 for short-rope activities.

Activities for Fitness Fun

Many activities and games that are teacher directed provide opportunities for children to jump and run. Children enjoy activities that are game-like and offer lots of opportunity to move. Music also provides for additional enjoyment. See figure 9.7 for sample activities.

Parachute Fitness

The parachute is a popular item with elementary school children and provides an excellent medium for enhancing physical fitness. Fitness routines can be developed through exercise movements with

Appropriate rope length promotes proper technique for skillful rope jumping.

children holding on to the parachute with one or both hands or locomotor movements in clockwise or counterclockwise directions. See figure 9.8 for fitness activities performed with a parachute.

FIGURE 9.5

Jumping a Short Rope (Self-Turned)

1. Stand with good posture, a jump rope handle in each hand, with the rope touching the ground behind the heels. Elbows are kept close to the body. Eyes are looking ahead.

2. Lift for the jump by straightening the knees. The jump should be about 1 inch in height. The jump needs to be only high enough to let the rope pass beneath the feet.

3. The wrists supply the force to turn the rope. With the elbows kept close to the body, small circles are drawn with the rope.

4. Landings should be made on the balls of the feet with the knees slightly bent. Feet should be slightly apart as they take off and land together.

FIGURE 9.6

Short-Rope Activities ⊙

The following are short-rope activities listed in order from least difficult to more challenging:

1. Helicopters: Hold both rope handles in one hand, elbow close to the side. Use small circular wrist movements to swing the rope, which makes a rhythmic sound as it hits the floor on each turn. Make low jumps each time the rope hits the floor.

2. Toe Catch: Start with rope at heels. Swing it overhead and catch it under the toes.

3. Single jump: Jump once, off both feet, for every turn of the rope.

4. Two-foot basic jump: Starting with rope at the heels, jump over the rope, feet together, making low jumps approximately 1 inch off of the floor.

5. Scissors: Start with feet together. On the first turn of the rope, jump feet apart so that the right foot is forward. On the second turn of the rope, jump so that the left foot is forward. Continue alternating right foot forward and left foot forward.

6. Straddle: Jump and land with feet apart. Jump and land with feet together.

7. Straddle cross ("X"): Jump to a straddle position, keeping feet shoulder-width apart. Then jump again and cross the legs. Alternate the leg in front with each cross.

8. Jogging step: Step over the rope first with the right foot and then the left. Continue to alternate feet, taking one step for each turn of the rope.

9. Rocker: Start with one foot forward; keep that foot in front. As the rope passes under the front foot, shift weight or rock to the front foot, leaning slightly forward and lifting the back foot up for the rope to pass under. Rock from the front foot to the back foot, leaning slightly backward for the rope to pass underneath.

10. Single-side swing and jump: Swing the rope, held in both hands on one side of the body, then open it and jump over it. Swing the rope to the other side, then open it and jump over it. Continue the "swing right jump, swing left jump" pattern.

Creating a Safe and Supportive Environment

It is important that children be successful during physical activity and build positive self-perceptions and self-confidence. To ensure that children achieve success and retain their intrinsic enjoyment of physical activity, consider the following recommendations when teaching fitness to children:

- Do not group students by gender ("boys here and girls there").

- Do encourage students to work with different partners and within diverse groups.

- Do not allow students to make comments or take actions that are hurtful to others.

- Do encourage students to be supportive of peers by making positive comments; encourage their efforts and acknowledge their accomplishments.

- Do not use physical activity as punishment.

- Do find ways to make physical activity fun for all children.

- Do find ways to make all children feel that they are included and respected.

- Do help children realize that learning involves making mistakes and that it is okay to make them; mistakes happen, and that's okay.

- Do help children understand that improvements in fitness or the components of fitness do not occur quickly but instead gradually over time through regular physical activity.

FIGURE 9.7

Fitness Activities

In, Out, Around (Grades K-3)

Equipment: Music, whistle, one hula hoop for each child.

Organization: Scatter the hoops throughout the area, leaving enough room on the outside for students to jog. Children should also be in scatter formation throughout the play area, standing outside of the hoops.

Procedure: Determine three signals, such as the following:

- One short whistle—travel throughout the area.
- Two short whistles—jump in and out of a hoop.
- Three short whistles—run around the outside of the hoop area.

When the music begins, children perform a locomotor movement, traveling throughout the area without touching the hoops. When the whistle sounds two short whistles, each child finds a hoop and begins jumping in and out on both feet. On one short whistle sound, the children begin traveling throughout the area again. On three short whistles, they jog around the outside of the hoop area. Continue the activity alternating the whistle signals.

Jump and Jog (Grades 2-5)

Equipment: Music, cones, and one jump rope for every two children.

Organization: Set up cones in a large oval, leaving enough room on the outside for children to jog. Divide children into pairs, with each pair getting a jump rope. The child with the rope stands inside the oval; the other child stands outside the oval.

Procedure: The child on the outside of the oval jogs around the cones counterclockwise while the partner jumps rope in place. Give a signal to switch, such as when the music stops or after 30 to 60 seconds.

FIGURE 9.8

Parachute Activities

The following are fitness activities performed with a parachute:

1. Standing facing the parachute and holding with both hands, do deltoid lifts by raising the parachute with arms extended forward.
2. Standing with right side to the parachute and holding it with the right hand, do lateral deltoid lifts by raising the right arm. Repeat on left side.
3. Jog in a clockwise direction while holding the parachute in the right hand.
4. Shake the parachute.
5. Raise the parachute over the head and then lower to the ground.
6. Slide counterclockwise while holding the parachute with both hands.
7. Sit, holding the parachute with both hands, and perform curl-ups.
8. Place several balls on the parachute, and shake the parachute to send the balls high into the air.
9. In push-up position, shake the parachute with one hand, then the other.
10. Skip while holding the parachute with one hand.
11. Standing facing the parachute and, holding it with one or both hands, do bicep curls.

SUMMARY

1. Physical fitness relates to the ability to perform physical activity.

2. Components of health-related fitness include aerobic capacity, body composition, flexibility, muscular strength, and endurance.
   - Aerobic capacity or cardiorespiratory fitness is the ability of the heart, blood vessels, and lungs to supply the body with oxygen and nutrients during exercise.
   - Body composition is the ratio of body fat to lean body tissue.
   - Flexibility is the range of motion at a joint.
   - Muscular strength is the capacity of a muscle to exert force.
   - Muscular endurance is the capacity of a muscle to perform for an extended period of time.

3. The basic principles of training are the overload principle, specificity of exercise, and progression.

4. There are two approaches to fitness. The exercise prescription orientation approaches fitness through training. The active lifestyle orientation takes a physical activity approach.

5. Elementary school children should develop and maintain fitness through participation in a variety of physical activities.

6. To promote the development of a physically active lifestyle, fitness activities must be fun and enjoyable for children.

7. Two fitness test batteries for assessing youth fitness are Fitnessgram and the President's Challenge. It is more important to emphasize regular participation in physical activity than a child's fitness score.

CHECKING YOUR UNDERSTANDING

1. What is physical fitness? Describe two types.

2. Name and describe the five components of health-related fitness.

3. What are the principles of training, and how do they relate to developing fitness?

4. Describe five harmful stretches and identify safe alternatives.

5. Identify five guidelines to follow for health-related fitness testing.

6. Compare and contrast the exercise approach and the lifetime activity approach to developing and maintaining fitness.

RESOURCES

Be a Fit Kid

http://kidshealth.org/kid/stay_healthy/fit/fit_kid.html

The Cooper Institute—Fitnessgram/Activitygram

www.cooperinst.org/products/grams/index.cfm

Fit Kids Challenge

www.fitkidschallenge.com/

The President's Challenge

www.presidentschallenge.org/

Hinson, C. (1995). *Fitness for children.* Champaign, IL: Human Kinetics.

REFERENCES

American College of Sports Medicine. (1998). Position stand. The recommended quantity and quality of exercise for developing and maintaining cardiorespiratory and muscular fitness, and flexibility in healthy adults. *Medicine and Science in Sports and Exercise*, 30(6), 975-991.

Council on Physical Education for Children. (2000). *Appropriate practices for elementary school physical education: A position statement of the National Association for Sport and Physical Education.* Reston, VA: Author.

Morrow, J.R. Jr., Jackson, A.W., Disch, J.G., & Mood, D.P. (2005). *Measurement and evaluation in human performance* (3rd ed.). Champaign, IL: Human Kinetics.

National Association for Sport and Physical Education. (2005). *Physical best activity guide: Elementary level* (2nd ed.). Champaign, IL: Human Kinetics.

Ratliffe, T., & Ratliffe, L. (1994). *Teaching children fitness: Becoming a master teacher.* Champaign, IL: Human Kinetics.

U.S. Department of Health and Human Services. (1996). *Physical activity and health: A report of the surgeon general.* Atlanta: U.S. Department of Health and Human Services, Centers for Disease Control and Prevention, and National Center for Chronic Disease Prevention and Health Promotion.

10

Administering the Elementary School Physical Activity Program

OVERVIEW

The opportunities for physical activity provided for students during recess (chapter 6), as well as those provided by the classroom teacher as breaks during the school day (chapter 5), have been discussed in previous chapters. Schools may also want to require participation in a morning exercise program (chapters 4 and 5). This chapter focuses on the administration of a physical activity program and on how to organize and deliver physical activity opportunities for children that are *voluntary* as before-school, after-school, or lunchtime programs or special events.

CHAPTER OUTCOMES

This chapter will help you

- identify the needs of students in your school for physical activity and the resources you have to meet those needs,
- identify who is responsible for the planning and conduct of a physical activity program,
- distinguish between those activities appropriate for younger students and those appropriate for older students,
- recruit and train staff to conduct the program,
- work with the community to ensure that all students are participants in physical activity,
- conduct the program in a developmentally appropriate way,
- fund the physical activity program, and
- reinforce participation.

IN THIS CHAPTER

Many children in today's elementary schools have the opportunity to participate in youth sport programs provided by the community. These programs present in-depth opportunities for children to acquire skills in team sports like soccer, youth football, basketball, and baseball or softball and individual sports like swimming, gymnastics, and tennis. They have become more and more expensive for parents, making it increasingly difficult and in many cases impossible for many children to be participants. Children also tend to specialize in one or two sports, limiting the experiences of an age group that probably should not be specializing but instead participating in a wide variety of types of physical activities. The school physical activity program should focus on providing all children the opportunity to be participants in many different physical activities through after-school, before-school, and lunchtime programs (chapter 11).

Opportunities for physical activity within a community vary widely from community to community. The school does not need to compete with these programs but rather should work with the community in several ways. Schools can (1) facilitate the participation of students in community programs and events; (2) supplement community programs by providing a wider range of activities of interest, particularly for those students who may not be interested in competitive sport or who for family reasons or financial reasons cannot participate; and (3) help students feel a school affiliation by running school events.

Who Is Responsible for the Physical Activity Program of the School?

The state of South Carolina has legislated that every elementary school appoint a physical activity director to plan the program and ensure that every student in the school gets at least 30 minutes of combined physical education and physical activity a day. In most cases this person is a physical education teacher. However, the physical education teacher cannot function in this role without the input and support of others in the school setting. Figure 10.1 reflects one physical education teacher's efforts to work with classroom teachers to increase the physical activity levels of students at her school, and the CD-ROM also shows a brochure designed to help teachers. A physical activity program is a *school* program that is the responsibility of the entire school and not the sole responsibility of the physical education teacher. School administrative and faculty support is critical to the success of any program. The support of the school wellness council (see chapter 2) will also be critical. While it is likely that the initiative for setting up a comprehensive physical activity program will come from either the school administration or the physical education teacher, responsibility for the design and conduct of the program needs to be assigned to an established committee. Figure 10.2 lists the potential participants of a school physical activity committee.

FIGURE 10.1

Working With the Classroom Teacher

As the school physical activity director, Cindy Wilkerson shares how she convinced teachers to increase physical activity in the school day. Cindy is the physical education teacher at Springdale Elementary School in West Columbia, South Carolina. Here's how Cindy describes an in-service session she conducted with teachers.

During a full-day teacher in-service, I shared with teachers the research supporting the need to increase physical activity in a child's day. I emphasized the connection between physical activity and academic success. The faculty learned how to best create, collaborate on, and implement activities for their classrooms. They were excited about using movement as a way to enhance what they were already teaching. In grade-level groups the teachers were to come up with examples to share with others. These are a few of their examples:

■ The third grade teachers teach the concept of perimeters. They decided that students could walk the perimeter of a rectangle to music and sing a *High School Musical* song.

■ Our third grade curriculum includes South Carolina history. The teachers decided that they could incorporate our state dance, the Shag, into a lesson by playing beach music, tying strips of cloth to individual desks to use as a partner, and teaching the students basic shag steps. How well the students got the dance was not going to be the concern, just that they were moving to the music and aware of the popularity of the dance.

■ The fifth grade curriculum includes alliteration. The teachers decided to use a song that I had learned at a youth retreat called "Alive, Awake, Alert, Enthusiastic"; at the end of a verse, students would shout out an onomatopoetic word accompanied by movement (e.g., shout "Bam!" and stomp their foot and throw their hands in the air).

I also shared activities with the teachers and had them participate:

■ In kindergarten, students are taught "popcorn words" to help them with reading. To share this idea with the faculty, I read from a book, and they would jump up out of their seats every time they heard a popcorn word.

■ We participated in an activity called Acid Lake that requires teamwork. This type of activity is a great way to start the school year and set the tone for a cooperative learning environment.

These are some ideas for a schoolwide focus:

■ *Documenting out-of-school physical activity.* Students are asked to document any time they are active at home, for example when playing outside, walking, participating in soccer practice, dancing, or bicycling, or when doing chores such as vacuuming, raking, helping to plant a garden, or washing the car. The objective is to raise awareness of what students are doing at home. Students are responsible for keeping up with their recording sheets and turning them in weekly. The two students that have the highest number of minutes each week are recognized during morning announcements.

■ *Staying hydrated.* We discussed the importance of nutrition and of allowing students to keep water bottles at their desk. Many studies show the importance of hydration to retention of information.

■ *Communicating to parents.* We decided as a faculty to partner with the home to provide the best possible environment for our children. One plan was to send out weekly brochures with important information about nutrition and movement, as well as other types of information that we feel is relevant to the well-being of children.

This was our first-year plan, but many teachers have expressed an interest in continuing to improve and expand our schoolwide physical activity program next year.

The nutrition and movement brochures were used to help teachers with the process. See brochure.pdf on the CD-ROM.

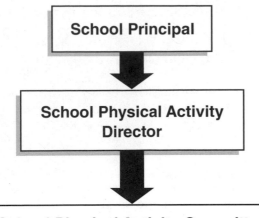

School Principal

School Physical Activity Director

School Physical Activity Committee

- School wellness council member
- Parent
- Community recreation leader (public)
- Community recreation leader (private)
- School officer (PTA/PTO)
- Classroom teacher

Figure 10.2 Administrative flowchart for a physical activity committee.

These are the responsibilities of the school physical activity committee:

- To do an analysis of student needs on a regular basis
- To make recommendations to the school principal on the policy governing the physical activity program
- To plan the program
- To oversee the conduct of the program

The school principal will have the ultimate responsibility for the program and thus will be a key player in approving any policy decisions made by the school's physical activity committee. The school principal will not have the professional expertise needed to plan an appropriate program for children and to conduct a program, making the school faculty and particularly the physical education teacher(s) key players in establishing policy. It is important to establish policies for the program in relation to these questions:

- What types of activities will be provided (after school, lunchtime, before school, special events [see chapter 11])?
- How will the program be staffed?

- Will contracts with community agencies and facilities be permitted?
- Will community personnel be recruited for participation?
- Will physical education teachers and other school personnel be pursued to conduct the program?
- How will the program be funded?
  - By participants in the program (either all, or based on need)?
  - By school funds?
  - By grants?
  - By fund-raisers?
- Will you pay the staff or use volunteers?
- Will you use professionals or nonprofessionals?
- Who will do the scheduling and administration of the program (staffing, paperwork, records, and so on)?

Answering all of these important questions before the establishment of a comprehensive program is the responsibility of the physical activity committee.

Clearly defining the roles of the physical education teacher, classroom teacher, physical activity committee, and administrator is important. The degree to which complex policies and procedures need to be established, as well as the complexity of the administrative structure governing the physical activity program, will depend on the size of the program, the number of people involved in running the program, and the nature of their involvement. Beginning programs run primarily by the physical education teacher with the help of a few parent volunteers will not need a complex organization. The physical education teacher plans most of the program; gets approval for the program from the school principal; recruits parents, other teachers, and volunteers for activities and events; and reports to the school administrator. As the program grows, clearly defining the roles of teachers, parents, and administrators becomes more important. As programs increase in size, they should have policies and procedures regarding the following:

■ **Administrative responsibility.** Who is in charge of what aspects of the program? Who has the authority to initiate or say that the school will run or participate in a particular program? Who will recruit staff? Fire staff? Establish and administer the budget? Require the participation of other teachers? Establish policy?

■ **The use of volunteers and nonteachers.** Who may work with students? How will these people be recruited? What will be their qualifications? Whom will they report to? Will they need to be supervised? What kind of training will they need? What is the legal liability of the school? What documents need to be in a personnel file? How will these personnel be evaluated?

■ **Transportation issues.** What transportation is available for travel outside the school to special events or community facilities or for after-school programs? How much will it cost? If parents provide transportation, what qualifications do they have? What are the legal liabilities involved in school or volunteer transportation?

■ **Budget issues.** Regardless of the source of income for a program, policies and procedures need to be established regarding the way funds are procured and the way they are spent. While states usually have very specific policies regarding the use of state funds, monies collected either by fundraising or by charging participants must be handled with consistent policy. Who pays what for what services? How are salaries or salary supplements decided? What forms for collecting funds or hiring or paying people need to be on record?

Analyzing the Opportunities for Participation and the Level of Participation

Before decisions are made about what to offer in a school physical activity program, an analysis of who is participating in the community and what they are participating in needs to be performed. In communities where the youth program in a sport or activity is very strong and students in a school are largely participants, there is probably not a need to duplicate that activity. Organized sport in most communities, however, is limited to a few activities offered through either recreation leagues or commercial groups; and in many lower-income schools, a very small percentage of students are participants. Youth sport programs are also limited to a season. Children may play soccer in the fall and do nothing the rest of the year. Doing an analysis of the population of the school in terms of participation in youth sport, as well as an analysis of what the community offers, will help identify potential voids in student opportunity for participation and the types of experiences needed.

One of the first things program administrators need to do is to analyze (1) what students are already doing with respect to physical activity, (2) what opportunities the community provides that

students are already participating in, and (3) what resources the school may have for supplementing those opportunities. An analysis of the opportunities for the school's students to participate in physical activity, under the auspices of the school or in the community, will help the physical activity program committee and administrator decide on the specific needs for programming. Figure 10.3 is an example of a physical activity questionnaire sent home to parents to get information on the level of participation in physical activity of students. Analyzing the information that you receive will allow you to set priorities to determine an action plan.

It is very likely that the needs of the primary grades will be different from those of the intermediate grades. It would be a good idea to consider a plan that divides the school population into kindergarten and first, second and third, and fourth and fifth grades.

What Are the Needs of Different Age Groups?

Older children (grades 4 and 5) will need and want to participate in more organized types of activities than younger children. Intramural and

Figure 10.3 Sample physical activity parent questionnaire.

club activities that afford the student opportunities to learn and apply skills are appropriate. For most children in this group, instruction, performance, and competition are attractive. Younger students will need opportunities to just play.

Activities Appropriate for Older Students

When you have surveyed parents to gather information on the participation of students in your school, you will probably find that a lot of students participate in youth sport clubs offered by community public and private organizations. You want to make sure that you are providing enough variety to attract the students who would not normally participate in these community activities. Intramural team sport activities are certainly appropriate; but jump rope clubs, gymnastics, walking or jogging clubs, swimming, tennis, golf, and dance clubs are examples of the kinds of activities that older elementary children not involved in sport are likely to find enjoyable. Activities can meet one or two times per week, and the seasons should be short to maintain interest. Intramural and club activities for this age group should also include instruction, and competition should be deemphasized. The following are kinds of organized and voluntary activities appropriate for upper elementary students:

- *Tournaments:* Short competitions between teams (e.g., Four Square, tetherball, pickleball)

- *Contests:* One-time events—competition in a specific skill (e.g., free throw contest, slow bicycle race, softball throw for distance, football kick for distance)
- *Clubs:* Long-term participation in an activity, usually individual activities (e.g., walking club, swimming, tennis)
- *Special events:* One-time or short-term events (e.g., 5K marathon, field trips)
- *Community opportunities:* After-school YMCA programs, golf, church leagues, swimming, recreation center activities

Activities Appropriate for Younger Students

Younger students (grades K-3) will primarily need opportunities to be active. The program provided for younger students will involve low organization kinds of games, as well as loosely structured but supervised opportunities for children to use both manipulative equipment and large playground and gymnastics equipment and to organize their own play (see chapter 7).

What Resources Does the School Already Have?

The best place to start in thinking about what resources you need is considering those you already have. The skills and willingness to be a participant

A program about walking your child to and from school can eliminate much of the line up of cars waiting for over an hour to drop students off and pick them up from school.

on the part of the faculty at a school will be your biggest resource. What skills do the classroom teachers, administrators, and support staff have that can be used in the program?

Most elementary schools have an indoor gym and one or more large all-purpose rooms, a cafeteria, and classrooms that can be used before or after school. They will also have a blacktop area outside (many with basketball courts), tetherball posts, and field space (usually a soccer and baseball field). It is also frequently possible to block off parking areas after school for added blacktop space.

There are two potential sources of equipment if funds are limited. The first is the physical education program; the second includes the secondary schools in a district and community agencies or commercial operations. Many of these latter are more than willing to let you have equipment for a short period of time if it is cared for and returned in a timely manner.

Scheduling Activities of the Program

Identifying when the activities will be provided is an important factor determined largely on the basis of local issues. All opportunities should be explored.

After School

Whereas most secondary programs find themselves competing with athletic teams for the use of physical education facilities, elementary schools are in a different position. For most elementary schools, competition for facilities is not a problem, making after-school programs a real possibility depending on the need for late transportation for students. In cases in which the majority of students walk to school, the after-school time slot is ideal, particularly in elementary schools that have an early start. In this situation, before-school programs would have to be very early and therefore less desirable.

After-school programs can also be provided by the community. The physical activity committee of the school can make arrangements with both public and commercial providers to run programs targeted to this age group. Instructors may be willing to come to the school. Schools will also want to take advantage of facilities in close proximity but should not be limited by distance if transportation can be provided or if parents are willing to take their children and perhaps others to those venues.

Before School

Many schools offer opportunities for students to come to school early to be participants in physical activity. Before-school walking programs, open gyms, circus skills programs, obstacle courses, and jump roping clubs have become common. When programs are at least 30 to 40 minutes in length, club and intramural types of activities can also be organized.

Lunchtime

Most elementary school–aged children eat fast. It is recommended that children have at least 20 minutes to actually eat their lunch after getting it. This means that standing in line waiting to be served does not count. When more than 45 minutes or an hour is provided for the lunch break in the school day, opportunities for physical activity can be offered during this time. For younger children, this might mean a structured play time of games, opportunities to use manipulative equipment, a walking club, or just an additional recess time. For older children, intramural and club activities can be provided as well.

Special Events

Community special events that focus on physical activity have received a great deal of attention because of the obesity crisis. Child-level marathons, walkathons, bicycle rides, dance-a-thons, walk-your-child-to-school events, and "Be Fit" campaigns flood the media in most communities. Elementary school physical activity programs should be taking advantage of these opportunities by organizing and facilitating the participation of children at a school.

In the past, schools have not done a great deal to promote community opportunities for participation in physical activity. Doing so would help schools achieve their objective to get students involved in physical activity and would help build the resources of many communities for physical activity. When community recreation centers are used and when community activity events have a high level of participation, everyone wins and the community begins to build a culture of being physically active.

When elementary students become participants, parents usually have to be involved in community opportunities. On the one hand this is an advantage. It is a disadvantage because it means that children with parents who can't be involved lose

Community agencies can play a major role in increasing physical activity. Schools need to facilitate that participation.

the opportunity to participate, making the school's role in programming for physical activity even more important.

School programs can increase student participation in special community events by

- informing children, teachers, and parents of the opportunities;
- recruiting faculty to participate;
- signing students up for participation;
- facilitating the transportation issues with school accommodations or parent volunteers;
- organizing school participation at the event; and
- reinforcing the participation of both children and parents.

Budget

Because most physical activity programs do not have an extensive budget, the process of planning the budget is relatively simple. A lot of what you are able to do, beyond using volunteers and using the equipment and facilities of the school, will depend on the financial resources that are devoted to the program or can be raised to support the program.

The biggest expense you will have is staffing the program. You will need people not only to run the activities but also to supervise the program and do the administrative duties of record keeping, payroll, and so on that are connected with large programs. Most of the staff you have will be volunteer and may be willing to work without pay or for a small honorarium. The director of the program (usually the physical education teacher) will need to be paid a salary supplement similar to that received by coaches of athletic teams in the district. You will need funds to pay for transportation if it is to be provided for after-school programs at the school or special events in the community. You will also want to have funds for advertising. If you plan on including activities that require equipment different from that of the physical education program, you will need to have an equipment budget. It is also reasonable to assume that using the physical activity program's equipment will make it important to replace the equipment more often in the physical education program.

The best situation would be to have the school provide funds to meet the budget requirement of a well-run program. In most cases, physical activity programs will need to think about ways to raise additional funds to do the kinds of things they want to do. Fortunately, parents of children in the elementary age group are the most supportive of school programs. The following alternatives for increasing your budget should be considered:

- **School budget.** Many schools can afford to put aside a reasonable amount of money to pay for an activity program that meets the needs of all students in a school.

- **Participation fees.** Students can be charged a nominal fee for participating in an activity, particularly those that are offered before or after school or outside of the school campus. For activities such as bowling or skating at a rink where there is a charge for the program or equipment, student fees may not be a choice. Fees are discriminatory against students who cannot afford them and should be avoided if possible, or reduced or waived under particular circumstances. Many before- or after-school programs provide scholarship funds for indigent families and base the fee requirements on the same information used for meal programs.

- **Fund-raising.** Physical activity programs may have to raise their own funds to conduct the kinds of programs they would like. Elementary school children and parents are accustomed to raising funds for school programs and are often very generous in their contributions. These efforts can be targeted to include events within the school, in which case you would raise funds from the students; efforts outside of the school can involve solicitation of funds from the community. These are some of the many potential approaches to fund-raising:

- Selling products (fruit, magazine subscriptions, stationery, and so on)
- Guessing contests (how many golf tees in the bowl, how many ID cards in the bowl?)
- Class competitions
- Selling jump ropes at the school bookstore
- Faculty–student games
- Field Day T-shirts
- Concession stands at community events
- Carnivals
- Tournaments, for example a golf or tennis tournament
- Garage sale, bake sale
- Healthy drink or snack machine profits
- Sponsorship—monetary or prize donations from businesses and individuals to directly

support the program as a whole or a specific event with the intent of visibility for their products (e.g., World of Music Dance-a-Thon, Harris Chevrolet Basketball League).

The physical activity program council should be given the responsibility of deciding how to raise funds and conducting the fund-raising efforts.

Planning the Program

All good programs start with both a short-term and a long-term plan. The long-term plan should create a vision of what you want the program to be—eventually. The short-term plan specifies actions that you will take first. After you have done a needs assessment, explored the potential for facilities within the school, explored the potential relationships with the community, and explored some potential funding possibilities, you are ready to create a vision of what a long-term plan might be for your program. Figure 10.4 describes the long-term plan for one elementary school.

There are several important ideas to keep in mind when planning a yearly program that are critical to its mission to involve all students in the school in physical activity.

■ *Not all children are interested in the same types of activities.* If you want to reach a large number of children, you will need to offer a range of different types of activities. Team sports, individual activities, free play, dance, leisure-time activities, and fitness-oriented activities will appeal to different students.

■ *Programs need to emphasize participation and not competition.* The school physical activity program is not a youth sport coaching opportunity. Unlike youth sport programs that often tend to overemphasize competition and stress performance, the school program needs to be inclusive of all levels of ability and emphasize the "fun" of participation regardless of how good someone is. The program should never eliminate students who want to be participants.

■ *Events that involve parents are ways to get families to participate.* Although single events like a bowling night, skating night, walkathon, or camping trip are unlikely to provide the regular physical activity students need in and of themselves, they have to the potential to interest families in being participants in these activities on a more regular basis.

■ *Programs need to be short-term.* Long seasons of participation in one activity are inappropriate for most young children. Short seasons with many choices during the year are more appropriate. Some will be okay with a commitment that involves a

Selling t-shirts can be a good fundraiser and an excellent way to promote your program.

FIGURE 10.4

Shady Oak Elementary School Long-Term Physical Activity Plan ⊙

Resources

Number of students: 700

Facilities: One double gym, one all-purpose room, blacktop area with two basketball courts, softball field, large grass field (two soccer fields), school cafeteria, large music room

Personnel: Two physical education teachers, two classroom teachers (one with an interest in fitness and one with an interest in children's dance), 20 parents willing to volunteer two days a week each for a period of six weeks

Funding: Secretarial help provided by the school; PTA fund-raiser for children who cannot afford to pay $1 per session; and scholarships for community participation for children who cannot afford to pay

Before-School Program

Initial (first year):

Walk Around the World (parents invited), all levels

Subsequent years:

Exercise to music (parents and teachers invited), all levels

Lunchtime Program

Initial and subsequent years:

Four Square and tetherball Friday tournaments, upper grades (eight weeks)

Walk and talk program, all levels (continuous)

Organized sign-up: hopscotch, tetherball, Four Square, disc golf (several activities offered on a rotating basis)

Lunchtime aerobics (four weeks in fall, winter, and spring)

After-School Program

Initial—school offerings:

Fall Speedball (small sided), upper grades
   Gymnastics, upper grades

Winter Basketball, upper grades
   Jump Rope for Heart, upper grades
   Dance club

Spring Disc golf, upper grades
   Teacher-pitched softball, upper grades

Subsequent years—school offerings:

Fall Pickleball
   Aerobic dance
   In-line skating

Winter   Fencing (parent skills)

             Volleyball

Spring   Golf

             Tennis

             Archery

Community

These are current community offerings and school events held in the community that will be made available through scholarships to any child who wants to participate:

Fall   Soccer (at recreation center), upper grades

            Fall community marathon/walk

            Swimming (at recreation center), upper grades

            Cycling club, upper grades

Winter   Gymnastics (at gymnastics center), all levels

            Dance club (at church), upper grades

            Bowling night

            Basketball (at church), upper grades

            Ice skating (ice rink)

Spring   Hiking club (community organization), all levels

            Little League

            Tennis

couple of times a week. Some may drop by occasionally for a variety of reasons.

■ *Instruction will be necessary.* Most secondary intramural and after-school programs are organized so that students "play" the game or just do the activity. Although the physical education program should be giving students the skills they need to participate, most elementary-aged students will not have the skills to just play the game and will need instruction followed by opportunities for small-sided game play.

■ *Clubs are more successful if they have a culminating event.* Gymnastics, dance, circus, rope jumping clubs, and so on are more successful if they end in a performance or competition and can be used as an all-school event such as an assembly or evening PTA program.

Staffing the Program

The more activities you offer, the more you will need to provide adult supervision. The first source of staff should be certified teachers. Your first source should be physical education teachers and student teachers, as well as other teachers and staff within the school who have the interest or skills for an activity or are willing to volunteer their assistance with fund-raising activities and promotional efforts. Retired teachers within the community are often willing to work with a program if it does not become a full-time job for them.

A second source of staff is community volunteers with specialized skills or community volunteers with interest in and support for the program who can be trained to help. High school students or college students are another source of volunteers. Community instructors in commercial or public facilities who are committed to promoting their activity are often willing to spend a few weeks at a school to initiate interest in their facility.

The last source of staffing would be paid instructors with specialized skills. These programs may have to charge for participation and give scholarships for students who cannot afford to pay. Most instructors with specialized skills are willing to work for minimum salaries as a contribution to the school's efforts.

Hiring Volunteers

Volunteers within a school program present some problems that can be avoided if you have clear procedures and policies for hiring them. Many well-intentioned volunteers are not prepared for the policies and important procedures of a school that are designed to protect children and protect the school from liability issues in case students are injured. Volunteers should not be hired out of convenience (e.g., because they know somebody in the school). They should be recruited from the population of the community, should fill out a formal application, and should be hired based on their qualifications for a formalized job description and the recommendations they submit with their application. Volunteers should be required to sign a formal contract that clearly identifies the role and responsibilities of the school and the person being hired. A more formal process may deter some good candidates from applying but will ensure that you are getting the best people for the job.

You can recruit volunteers through the school Web site, flyers sent home, or community newspapers or by targeting groups that you know have specialized skills like a community dance group. Chapter 14 shows an example of a recruitment flyer that can be used to solicit volunteers for your program (figure 14.4). The best time to recruit volunteers is in the spring or summer before the school year begins so that the full program can be planned and so that volunteers can plan their own schedule. Having a physical activity program school committee will help a great deal in the planning and conduct of the recruitment and hiring process.

One of the best ways to begin the hiring process is to ask all people who may have an interest in working in the program to come to a meeting at which you explain what the program is, why it is important, and why you need their help. This meeting will also give you an opportunity to communicate the various job descriptions, responsibilities, and school policies in terms of working with volunteers. Volunteers should be asked to fill out an application, and you will need to begin the process of interviewing candidates who seem most qualified.

The interview is important: You should look at it as an opportunity to find out how highly qualified for the job a person is and also as an opportunity for the applicant to find out more about the job and decide if he or she is willing to meet the obligations of the position. Schedule interviews at times that are convenient for the applicants. Use the interview as an opportunity to explain the whole program, why it is important, and what you hope to "build" over time. Go over the job description and the qualifications you are looking for. Try to get a sense of whether the person you are interviewing has the personal skills needed for the position and the time needed to make a commitment to the program. When thinking about the people you are willing to have work with students, consider the following: Why does the person want to do this? Are these reasons compatible with the intent of the program? Does the candidate have the necessary credentials for this particular position or for a different one? How much training will the candidate need? Do you see the candidate staying with the position? Does the candidate relate well to other adults and to students? Is the candidate a good role model? Are the candidate's references positive, and are the people who supplied the references qualified to know whether the candidate can do the job or not? Is the candidate willing to undergo an official background check?

Training Volunteers

After hiring volunteers, it is important to meet with them as a group. This will give you an opportunity to build a sense of "team" and to share with them the goals of the program and information they will need to fulfill their responsibilities. They will need to know things such as these:

- Where to call if I can't make it
- Where to sign in and sign out of the building
- What dress is appropriate for the activity
- Where I get the equipment I need
- What to do if a student is injured; for an after-school program, what to do if a parent doesn't pick up a child
- Whom I report to if I have a problem

Protocols for attendance and record keeping, reporting equipment failures, and so on are all items that can be communicated in a training session and in writing in the form of a "handbook," as well as explained in a training session.

People who don't work in schools are also not usually familiar with polices regarding sexual harassment, injury procedures, HIV (human immunodeficiency virus) policies, and liability issues. They will need to be made aware of all of these issues. Legal liability issues are very real for schools since the schools are entrusted with the care of children and are expected to act in the children's behalf. Physical activity programs in and of themselves pose some risk. You can be held liable for injuries that a claimant suffers under your care if you are shown to be negligent in carrying out what is customary practice to protect a person against injury (breach of duty). Customary practice is what a reasonable and prudent person would do in the same situation. Negligence refers to doing something that a reasonable, prudent person in your field would not do. Volunteers need to know what is customary practice in the situations for which they have responsibility.

Although the job description will help, anyone you hire to do a job needs to know very specifically what you expect of him or her. Most people fail to do what they are supposed to do in a job not because they are trying to get away with something but because they don't know what they are supposed to do. Volunteers also need specific training for a job. You will want them to "buy into" the idea that participation needs to be made a positive and safe experience for all students regardless of who they are. You cannot put volunteers in a position and expect them to know what to do without support. Either the program director or another person familiar with the job should work alongside a new volunteer for the first couple of days of the job. Once you get your program going, you will be able to have previous volunteers train new ones. Although initially the process is time-consuming, it is essential.

Working With Volunteers

In many cases it is not difficult to recruit volunteers for the first years of a program. Maintaining the willingness of volunteers to stay with you over a long period of time will depend on how you treat them. Volunteers should be treated as members of a team. They should be assigned to a job that they have the skills for and interest in. If they volunteer to do one job, you don't want to put them in a situation in which you are asking them to do something quite different that they may be overqualified for or don't have the skills and interest to do. Use the talents that people have. Do not try to convince volunteers that they should give more time than they agree to. Make sure that if they say they will put in 2 hours a week, you do not give them a job that takes 4 hours or more a week. The program should have mechanisms through which volunteers can get their questions answered and that also provide input into their jobs and the program as a whole.

Volunteers have to be supervised. They cannot be sent off to do a job and forgotten. Periodically meet with all of the volunteers to get their input and to share any issues that may have come up in the program that need to be addressed.

Reinforcing Participation

Programs will be more successful if participation is reinforced in some way. Programs can reinforce participation in the following ways:

- The classroom teacher and physical education teacher can bring attention to those students who are participants.
- Information about successful participation can be posted in the school, including on the gym wall, or through the school Web site.
- T-shirts given to participants will draw attention to the program.
- Programs and events can be included in school morning announcements.
- Students who are participants can be asked to recruit a friend.
- A school newspaper sent to parents can advertise and reinforce participation.

While awards and prizes can reinforce participation, they should be used with caution. The awards

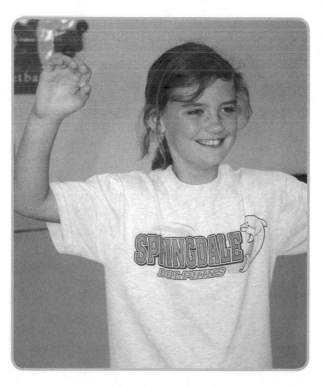

Any prizes or awards with the school logo will draw attention to the program.

program you design should be reflective of the goals of your program. The major goal of most physical activity programs includes participation and the development of participants whose personal characteristics contribute to their own enjoyment in participation as well as that of others. While awards should not be the major goal of participation, good performance, good effort, and good character should be rewarded and recognized.

Evaluating Your Program

A large and comprehensive physical activity program takes time to develop. It takes time to put the pieces in place that are essential to the conduct of the program. It takes time to get the support you need so that the program is not a "one-man show," and it takes time for students and parents to see the value of the program and seek to participate. The program needs to be evaluated each year in terms of its mission. Who is participating in what activities over the scope of the program? Is the program offering the kinds of activities that attract the targeted population—students who are not normally physically active? Does the program have the kind of support it needs in terms of resources—adequate staff, equipment, facilities? What is the perception of the students, faculty, and parents toward the program? All of these issues are part of a comprehensive evaluation that should be conducted to form the basis of planning for future years.

SUMMARY

1. The voluntary physical activity program should supplement and not duplicate the opportunities provided to children for physical activity outside of the school day.

2. A physical activity committee should plan and conduct the physical activity program for a school.

3. Planning for a physical activity program involves assessing needs, developing policies, and establishing a method of funding the program.

4. The program for younger students will be loosely structured around opportunities to be physically active.

5. Activities can be scheduled before school, after school, and at lunchtime.

6. Volunteers will probably be needed to conduct a comprehensive program, and they need to be hired and trained in a formal way.

7. Programs can be funded as part of the school budget, using participation fees, or through fundraisers.

CHECKING YOUR UNDERSTANDING

1. How can schools work with communities to meet the needs for student participation in physical activity?

2. Who should be on the physical activity committee?

3. How do the needs of younger children and older children differ for physical activity?

4. For each of the times during the day when structured physical activities can be scheduled, what are the advantages and disadvantages?

5. Explain three factors that must be considered in planning the physical activity program.

6. What are the advantages and disadvantages of working with volunteers in a program, and what do you need to do to avoid the disadvantages?

7. How can a physical activity program be funded?

8. What can schools do to reinforce participation in the physical activity program?

RESOURCES

After School Physical Activity
www.afterschoolpa.com

Promoting Health: Strategies
www.cdc.gov/HealthyYouth/PhysicalActivity/promoting_health/strategies/afterschool.htm

National Association for Sport and Physical Education Intramural Guidelines
www.aahperd.org/NASPE/pdf_files/pos_papers/intramural_guidelines.pdf

Assessment of an After-School Physical Activity Program to Prevent Obesity Among 9- to 10-Year-Old Children: A Cluster Randomized Trial
www.ncbi.nlm.nih.gov/pubmed/17895883

California After School Physical Activity Guidelines
www.cde.ca.gov/ls/ba/as/documents/paguidelines.pdf

Byl, J. (2002). *Intramural recreation: A step-by-step guide to creating an effective program.* Champaign, IL: Human Kinetics.

Mull, R., Bayless, K., & Jamieson, L. (2005). *Recreational sport management* (4th ed.). Champaign, IL: Human Kinetics.

National Association for Sport and Physical Education. (2002). *Guidelines for after school physical activity and intramural sport programs.* Reston, VA: Author.

11

Programs Before, During, and After School and Special Events

OVERVIEW

This chapter addresses how before-, after-, and during-school events can be planned and scheduled to provide all students opportunities to be active and to use skills learned in physical education class as well as to learn new ones. Before-, after-, and during-school physical activity events give students additional opportunities to accumulate the minimum daily recommendation of 60 minutes of physical activity. The school physical activity program should offer students a variety of extracurricular activities including activity clubs, intramurals, single school events, and community events. What distinguishes these experiences from other aspects of the physical activity program is that they are voluntary.

CHAPTER OUTCOMES

This chapter will help you

- identify various responsibilities in implementing a physical activity program;
- identify ways in which activity clubs, intramurals, and single and community events can provide opportunities for physical activity;
- describe how the physical activity program can provide a variety of activities for a wide range of ability levels;
- initiate a school walking program;
- identify ways to track physical activity; and
- plan a yearly physical activity program.

IN THIS CHAPTER

Many young people are not physically active outside of school. Among children between the ages of 9 and 13 years, 61.5% do not participate in any organized physical activity during nonschool hours, and 22.6% do not engage in any free-time physical activity, according to 2002 data from the Youth Media Campaign Longitudinal Study (YMCLS) of the Centers for Disease Control and Prevention (CDC) (2003). According to data from the CDC's Youth Risk Behavior Surveillance System 2007 survey (2008), 35.4% of students watched television 3 hours or more on an average school day. Children are not physically active at home. Many children are not allowed out of the house for safety reasons when they return home from school. Therefore, school physical activity programs are critical to ensure that all children have access to regular physical activity.

Schools are in a position to affect the physical activity levels of the many children in attendance. Physical activity programs in schools ensure the occurrence of physical activity and educate students on the importance of regular physical activity. Schools have the potential to influence large numbers of children in developing lifelong physical activity patterns.

To Structure or Not to Structure

In planning before- and after-school physical activity programs, the school physical activity committee (see chapter 10) must decide whether the program will be structured, with staff-directed activities, or not structured, with opportunity for child-directed activities or free play. The decision may be to include both structured and nonstructured or open-gym opportunities. One option is for the K and first grade program to offer organized free play and for the grades 3, 4, and 5 program to be structured. Another option is to designate one area for child-directed activities and another for programmed or instructional activities. Whether the program is structured or not, children should have the opportunity to participate in a variety of developmentally appropriate physical activities in a safe environment.

Administrative Duties of the Program

Once the school physical activity committee has taken responsibility for designing the physical activity program, the responsibilities for running the program must be delegated. The physical education teacher/physical activity director or a hired staff may be responsible for implementing the program. Delegating specific responsibilities to certain individuals involved in putting the program into action is crucial to running an effective program. Physical activity staff members or volunteers should be responsible for

- ensuring that events begin and end at scheduled times,
- ensuring that designated activity areas are safe (e.g., provide adequate space for the activity, free of debris and potential hazards),
- seeing that the activity area is prepared with enough equipment to accommodate all participants and that nets or goals are set up before student arrival,
- returning the activity area to its original state by taking down nets and goals and returning equipment to storage,

- supervising children during activity,
- supervising children who arrive early or whose ride is late to pick them up,
- administering first aid during the activity or event,
- unlocking or securing the facility, and
- enforcing standards of behavior.

Providing a Variety of Opportunities

A physical activity program should offer students a variety of organized and voluntary physical activities. A diverse selection of sports and recreational activities should be available for students with a wide range of abilities with the intent of meeting the needs of every student in the school. Different types of activities may be provided through activity clubs, intramurals, single events, and school and community events.

Activity Clubs

Activity clubs are typically organized by interest in a particular activity such as soccer, in-line skating, gymnastics, dance, or bicycling; or they can be designed to accommodate a larger percentage of the school population in terms of physical ability and developmental appropriateness, for example through walking, running, fitness, or jump rope clubs. Clubs can be scheduled to meet one or more times a week before, during, or after school. Activity clubs enable students to build upon existing skills and learn new skills for an activity of particular interest. A jump rope club such as the one described in the sidebar offers this type of opportunity; see "The Magic of Jumping" by Kathy Kent, an elementary physical education teacher. Kathy Kent also shares her suggestions for starting a jump rope club in the sidebar "Tips to Help You Start a Jump Rope Club."

The Magic of Jumping: Why Jump Rope (Activity) Clubs Are Important

I have been a health and physical education teacher for over 25 years. I am a veteran teacher from the "trenches." I have served in schools that had excellent facilities and opportunities for students, and also in schools that had no budget whatsoever for physical education, intramurals, or sports. I have worked with children of all ages and coached many teams in the public and private sectors. However, I would have to say that in all my years of experience, coaching a jump rope team and sponsoring a jump rope club at an elementary school as a volunteer was the most rewarding of all. Of course, the rewards were not monetary; they were intrinsic. No teacher in the school was greeted as warmly as I was when I arrived each day! I would have a sea of smiling faces waiting for me to unlock the gym so that the children could jump for 20 to 30 minutes before school started. And no one was missed more than I was on a day I had to be absent. "Where were you, Mrs. Kent? We missed Skippers yesterday!"

I have often wondered why kids like to jump or to be in the gym so much. What is their motivation? Why are they so eager? There may be many reasons to explain their enthusiasm, but I think self-accomplishment is the key. There is an inner sense of pride when anyone learns something new. Synonyms for the word "accomplish" are "realize," "achieve," and "do." What greater feeling in the world is there than realizing that you have achieved something you have been trying hard to do? In so many situations, I observed my students as they worked on skills and routines, trying over and over until they got it right, only to go on to the next difficult task to try and try again. Each time I would see glimmers of pride on their faces when they realized that they had learned something new . . . that they had accomplished something on their own. A child may be taught and coached by others, but only the individual can have the thrill of self-accomplishment. If you have heard a child say, "Watch me! Watch me!" you have shared in that child's moment of glory. When you witness the wonderment and joy that children express when they accomplish a task, it is like magic. This is magic that can happen when people are willing to devote time and effort to sponsoring a club or group.

Take the time, and realize the magic of jumping. It is so important!

Tips to Help You Start a Jump Rope Club

I have often had people ask, "How do you start a jump rope club?" Here are some of the questions you will want to ask yourself about starting a club, followed by some suggestions that have worked for me.

1. Time: Do I have time in my schedule to give?
   - Before school? After school? During the day (activity period)?
   - Once a week? Twice or three times per week? Every day?

I volunteered my time for 30 minutes before school each day. Some coaches give 1 hour once a week. This is entirely up to you.

2. Support: Will this activity be supported by my school?
   - Will my principal allow this activity?
   - What are the legal liabilities involved?
   - Would a jump rope club interfere with other clubs or activities (chorus, student council, and so on)?
   - Will parents support my efforts by bringing kids early or picking them up later?
   - How much space do I have? How many students can I accommodate?

I had my group meet before school so I could include bus riders. Car riders had to make arrangements to arrive early. Students who ate breakfast in the school cafeteria could come 7 minutes late.

3. Interest: How many students are interested?
   - Survey each of your classes by a show of hands.
   - Issue invitations: Give a 1-minute jump challenge (have students work with a partner; have both students count each turn of the rope as one person jumps; time for 1 minute—do not count misses; compare and report the number of jumps). This works well for third through fifth graders. For K through second graders, make note of skilled jumpers observed in physical education class. I sent the invitation to the child's parents to get their permission and also to explain expectations, procedures, and rules. The invitation would be signed by the child and the parent and then returned.

I usually had more students who wanted to be Skippers than I had room in the gym to safely accommodate, so I required a tryout consisting of a 1-minute speed jump and various jump skills. This assessment served as an important tool to determine the serious jumpers and also to justify participation to parents or teachers.

4. Motivation: How will I keep my students motivated?
   - Performances! This was a big motivator for the Skippers. Plan performances for PTA night, community festivals, health fairs (to promote physical activity and heart health), nursing homes, or other special events. Create your own "PE Fun Night." Be aware that transportation will be your biggest problem. In my situation, parents drove their own children to the event and I met them there. (Check on your district's policy regarding transportation.)
   - Incentives: Use stickers, coupons from local restaurants, jump ropes, T-shirts.
   - Challenge charts: Students write their name on a poster after accomplishing various levels of skills.
   - School records: Post records such as most jumps in a minute, most double unders, most rump-bumps, most jumps without a miss, most crisscross, and most Double Dutch.

Walking clubs facilitate social development.

Walking clubs have also become quite popular and provide an opportunity for students of all ages and fitness levels to be physically active. Walking is safe and simple and does not require a lot of expensive equipment. Walking clubs are fairly easy to initiate. A walking course can be set up on the school grounds, for example around the playground or a field. Walking courses can also be set up around a neighborhood. The space that is available will influence the length of the course. A half mile is an ideal distance for a walking course, allowing for supervision of students, for short fitness breaks, and for tracking walking distances of individual students or determining the number of miles accumulated by a class. Courses should be defined using permanent fixtures, such as tires or posts, or painted markings on asphalt or concrete. Specific directions, markings, and mileage should be identified for different routes. Walk the course with students to point out and familiarize them with the exact route. The following are some guidelines for children to follow so that they are safe while walking:

- Wear walking shoes or comfortable, supportive footwear such as tennis shoes or running shoes.
- Wear loose-fitting, comfortable clothing and layer it to adjust to changing temperatures.
- Use proper technique to avoid injury (see figure 11.1).
- Hydrate prior to and following exercise. Additional water will be needed on hot and humid days.
- Walk with someone; it is good to have others around when you are out walking.

Intramurals

The intramural program, as well as other physical activity opportunities, should extend and complement the physical education program. Intramurals typically involve dual or individual and team activities. Sample activities are pickleball, three-on-three basketball, Four Square, tetherball, modified volleyball for grades 4 and 5, and parachute games and T-ball for the lower grades. Intramural opportunities and club activities may include options for free play, instructional activities, or opportunities to play or participate in staff-directed activities.

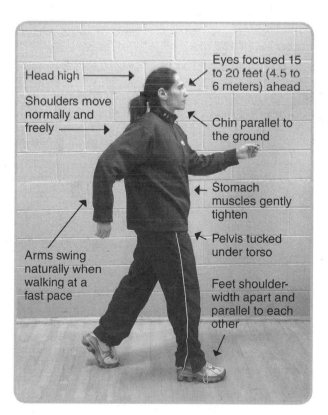

Figure 11.1   Proper walking technique. Walk with smooth movements. As you walk forward, roll your foot from heel to toe. Avoid coming down hard with your heel on the ground.

When selecting intramural activities, consider the activities included in the physical education curriculum, the skill levels of students, and student needs and interests (see chapter 10 for questionnaire). If students learn soccer skills in physical education class, then intramurals can provide an opportunity for them to practice those skills. If a sport or an activity is not part of the physical education curriculum, students will not know the skills involved; thus the activity will be inappropriate for game play without some initial instruction. For example, if badminton is not part of the physical education curriculum, badminton intramurals would need to include instructional activities before modified game play could be a successful and enjoyable experience for students.

Apart from instruction for new or novel activities, instructional opportunities for younger or less skilled students should be available. Merely setting up opportunities for game play will not provide a positive physical activity experience for students who have not acquired the skills needed for continuous game play. A gymnastics club for all ages will need to provide not only the opportunity to perform skills but also instruction and structured practice. Younger and less skilled participants will require more staff-directed and instructional opportunities for successful participation in many sport-related and recreational activities. In addition, games and equipment will need to be modified to fit the abilities of most elementary school students.

Upper elementary students developing skills for game play should be provided with opportunities to play the game. Game play for some activities may require the formation of teams. As indicated in chapter 7, there are many ways to form teams that do not compromise a student's self-esteem or create the potential of public humiliation as with the traditional method of having captains choose team members. See chapter 7 and visit PE Central (www.pecentral.org/lessonideas/ViewLesson.asp?ID=259) for a variety of appropriate ways of forming groups or teams. Change the makeup of teams often to give students the chance to play with different team members.

When allowed to select and play a game, for example during open gym or recess, elementary school students will typically opt to play cooperatively, with no concern for keeping score. When students learn a skill such as striking a ball with a racket, they want to see how long they can keep the ball going across the net before someone misses. Students should have the option of cooperative, self-testing, or competitive play. If there is interest in both competition and cooperative play, set up a play area for each. Teams should also be formed based on the skill level of play. If students involved in an event vary widely in age, players should be grouped within two years of each other (e.g., 6- and 7-year-old students are close enough in size and skill, but typically an 8-year-old would have an unfair advantage over 6-year-olds). If competitive play calls for refereeing, this role may be filled by a staff member or an older student, or upper elementary students may be taught to officiate their own games.

Single Events

Single events may include activities such as fundraisers, field days, and marathons that have special categories for children. Single events provide opportunities for schoolwide participation in physical activity. The following are among the more common single events that enable schools to encourage participation.

Jump Rope for Heart Jump Rope for Heart (JRFH) is an educational fund-raising program jointly sponsored by the American Heart Association (AHA) and the American Alliance for Health, Physical Education, Recreation and Dance (AAHPERD). Jump Rope for Heart engages elementary students in jumping rope while raising funds for lifesaving heart and stroke research. Students ask for donations from family and friends and receive thank-you gifts based on the dollars they raise. This educational program teaches students that the risk of heart disease and stroke can be reduced through a healthy and physically active lifestyle. It also promotes the value of community service to students and their families. Schools participating in JRFH receive everything they need to conduct the event, including jump ropes and an educational kit with heart-healthy curriculum and activity ideas. Schools are eligible for gift certificates for free physical education equipment based on the amount of money raised. The rope jumping event can be introduced in the physical education class and scheduled before school, after school, or as a schoolwide event during the school day. It should not take place during physical education classes but should provide an additional opportunity for students to be physically active and use the jumping skills learned in physical education. The Web sites of both the AHA and AAHPERD have links to Jump Rope for Heart.

School Walk for Diabetes The American Diabetes Association sponsors a program called School Walk for Diabetes (SWFD) that is appropriate for students in grades K through 12. Participants typically walk a few miles. This fund-raising program helps in the search for a cure for diabetes and also to raise awareness of the disease, whose incidence is rapidly increasing. Upon registering your school, you will receive a coordinator's packet complete with materials needed for organizing the schoolwide event. November is American Diabetes Month and provides the perfect backdrop for the walking event. The fourth Tuesday in March, Diabetes Alert Day, would also be an appropriate date for holding the event.

Field Day What spring day do elementary students look forward to? Field Day! Unfortunately, the physical education teacher may not share such enthusiasm, especially if he or she is the sole orchestrator of this schoolwide event. The physical activity committee should include a field day as part of the physical activity program. Field Day should promote healthy competition, fun, enjoyment, and cooperation. Along with the physical education teacher, parents, other teachers, and various volunteers should share in carrying out the many duties involved in a successful field day:

- Designing developmentally appropriate events and activities for different grade levels
- Scheduling events
- Making and collecting materials and equipment for events and activities
- Setting up and taking down the field or activity areas
- Running events (e.g., starting and stopping, giving directions) and supervising them
- Moving students from one event to another
- Providing water, first aid, and bathroom breaks

School Events

Many school events can offer students in every grade an opportunity to accumulate physical activity minutes. School events may include morning exercise, active transportation, and walking initiatives.

Morning Exercise

Many students begin the school day with idle time sitting in the gym, the cafeteria, or another location designated for bus holding or early arrivers. These students ride early buses or are dropped off at school by parents on their way to work; they must remain seated and quiet as they are monitored by teachers whose morning duty is to supervise the area. Rather than overseeing students to keep them seated and inactive, use this opportunity for students to begin the day with a bout of physical activity.

Once students arrive in the classroom and just prior to the start of instruction, schoolwide announcements take place in many elementary schools. Announcements or morning news is often delivered through the public announcement system to all classrooms. The schoolwide televised news program provides an opportunity for schoolwide physical activity. A segment of a children's fitness video or student-led physical activity can be included to prepare students for the instructional day. Many videos and DVDs have been designed for classroom workouts. (See resources identified at the end of this chapter.) You may also want to consider student designed recordings for activity breaks. Using the dance steps identified in chapters 8 and 5, students can create dance videos or DVDs for physical activity breaks. Children enjoy performing for others; by having them produce videos or DVDs, we enable them not only to create and perform dances but also to engage others in physical activity. Another option is to have live activities, exercise, or dance sessions led by your students.

Chapter 4 provides an example of a morning exercise program in Oregon that the entire school participates in (faculty and students) in the gym to start the day. While for many schools this would not be a possibility, if a school has a large enough facility, the benefits of physical activity and "team building" in this way far outweigh the time spent.

Active Transportation

Students who walk or bike to school generally expend more energy overall throughout the day (Tudor-Locke, Ainsworth, & Popkin, 2001, 2003; Cooper, et. al, 2003), and this may particularly help overweight students (Rosenberg et al., 2006). In efforts to increase physical activity levels and reduce childhood obesity along with reaping the many other benefits of walking (see sidebar, "Benefits of Walking"), several organizations have developed programs that encourage children to walk to school. A popular walking program is the KidsWalk-to-School program (see the sidebar, "KidsWalk-to-School Program") developed by the Department of Health and Human Services CDC.

Many years ago it was not uncommon to see children walking or riding their bikes to school. Today this is much more rare. The reasons include such barriers as increased distances that children must now travel, the fear of child abduction and

Walk-to-school programs encourage students to be active before school.

Benefits of Walking

Walking is a low-impact exercise with many health benefits. Whether one is walking for transportation, as a recreational activity, or for fitness, the benefits are numerous:

- Weight management
- Reduction in blood cholesterol
- Control of high blood pressure
- Decreased risk of heart attack
- Decreased risk of stroke
- Reduced risk of type 2 diabetes
- Reduced symptoms of depression and anxiety
- Overall feeling of well-being and elevated mood
- Strengthening of muscles
- Strengthening of bones and reduced risk of osteoporosis

other crimes, and concerns about traffic issues and weather. Only 13% of all trips to school are made via walking and bicycling. According to the CDC, for school trips of 1 mile (1.6 kilometers) or less, a low 31% are made via walking, and within 2 miles (3.2 kilometers) of school, 2% are made via bicycling. To overcome these barriers, the KidsWalk-to-School program suggests the Walking School Bus (www.walkingschoolbus.org) or Bicycle Train, whereby children travel in groups accompanied by one or more adults. Many resources (www.cdc.gov/nccd-php/dnpa/kidswalk/resources.htm) are available through the KidsWalk-to-School program that will help you organize and implement a walk- or bike-to-school program in your community. For additional programs and resources, see the Web resources at the end of this chapter.

Walking Initiatives

Setting goals such as walking a particular distance as shown on a map can inspire students to walk. A schoolwide incentive of a designated amount of mileage can motivate students to accumulate miles on a route across an area, a state, the United States, or another country. Students can accumulate miles while walking at designated times or even during nonschool hours. Distances can be recorded by laps, miles, or steps. Mileage can be tracked on a classroom chart or a Web site. Several Web sites are available for online tracking of steps or other physical activity. Many programs have set up competitions between schools or between classes within schools to make the walking programs more fun for students. Some of these programs have been organized nationally through Web sites such as PEcentral and NASPEtalk.

KidsWalk-to-School Program 💿

The following are the goals of KidsWalk-to-School:

- Encouraging children to walk and bicycle to and from school
- Increasing awareness of the importance of regular physical activity for children, improved pedestrian safety, and healthy and walkable community environments
- Mobilizing communities to work together to create safe routes to school

The following are anticipated benefits of the KidsWalk-to-School program:

- Increased levels of daily physical activity for children
- Increased likelihood that children and adults will choose to walk and bike for other short-distance trips
- Improved neighborhood safety
- Fewer cars traveling through the neighborhood
- Fewer cars and less congestion at the pickup and drop-off points at the school
- Friendlier neighborhoods as people get out and about interacting with one another

See www.cdc.gov/nccdphp/dnpa/kidswalk.

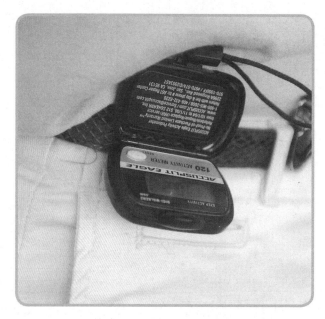

Figure 11.2 Pedometers can be motivating tools.

Logit is a pedometer step logging program that allows you to participate in a hike across the United States as an individual or with a group or class by logging in your steps (www.peclogit.org/logit.asp). Pedometers are commonly used devices for assessing step counts (see figure 11.2). The concept of measuring physical activity can be abstract for children. Using pedometers provides children with a concrete measure of physical activity by recording step counts. Pedometers also provide accountability for physical activity by demonstrating that students are indeed physically active. Most pedometers have a pendulum mechanism that measures the up-and-down motion of the hip when steps are taken.

The physical education teacher will most likely introduce students to pedometers. Beyond physical education, pedometers can be used to measure daily physical activity and to promote physical activity outside of the physical education class. When introducing students to pedometers, teach how to wear them and give guidelines for their use:

- The pedometer should be firmly attached to the body, clipped along a belt or a waistband so that it is in line with the knee.
- Explain that shaking the pedometer will have an adverse effect on its accuracy. Allow students to give the pedometer one gentle shake to see how it registers a step; then initiate the "you shake it, I take it" rule.
- Allow students to check pedometers out and wear them for three or four days and record daily steps. This will allow them to establish a baseline or average daily step count that can be used to set physical activity goals.

Experts recommend 10,000 steps a day to achieve good health. This is equivalent to walking about 5 miles (8 kilometers). The Presidential Active Lifestyle Award (PALA) recognizes adults who are active at least 30 minutes a day or if they walk 10,000 steps a day; youth ages 6 to 17 are eligible for the PALA if they are active for 60 minutes a day or walk 11,000 steps a day (girls) or 13,000 steps a day (boys). The President's Challenge interactive Web site www.presidentschallenge.org/ allows people to track their physical activity level by participating in a variety of activities.

Activitygram, which accompanies Fitnessgram (see chapter 9), provides information regarding physical activity patterns in the form of a report based on physical activity guidelines. Introduced in 1999, Activitygram is a behaviorally based physical activity assessment tool that provides a three-day record of activities performed during each 30-minute period. The report includes the following types of information:

- Total number of minutes of activity each day as compared to a goal of 60 minutes
- Periods of time each day spent in activity
- Types of activity

Activitygram enables you to promote awareness about the importance of physical activity and fitness, as well as activity levels of children in grades K through 12, and to help students develop patterns of lifelong, health-promoting physical activity. (The program is also appropriate for use with young adults up to age 30.) It also provides an activity log for recording steps from a pedometer (www.fitnessgram.net/overview). Activitygram focuses on regular participation in moderately intense physical activity (see figure 11.3 for sample report). No distinction is made between moderate and vigorous physical activity, which reinforces the notion that physical activity does not have to be vigorous to be beneficial. Students who achieve 60 minutes each day reach the Healthy Activity Zone.

Community Events

The physical activity committee should work in tandem with area community centers, YMCAs, parks and recreation departments, tennis clubs, karate studios, and bowling alleys. If committee members are informed of community events, they are better able to promote the events to students. Physical education teachers can play a role in facilitating the participation of students in community activities by making students and parents aware of the potential to participate and reinforcing students who are participating. Some teachers may want to invite community representatives to school or play a role in registering students for participation.

If funds are available, community facilities can be used to outsource school-sponsored programs. If the school plans to provide opportunities for students to swim or play tennis and the campus does not have a pool or tennis courts, these programs can be conducted at another location.

A culmination of a walk or jog club is participation in a community event.

ACTIVITYGRAM®

Fitness, Felicia
Felicia Fitness: 01/31/2005

MINUTES OF ACTIVITY

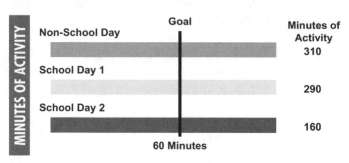

Goal

Minutes of Activity

Non-School Day — 310

School Day 1 — 290

School Day 2 — 160

60 Minutes

MESSAGES • MESSAGES • MESSAGES

The chart shows the number of minutes that you reported doing moderate (medium) or vigorous (hard) activity on each day. Congratulations, your log indicates that you are doing at least 60 minutes of activity on most every day. This will help to promote good fitness and wellness. For fun and variety, try some new activities that you have never done before.

TIME PROFILE

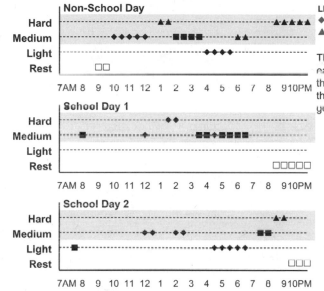

Non-School Day

Hard / Medium / Light / Rest

7AM 8 9 10 11 12 1 2 3 4 5 6 7 8 910PM

School Day 1

Hard / Medium / Light / Rest

7AM 8 9 10 11 12 1 2 3 4 5 6 7 8 910PM

School Day 2

Hard / Medium / Light / Rest

7AM 8 9 10 11 12 1 2 3 4 5 6 7 8 910PM

LEGEND:
◆ Most of the time (20 minutes)   ■ All of the time (30 minutes)
▲ Some of the time (10 minutes)   ☐ TV/Computer Time

The time profile shows the activity level you reported for each 30 minute period of the day. Your results show that you were active both during and after school and that you were also active on the weekend. Keep up the good work.

ACTIVITY PROFILE

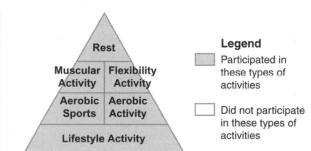

Rest

Muscular Activity / Flexibility Activity

Aerobic Sports / Aerobic Activity

Lifestyle Activity

Legend

☐ Participated in these types of activities

☐ Did not participate in these types of activities

The activity pyramid reveals the different types of activity that you reported doing over a few days. Your results indicate that you participated in regular lifestyle activity as well as some activity from the other levels. This is great! The variety in your program should help you stay active.

Your results indicate that you spend an average of 1 hours per day watching TV or working on the computer. While some time on these activities is okay, you should try to limit the total time to less than 2 hours.

ACTIVITYGRAM provides information about your normal levels of physical activity. The ACTIVITYGRAM report shows what types of activity you do and how often you do them. It includes the information that you previously entered for two or three days during one week.

© 2005 The Cooper Institute

Figure 11.3   Sample Activitygram computer report.

Planning Events in Advance

The before-school, during-school, after-school, and special events of the physical activity program should be planned in advance like other curricular areas. The yearly plan should be in place prior to the start of the school year, providing the calendar for the clubs, intramurals, and special events that will be part of the school physical activity program. Planning in advance allows you to make sure that you are offering students a variety of activities as well as a variety of formats. Offering children both structured or instructional activities and opportunities to select their own activities (e.g., open gym) is a way to achieve variety through the use of different formats. Table 11.1 is an example of a yearly plan organized by grade level.

Planning for the next school year will be more effective if you track the participation of students in your program. You need to know who participated in what activity and to be able to identify students who are not participating. Using the Activitygram (part of the Fitnessgram program) several times a year will help you identify students who may need to be specifically targeted for special programming.

SUMMARY

1. Whether activities are structured or non-structured, many responsibilities are involved in implementing a physical activity program, including preparing, equipping, and supervising activity areas.

2. Activity clubs that meet one or more times per week provide physical activity opportunities of interest and may be designed to accommodate a wide range of student abilities.

3. Walking clubs are very popular because they are simple to initiate, accommodate a wide range of abilities, provide an ideal activity for obese children, and confer numerous health benefits.

4. Intramural programs provide students of all ability levels with opportunities to voluntarily participate in sport-related and recreational activities.

5. When planning an intramural program, consider activities that extend and complement the physical education program, the skill level of students, and student interest.

6. The intramural program should include instructional opportunities for new or novel activities and also offer instruction for younger or less skilled participants.

7. Single events such as Jump Rope for Heart and School Walk for Diabetes provide opportunities for physical activity.

8. Morning exercise videos, walk- or bike-to-school programs, and schoolwide initiatives provide opportunities for physical activity.

9. Setting goals and tracking physical activity through charts displaying accumulated individual or class mileage, logging information on a Web site, or using pedometers to count steps motivate students to be physically active.

10. The yearly physical activity plan should be in place at the start of the school year and should include a variety of activity formats (e.g., clubs, intramurals, special events) and a variety of sport-related and recreational activities.

CHECKING YOUR UNDERSTANDING

1. What responsibilities are involved in implementing a physical activity program?

2. Describe how a school physical activity program can be designed to provide a variety of activities for a wide range of abilities.

3. How would you go about initiating a walking club or a jump rope club at your school?

4. What guidelines should be followed to keep students safe while walking?

5. How would an intramural program for lower elementary school grades differ from the intramurals offered for upper grades?

6. Describe two different ways in which physical activity can be monitored.

7. How can community events be incorporated into the school physical activity program?

8. Describe the characteristics of a good yearly physical activity plan.

RESOURCES

Pangrazi, R.P., Beighle, A., & Sidman, C.L. (2007). *Pedometer power: Using pedometers in school and community* (2nd ed.). Champaign, IL: Human Kinetics.

Afterschool.gov
http://afterschool.gov/

After-School Physical Activity Web Site
www.afterschoolpa.com/home.html

BAM! Body and Mind
www.bam.gov/sub_physicalactivity/index.html

TABLE 11.1

Yearly Plan for Physical Activity Program

Month	K to1	Grades 2 to 3	Grades 4 to 5
SEPTEMBER			
Intramurals	Open gym	Four square	Four square
Clubs	Walking club	Walking club	Walking club
Special events			
OCTOBER			
Intramurals	Parachute play	Soccer skills	Modified soccer
Clubs	Walking club	Walking club	Walking club
Special events	Family fitness night	Family fitness night	Family fitness night
NOVEMBER	National diabetes month		
Intramurals	Tag games	Paddle activities	Pickleball
Clubs	Dance club	Dance club	Dance club
Special events	School walk for diabetes	School walk for diabetes	School walk for diabetes
DECEMBER			
Intramurals	Beanbag activities	Long and short rope activities	Long and short rope activities
Clubs	Dance club	Dance club	Dance club
Special events	Dance night	Dance night	Dance night
JANUARY			
Intramurals	Open gym	Floor hockey	Floor hockey
Clubs	Jump rope club	Jump rope club	Jump rope club
Special events			
FEBRUARY	American heart month		
Intramurals	Tossing and catching activities	Dribbling, passing, and shooting skills	Basketball
Clubs	Jump rope club	Jump rope club	Jump rope club
Special events	Jump rope for heart	Jump rope for heart	Jump rope for heart
MARCH			
Intramurals	Kicking activities	Martial arts	Martial arts
Clubs	Jump rope club	Jump rope club	Jump rope club
Special events			
APRIL			
Intramurals	Tee-ball	Whiffle ball	Whiffle ball
Clubs	Running club	Fitness club	Fitness club
Special events	Family fitness night	Family fitness night	Family fitness night
MAY	National physical fitness and sports month		
Intramurals	Open gym	Deck ring activities	Volleyball
Clubs	Running club	Fitness club	Fitness club
Special events	Field day	Field day	Field day

CDC's Kidswalk

www.cdc.gov/kidswalk

Educational Record Center

www.erckids.com

Fit for Life—After-School Physical Activity and Obesity Prevention Program

www.ronjones.org/Health&Fitness/FitforLife/index.html

Fit Kids

www.fitkidsnc.com/SeeLearnDo.aspx

Fitness Finders (Mileage Club)

www.fitnessfinders.net

International Walk to School

www.iwalktoschool.org

Jump Rope for Heart

www.americanheart.org/presenter.jhtml?identifier=2360

National Center for Safe Routes to School

www.saferoutesinfo.org

PE Central

www.pecentral.org/

Physical Activity Brochure

www.cdc.gov/healthyyouth/physicalactivity/brochures/pdf/principal.pdf

Powerful Bones. Powerful Girls.

www.girlshealth.gov/bones/

Recharge! Energizing After School

www.actionforhealthykids.org/special_after.php

School Walk for Diabetes

http://schoolwalk.diabetes.org/site/PageServer?pagename=SW_homepage

Walk and Bike to School USA

www.walktoschool.org

Walk4Life—WalkSmart Active Schools

www.walk4life.com/movementworks/walksmart.aspx

REFERENCES

Centers for Disease Control and Prevention. (2003). Physical activity levels among children aged 9-13 years--United States, 2002. *Morbidity and Mortality Weekly Report*, 52(33).

Centers for Disease Control and Prevention. (2008). Youth risk behavior surveillance--United States, 2007. *Morbidity and Mortality Weekly Report*, 57(4).

Cooper, A.R., Page, A.S., Foster I.J., & Qahwaji, D. (2003). Commuting to school: Are children who walk more physically active? *American Journal of Preventive Medicine*, 25, 273-6.

National Association for Physical Education and Sport. (2005). *The physical best activity guide: Elementary level*. Champaign, IL: Human Kinetics.

Rosenberg, D.E., Sallis, J.F., Conway, T.L., Cain, K.L., & McKenzie, T.L. (2006). Active transportation to school over 2 years in relation to weight status and physical activity. *Obesity*, 14(10), 1771-1776.

Tudor-Locke, C., Ainsworth, B., & Popkin, B. (2001). Active commuting to school; An overlooked source of children's physical activity? *Sports Medicine*, 31, 309-13.

Tudor-Locke, C., Ainsworth, B., Adair, L., & Popkin, B. (2003). Objective physical activity of Filipino youth stratified for commuting mode to school. *Medicine and Science in Sports and Exercise*, 35(3), 465-471.

PART III

The Secondary Physical Activity Program

12

The Comprehensive Physical Activity Program for the Secondary School

OVERVIEW

This chapter sets the stage for the secondary school physical activity program. It describes the need for the program; explains differences between the physical education, athletic, and physical activity program; and outlines some of the choices administrators and those responsible for conducting the program need to make in establishing the program.

CHAPTER OUTCOMES

This chapter will help you

- identify the need for the return of physical activity programs for the secondary school and their importance for today's secondary student;

- describe the characteristics of a good middle school and high school physical education program and the differences between a physical education program, a physical activity program, and an athletic program;

- identify the importance of the school administration and physical activity director in conducting the secondary physical activity program;

- understand the reasons people participate in physical activity and the implications of that knowledge base for designing a physical activity program;

- explore opportunities that can be provided for students before and after school, during the school day, and through community-based activities outside the school; and

- explore the advantages and disadvantages of mandating physical activity for every student.

IN THIS CHAPTER

Although a very small number of schools in the United States have developed the kinds of comprehensive physical activity programs outlined in previous chapters for elementary students, even fewer have considered how to meet the needs of the secondary student. Most secondary schools have assumed that the normal physical education requirement and the athletic program meet the responsibility of the school to provide activity for students. They do not. Physical education time is limited, and the athletic program serves the needs of a very small minority of the more highly skilled students. The students who need the school to provide opportunities for physical activity are ill served by the present programs.

Secondary programs must look at the need to provide all students with opportunities to be physically active. A comprehensive school physical activity program is designed to meet the needs of all students in the school through

- a standards-based required physical education program,
- an inclusive athletic program,
- an elective physical education program,
- intramural and club activities,
- school special events, and
- community collaboration.

What Are the Needs of the Secondary Student?

More than half of American adolescents are not vigorously active on a regular basis (U.S. Department of Health and Human Services [USDHHS], 1996). Minimal standards for health suggest that the adolescent engage in at least 30 minutes of moderate to vigorous activity each day. The surgeon general's report on physical activity and health (USDHHS, 1996) indicates that the physical activity levels of students decline rapidly once they leave the elementary school and the childhood years. This decline is greater for girls than for boys. More than 70% of boys at 12 years of age participate in vigorous physical activity. By the time boys are high school seniors, this figure is reduced by over half, to about 29%. The profile for girls starts lower and ends lower. Inactivity is more prevalent among girls and particularly among black females. The Youth Risk Behavior Surveillance System (Centers for Disease Control and Prevention, 2008) showed that 65% of high school students do not participate in 60 minutes or more of daily physical activity. In contrast, 25% play video games for 90 minutes or more daily, and 35% watch TV for 90 minutes or more daily.

Although everyone supports the important role that physical activity plays in the lives of children, few have considered the consequences of a lack of physical activity in adolescence. The physical activity patterns of adolescents are important because they play a major part in establishing adult patterns of participation. They also have a direct effect on the current health status of the adolescent. The periods of rapid growth experienced by adolescents make physical activity an essential component of their lives. For the adolescent, physical activity

- helps build and maintain healthy bones, muscles, and joints;
- helps control weight, build lean muscle, and reduce fat; and
- prevents or delays the development of high blood pressure and helps reduce blood pressure in some adolescents with hypertension (USDHHS, 1996).

Comprehensive school physical activity programs can not only provide for the daily needs of students for physical activity and encourage lifelong participation; they also have the potential to positively affect student attitudes toward school and academic work. Sport and physical activity is a large part of our culture. Nonparticipants are at a real disadvantage in terms of their potential quality of life.

How Did We Get Here?

The decline in physical activity of adolescents has mirrored the decline in physical activity for children and adults, with some special, more recent conditions that make it more difficult to motivate preadolescents and adolescents to engage in physical activity. Physical activity is competing for the time of an age group with many choices. Parking lots at high schools are filled not with student bicycles but with student cars. Computer games, cell phones, portable media players, and computer online activities have found not only willing participants but in many cases addicted participants. These adolescents are engaged, but not physically.

Many adolescents are working and are using their spending money to support their "toys" and what seems like an insatiable appetite for fast food and constant communication with each other. On the other hand, their needs to pursue their own identity and become comfortable with their own physicality and sexuality are no different than for any other generation of teens. Today's teen has not

only more choices but also more freedom to choose. Providing opportunities for this population to choose wisely is the responsibility of everyone who works with adolescents.

It is the responsibility of parents, communities, and schools to offer opportunities for adolescents to make good choices about how they spend their time. Because schools have a captive audience and a long-term involvement with students, it is the school program that must have a primary responsibility for *initiating* efforts to increase levels of physical activity of this age group. Parents and communities can and must play a major role, but school policies and programs that involve parents and communities are likely to be more effective than any single effort by any other group.

The decline in physical activity levels of students has mirrored the decline in physical education programs. One effective way to meet both the long-term (education for a physically active lifestyle) and short-term (daily physical activity) needs of this age group for physical activity is to provide students with daily physical education each year of middle school and high school. While some states have a one-year requirement for physical education in high schools and a few have a two year requirement, some have no requirement (National Association for Sport and Physical Education [NASPE] and American Heart Association, 2006). The range in requirements is even greater for middle school. The NASPE recommends that secondary students have 225 minutes a week of physical education (average 45 minutes per day). While almost all eighth graders take at least one semester of physical education, only about 34% of high school seniors take physical education (Johnston, Delva, & O'Malley, 2007). Given that there is not likely to be an immediate and dramatic change in the number of schools providing daily physical education for students in grades 6 through 12, schools must look to other types of programs to increase participation in physical activity.

School Wellness Policies

The Child Nutrition and WIC Reauthorization Act of 2004 (PL 108-265) required all school districts with federally funded school meal programs to develop and implement wellness policies by the 2006-2007 school year (USDHHS, 2004). These wellness policies must include goals and policy for physical activity and a plan to measure implementation. Because the wellness efforts of a district are to involve a wide range of school and community personnel, those personnel should be a primary resource for initiating comprehensive school physical activity programs that include physical education and before-, during- and after-school efforts (see chapter 2 for a full discussion of school wellness policies).

As part of a school wellness policy, a physical activity director should be appointed. The most logical person to fill this role is a physical education teacher, but other alternatives should be considered as well. It may be that schools want to appoint a part-time person whose responsibility is exclusively to coordinate the physical activity program of the school. Although physical education teachers are expected to take the lead in the development of comprehensive school physical activity programs, they cannot be expected to be successful operating in isolation of the support of other school personnel and school and district policy.

The School Physical Activity Program: Physical Education

Students who participate in good physical education programs are more likely to be physically active and remain physically active into their adult years (Fairclough & Stratton, 2005; Sallis et al., 1997; Strong et al., 2005). Physical education programs at the secondary level not only give students opportunities to be physically active; they also have the responsibility to educate students for a physically active lifestyle. In this way they differ substantially from other aspects of a comprehensive school physical activity program and are essential to any efforts to increase levels of physical activity of the adolescent. There are four essential elements of quality physical education regardless of the school level:

- Opportunity to learn
- Meaningful content
- Appropriate instruction
- Student and program assessment (NASPE, 2004)

The Middle School Physical Education Program

In 2009, NASPE published *Appropriate Practices for Middle School Physical Education*. In this position statement, the association describes many characteristics of a good physical education program that should exemplify good physical education at all levels:

- A positive and psychologically and physically safe learning environment for all students

- Sequential instruction based on the national standards
- High expectations for achievement
- Maximum participation
- Content planned and selected to develop identified learning objectives in motor skills, health-related fitness, concepts in the disciplines of physical education and fitness, self-responsibility, and valuing physical activity
- Specific instructional feedback on what is to be learned
- Integration with other subject areas when the content of the physical education program is not compromised
- Regular assessment and reporting of student progress
- An emphasis on lifestyle changes to promote physical activity

What is perhaps unique to the middle school in relation to the physical education curriculum is the attention paid to

- individualized instruction;
- cooperative learning experiences;
- a broad range of activities that include all of the movement forms and fitness;
- longer units that allow for the development of complex skills;
- grouping of students for both social reasons and physical reasons;
- developing self-awareness, leadership, caring for self, and respect for others;
- fitness testing and development; and
- encouraging the use of community resources.

Middle school programs should be standards based. The national standards for middle school physical education are presented in figure 12.1, along with the expectations for outcomes. A more detailed discussion of curriculum issues and appropriate curriculum for this age group can be found in *Designing the Physical Education Curriculum: Promoting Active Lifestyles* (Rink, 2009).

The High School Physical Education Program

Although there are many good high school programs of physical education, many programs are a "turn-off" to physical activity. They do not have to be. What characterizes good programs has been described in the NASPE publication

FIGURE 12.1

National Standards and Emphases for Middle School Students

Standard 1: Demonstrates competency in motor skills and movement patterns to perform a variety of physical activities.

- Achieve mature forms of basic skills.
- Participate with skill and achieve competence in the basic skills of a variety of sport, dance, gymnastics, and outdoor activities.
- Use skills and tactics successfully in modified games or activities of increasing complexity.

Standard 2: Demonstrates understanding of movement concepts, principles, strategies, and tactics as they apply to the learning and performance of physical activities.

- Identify critical elements of sport-specific games and activities that characterize good performance.
- Identify basic tactics of both invasion and net activities and how to use them effectively in modified game situations.
- Know the basic principles of conditioning for a sport or activity.
- Identify principles of good practice.
- Use information from the disciplines as well as feedback from others to improve performance.

Standard 3: Participates regularly in physical activity.

- Understand the importance of being physically active on a daily basis.
- Be a participant in physical activity on a daily basis.
- Understand one's own interests and abilities in terms of physical activity.
- Make lifestyle choices to be physically active.

Standard 4: Achieves and maintains a health-enhancing level of physical fitness.

- Be able to set personal goals and assess the extent to which one has achieved those personal goals.
- Have the skills to assess one's own cardiovascular endurance.
- Meet the standard for fitness identified for one's age group.
- Identify the relationship between regular participation in physical activity and fitness.
- Identify the health related benefits of physical activity and fitness.
- Be very comfortable with identifying and using the components of fitness to talk about one's own fitness status and to identify what one can do to improve or maintain one's own personal fitness levels.

Standard 5: Exhibits responsible personal and social behavior that respects self and others in physical activity settings.

- Interact with others in a positive way regardless of skill level, gender, or status within the group.
- Accept responsibility for conducting oneself in a safe and productive manner in class.
- Work independently.
- Demonstrate respect for self and others.

Standard 6: Values physical activity for health, enjoyment, challenge, self-expression, and/or social interaction.

- Value physical activity for positive personal effects of that activity.
- Identify different positive effects of participation in different kinds of physical activity.
- Use movement to express feeling.
- Identify personal likes and dislikes regarding physical activity in terms of their personal effects and in terms of the kinds of activities that are personally attractive.

Appropriate Practices for High School Physical Education (2009). A good high school program

- is a planned sequential program based on state and national standards;
- includes motor skill development, physiological and biomechanical principles, and an emphasis on health-enhancing physical activity;
- is designed to promote a physically active lifestyle;
- includes regular assessment and reporting of student progress;
- includes the development of lifestyle changes to promote physical activity;
- includes skill-related and health-related components of fitness;
- has high expectations for achievement; and
- includes maximum participation.

One of the most essential characteristics of a good high school program is the opportunity for students to choose activities according to their needs and interests. There is great diversity in the types of activities that students find enjoyable. Many successful programs have moved to "choice" programs in which students sign up for an activity of their choosing for a quarter or a semester. The longer time frames allow teachers to create instructional units that have the potential to develop competence in an activity. Students are more likely to be engaged and active participants in an activity when they have made the choice to learn the activity and are helped to become competent in that activity.

The second unique characteristic of high school physical education programs is the emphasis on discipline knowledge, particularly for programs that have more than a semester or a year of physical education. The traditional disciplines in physical education include knowledge in motor learning, motor development, exercise physiology, sport psychology, and biomechanics. The intention is not to make physical education an academic subject, but rather to use discipline knowledge to facilitate student learning and understanding of movement and fitness for a lifetime of physical activity. High school programs emphasize cognitive knowledge that is essential in order for students to take independent responsibility for their level of fitness through either an activity or an exercise model. These are skills that students need and will use through the life span, and are often taught with a textbook and either as a separate unit within the program or as content integrated with other units. Many useful texts and programs are designed to help students develop personal responsibility for their fitness and

Physical education programs at the high school level should help students develop skills for participation.

levels of activity; an example is the text *Fitness for Life* (Corbin & Lindsey, 2007).

The national content standards for high school physical education and the important outcomes for high school students are listed in figure 12.2. A more detailed discussion of appropriate curriculum for this age group and issues involved in planning the curriculum is presented in *Designing the Physical Education Curriculum: Promoting Active Lifestyles* (Rink, 2009).

FIGURE 12.2

High School National Standards and Emphases

Standard 1: Demonstrates competency in motor skills and movement patterns to perform a variety of physical activities.

- Perform basic and advanced skills and tactics to participate in one activity from three of the following types of physical activities: aquatics, team sports, dual sports, individual sports, outdoor pursuits, self-defense, dance, and gymnastics.

Standard 2: Demonstrates understanding of movement concepts, principles, strategies, and tactics as they apply to the learning and performance of physical activities.

- Understand and increasingly apply discipline-specific knowledge to enhance performance.
- Design a personal activity plan to improve health-related fitness according to scientific knowledge.

Standard 3: Participates regularly in physical activity.

- Understand the relationship between physical activity and a healthy lifestyle through the life span.
- Possess the skills, knowledge, and disposition to maintain a high level of physical activity independently.
- Participate regularly in physical activity.
- Identify community resources for participation in physical activity.

Standard 4: Achieves and maintains a health-enhancing level of physical fitness.

- Independently apply training principles to maintain or improve a level of fitness.
- Assess personal fitness status.
- Meet the health-related fitness standards as defined by Fitnessgram.
- Achieve personal fitness goals after a period of training.
- Identify the specific benefits of being fit.

Standard 5: Exhibits responsible personal and social behavior that respects self and others in physical activity settings.

- Positively influence the behavior of others in physical activity settings.
- Develop a personal philosophy of participation that is inclusive of others of different ages, ability, gender, race, ethnicity, socioeconomic status, and culture.
- Hold oneself personally responsible for safe practices, settling conflicts in a positive way, rules, procedures, and etiquette in physical activity settings.

Standard 6: Values physical activity for health, enjoyment, challenge, self-expression, and/or social interaction.

- Identify the potential values of different kinds of activities.
- Identify the activities that provide personal pleasure and why they provide pleasure.
- Be willing to learn new activities.

While almost 91% of all eighth graders take physical education, only about 34% of high school seniors do; and this number drops considerably in low socioeconomic status schools.

The School Physical Activity Program: Interscholastic Sport

There was a time when many high school and middle school programs looked at opportunities for students to engage in physical activity in terms of a foundation built in daily physical education programs. There were also opportunities for all students to engage in intramural and club activities and for the more highly skilled to engage in athletic programs. There was a time when middle schools students in particular were protected from the highly structured and highly competitive athletic programs of high schools because of the potential negative effects of that participation on this age group and the resulting lack of opportunities for students who "don't make the team." Intramural participation of eighth grade students is 24% for boys and 21% for girls. This declines to 16% for boys and 13% for girls through high school (Johnston, Delva, & O'Malley, 2007). The recent trend that moves away from providing physical activity opportunities for the larger school population and toward the dominance of school athletic programs for only the highly skilled is a major problem. This trend makes it difficult to increase the physical activity levels of the larger population. Not only does this emphasis exclude opportunities for a large number of students to participate; it may not be in the best interest of the students who do participate. This is particularly true for the middle school student.

In 2002, NASPE issued a position paper with the following recommendations for the middle school:

The most appropriate practice for middle school sport and physical activity programs is to provide a comprehensive array of after-school programs to meet the diverse experiences, interests, and ability levels of students. These programs must always be based on the needs of middle school students and should include intramurals, activity clubs (e.g., sport, dance, exercise), special events, and open gym days/nights. Such programs should take precedence over interscholastic sports competition. The activities offered through after-school programs should include those introduced in middle school physical education classes as well as novel programming concepts that may capture the interests of diverse groups of middle school students. All students should be encouraged to participate in such after-school programs regardless of their ability and prior experience with organized sports. The primary purposes of these programs are to provide opportunities for students to:

1. improve self-esteem and feelings of competence through positive interactions with their peers and adults
2. acquire new skills and refine those previously learned
3. learn to function effectively as members of a team or group
4. improve personal health and fitness levels
5. have fun and enjoy physical activity

Recommendations for interscholastic sports for this age group are presented in the sidebar, "Recommendations for Middle School Interscholastic Sport Programs." While these recommendations reflect a concern for the development of the middle school child, many of the ideas expressed are appropriate for high school students as well. This is particularly true for the recommendation to provide opportunities for all who may want to participate. Recommendations for high school after-school and intramural programs can be found in the 2002 NASPE publication, *Guidelines for After School Physical Activity and Intramural Programs*.

It is the position of the authors of this text that both a developmentally appropriate athletic program and other opportunities for physical activity for the larger school population can and should be part of a good school physical activity program. We fully recognize that the decision to provide opportunities for students other than just the highly skilled is a value judgment and that it is critical for policy makers who have to make the hard decisions to consider the implications of their decisions. The following scenario highlights the political nature of these decisions.

The principal of Summer Middle School recognized the developmental nature of the middle school and the importance of providing opportunities for all students to participate in the after-school sport programs of the school. She designed the program so that there would be as many teams as needed to facilitate the participation of everyone who wanted to play, and provided the time and staff to run the program. Before the program was even started, parents of the more highly skilled called and were not supportive. They felt that their more highly skilled students would have a better chance of playing high school athletics if there was only one team. They would get more playing time and the full attention of the coach. The principal went back to a highly selective one-team model.

Recommendations for Middle School
Interscholastic Sport Programs

If middle schools decide to offer interscholastic sport programs, they should be progressively phased in and should be both recreational and competitive. The following guidelines from the National Association for Sport and Physical Education (2002) should be followed:

- The types of interscholastic sports offered to middle school students should be carefully considered. Sports that encourage students to concentrate on personal improvement (e.g., track and field, swimming, and so on), accommodate large numbers of participants, and are inherently safe (e.g., small sided soccer in modified space; pickleball) should take precedence over contact sports or sports that require extensive amounts of equipment or space.

- If interscholastic sports are offered at the middle school level, they must address the unique characteristics of middle school students. Therefore, playing rules, equipment, field dimensions, and so on must be modified to accommodate the ability levels and capacities of the participants. Middle school athletic programs must not attempt to imitate those conducted at the high school level. Safety and developmental appropriateness must be the primary concerns. In addition, middle school athletic programs should have skill refinements, basic tactics, and effective team membership as their primary goals instead of winning or entertaining spectators.

- All students who want to participate and are willing to make the commitment necessary for team membership should be allowed to participate in interscholastic sports at the middle school. An exclusive interscholastic program (cutting) has no place at the middle school since it contradicts the very tenets on which the middle school was founded. A variety of policies can be implemented to overcome any and all obstacles related to achieving this goal.

- Even if interscholastic sports are offered at the middle school, after-school programs that are more recreational and intramural should continue to be offered since they are more consistent with the overall philosophy of the middle school and accommodate larger numbers of students. Interscholastic sports can

  - 1. provide a "transitional experience" so they become accustomed to staying after school to participate with classmates;
  - 2. introduce them to sports that they might have been previously unfamiliar with;
  - 3. bolster confidence and self-esteem by letting students experience equitable competition and developmentally appropriate activities;
  - 4. allow them to participate in an environment that is less structured and less demanding than typically found in interscholastic sports.

Clearly it takes strong leadership for policy makers to do what is right, and it is not always easy to take the high road in the face of particularly vocal minorities. The conduct of these programs is discussed in the chapters that follow.

Scheduling the Physical Activity Program

In order to meet the needs of all students in a school, the implementation of a physical activity program for this age needs to consider all possibilities for scheduling, including programs during the school day, before- and after-school programs, and community-based programs outside the school.

Programs During the School Day

Unlike elementary school schedules, middle school and high school schedules are tightly structured. If students have any time during the regularly scheduled school day, it is most likely to be at lunchtime or during a "study hall." Several alternatives exist for programs conducted during the school day, including elective physical education, lunch programs, and study hall alternatives. A full discussion of these alternatives and their contributions appears in chapter 14.

Elective Physical Education

In the face of reduced requirements for physical education, many high school programs have established elective programs of physical education. Students can register for elective programs that either carry additional credit for graduation or do not carry credit. While some of these programs have been designed for the athlete, many have not been. When the physical education required program is well conducted, a large number (up to 65%) of high school students will choose to participate in the elective program. Successful programs will offer students an opportunity to choose activities that they have not been exposed to in the required program, as well as opportunities to participate in activities designed to develop and maintain fitness. Students register to take a physical education course after completion of the required physical education course when they sign up for the rest of their course work. Elective physical education programs need to include a wide range of courses that appeal to the diversity of interests of this population. Students who have had a required physical education course should not be permitted to sign up for the same experience but should be encouraged to take a different course. In some cases, elective physical education programs find themselves competing with elective course work in other content areas or running into policies that require students who are not doing well academically to take additional academic courses. Elective programs require the support of administrators who recognize the value of students having the opportunity to be physically active during the school day.

Lunch Programs

Many schools have found that they can run walking clubs, intramural programs, club activities, or "free gym" during lunchtime. Many students are sent outside after a quick lunch to do nothing but "hang out." Many of these students would much rather be engaged in more meaningful activity. Setting up facilities for a school fitness center would attract many students who sit and do nothing during their "free period." Fitness and weight training facilities should be open to students during the lunch hours.

Before- and After-School Programs

While it is common in most secondary schools for athletic teams to practice and play after school hours, opportunities for nonathletes have been largely crowded out by increased opportunities for highly skilled participants of both genders. Intramural opportunities and club activities engaging a large number of students in physical activity were at one time a commonplace part of school programs. They need to be again.

Competition for facilities and for teachers to conduct intramural and club activities is most certainly a hindrance to any efforts to reestablish these programs. Perhaps what is most key to their reestablishment is a change in perspective of what is important. Athletics is an important part of school physical activity programs and our culture. Surely any effort to reduce or eliminate athletics would be met with a great deal of resistance, and it should be. The important concept is that athletics do not have to be reduced or eliminated in order to meet the needs of the larger population of the school for physical activity. Before- and after-school physical activity programs for the larger school population can be in addition to school athletic programs rather than replacing them. To make this happen, coaches, teachers, and administrators must sit down and establish policies that will create a win–win orientation to their efforts. Comprehensive high schools have many indoor and outdoor teaching stations available to them. These are not all used all the time by athletics. Intramural soccer or basketball programs do not have to be run during soccer and basketball season. A large number of indoor and outdoor facilities sit empty before and after school and at various times during the school day. A full discussion of these issues is provided in chapter 13, "Planning the Secondary Physical Activity Program."

Involving the Community and Mandating Physical Activity

South Carolina was one of the first states to implement state-level assessment for physical education programs. One of the requirements for high school students in this program is that they participate in moderate to vigorous physical activity outside the physical education class on a regular basis for a period of at least six weeks during the school year. Students can choose to participate in after-school programs or programs of their choice in the community. They establish a contract with the physical education teacher that indicates an adult contact for confirmation of participation. The physical education teacher confirms participation with the adult.

A study done by Heidorn (2007) on the outside-of-class participation requirement was most sup-

Physical activity programs at the high school level should offer a wide variety of activities.

1. A staff person assigned as the physical activity *broker*. This can be the physical activity director or another person whose job it is to connect all students to an activity (or activities) of their choice either within or outside the school. It is also the job of this person to communicate choices to students and monitor student compliance.

2. A wide range of opportunities for students to meet the requirement within the school.

3. Strong community relations that engage the cooperation of churches, parks, recreation centers, and fitness centers to provide opportunities for students to meet this requirement and to work with the school to administer the programs.

4. Communication that solicits the cooperation of parents, other school personnel, and students.

The School Physical Activity Program: A Comprehensive Perspective

While there is likely to be great variation in the potential to create opportunities for a physical activity program for secondary students, good programs will also have much in common. The sidebar, "The Physical Activity Program of New Age High School," describes the vision of one school for an effective physical activity program. The scenario depicted is not an unreasonable expectation for schools. Minimally effective physical activity programs should

- begin with a good physical education program;
- have administrative support;
- have a designated physical activity director;
- work in conjunction with the school wellness policies and programs;
- meet the diverse needs and interests of the total student body;
- provide opportunities for structured and nonstructured activities in activities *relevant to and valued by* the students in a particular school before school, after school, and during the school day;
- consider the development of policies that mandate participation; and
- involve communities and parents.

portive of the effort. Interviews with students indicated that students mostly enjoyed the requirement and did participate in the activities they had chosen. Teachers involved in the study perceived that the requirement was having an impact on students, that it was a necessary requirement, and that most students were honest when reporting their participation. Key to the program's success were accountability and student choice. Contracts with students were established; adults verified student participation, and students were free to choose to be active in any way they wished.

Mandating participation in physical activity can be an effective way to meet students' needs for weekly participation in physical activity when requiring physical education every year is not a possibility in a school. In order for a mandated program of physical activity to work on a large scale, several key components have to be in place:

The Physical Activity Program of New Age High School

The district wellness committee of Bandoline County gave the physical education faculty and administrators of New Age High School the task of developing a physical activity program for their students. The first thing this group did was to establish a goal and vision for what they wanted to do. *Every student in their school would participate in at least 30 minutes a day of moderate to vigorous physical activity.* They brainstormed ways in which this could be accomplished:

- Create a policy that *requires* each student to participate daily in 30 minutes of vigorous activity through the programs of either the school or the community.
- Designate a school physical activity director to "broker" student choices and coordinate the efforts, as well as monitor the program. Because this was a large high school, a full-time faculty member would be hired.
- Designate a physical activity council consisting of representatives from physical education, other faculty members, parents, student government representatives, the community, and administrators.
- Provide before- and after-school intramural and club opportunities that would change periodically and could be conducted by community and parent volunteers with an interest in the activity.
- Establish before-, during-, and after-school facilities and programs for fitness-centered activities (weight-lifting, aerobic activities).
- Invite all churches, recreation centers, community clubs with interests in physical activity, YMCA/YWCA, state and national parks, and commercial organizations offering physical activities to meet with the physical activity director about providing students opportunities outside of the school setting.
- Establish a Web site to communicate policies and opportunities to students and parents.
- Inform parents of the requirement, its intent, and opportunities provided to students.

The planning committee collected data on student, faculty, and community interests; established a time line for implementation; and developed a potential three-year budget. They took their plan first to the district wellness committee to get support and then to the district school board. They suggested a three-year trial period and made the decision to apply for a state grant to begin the program.

The Physical Activity Director of the Secondary Program

The role of the physical activity director in secondary schools is quite different from that in the elementary school. The physical activity director of the elementary school program is likely to see as his or her major responsibility working with classroom teachers to ensure that students have 30 minutes of moderate to vigorous physical activity a day. The physical activity director of the elementary school will also be engaged in running and organizing before- and after-school programs and special events. Classroom teachers will be encouraged to provide activity breaks during their classes. Physical education teachers, coaches, and classroom teachers with special interests in particular activities, as well as adults from outside the school, will have a major responsibility for the program the school offers.

Like the physical activity director of the elementary school, the physical activity director of the high school needs to work with classroom teachers to help them provide physical activity breaks from academic work. This is particularly true in schools on a block schedule. Primarily, the physical activity director of the high school program needs to see his or her mission as providing a wide variety of opportunities for activity and connecting all students with the opportunity to participate in moderate to vigorous physical activity of their choice. In order to conduct the program, the physical activity director will need release time or minimally a salary supplement, depending on the size of the school and extensiveness of the program. High school physical activity directors must truly see themselves as a *broker,* with a major responsibility to connect every student to an activity that the student views as meaningful.

Administrative Support

No effort to establish a school physical activity program can succeed without the personal and financial support of the school administration. While federal law can mandate that schools have a policy, without the support of the administration, policy is not likely to be implemented. Administrators need to share the goal, participate in creating the vision, and provide the needed resources and leadership to make it happen.

The physical activity program of the school can potentially have a far greater impact on a large number of students than many club or athletic programs that are presently supported by schools. Although increasing physical education time is still an ideal way to increase the levels of physical activity for this population, establishing physical activity programs is likely to be a less expensive alternative. Involving the community and parents has the potential of garnering support needed for other efforts of the school.

One Size Does Not Fit All

One of the biggest challenges in conceptualizing a good physical activity program for a secondary school is the idea that by the time students reach their teen years they are very diverse, both as to why they choose to participate in physical activity and as to what activities they choose. It is a challenge to provide structured and nonstructured opportunities for activities *relevant to and valued by* the students in a particular school before, after, and during the school day. One of the classic works in physical education curriculum theory (Jewett & Mullan, 1977) suggested that people are motivated by different purposes in their movement experiences. This work indicated that the following reasons for participation are usually critical to the choices people make to be participants in a physical activity program:

- **Physiological efficiency:** improving and maintaining my fitness and skill
- **Psychological well-being:** joy of movement, release of tension, self-understanding, challenge, self-perception
- **Social interaction:** teamwork, competition, leadership, sharing ideas and feelings with others
- **Cultural:** participating in what is important to my culture or society

Some of these ideas are probably somewhat age related. For example, as we get older, maintaining physiological function becomes more important; for young children it seems easier to find joy just in moving for its own sake, and many teens are motivated by the need for social interaction. On the other hand, secondary students are likely to find personal meaning in all of the reasons listed, making it essential that we have a wide variety of offerings from which they can choose. Table 12.1 attaches potential choices for activities to

TABLE 12.1

Meeting the Diverse Needs of Students

The why of participation	Potential activities
Physiological efficiency: Improve and maintain skill and fitness	Walking, jogging, aerobic dance, strength training, instructional classes in a skill, self-defense
Psychological well-being: Release tension, experience enjoyment and challenge, increase self-understanding and a positive self-perception	Dance, individual sports and activities, martial arts, yoga, aquatic activities, walking, jogging
Social interaction: Experience teamwork, competition, leadership, being with friends, sharing ideas and feelings, sense of belonging	Team sports, individual sports, and activities with "my friends"
Cultural: Participate in what is important to one's culture; "belonging"	Activities common to a community or ethnic group (e.g., baseball in a baseball family, badminton in a badminton family); activities common to an age group (e.g., skateboarding, snowboarding, bicycling)

these ideas. A comprehensive program of physical activity recognizes that if all students are to be given opportunities for active participation that is meaningful to them, it is essential to include all of these types of activities.

Colleagues in recreational sport who have always had to deal with voluntary participation have wrestled for a long time with trying to meet the needs of a very diverse population. Figure 12.3, from the work of Mull, Bayless, and Jamieson (2005), presents continuums for a variety of factors that account for that diversity. Good physical activity programs will have to consider these factors in their planning as well. It will take a very comprehensive program to meet the needs of a student population whose interests span these reasons for participation. Meeting the needs for all students who will fall at different ends of the continuums is a challenge.

Informal	Formal
Organizational design	

Simple	Complex
Rules and regulations	

Low	High
Skill performance	

Minimum	Maximum
Physical exertion	

Relaxed	Intense
Mental concentration	

Low	High
Risk	

None	Numerous
Rule modification	

Low	High
Emphasis on winning	

Figure 12.3   Degrees of recreational sport participation.

SUMMARY

1. Once they leave elementary school, children show a rapid decline in their level of physical activity.

2. Physical activity has many growth and development as well as health advantages for adolescents.

3. Schools have a primary responsibility for increasing the physical activity of adolescent students.

4. The cornerstone of a good physical activity program is a good physical education program.

5. Opportunity to learn, meaningful content, appropriate instruction, and student and program assessment are the essential elements of a good physical education program.

6. School athletic and physical activity programs serve different needs.

7. After-school programs for students can improve self-esteem and competence, give students the opportunity to acquire and refine skills, help them learn to function as members of a group, improve their personal fitness levels, and provide an opportunity to have fun participating in physical activity.

8. The physical activity director of the secondary school should be a *broker*, ensuring that every student is connected to a positive physical activity experience.

9. Physical activity programs and athletic programs can share facilities within the school.

10. Elective physical education is one way to provide students with daily opportunities for physical activity.

11. Mandated programs for physical activity may be a way to help students establish daily routines for physical activity.

CHECKING YOUR UNDERSTANDING

1. What are the needs for physical activity for the adolescent student?

2. What factors influence the lack of physical activity among today's youth?

3. What are the characteristics of a good physical education program for middle school and high school students?

4. What is the difference between school athletic programs and school physical activity programs?

5. What are the characteristics of an effective physical activity program?

6. What are the responsibilities of the physical activity director of the middle school program and of the high school program?

7. What are the most common reasons that adolescents participate in physical activity?

8. For each of the times of the day when the physical activity program can be scheduled, what are the advantages and disadvantages?

9. What has to be in place to effectively run a mandated physical activity program?

RESOURCES

American Academy of Pediatrics: Policy on Organized Sports for Children and Preadolescents

www.aap.org/healthtopics/sports.cfm

American Academy of Pediatrics. (2001). Organized sports for children and preadolescents. RE0052. Available at http://aappolicy.aappublications.org/cgi/content/full/pediatrics;107/6/1459.

Burns, P. (1993). Meeting the sports needs of all young people. *Scholastic Coach*, 62(8), 4, 6.

National Association for Sport and Physical Education. (2002). *Co curricular physical activity and sport programs for middle school students* [Position paper]. Reston, VA: Author.

New York State Public High School Athletic Association. (2000). *Handbook for modified athletics, grades 7, 8, 9.* Delmar, NY: Author.

Powers, H.S., Conway, T.L., McKenzie, T.L., Sallis, J.F., & Marshall, S.J. (2002). Participation in extracurricular physical activity programs at middle schools. *Research Quarterly for Exercise and Sport*, 73(2), 187-192.

Young, D.R., Felton, G.M., Grieser, M., Elder, J.P., Johnson, C., Lee, J., et al. (2007). Policies and opportunities for physical activity in middle school environments. *Journal of School Health*, 77(1), 41-47.

REFERENCES

Centers for Disease Control and Prevention. (2008). Youth Risk Behavior Surveillance – United States, 2007. Available at www.cdc.gov/HealthyYouth/yrbs/pdf/yrbss07_mmwr.pdf. Accessed on September 2008 .

Corbin, C., & Lindsey, R. (2007). *Fitness for life.* Champaign, IL: Human Kinetics

Fairclough, S., & Stratton, G. (2005). Physical education makes you fit and healthy: Physical education's contribution to young people's physical activity levels. *Health Education Research*, 20(1), 14-23.

Heidorn, B. (2007). The effectiveness of an outside of school physical activity requirement for high school students. Doctoral dissertation, University of South Carolina, Columbia.

Jewett, A., & Mullan, M. (1977). *Curriculum design: Purposes and processes in physical education teaching-learning.* Reston, VA: American Alliance for Health, Physical Education, Recreation and Dance.

Johnston, L., Delva, J., & O'Malley, P. (2007). Sports participation and physical education in American secondary schools: current levels and racial/ethnic and socioeconomic disparities. *American Journal of Preventive Medicine*, 33(4s), 178-186.

Mull, R., Bayless, K., & Jamieson, L. (2005). *Recreational sport management* (4th ed.). Champaign, IL: Human Kinetics.

National Association for Sport and Physical Education. (2002). *Co-curricular physical activity and sport programs for middle school students* [Position paper].

National Association for Sport and Physical Education. (2002). *Guidelines for after school physical activity and intramural sport programs.* Reston, VA: Author.

National Association for Sport and Physical Education. (2004). *Opportunity to learn standards for high school physical education.* Reston, VA: Author.

National Association for Sport and Physical Education. (2009). *Appropriate practices for high school physical education.* Reston, VA: Author.

National Association for Sport and Physical Education. (2009). *Appropriate practices for middle school physical education.* Reston, VA: Author

National Association for Sport and Physical Education and American Heart Association. (2006). *2006 Shape of the nation report: Status of physical education in the USA.* Reston, VA: National Association for Sport and Physical Education.

Rink, J. (2009). *Designing the physical education curriculum. Promoting active lifestyles.* Boston: McGraw-Hall.

Sallis, J.F., McKenzie, T.L., Alcaraz, J.E., Kolody, B., Faucette, N., & Hovell, M.F. (1997). The effects of a 2-year physical education program (SPARK) on physical activity and fitness in elementary school students. *American Journal of Public Health*, 87, 1328-1334.

Strong, W., Malina, R., Blimkie, C., Daniels, S., Dishman, R., Gutin, B., Hergenroeder, A., Must, A., Nixon, P., & Pivarnik, J. (2005). Evidence based physical activity for school-age youth. *Journal of Pediatrics*, 146(6), 732-737.

U.S. Department of Health and Human Services. (1996). *Physical activity and health: A report of the surgeon general.* Atlanta: U.S. Department of Health and Human Services, Centers for Disease Control and Prevention, National Center for Chronic Disease Prevention and Health Promotion.

U.S. Department of Health and Human Services. (2004). Section 204 of Public Law 108-265—June 30, 2004, Child Nutrition and WIC Reauthorization Act of 2004.

Planning the Secondary Physical Activity Program

OVERVIEW

As emphasized throughout this book, physical activity programs should be planned to meet the needs of the whole school population. While most programs will need to start small and grow as student interest and institutional capacity grow, administrators of programs need to think through the potential of their school to offer a wide range of opportunities for students. This chapter is designed to help physical activity directors plan a physical activity program.

CHAPTER OUTCOMES

This chapter will help you

- determine student needs and interests in relation to the school physical activity program,

- identify procedures for procuring facilities and equipment for the program,

- identify the potential components of the physical activity program and scheduling issues,

- describe the difference between middle school and high school physical activity programs,

- describe procedures for administering the program and hiring and supervising staff, and

- identify different ways in which the physical activity program can be promoted.

IN THIS CHAPTER

Sometimes the intramural program is considered to be the physical activity program. The specific meaning of the term intramural is "within the walls." Traditionally in many schools the term "intramural" has been used to refer to competition between teams organized within the school. This text uses the term "physical activity program" rather than "intramural program" to distinguish the physical activity program from the instructional physical education program, as well as to include all school initiatives aimed at increasing the physical activity levels of students and not just competitive activities or those conducted on the school campus. Although the physical education program is the foundation of a good physical activity program, a comprehensive physical activity program is an extension of the physical education program and has as its purpose meeting the needs for daily physical activity of secondary students in a way that develops a physically active lifestyle. The intramural program is just one component of the physical activity program.

Although requiring participation in the program is an idea that deserves exploration (see chapter 12), participation in physical activity programs is usually voluntary. To attract students, the program must be conducted so as to offer a wide range of attractive options for participation. Because the intent is not only to provide students with opportunities for daily physical activity but to do so in a way that encourages a physically active lifestyle, the program must offer fun and enjoyable activities that are meaningful experiences for the students.

The Goals of an Inclusive Program

In chapter 12 we alluded to the idea that all students don't find the same types of activities meaningful and enjoyable. This is particularly true of the secondary student, and even more so of the physically inactive "at-risk" population that needs to be targeted in a comprehensive physical activity program. While the athletic programs of schools have for the most part met the needs of the more highly skilled through highly competitive activities, the rest of the school population has been left largely underserved in terms of opportunities for physical activity.

The needs and interests of this age population in relation to physical activity are highly diverse. Planning a physical activity program requires the planners to think in terms of the impact of that diversity on what they do. The goal of the program should be to connect *each* student in the school with physical activity that he or she finds meaningful in order to meet the immediate needs for daily physical activity, and to do so in a way that develops a long-term physically active lifestyle.

While physical education programs and comprehensive physical activity programs are both concerned with developing a physically active lifestyle, they are conducted and evaluated with a different intent. The physical education program is conducted as an instructional program and evaluated in terms of what students learn; physical activity school programs have had as their goal making physical activity fun and building student leadership and character to develop a physically active lifestyle. Physical activity programs should be evaluated in terms of the extent to which they promote the physical activity of the entire student body.

Designing a comprehensive program inclusive of the needs and interests of all students, in a way that connects each student to a physical activity, is not easy and until the recent obesity crisis has largely not been a concern of the school. Where programs have existed, they have not targeted the inactive. In an inclusive program, each student can find activities that he or she sees as meaningful and enjoyable, and all students have an equal opportunity for participation. When thinking about planning for an inclusive program, it is helpful to consider whom you want to include. An inclusive program will meet the needs of the following groups that are often left out of athletic programs:

- Students who want to focus on fitness activities
- Students with some skill who have been left out of the athletic programs and want to participate in competitive activities
- Students who are less skilled or less competitive and want to participate in nontraditional activities that don't require a lot of skill
- Students who may want to develop skills in activities not traditionally offered by physical education programs
- Female students who want to participate in sport within programs that have few opportunities for girls, or in more traditional gender-related activities such as dance
- Students who have been unsuccessful in physical activities and largely have chosen not to be participants
- Special needs students for whom activities must be modified
- Students who want to be involved in physical activity for social reasons

Each of these groups has unique needs for programming. Table 13.1 identifies kinds of activities that may attract different groups of students. As you begin your programming efforts and put the program together, you will want to review this list

TABLE 13.1

The Inclusive Physical Activity Program

Student group	Potential interest
Students who want to focus on fitness activities	Walking/jogging clubs, open weight room, aerobic dance, community fitness centers
Students with some skill who have been left out of the athletic programs and want to participate in competitive activities	Intramural competitive programs with leagues and tournaments, open gyms
Students who are less skilled or less competitive and want to participate in nontraditional activities that don't require a lot of skill (some will like team and some will like individual activities)	Modified sport games (e.g., throw volleyball, scooter basketball); individual activities (e.g., disc golf, archery)
Students who may want to develop skills in new activities not traditionally offered by physical education programs, particularly adventure activities	Clubs and community opportunities (e.g., wall climbing, kayaking, low-element challenge courses)
Female students who want to participate in sport or more traditional gender-related activities such as dance	Girls-only intramural competitive programs with leagues and tournaments; gymnastics and dance clubs, aerobic dance
Students who have been unsuccessful in physical activities and choose not to participate	Walking clubs, activities that don't require a great deal of skill, fitness activities
Special needs students for whom activities should be modified	Activities that students choose and that are modified when they get there; Special Olympics program that students can be connected to; special programs if the population is large enough
Students who want to be involved in physical activity for social reasons	Examples: walking/jogging, golf, doubles tennis, bocce ball, croquet

and ask yourself whether the needs of each of these groups are being met by what you do. Planning the program will require you to assess student needs and interests and establish a baseline for the facilities, equipment, and personnel you have and will need in order to run the program. This chapter is an overview of those responsibilities. Chapter 14, "Administering the Physical Activity Program," describes each of these functions in more detail.

Determining Student Needs and Interests

One of the first things that planners may want to do is to establish a baseline of student needs and interests. This can be done using a variety of sources of data, but student focus groups representing a small random sample of the student population and surveys are usually effective. Student focus groups

are conducted by inviting a group of students (usually not more than 10-15 in a group) to share their perspectives on what their primary interests might be for participation. Large schools may have to invite several groups of students in order to get the representation needed. Focus groups allow you to get the students' perspective on the kind of program they would like to see. Figure 13.1 outlines some questions the focus group leader may want to ask students. Based on the findings from the focus groups, a more comprehensive student survey similar to the one suggested in figure 13.2 might be given to the entire school population.

Getting the student perspective is important when you are beginning to plan a program. The focus group will give you the student perspective. Through the use of interest surveys, you can determine the kinds of programs you will need to meet the interests and needs of all students. If all

---

FIGURE 13.1

Student Interest Focus Groups

1. What activities do you participate in after school that you really enjoy?
2. Which of the following types of activity opportunities would you participate in if provided?
   - Fitness center for weight training
   - Fitness center or time for cardiorespiratory workout (jogging, aerobic dance, step climbers, bicycles)
   - Open gym to just shoot hoops
   - Three-versus-three basketball tournaments
   - A club for a new activity like fencing
   - A dance club
   - Ultimate pickup games or tournament
   - Disc golf
   - Golf lessons at the golf course
   - Bowling at the bowling alley
   - Tennis tournament, tennis open courts
3. If you want to be a participant in these activities, when is the best time to offer them?
   - Before school
   - After school
   - Lunch
   - Your free period
4. Would you prefer to participate with mixed-gender groups (boys and girls together) or with girls and boys separate?

FIGURE 13.2

Student Interest Survey

Name _____   Date _____

Year in school _____   Student ID # _____

When would you most like to come to participate in physical activity?

_____ Before school _____ Lunchtime _____ During my free period _____ After school

Rate each of the following activities in terms of your interest in participating. A "5" indicates a high interest a "0" indicates no interest. Put a check in the column that has a "?" if you do not know what the activity is. Check in the "B" column if you have done the activity before.

Activity	0-5	?	B	Activity	0-5	?	B
Aerobic dance				Volleyball (3 v. 3)			
Touch football				Paddleball			
Badminton				Pickleball			
Tennis				Rugby			
Baseball				Wrestling			
Ultimate				Skateboarding			
Fencing				Kayaking			
Field hockey				Rock climbing			
Lacrosse				Backpacking			
Bowling				Sailing			
Golf				Skiing			
Martial arts				Team handball			
Table tennis				Social dance			
Disc golf				Jazz dance			
Weightlifting				Modern dance			
Track and field				Handball			
Gymnastics				Archery			

Figure 13.2   Sample student interest survey.

students are surveyed, the data will show you how many students are interested in particular activities and which students are interested in what activities. One of the biggest problems you are likely to have is that in most schools, a program that is just beginning cannot meet all these needs and interests. You will want to set priorities based upon gaining maximum participation. If each student is surveyed and you can attach names to the survey, you will also be able to target particular groups not presently being served by school or community programs. You will need to establish priorities that juggle student interests with resources available; these are not easy decisions but nevertheless decisions that have to be made.

What Facilities Do We Have and Need?

Facilities are likely to be the biggest inhibitor of what you can do with a secondary physical activity program. You will need to think in terms of working with the facilities that are available, when they are available, and using alternative spaces and community resources. Because facilities are such a big part of decisions regarding what you can offer, you may find yourself walking around your school making lists of what potential activities can be offered in what location.

Many facilities will have to be coordinated with the schedules of both the physical education program and the athletic programs of the school. Can physical education classes be scheduled so that the gym is empty during lunchtimes? Can you use the weight rooms when classes aren't scheduled and athletic teams are not using them for training? Does the gym sit empty in the afternoons when outdoor teams are practicing, and do the fields sit empty when indoor teams are practicing? Can you run activities directly after school in the gym while athletic teams are doing conditioning or "classroom" activities? Can athletic teams wait 45 minutes after school to begin their practices? All of these issues need to be part of a program coordinated with both the athletic and the physical education programs. Many of the faculty who run these programs will be supportive of the need for a physical activity program for the larger school population, but some will not. Selling the idea that a comprehensive physical activity program is just as important as the current well-established athletic program may take some time, but will be a lot easier if the program is designed as a district wellness council project and if the administration is supportive. This means that any attempt to negotiate space needs to be done with the administration.

Finding appropriate facilities to run a program may also mean that you have to think in terms of alternative areas within the school campus. Many activities do not require a gym but merely a space larger than a single classroom (e.g., dance, fencing, and golf). School all-purpose rooms, cafeterias, stages, and large hallways are not ideal but are acceptable when ideal facilities are not available. Many schools now have weight rooms, fitness rooms, strength rooms, and cardio rooms that can be utilized before school, after school, at lunchtimes, and at times during the day when no classes are scheduled in these facilities. Outdoor spaces have the same potential. If you don't have a gym for volleyball, can you set up courts outside? Climate will also determine what facilities are available. If the weather is good, most sports and activities can be conducted outside. If snow is on the ground from October to March, all sorts of winter contests and events are possible (e.g., snow sculpture contests, snowman contests, games like King of the Hill), as well as winter sports such as snowshoeing, skiing, and winter hiking. The Web sites listed at the end of this chapter can provide teachers with a great deal of help in setting up a curriculum of outdoor winter sports.

Programs also need to consider the available community resources. Public and commercial recreation and sport groups are anxious to educate students to be physically active and particularly anxious to have young people develop an interest in their activities. The physical activity programs of the school should not seek to duplicate opportunities in the community but rather should work with the community to connect students to these opportunities. Many parks, recreation centers, golf courses and driving ranges, fitness centers, bowling alleys, and pools may be available within close proximity to the school. Many high school students today have their own transportation. Middle school students may need transportation to these facilities. Setting up a program requires school personnel to work with the community, not only in terms of using the facilities but also in terms of recruiting personnel to work in the program.

It would be very wise for program administrators to meet with community leaders and providers as part of the process of setting up a program. The purpose of such meetings is to share the objectives of the program, solicit input into it, and investigate the possibilities for cooperative arrangements. Such arrangements might involve the following:

- Program leaders providing students with material on community participation possibilities (where, what, how much?)

- When a cost is involved, community providers sponsoring students for a period of time (e.g., free membership for a semester)
- Community providers agreeing to conduct a club for the activity either at the school or at the community facility
- Community leaders coming to the school and talking to student groups about participation

What Equipment Do I Need?

Programs need to be planned in terms of equipment that is available or is possible to obtain. Regulation equipment for many activities is not necessary; and a lot of community organizations are willing to donate older equipment, let you borrow theirs for short periods of time, or lease it at reduced rates. Schools can also share equipment within and between districts. There is no need to run the same activity at the same time. District offices may house equipment to be checked out by individual schools.

Structuring the Program

When you have some idea of student interests and the resources that you will have to run your program, you need to think about the different components of the program. Most people think in terms of intramural programs as competitions between

Many weight rooms are empty a large part of the day and can be opened to the school population.

teams within a school. In order to meet the diverse needs of a school population, when you consider the physical activity program of the school you should think more broadly, about elements such as these:

- *Open facilities:* Fitness areas, weight rooms, and open gyms—many students will come to participate in "pickup" games and activities when facilities are available
- *Tournaments:* Short competitions between teams (e.g., table tennis tournament)
- *Leagues:* Long-term competitions between teams (e.g., basketball or pickleball)
- *Contests:* One-time events—competition in a specific skill (e.g., free throw contest, dance contest)
- *Clubs:* Long-term participation in a particular activity, usually individual (e.g., social dance, skiing or cycling)
- *Special events:* One-time or short-term events (e.g., 5K marathon, field trips)
- *Community opportunities:* Health club participation, golf, church leagues

You do not want to duplicate the opportunities in the community if they are available and open to all students. You want to facilitate student participation in these activities, which will do much to help students make the transition from within school to out of school and a physically active lifestyle. If there is a special marathon, cycling event, Thanksgiving dance, or backpacking event, you should be thinking about working with the community to facilitate the participation of your students. You can begin your planning by taking the interest surveys of students and blocking out where their interests may be met by the community and where you may need to provide programs not available in the community. Table 13.2 is a rough draft of a program outline.

Issues Related to Timing

How long should a league season be? When is the best time to hold an event? In deciding how long to run a competition between teams or a club activity, you will want to plan so that you do not lose student interest before the activity culminates. Seasons for middle school students will probably be shorter (two weeks) than for high school students (four to six weeks). There are no hard-and-fast rules about how long a season should be, and the decisions you make need to be based on your experience with the program and on the relationship of a particular activity to other offerings within the program.

Scheduling of single events is best coordinated with school calendars, holiday schedules, and community activities. You don't want to compete with other school or community events for student participation.

TABLE 13.2

Program Plan: South High School

Type of event	When offered
Open facilities (weight room before school and at lunchtime, gym before school and after school)	September-June
TOURNAMENTS	
Pickleball	September
Miniature golf	October
Table tennis	November
3 v. 3 volleyball	January
Wiffle ball	February
Four Square	March
Horseshoes	April
Tennis	May
Archery	June

(continued)

TABLE 13.2 *(continued)*

Type of event	When offered
LEAGUES	
3 v. 3 basketball, girls and boys	September-October
7 v. 7 soccer, girls and boys	October-November
Ultimate, coed	November-January
Golf, coed	March-April
Bowling, coed	February-March
3 v. 3 basketball, girls and boys	March-April
CONTESTS	
Free throw contest, girls	September
Free throw contest, boys	September
Jogging contest, total miles	October
Pogo stick contest	November
Hula hoop contest	December
Dance marathon	January
Cup stacking	February
Sit-ups and push-ups	March
Jogging, total miles	April
CLUBS	
Taekwondo	November-February
Archery	April-June
Cycling	September-October
Line dancing	November-January
Walking	September-June
Tai chi	January-March
Pilates, yoga	September-December
SPECIAL EVENTS	
Orientation to program	September
Community walk/run	April
Thanksgiving hop	November
Rafting field trip	October
Snowmobiling Snowshoeing Winter hiking	January
COMMUNITY OPPORTUNITIES	
Rec center basketball	
Fitness center aerobics	
Church league softball	
Bowling league	

Differences Between Middle School and High School Programming

There will be significant differences between high school and middle school in terms of the types of activities you provide, the length of time activities are run, and the amount of support you will need to run the activities. Middle school students need more opportunities to explore activities they have not done before. Most do not have the skills to play regulation sports. Middle school students may need some initial instruction and will need more supervision. Leagues will involve sport activities that are very small sided and modified. Students in the middle school find participation in low-skill contests and low organization kinds of activities more enjoyable than older students do. They may participate in contests that adults and high school students think are *silly*. Planning a middle school program will involve a variety of activities and shorter-duration interest groups.

High school students are able to participate more independently in activities that they have already been introduced to in or outside of physical education. If they have been well prepared in physical education, they should be able to play regulation forms of most sport activities but will still enjoy more small-sided contests with greater opportunity to "touch the ball." They will want to develop skill in club activities and to participate for longer periods of time to work toward a culminating event in the given activity. They will tolerate instruction and coaching in activities they have no experience in; and they are likely to be more attracted to all-school events like "dance-a-thons" or to activities more related to their adolescent culture than the typical field days or events that may capture the interest of the middle school student.

How Do Students Sign Up?

Different aspects of the physical activity program require different strategies for getting students signed up. There is no best method. If the physical activity program is going to be a required program, students will need to choose ahead of time what they want to participate in and will contract to participate in particular activities. Contracts can be for a quarter, a semester, or the entire year (see chapter 14). For an "open facility" that is available on a first come, first served basis, no sign-up procedures are required. For a strictly voluntary program, you will have to make a decision about how to sign students up. Since most people who run physical activity programs have other full-time jobs, you want to make the process efficient. At the same time, to maximize participation, you want to make signing up an easy process for students.

Open Participation

Most schools will want to designate and schedule particular groups for open participation at different times. The weight room might be designated for girls only on some days and for boys only on other days. Lunch intramurals might be scheduled for sixth grade on Monday and Wednesday and for seventh and eighth grades on Tuesday and Thursday. A gym might be "girls only" on Tuesday, "boys only" on Thursday, and open on other days. Not knowing how many students will show up at any one time may require you to make some quick adjustments in the activity planned; but with experience in the program you will be able to better predict how many students you may need to accommodate at one time. An advantage of open participation is that it gives students the option of showing up or not showing up. The decision is theirs. Required programs and more structured activities, particularly team activities, create more student responsibility for attendance.

Team Activities

Regardless of whether the activity is scheduled as open participation or whether students sign up in advance, if the activity involves teams, your guiding principle should be equal distribution of skill and ability. Balancing teams sometimes creates a problem because students often want to participate with their friends. The value of competition and the fun for most people in competitive events rest with the idea that each person or team has an equal chance of winning and losing and that the outcome is unknown. When the outcome is known ahead of time and the same people win and the same people lose, those on the team that have little chance of winning are likely to not want to participate, and the fun of the competition is decreased for all.

In open participation, students usually can organize themselves into "pickup teams." The supervisor must watch carefully to make sure that students who have shown up are not excluded or made to feel excluded by the way in which teams are chosen. Rules of "next up" need to be established by the students or supervisor. Student groups in these situations can decide on their own rules and conduct the activity independently for the most part.

For team activities, students can also sign up as a team. Sometimes teams represent grade levels, homerooms, or particular groups within the school.

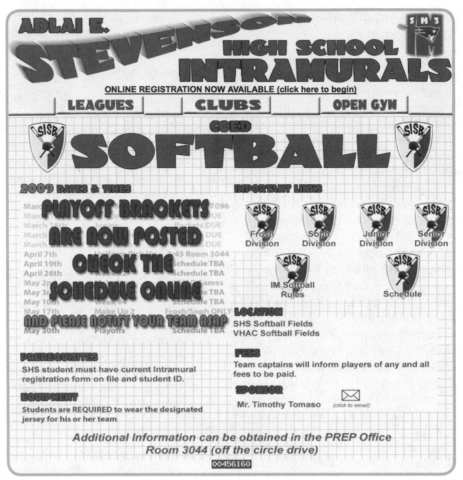

Many high schools have their own Web page to keep students abreast of opportunities and current information on the program.

Mostly, students at the secondary level want to play with their friends. Again, the issue of balanced teams must be weighed against the idea of giving students the opportunity to form their own teams. If individuals sign up to participate, the administrator has more control over balancing the skill levels of the teams. One method that seems to work is to have the group select captains and for the captains to meet with the administrator to select balanced teams. Selection of teams should be a private process and not one in which participants may be publicly humiliated. Captains usually pick the students who are their friends, but the process also has some advantages with regard to balancing the teams.

Clubs

Students should sign up ahead of time to join a club. When the club will meet, how long it will meet, and the requirements for membership should be clear. Club activities are based on the idea of sustained participation over a period of time. Many club activities include not only participation but also instruction in the activity on the assumption that people want to get better at that activity. If an activity for the club changes, some members may find that they do not enjoy the new activity and should be permitted to drop their membership. Clubs can meet at the school or can use community facilities and equipment. Good programs give students the opportunity to recommend adding a club if enough students demonstrate interest.

Special Events

Some special events require students to sign up ahead of time, and some do not. If the event involves registration, preparation of facilities or equipment, or limited enrollment (e.g., field trips such as kayaking, bicycle touring, marathons), students will need to sign up in advance. Most special events held at the school (e.g., dance-a-thons, Circus Night) will not require prior sign-up.

Staffing the Physical Activity Program

In an ideal world, there would be enough trained professionals in physical education or recreation within a school setting to staff a complete comprehensive physical activity program. In most schools the ideal is not the reality. Two kinds of skills are needed to staff a program. For some activities you will need staff with highly specialized skills in the given activity (e.g., aquatics, taekwondo, archery, Pilates, tai chi), particularly when safety is an issue. In other cases you will need a staff that you can train to organize and run the activity (e.g., jogging program, three-on-three basketball, dance contest). There are six main sources of staff:

- Physical education teachers and student teachers within the school who have the skills for an activity
- Other teachers and staff within the school who have the interest or skills (or both) for an activity or are willing to volunteer their assistance with fund-raising and promotional efforts
- Community volunteers with specialized skills
- Community volunteers with interest in and support for the program who can be trained to help
- Community paid instructors
- Students

If you could pay salary supplements to teachers and honorariums to volunteers, it would be easier to recruit help. Some programs recruit volunteers for fund-raising and then pay people to conduct the program. For most programs, you will need to depend on convincing people that their efforts and time are worthy contributions to a much-needed program. Program leaders have to be patient with regard to the amount of time it takes to build a program and get people on board. The best recruitment tool you will have is a good program and a satisfied volunteer.

You not only have to recruit volunteers; you have to keep them involved. People with experience in volunteer efforts suggest the following:

- Do not try to convince volunteers that they should give more time than they have agreed to. Make sure that if they say they will put in 2 hours a week, you do not give them a job that takes 4 or more hours a week.

Why People Volunteer

- To help others and contribute to the community
- To use skills in a new setting
- To gain work experience
- To find new friends and form new relationships
- To develop a sense of accomplishment and self-worth
- To learn new skills
- To challenge themselves
- To contribute to a cause they hold dear
- To gain recognition for their abilities
- To help improve the quality of their community

- Use the talents that people have. Don't put an instructor in a record-keeping job. Find someone else to do the record keeping.

Knowing why people volunteer to do things is a good way to channel your efforts into a plan that works. The sidebar outlines why people volunteer. Find out which of these reasons is likely to convince a volunteer to contribute. When someone does volunteer for a job, you will be more successful in getting the individual to do it again if the beginning and ending for the responsibility are clear. For example, if a parent or someone else in the community is a good fencer, you might share that the club activity is for eight weeks, two days a week. You will not ask the individual to do anything until next year when you run the activity again. Volunteers do not want to feel trapped by their responsibilities and have no way out.

Many commercially run recreation organizations (e.g., tennis clubs, golf courses, dance studios) may very well be willing to volunteer their expertise for school programs that have the potential to build a customer base for them. These folks should be a primary target for school programs. Many may even be willing to allow students the use of their facilities without charge while they are participants.

Many volunteer jobs do not require a great deal of expertise, such as student record keeping, basic facility and equipment management, organizing teams for participation, keeping score, and refereeing. Students are good sources for many organizational functions of a program. Developing a leadership base of student assistants will not only help the students but will also provide invaluable help for the program. Some schools have established "clubs" of student leaders who are trained to conduct programs and given special opportunities. Student roles and responsibilities are described in detail in chapter 14.

Promoting the Program

The best program in the world can be ineffective because no one knows about it or because people do not have information about how to participate. Students need to know when, where, and how to participate; and the information you give them has to motivate them to want to participate. Promotional materials should make students aware that an opportunity exists, give students the information they need in order to participate, and create a sense of "I want to do this" (Byl, 2002).

Methods of Promotion

Once you get your program started, the student "grapevine"—student-to-student contact— is one of the most effective ways of promoting it. If the program is good, students will know about it. In today's media world there are many choices for promoting your program in a school setting, including those listed next. A checklist of promotional alternatives is provided in figure 13.3.

■ *Live presentations:* Members of your staff, teachers, or student representatives can talk to different classes in homeroom or at other times during the school day to communicate opportunities and information on participation. Many schools have orientation programs for new students or for returning students at the beginning of the school year. These are ideal times for face-to-face contact with students.

■ *Public address announcements and video presentations:* Many schools use morning or afternoon announcements on the public address system to communicate about school events. Some schools use a closed-circuit TV to do morning announcements. These are ideal formats for ensuring that all students are made aware of the opportunities for participation.

■ *Handouts, newsletters, flyers:* If budget permits, putting a piece of paper in someone's hand is an effective way to get a lot of information across in a way that allows the person to quickly retrieve the specifics of the communication to be used later. Handouts can be distributed to each student in a class in homeroom or put in places that all students frequent so that they can pick them up (cafeteria, hallways, entrances to school).

■ *The school newspaper:* Many schools (particularly high schools) have school newspapers or flyers that are distributed on a regular basis. Getting a "good spot" in the paper will ensure that most students get the information you want them to have.

■ *Web sites:* Your physical activity program should have its own Web site. The program Web

---

FIGURE 13.3

Promoting Your Program Checklist

■ Live presentations

■ P.A. announcements and video presentations

■ Handouts, newsletters, flyers

■ The school newspaper

■ Web sites

■ E-mail

■ Bulletin boards and posters

■ T-shirts and other prizes

site should be linked to the district or school Web site for easy access. Most districts have turned to Web masters to design and input the contents of the school Web site. You will need to work with these folks to make sure that what you want done is done correctly and on time. If more skilled help is not available, there are lots of programs for creating Web sites that are easy to use. It is even possible that students within your school already have these skills.

■ *E-mail:* E-mail is quickly becoming the media of choice for promotional efforts and advertising. If your school uses e-mail to communicate with students, you should consider using this avenue for promoting and providing information on your program. If you are permitted to set up a listserv of students or of previous participants in an activity, you should consider this direct contact an avenue of choice.

■ *Bulletin boards and posters:* Attractive posters placed in high-traffic areas are an effective way to get your message across if they are not competing with a lot of other written material to result in a media overload. The physical activity program should have a bulletin board that students know always has current information on opportunities for participation.

■ *T-shirts and other prizes:* If you have the funds, it is effective to create awards such as T-shirts or other items that bear the logo of the program or event. When worn or used by the student, these become an advertisement for the program.

Making Your Promotional Work Effective

There are some things you can do to target your participants and make your efforts at recruitment more effective. These ideas are critical for programs that are just trying to get started.

■ Communicate the benefits of the program to students using the language of the age group. Saying "Improve cardiorespiratory fitness" might not be as effective as saying "Come and have fun with your friends" or mentioning prizes to be given out.

■ Set the goal of reaching the greatest number of people with the least effort. Plan your promotional effort to use a systematic approach.

■ Communicate the inclusiveness of your program. Let students know they don't have to be skilled or even know anything about the activity to participate.

■ Encourage students who are participants to seek out those who are not. Have a prize for those who sign up the most new participants.

■ For high school students, appeal to their sense of trying new things and challenging themselves. Middle school students will be more motivated by "fun."

■ Keep your materials up to date. Take down items such as posters for events that have already happened. Keep the Web site current. For events that have not yet occurred, give students plenty of time to make plans to attend.

■ Get help to make your materials look "professional." Everything you send out should be visually appealing. Color and photographs are obvious pluses. If your budget is limited, look to volunteers or staff and faculty in the school for help. Design and use a consistent logo.

SUMMARY

1. The needs of all students, particularly those "at risk" in terms of physical activity, must be a priority for planning the secondary physical activity program.

2. The initial step in planning the program consists of determining student needs and interests and the facilities and equipment available.

3. Programs should be structured to provide a variety of opportunities including open facilities, tournaments, leagues, clubs, special events, and community opportunities.

4. Seasons for middle school students will be different than those for high school students and will need to include instructional opportunities.

5. The program can be staffed with physical education teachers and other school personnel, community volunteers, community paid instructors, or parents.

6. All sources of communication should be considered in promoting the program.

CHECKING YOUR UNDERSTANDING

1. What should be the primary goal in planning the physical activity program?

2. What are the potential interests of secondary students in relation to participation in a physical activity program?

3. How can you determine student needs and interests?

4. What facilities are likely to be available in the middle school and the high school setting?

5. How can physical activity programs coexist with athletic programs?

6. How can the physical activity program make use of community resources?

7. What kinds of opportunities should be considered in planning the physical activity program for secondary students?

8. What are the differences between an appropriate program for middle school students and one for high school students?

9. What potential sources for staffing a program should be considered?

10. Describe five ways a program can be promoted.

RESOURCES

Educators and Recreation Professionals

www.winterfeelsgood.com/winterfeelsgood.php?section=teachers

Introduction to Snow Sports (Snowshoeing & Nordic Skiing) Curriculum and PEP Grant Information

www.winterfeelsgood.com/winterfeelsgood.php?section=helpful&page=info_curriculum_fairfax

WinterKids Guide to Outdoor Active Learning

www.winterkids.org/GOAL/index.html

American Academy of Pediatrics. Clinical Report. (2007).The importance of play in promoting healthy child development and maintaining strong parent-child bonds. *PEDIATRICS*, 119(1), 182-191.

Burns, P. (1993). Meeting the sports needs of all young people. *Scholastic Coach*, 62(8), 4, 6.

Doyle, P. (2001). *Game on: 76 games and activities for kids 5-14*. Champaign, IL: Human Kinetics.

May, S. (2000) Volunteering – Back to basics. Profile (June-July): 3 In Byl, J. (2002). *Intramural Recreation: A Step by Step Guide to Creating and Effective Program*. Champaign, IL: Human Kinetics.

National Association for Sport and Physical Education. (2002). *Co-curricular physical activity and sport programs for middle school students* [Position paper]. Reston, VA: Author.

New York State Public High School Athletic Association. (2000). *Handbook for modified athletics, grades 7, 8, 9*. Delmar, NY: Author.

Powers, H.S., Conway, T.L., McKenzie, T.L., Sallis, J.F., & Marshall, S.J. (2002). Participation in extracurricular physical activity programs at middle schools. *Research Quarterly for Exercise and Sport*, 73(2), 187-192.

Stewart, C. (2005). Has the decline of intramural sports contributed to the youth obesity epidemic? *Journal of Physical Education, Recreation and Dance*, 76, 11-13.

Young, D.R., Felton, G.M., Grieser, M., Elder, J.P., Johnson, C., Lee, J., et al. (2007). Policies and opportunities for physical activity in middle school environments. *Journal of School Health*, 77(1), 41-47.

REFERENCE

Byl, J. (2002). *Intramural recreation: A step-by-step guide to creating an effective program*. Champaign, IL: Human Kinetics.

14

Administering the Physical Activity Program

OVERVIEW

As with most programs, the success of the physical activity program is largely dependent upon the manner in which it is administered. This chapter outlines some of the essential functions critical to administering a physical activity program (developing an administrative flowchart of responsibilities, staffing, ensuring the health and safety of participants, budgeting, and awards). The chapter begins with information that can be helpful in setting up a required program.

CHAPTER OUTCOMES

This chapter will help you

- describe how to set up a required physical activity program,
- identify the essential components of an administrative organizational flowchart,
- describe how to staff the physical activity program,
- identify the factors essential for positive relationships with volunteer workers,

- identify the potential safety factors and liability issues involved in a physical activity program,
- identify potential sources of income and expenditures for the physical activity program, and
- identify the factors related to a good awards system for the physical activity program.

Although it is becoming more common for classroom teachers at the secondary level to look for ways to provide activity breaks for students, particularly when schools use block scheduling, most secondary physical activity programs are conducted apart from classroom programs and the physical education program. They require policies and procedures and an administrative structure to ensure their success. The goal of the secondary physical activity program is the same as for the elementary program—to involve all students in the school in physical activity. Setting up a program to do this requires planning and administration skills.

One of the first decisions that needs to be made is whether the program will be a required one or a voluntary one. This chapter begins with a discussion of some of the issues involved in setting up a required program, and then focuses on administrative decisions common to all programs, whether voluntary or required.

Establishing a Required Program

As discussed in chapter 12, required physical activity programs are new to schools. Although many states have established laws to mandate physical activity apart from physical education at the elementary school level, only Tennessee and to a lesser extent South Carolina have attempted to mandate participation at the secondary level. Elementary programs must take time out of the school day to ensure that students are getting at least some physical activity. These programs are mostly conducted by classroom teachers and utilize a mandated recess, a model that will not work at the secondary level. Because secondary students are more independent in their free time, it is possible to expect them to be physically active outside the school day when activity during the school day is not an option. Setting up a required physical activity program that will work necessitates that you have several critical components in place, including policy that mandates the program, resources such that students have a wide variety of options from which to choose to be active, and procedures for accountability.

Establishing Policy

Schools, districts, or states must formulate policies that mandate participation in physical activity if a required physical activity program is to be established. Tennessee is considering requiring students to take one year of required physical education and to participate in a physical activity program for another year. South Carolina requires high school students to participate in physical activity outside the physical education program for a minimum of six weeks; this outside activity is a part of the physical education program. Both of these efforts are designed not only to help students become participants in physical activity but also to help them make the transition from required physical education to physical activity as a part of their lifestyle.

Beginning research on the South Carolina program indicates that students are very supportive. Heidorn (2007) reported that students mostly enjoyed the requirement and were honest and actually participated in the activities they said they did. Teachers in the study felt that the requirement was having an impact on students and was a necessary part of the physical education program. The study also showed that effective teachers held students accountable for the requirement, gave students a choice regarding their outside activities, maintained consistent contact with parents, and assisted students in finding time to be physically active.

Although individual schools can put policies in place, it is easier to enforce expectations and get support for a program if the policy is established at a level higher than the school (district, state). Programs that seek a requirement should do several things:

- Work with the district wellness council to get support
- Work with the state American Alliance for Health, Physical Education, Recreation and Dance (AAHPERD) organizations and health organizations to get state policy formulated
- Seek the support of the administration and parents for policy
- Start a voluntary physical activity program, make it successful, and then seek support for a mandated requirement

Develop a Program That Gives Students Many Choices

As discussed throughout chapters 12 and 13 of this text, there is a great diversity of needs and interests among secondary students. If a required program is instituted, it must allow for the greatest flexibility in student options for meeting the requirement. That would mean that students should be allowed to choose to participate in programs in the school as well as outside the school. Examples of both are listed in table 14.1.

Table 14.1 does not include many traditional physical education activities, but it certainly could. It was designed to emphasize the different intents of a physical activity and a physical education program in terms of what one might consider appropriate experiences. While a hunting club would rarely be a school activity, if students are getting up at five in the morning and hiking into the woods to hunt on a regular basis and if this is an interest of theirs, a hunting club should be supported as meeting the requirement. Physical activity programs developed in such a way that they are consistent with the guidelines presented in chapter 13 should be more effective in helping students with mandated requirements.

Accountability for Student Participation

It is not enough to have a policy that mandates participation in physical activity. Without accountability for that participation, the program is likely to be unsuccessful for a large number of students and probably the very students you hope to reach the most. If the program is run entirely through the school, with the cooperation of community agencies and organizations, you can have better control over signing students up and making sure that they are participating. The stronger programs will probably want students to have more choices outside the school. In any case, you will need a contract signed by the student and an adult, parent, or guardian that commits the student to participating in particular activities. You will also need an adult confirmation sheet indicating that the student has participated. Examples of these are shown in figures 14.1 and 14.2. These contracts and confirmation sheets need to be checked in order to give the student credit for meeting the requirement. All forms should be available online for students.

TABLE 14.1

Physical Activity Options Inside and Outside the School

Sample options inside the school	Sample options outside the school
Athletic programs	Hunting clubs
Marching band	Community youth sport
Walking clubs	Church leagues
Sport clubs	Fitness centers
Intramurals	Structured aerobic groups
Elective physical education	Camping
Junior ROTC	Hiking
Dance and cheer teams	Snowboarding and skiing

FIGURE 14.1

Student Contract to Participate

Student Contract for Outside Activity Participation Form

To be completed by the student:

Student name _____ Gender _____ Student ID # _____

Requirement: The student will choose at least one activity to participate in two times a week for each week of the school year.

Fill in the blanks with the activity or activities listed in which you will participate to meet the physical activity requirement.

- You may use the codes provided to complete this form.
- For outside-of-school choices, a copy of this form will be sent prior to each report card date to the confirmation person(s) you list.
- Activities inside of school will be confirmed with attendance records.
- You may fill out the form for the year or by quarters.
- Due dates: September 7, November 3, January 4.

September
Week 1 _____ Week 2 _____ Week 3 _____ Week 4 _____

October
Week 1 _____ Week 2 _____ Week 3 _____ Week 4 _____

November
Week 1 _____ Week 2 _____ Week 3 _____ Week 4 _____

December
Week 1 _____ Week 2 _____ Week 3 _____ Week 4 _____

January
Week 1 _____ Week 2 _____ Week 3 _____ Week 4 _____

February
Week 1 _____ Week 2 _____ Week 3 _____ Week 4 _____

March
Week 1 _____ Week 2 _____ Week 3 _____ Week 4 _____

April
Week 1 _____ Week 2 _____ Week 3 _____ Week 4 _____

Figure 14.1   Student contract to participate.

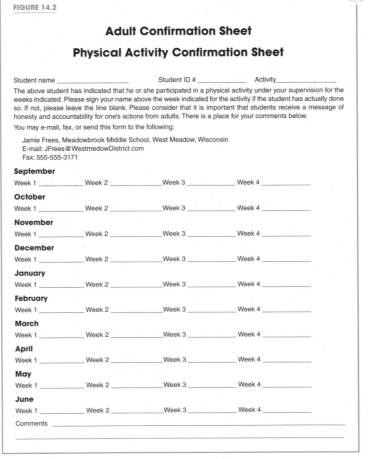

FIGURE 14.2

Adult Confirmation Sheet

Physical Activity Confirmation Sheet

Student name _____ Student ID # _____ Activity_____

The above student has indicated that he or she participated in a physical activity under your supervision for the weeks indicated. Please sign your name above the week indicated for the activity if the student has actually done so. If not, please leave the line blank. Please consider that it is important that students receive a message of honesty and accountability for one's actions from adults. There is a place for your comments below.

You may e-mail, fax, or send this form to the following:

Jamie Frees, Meadowbrook Middle School, West Meadow, Wisconsin
E-mail: JFrees@WestmedowDistrict.com
Fax: 555-555-3171

September
Week 1 _____ Week 2 _____ Week 3 _____ Week 4 _____

October
Week 1 _____ Week 2 _____ Week 3 _____ Week 4 _____

November
Week 1 _____ Week 2 _____ Week 3 _____ Week 4 _____

December
Week 1 _____ Week 2 _____ Week 3 _____ Week 4 _____

January
Week 1 _____ Week 2 _____ Week 3 _____ Week 4 _____

February
Week 1 _____ Week 2 _____ Week 3 _____ Week 4 _____

March
Week 1 _____ Week 2 _____ Week 3 _____ Week 4 _____

April
Week 1 _____ Week 2 _____ Week 3 _____ Week 4 _____

May
Week 1 _____ Week 2 _____ Week 3 _____ Week 4 _____

June
Week 1 _____ Week 2 _____ Week 3 _____ Week 4 _____

Comments _____
_____

Figure 14.2   Adult confirmation sheet.

Middle school students need an opportunity to develop specialized skills.

Consequences for nonparticipation need to be established as part of policy. In most cases, the policy at the high school level should include graduation credit. Participation or lack of participation should be noted on the student report card. A failure to meet the requirement at the middle school level might result in repeating the experience in summer school.

Chapter 13 notes that the head of this program needs to be a physical activity broker. The job of the broker includes the following:

- Establishing a list of community resources (those that will set up special programs as well as those that do not) and school-run choices for the students
- Communicating to the student in writing, on the Web site, and through special orientation programs:
  - The expectations of the requirement
  - The potential possibilities for participation
  - Reasons for the importance of participation
- Counseling students who are having difficulty making choices—making sure there is a place for each student in an activity of interest
- Establishing deadlines for submission of contracts and confirmation forms

- Maintaining student records:
  - Student compliance
  - Student interest
    Student evaluations of their experiences

Administering Required and Voluntary Physical Activity Programs

Regardless of whether you have decided to make your physical activity program required or voluntary, you will need to

- establish a flowchart of responsibilities for the program,
- staff the program,
- ensure the health and safety of participants,
- develop and manage a budget, and
- establish a system of awards.

Establishing a Flowchart of Responsibilities

Whether the physical activity is voluntary or required, a well-established program will have an administrative flowchart of responsibilities. Programs just beginning might have only the physical activity director responsible to the school principal (figure 14.3). Well-established and inclusive programs will want to have a physical activity program council, which should include the following:

- The school administration
- The physical activity director (broker)
- Representatives from the school wellness council
- Representatives from the physical education and athletic departments
- Student representatives
- Volunteer representatives
- Parents

All of these people can help with gaining and maintaining support for the program and provide input with different perspectives that will help make the program better. They can be used in the planning stage as well as throughout the conduct of the

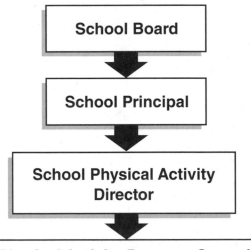

Figure 14.3   Flowchart of responsibilities.

program. They can be a "workforce" that gets some things done so that the physical activity director does not shoulder the burden of all aspects of the program, and they will be very useful in setting up fund-raising projects to support the program. The responsibility of the council should be to recommend policy to the administration and to oversee the program budget.

Staffing the Physical Activity Program

Beginning programs will want to make a list of facilities and potential program offerings within the school and in the community (chapter 13). Then it will be necessary to find people to conduct the activities. A major assumption—if your beginning program is like most—is that you will not have an extensive budget for conducting the activities you want, so you will need to make some hard choices based on meeting the diversity of needs. You will most likely have to depend on a lot of volunteer help or use the faculty within the school.

Hiring volunteers presents its own problems. The tendency is for schools not to recruit but rather, out of convenience, to hire people they know or people who have had a relationship with the school. Volunteers should be hired in a more formal way to ensure their success and their contributions to the program.

After the initial program is planned, the director should begin to advertise for people with particular skills. Job descriptions should be established that communicate very carefully the qualifications of the job, the responsibilities of the job, and the procedures that will be used for hiring. Job descriptions can be put on the school Web site or on the Web site of the physical activity program. An example of a job recruitment flyer is shown in figure 14.4. All candidates should be interviewed by the physical activity program director, should be required to submit recommendations, and should have an official background check. Summer would be a good time to recruit and hire staff for the coming school year (a good summer job for the program administrator). Although this more formal process may deter some good candidates from applying, it will do much to prevent programs from hiring well-intentioned people who simply don't have the skills needed for a job.

Hiring Volunteers

Once you have applications for a job, you will want to interview the candidates who seem most qualified for the position. The interview is important because it not only should give you a chance to find

FIGURE 14.4

Job Description Flyer

Meadowbrook Middle School

Physical Activity Program Volunteers Needed

Volunteers are needed to help conduct the school physical activity program. The purpose of the program is to provide opportunities for children of the school to increase the amount of physical activity they get during each day. We need your help with the following jobs:

Club Activities

If you have a skill you would like to share with students who are interested in learning the skill, we need your help. Clubs will meet twice a week for eight weeks for one hour either at the school or at a community facility. Clubs can meet before school, at lunchtime, or after school depending on your schedule. The following clubs are being considered:

- Tennis
- Golf
- Archery
- Fencing
- Wall climbing
- Skateboarding
- Social dance
- Line dancing

Your responsibility would be to run the club with the help of the physical activity director.

Intramural Activities

Intramural activities will meet during lunch, before school, and after school. We need volunteers with experience in the activity to run practices, organize and conduct leagues, and officiate. Each league will meet twice a week (Monday and Wednesday or Tuesday and Thursday) for six weeks. The following sports are being considered:

- Soccer
- Basketball
- Ultimate
- Touch football
- Team handball
- Badminton
- Disc golf

Figure 14.4   A sample job description flyer.

out who is the most qualified for the job but also should enable candidates to find out more about the job and decide whether they really are willing to meet the obligations of the position. For volunteers, schedule interviews at times convenient for them. Use the interview as an opportunity to explain the whole program, why it is important, and what you hope to "build" over time. Go over the job description and qualifications you are looking for. Try to get a sense of whether the person you are interviewing has the personal and professional skills needed for the position and the time needed to make a commitment to the program. When conducting the interview you should be trying to seek information on the following:

- Why does the person want to do this? Are these reasons compatible with the intent of the program?

- Does the candidate have the necessary credentials for the position or for a different one?
- How much training will the candidate need?
- Do you see the candidate staying with the position?
- Does the candidate relate well to others? Students?
- Is the candidate a good role model?
- Are the references the candidate gave positive, and are the references qualified to know whether the candidate can do the job or not?

Some districts and states have laws that govern who works in schools and how they are appointed or hired; for example, there may be laws requiring fingerprinting and background checks to determine if the candidate has ever been convicted of a crime.

It is important to determine what these state and local regulations are and how you will get assistance in complying with the regulations. All candidates should be asked to sign a contract that is a formal agreement between the school and the volunteer (figure 14.5).

Training Volunteers

For new employees or volunteers, it is important to have an orientation session that allows you to

- introduce all the members of the team to one another;
- give an overview of the total program and the goals and objectives of the program;
- share with new employees your flowchart of administration, with contact information;
- go over the handbook of policies and procedures (see figure 14.6); and
- deal with the specifics of issues like where someone should call if he or she can't make it, where to sign in and out of the building, and what is appropriate dress for the activity.

Items like protocols for attendance and record keeping and for reporting equipment failures can be communicated at the orientation session and in writing in the form of a "handbook," and also communicated in a training session. A sample index for a handbook is shown in figure 14.6. People who don't work in schools are also not usually familiar with polices regarding sexual harassment, injury procedures, and liability issues. They will need to be addressed both in the training program as well as written in the manual.

Although the job description will help, anyone you hire to do a job needs to know very specifically what you expect. Usually when people don't do what they are supposed to do in a job, the reason is not that they are trying to get away with something but that they don't know what is expected. Volunteers also need specific training for the job you want them to do. Even someone with a lot of experience lifting weights, for example, will need a formal introduction to safety and conditioning practices before supervising a weight room. You want people to buy into the idea that participation needs to be made a positive and safe experience for all students regardless of who they are. You will not be able to put a volunteer in a position and expect him or her to know what to do without support. Either the program director or another person familiar with the job should work alongside that person for the first couple of days. Once you get your program going, you will be able to have previous volunteers train new ones. Initially the training will be time-consuming, but it's essential.

Working With Volunteers

Everyone wants to feel appreciated, whether being paid or not. Volunteers should be treated as members of a team. They should be assigned to a job they

---

FIGURE 14.5

Contract for Employment

Name _____ Address _____

Phone number (day) _____ (evening) _____

E-mail _____ Social security number _____

I agree to perform the following responsibilities at Meadowbrook Middle School:

- Come to an orientation meeting of all physical activity program volunteers on September 4, 2010 from 7:00 p.m. to 8:30 p.m.
- Conduct an archery club at the school for as many as 25 seventh and eighth grade students on Monday and Wednesday morning from 7:30 to 8:30 from October 4, 2010 to October 30, 2010. I agree to come a half hour before the group meets to set up equipment and to stay a half hour after the club meets to put the equipment away.
- Establish safety rules for the activity and enforce them.
- Abide by the rules of the program and spirit of the program as defined in the handbook for volunteers.
- If I cannot make it to a session, I will notify the program director at least 48 hours in advance if possible.
- I will hold in confidence any information I receive about students, faculty, or other employees as a result of my participation in the program.

I agree that this contract may be terminated by either party for sufficient cause.

_____ Date _____

Volunteer signature

_____ Date _____

Physical activity program director signature

Figure 14.5 Sample contract for employment.

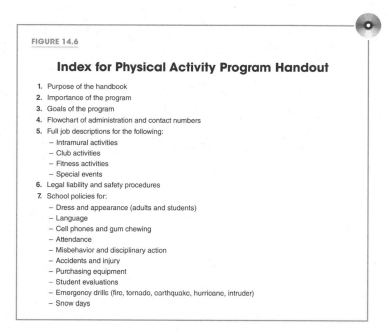

Figure 14.6   Index for physical activity program handout.

---

have the skills and interest for. If they volunteer to do one job, you don't want to put them in a situation in which you are asking them to do something quite different that they may be overqualified for or don't have the skills and interest to do. Mechanisms within the program should exist to enable volunteers to get their questions answered and also provide input into their jobs and the program as a whole.

Volunteers have to be supervised. They cannot be sent off to do a job and forgotten. The work of volunteers should be evaluated on a regular basis both by you and by the students. Figure 14.7 provides a sample form for the evaluation of volunteers that can be used for many different physical activity positions.

Ensuring the Health and Safety of Participants

Institutions and individuals today need protection against being held legally and financially responsible for what happens to those under their care. Physical activity programs by their very nature have an inherent risk. While it is unlikely that a student would be injured sitting at a desk, there is more risk to a student participating in a physical activity. Some activities have a greater potential of risk than others. For instance, kayaking or gymnastics involves a greater risk than jogging or a game of tennis. Many activities are appealing to participants because there is an element of risk, and you do not want to take all of that away. Nevertheless, you need to know how to protect yourself from being held liable for the injuries that might occur in your program.

What Can I Be Held Liable For?

You can be held liable for injuries that a claimant suffers under your care if you are shown to be negligent in what is customary practice to protect a person against injury (breach of duty). Customary practice is what a reasonable and prudent person would do in the same situation. Negligence refers to doing something that a reasonable, prudent person in your field would not do. Obviously much regarding what is negligent revolves around such issues as the age of the student and the specifics of the situation, which is why we have jury trials to decide cases. Programs that try to reduce the risk in activities by making sure that equipment and facilities are appropriate and in good repair, having written policies regarding safety, and training staff to work with those policies—reduce the incidence of injuries and have a better chance of not being held legally liable for those that do occur.

Creating a Risk Management Plan

Schools as state institutions will have a risk management plan, but it most likely will not be specific enough to meet the needs of your physical activity program. This section outlines what constitutes a good risk management plan for a physical activity program.

Assumption of Risk Forms   Programs will want to have participants and their parent or legal guardian sign a liability release form. Your school may already have these forms for the athletic program. The forms do not relieve you of criminal negligence, but they do communicate to the participant that there is some risk in participation, as well as participant

FIGURE 14.7

Evaluating Volunteers

Date _____   Responsibility of volunteer _____

Name of volunteer _____ Name of evaluator _____

Rate each of the following on a 5-point scale, with 5 meaning a real strength of this individual and 1 meaning a real weakness.

1-5	Characteristic	Comments
_____	Enthusiasm	
_____	Self-control	
_____	Appearance	
_____	Knowledge of activity	
_____	Knowledge of how to conduct the activity	
_____	Safe environment	
_____	Engaged students	
_____	Establishes a professional rapport with students	
_____	Attends to paperwork	
_____	Is organized	
_____	Enforces policies fairly and consistently	
_____	Models appropriate behaviors	
_____	Takes responsibility for equipment	

Recommendations _____

_____

_____

_____

_____

_____

Signed _____   Date _____

Figure 14.7   A sample form for evaluating volunteers.

responsibility for safe practice. A sample of a brief assumption of risk form is provided in figure 14.8.

Health Questionnaires   Most high school and middle school athletic programs require students and their parent or legal guardian to fill out a health questionnaire that might include the following:

- Information on heart and cardiorespiratory problems
- Medications that might affect participation
- Health conditions that might affect participation

Some programs require a physical for participation, although this requirement may be an inherent inhibitor to participation. The physical activity director should review these forms and follow up on any indication that a health problem could put the student at risk in the activity chosen.

Facilities Management   Facilities and equipment need to be selected with safety in mind. For example, you do not want to put a volleyball court next to a parking lot where students can go after a ball and be hit by a car, or locate an archery range in such a way that students are shooting arrows into a field where others are playing soccer. Children and youth are also very much affected by what is called an "attractive nuisance." Gymnastics equipment is an attractive nuisance, meaning that children cannot be expected to stay off of it. If you left gymnastics equipment out in a gym unsupervised and a student

---

FIGURE 14.8

Example of a Simple Assumption of Risk Form

Stoney Pointe Middle School
General Assumption of Risk and Release of Liability
After-School Physical Activity Program

I _____ give my permission for my student _____ to participate in the after-school sport program _____ being held at Stoney Pointe Middle School. In consideration of my participation in this program I agree to the following:

RISKS INVOLVED IN PROGRAM: While every attempt will be made to conduct the activity in a safe manner, sport participation carries with it some inherent risks.

HEALTH AND SAFETY: There are no health-related reasons that preclude the participation of the student.

ASSUMPTION OF RISK AND LIABILITY: Knowing the risks described above and in voluntary consideration of being permitted to participate in the activity, I agree to release the school and its employees from any claim of damages or injuries arising out of participation of my student in this program.

_____   _____
Signature of parent or legal guardian   Date

Figure 14.8   Example of a simple assumption of risk form.

got hurt on that equipment, you could be held liable even if you had told everyone not to play on it. Each site should be selected with the safety of participants in mind and monitored regularly for inherent risks.

Facilities and equipment management also means checking the playing surface, fixtures, lighting, and equipment for problems on a regular basis and making sure that you have emergency equipment available (e.g., a phone for getting help on the field). It is helpful to have formal procedures in place for activity leaders to go through to report any facility or equipment problems. Comments made in passing, like "Oh, by the way, there is a big hole on the field where they are putting in a post," are not helpful.

Emergency Procedures   Schools usually have emergency procedures for handling problems during the school day. These may or may not be appropriate for after-school or before-school hours or for activities held on fields or at community sites. Each activity supervisor should know what to do in case of an emergency. Students and parents should also know whom to call for information in case of an emergency, or in case problems arise related to a student's participation after he or she has left school.

Blood and Body Fluids   The recent emergence of problems related to the hepatitis B virus, as well as other viruses that can be passed through body fluids, has necessitated precautionary methods for dealing with any spilled blood or body fluids in physical activity settings. The idea is to protect not only the students with the problem but also other students who are participants. Guidelines of the National Collegiate Athletic Association (NCAA, 2000) and similar efforts are good ones to consider:

- All previous wounds or those that occur during participation must be covered.
- Caregivers must have the supplies to deal with blood and body fluids.
- It is everyone's responsibility in a program to report bleeding.
- Universal precautions (wearing latex gloves) should be taken to handle blood or body fluids.
- All areas and equipment contaminated must be thoroughly cleaned before participation resumes.
- All personnel should be trained in first aid and infection control.

Lightning   All participants must be moved to a safe shelter with an approaching storm and at the first sound of thunder or sight of lightning. Outside physical activity venues (e.g., golf courses, softball and soccer fields, lakes and rivers) are large open areas, making individuals who are on them the highest point and therefore a target for lighting. There should be no exceptions or arguments about how far away the sighted lightning was. If lightning is in view at all, leave the premises immediately.

Developing and Managing the Budget

In very simple terms, planning a budget means balancing your expenses with your income. Most school physical activity programs do not have much income, which means that you will have to decide the best use of any funds you do have and will not be overly involved in salary issues.

Expenses

While good physical activity programs can be conducted without a lot of expenses, particularly if the resources of the school are used and most help is volunteer, it would be nice to have funds to make the program really effective. Expenses for physical activity programs usually fall into the categories of paid positions, equipment, facilities, advertising, and awards and prizes.

■ **Paid positions.** Most programs have to rely on volunteer help. Fully developed programs will consider paid positions, which will increase the reliability and expertise of personnel.

– The physical activity director should be paid by the school either as a full-time employee or as a part-time employee hired specifically to direct the program.

– Part-time people are hired to perform specific duties with the program (secretarial help, instructors, supervisors, officials).

■ **Equipment.** Programs will want to gradually increase the amount of equipment available for conducting the program, as well as acquire the types of equipment that will allow expansion of program offerings. Very specific controls on the use and management of equipment will reduce your equipment budget considerably. In some cases it may be cost effective to rent equipment for a short season (kayaking, gymnastics, backpacking, rope climbing).

■ **Facilities.** Many schools do not have the facilities that would allow you to offer the kind of broad-based program you would like. Renting skating arenas, ice rinks, pools, and so on will make sense; and many facilities may provide them at a reasonable cost, which may be part of the budget of a program or part of a participation fee charged to students.

■ **Advertising.** Most programs advertise within the school using school resources. More professionally done banners, posters, and flyers are often more effective but more expensive.

■ **Awards and prizes.** For many events you will want to provide awards and prizes to participants. They don't have to be extensive but will add to the fun of the event. Community businesses may donate or reduce the cost of awards and prizes.

You will reduce your equipment budget considerably if it is organized and everyone assumes responsibility for maintaining it.

Revenue (Income)

The best situation would be to have the school provide funds to meet the budget requirements of a well-run program. In most cases, physical activity programs need to think about ways to raise additional funds to do the kinds of things they want to do. The following alternatives for increasing your budget need to be considered:

■ **Participation fees.** Students can be charged a nominal fee for participating in an activity, particularly those that are offered before or after school and outside of the school campus. For activities such as bowling or skating at a rink where a charge is likely for equipment or facilities, fees may need to be charged. If supervisors or officials for games are going to be paid, you may also have little choice but to charge a fee for students who elect that activity. Fees are discriminatory against students who cannot afford them and should be avoided if possible or should be waived under particular circumstances. However, many secondary students work and may be able to pay for fees out of their personal funds without relying on their parents or guardians.

■ **Fund-raising.** Physical activity programs may have to raise their own funds to conduct the kind of program they would like. These efforts can include events within the school, in which case you would raise funds from the students, or out of the school, from the community. The many potential approaches to fund-raising include the following:

- Selling products (fruit, magazine subscriptions, stationery, and so on)
- Guessing contests (how many golf tees in the bowl, how many ID cards in the bowl?)
- Class or individual competitions
- Carnivals
- Tournaments (e.g., golf or tennis)
- Garage sale or bake sale
- Healthy drink or snack machine profits
- Concession stands at school events
- Sponsorship—monetary or prize donations from businesses and individuals to directly support the program generally or a specific event with the intent of visibility for their products (e.g., World of Music Dance-a-Thon, Harris Chevrolet Basketball League)

The physical activity program council should be given the responsibility of deciding how to raise funds and of conducting the fund-raising efforts.

Establishing an Awards System

Awards are different from prizes. Whereas prizes are for single events, awards are earned over time. Prizes may also be given in the form of T-shirts or certificates just for participating. The awards program you design should be reflective of the goals of the program. The major goal of most physical activity programs includes participation and development of participants whose personal characteristics contribute to their own enjoyment in participation as well as that of others. While awards should not be the major goal of participation, good performance, good effort, and good character should be rewarded and recognized. You will need to balance the amount of emphasis you put on the award program, standings, and winning with your major goal, which is participation. While some students may check the standings of a league competition on a daily basis and be motivated by the competition, many others will be turned off by an emphasis on winning. Making sure that the award

Awards can reward good performance, good effort, and good character.

program does not become the goal of the activity is a difficult balancing act. With that in mind, you may want to consider the following in setting up your program of awards:

- Fair play or good sportsmanship
- Tournament and league winners and MVP
- Most improvement in a club or individual activity
- Outstanding skill or ability in a club or individual activity
- Outstanding referee
- The amount and consistency of participation

Award winners who are not participating in contests or leagues can be nominated by participants, supervisors, or referees. Awards can be presented at the event itself, at a school ceremony in which other school awards are given out, or at a separate event for just the physical activity program. As the program grows, the awards and the formality of their presentation will also grow.

SUMMARY

1. Required physical activity programs have the potential to connect students with opportunities in the community for physical activity and to make participation part of their routine.

2. Schools, districts, and states need policies that will create accountability for required participation.

3. Required programs should offer students a great deal of choice for participation.

4. Accountability is critical in order for a required program to be successful.

5. Policies need to be established for hiring and working with volunteers as well as for training volunteers.

6. Participation in physical activity puts students at some risk, which must be considered in the policies of a program and in relation to the manner in which a program is conducted.

7. A risk management plan, assumption of risk participation forms, health questionnaires, and emergency procedures should be a part of every program.

8. Programs can be funded with participation fees, school funds, or fund-raising projects.

CHECKING YOUR UNDERSTANDING

1. What are the advantages of required physical activity participation?

2. What do you need to consider in setting up a required participation program?

3. Describe the varied interests of secondary school students in relation to participation in physical activity.

4. How can you establish accountability for required participation in physical activity?

5. Who needs to be represented on the physical activity committee of a school?

6. How can a physical activity program be staffed?

7. What are important things to consider with the use of volunteers in a program?

8. How can a program protect itself from legal liability?

9. How can a physical activity program be funded?

10. What should be the intent of awards in a program?

RESOURCES

Example Web sites of High Intramural Programs

www.mtlsd.org/highschool/intramuralsports.asp
http://highschool.gardencity.k12.ny.us

Byl, J. (2002). *Intramural recreation: A step-by-step guide to creating an effective program.* Champaign, IL: Human Kinetics.

Mull, R., Bayless, K., & Jamieson, L. (2005). *Recreational sport management* (4th ed.). Champaign, IL: Human Kinetics.

National Association for Sport and Physical Education. (2002). *Guidelines for after school physical activity and intramural sport programs.* Reston, VA: NASPE.

REFERENCES

Heidorn, B. (2007). *The effectiveness of an outside of school physical activity requirement for high school students.* Doctoral dissertation, University of South Carolina, Columbia.

National Collegiate Athletic Association. (2000). Guideline 2H: Blood borne pathogens and intercollegiate athletics [Online]. Available at www.ncaa.org.

15

Conducting Intramural Sports

OVERVIEW

One of the largest components of a secondary school physical activity program is likely to be the intramural program. The purpose of this chapter is to help you organize and run an effective intramural program. Topics include when to hold intramurals, how to modify play for a maximum number of participants, how to develop student leadership to conduct the program, how to organize teams and individuals for competition, and how to use the intramural experience to promote positive behavior.

CHAPTER OUTCOMES

This chapter will help you

- distinguish intramurals from other parts of the physical activity program,
- identify the advantages and disadvantages of holding intramurals at various times during the school day,
- identify how to modify sports and games for different skill levels and ages,
- describe how student leaders can be used and trained to facilitate the intramural program,
- identify the advantages and disadvantages of different organizations for competition between players and teams, and
- describe how the intramural program can be designed to promote positive behavior on the part of the participants.

Many students will be interested in participating in competitive sport as part of a physical activity program. These events are referred to as intramurals and include opportunities to play both team and individual sports on a regular basis for a period of time (a season). Intramurals differ from athletics and many youth sport opportunities outside of the school in several important ways. First, they are held within the school. Teams do not play others outside the school. Second, the major goal is participation, not winning. Students of all skill levels are encouraged to participate because they enjoy the game, and winning is deemphasized. Although in the middle school there may be attempts in intramural programs to teach and improve player performance, the emphasis is on playing the game, not practice or instruction. A third aspect of intramural play that distinguishes it from athletics is that play does not have to be regulation. In fact, you will want to modify many aspects of the game to maximize participation, facilitate the participation of many teams or individuals, and provide developmentally appropriate play.

When to Hold Intramurals?

Intramurals can be held before school, at lunchtime, or after school or at all of these times, depending on the staff and facility resources available. The advantage of holding intramurals at lunchtime for many schools is that they are then available for all students. The disadvantage is that student time and facilities are likely to be limited for indoor activities during this time block. Lunchtime activities may be appropriate for middle school students. The need

for longer periods of play and involvement is not as important for this age group as it is for high school students. High school students are likely to lose interest if they just get started in an activity and have to quit and go to class.

Before- and after-school programs also have their own set of problems, depending on the number of students who are bused to school. Unless an activity bus is provided, students who are bused to school may not be able to come early or stay late. The decision to hold before-school programs is in part dependent on what time school starts. In some districts, elementary schools begin before high school; in others, high school starting times are earlier than for middle or elementary schools. Before-school activities would be ideal for high school students who mostly take cars to school. However, the program will need to attract an age group that often finds it more important to "sleep in." After-school programs are often limited by the competition with athletics for facilities and in high schools with teenagers' work schedules. Most professional organizations recommend that intramural activities for the middle school student take precedence over athletic opportunities. The idea is that both needs should be served but that the priority should be to maximize participation and not eliminate students from involvement.

Modifying Play

The official rules of sport standardize the number of players, equipment, court and field size, time, scoring, and other particulars regarding what a player can and cannot do. None of these are sacrosanct;

they should be considered open to change if this will facilitate participation and be developmentally appropriate. In most cases the modified forms of these sports should be taught as part of the physical education program, which should make the transition to intramural play easier particularly for those who play youth sports outside of school and play with official rules or different rules.

Number of Players

One of the first ideas that program planners should consider is changing the number of players on a team. Less skilled players, particularly most middle school students, will profit from basketball games that aren't 5 versus 5 and soccer games that aren't 11 versus 11. In fact, many high school students prefer 3-versus-3 basketball games held on half-court. Having fewer players gives students more opportunities to be active in the game and also allows you to reduce the regulation play area for a sport. It is not uncommon to go to a recreational facility and find adults on a soccer field who choose the smaller field, usually used by younger players, instead of the regulation-size field next to it. In most cases, regulation-size play areas require a great deal more skill and physical conditioning.

For coed play, leaders may want to specify how many girls and how many boys need to be on a team. In mixed-grade-level teams, the issue may be how many seventh graders have to be on a team of seventh and eighth graders.

Equipment

Most sport associations have recommended smaller equipment for younger students. Girls should not be expected to play with basketballs appropriate for boys. Middle school students will benefit from smaller basketballs and perhaps even trainer volleyballs. Equipment needs to be available that is developmentally appropriate. Developmentally appropriate equipment is equipment that elicits a mature skill pattern; if the equipment elicits less than a mature skill pattern, it needs to be changed.

Court and Field Size

Most intramural programs will not have the facilities to accommodate the number of participants they would like to using regulation play areas. If the choice is fewer participants and less play on regulation-size play areas versus more participants using a modified play area, programs should choose to modify the play areas and maximize participation. If the goal is to make participants out of the students who sign up for your program, the message that they don't need anything official to play

Intramural sports played with small-sided games give more students an opportunity to be active.

a sport is probably a good one. Perhaps they will choose to play badminton at home over a rope, or floor hockey on the driveway. Net activities can actually be played over a rope with cones and poly spots and lines as boundary markers. Soccer or any other invasion game (hockey, lacrosse, Ultimate, team handball) can be played on any field size with cones, goals, and lines. Basketball can be played half-court.

The size of the playing field and goals can also affect the game in terms of advantaging the offense or the defense. Larger soccer goals allow for more scoring. Smaller playing fields or courts make it easier for the defense and more difficult for the offense. Smaller courts for net activities require less force production skill but more control.

Time

In order to allow all teams to play more games, the official time of most games will need to be modified. Although time may vary from sport to sport, to give students the physical activity they need, participation should include at least 30 minutes of physical activity a day and be balanced with the need to give students a meaningful competitive experience. Students do not have to play a full match of tennis or for regulation time in most sports in order for the experience to be meaningful, but you will want to make sure that all students play enough to make their time investment in participation worthwhile.

Changing the Rules

Many of the rules that govern what a player can and cannot do in a game can be modified to meet the needs of the game, but these modification should be clear to the participants. When students play these games informally outside of school, they often devise their own rules. Program leaders can make rules governing how many hits are necessary in volleyball before a player can send the ball over the net. They may require two passes before a player can shoot or require that girls touch the ball before you can score. Each of these modifications is designed to promote maximum participation and inclusion of all players. For younger players, officials may be trained to be liberal in enforcing rules regarding "traveling" in basketball or "lifting" in volleyball. What should not be modified are rules that ensure the safety of participants like "high sticks" in hockey and physical contact rules in touch football.

Rules should be changed to accommodate the skill level of the participants. The purpose should be to change rules that inhibit the free flow of the game. When games are stopped for rule violations

on almost every play, the game is no longer fun. If students do not have the basic skills for a game, program planners need to consider whether that game or that form of the game is an appropriate choice for the program. They also need to consider whether or not the program should be accompanied by clinics that will give students the skills. These are more likely to be needed and appropriate at the middle school level.

Student Leadership

One of the objectives of a student physical activity program should be to develop student leadership skills, not only because of the contribution the experience makes to the development of the student but also because programs need student leaders for more efficient conduct. As a young high school student, the author was a member of the Physical Education Leaders Club. As leaders we took attendance during class, assisted with officiating and instruction, helped with equipment, and had various roles in the intramural program. We were also given special privileges. We wore white uniforms when everyone else had blue, met once a week and had opportunities to participate in activities not part of the standard curriculum (e.g., roller skating on the gym floor, fencing), had an induction ceremony and banquet for new members, and got to march in the Memorial Day parade in our striking blue blazers with gold piping. Many of the opportunities for groups like these to interact with adults and develop character and responsibility have been increasingly reserved for athletic teams. A well-conducted physical activity program can begin to make them available to a larger number of students.

Student leaders can serve a variety of functions within the intramural program: They can be representatives on the physical activity program council, captains of teams, and officials. They can also help in promotion and in any administrative function of the program, including making announcements, setting up and taking down equipment, taking attendance, and record keeping. The older the students, the more responsibility they can be given and the more independently they should be able to function.

Student leaders and officials can be recruited from physical education classes or by means of an open advertisement requesting volunteers, or they can be handpicked by the program administrators. Middle school programs are likely to need more help and should consider asking high school students to come work with the younger students.

Regardless of the responsibilities you are willing to give students, they need to be trained. Middle or high school programs that have an elective physical education program can consider a special section of physical education dedicated to training student leadership for the program. This would be ideal. When a special class is not possible, meetings will have to be set up for handpicked or volunteer student leaders. Physical education teachers can also begin the process of training students for leadership within the required physical education class by giving students with interest and potential the opportunity to lead and assist classes.

Student leaders need to be recognized for their efforts in some way. If you can organize a "club" or give the students some distinct identify (special T-shirts), this will go a long way toward building a sense of belonging and commitment necessary to sustain a program. Once you get a program of student leaders established, experienced students will be a great help in training new students.

Officials

When it comes to leadership, having an adequate number of qualified officials for games is likely to be one of the biggest challenges in running an intramural program. Student athletes who play a sport for the school or outside the school have the skills and are often willing to assist with officiating. Parent and community volunteers are also a source of officials. Physical education programs that take a *sport education* approach to a sport unit actually train officials as part of the physical education class, which enables another program to ask each team to supply an official for a day of competition. Some programs may need to take time to train students to be officials or to teach students how to officiate their own games without disputes.

Good officiating prevents much of the conflict in games. As a program administrator you can do a great deal to enhance the quality of officiating and decrease conflicts, including the following:

- Training the officials to respond consistently, decisively, and assertively
- Having the officials evaluated (by supervisor and players)
- Providing officials with professional attire and equipment
- Supporting the officials in conflicts with players and disciplining players who cannot accept the decisions of officials
- Making sure all players have access to game rules (have captains go over the rules at the beginning of the season with their team and make sure the rules are posted where everyone can see them)
- Having officials explain a rule to players or teams that are having trouble with the rule

Team Captains

How team captains are selected depends on how students sign up to participate. If participation is open, captains can be elected by the players, meet privately with the supervisor, and then choose teams. With younger groups, the supervisor may want to choose the captains and in some cases the teams to ensure that teams are of equal ability. If teams sign up as teams, they can elect their own captain.

Team captains have a variety of roles to play that must be communicated to them:

- Making sure that the team members know when they are going to play and that they show up for the game
- Sharing what the rules of play will be
- Maintaining the fair play and behavior standards of the program
- Obtaining equipment and putting it away after a game
- Making sure that team standings are reported and posted correctly
- When there are substitutes, deciding who will play when and in what position, and making sure that everyone gets equal playing time

Organizing the Competition

As part of the physical activity program you will want to organize individual players in individual or dual sports and organize teams in team sports for competition. There are many alternatives for doing so. The information in this chapter will help you set up leagues and tournaments that best meet the needs of the program you are conducting.

The first decision you will need to make is whether or not teams will have some permanent status or whether they should be "pickup" teams formed when students arrive. Younger middle school students may be more attracted to less formal organizations. Many high school students will prefer a more permanent and long-term arrangement. Another alternative is to offer both. Run one program that is less formal and another program as a league, and let the students choose. Students will also have an opportunity for less formal participation if a portion of your program is "open gym" and they can decide when they get there what they want to do and whom they want to do it with.

Tournaments are usually considered more short-term (several days) and *leagues* more long-term competition between teams (weeks). In a physical activity program, your primary objective is to make sure that the competition is a valuable experience for all by making the teams even. Once you have the teams, you will need to set up the league or tournament. There are alternative formats for setting up competition that arrives at a "winner." Each of these formats has both advantages and disadvantages.

Round Robin Format

One of the most useful formats for organizing play for intramural competition is the round robin tournament. In this format each team plays every other team. Which team you play next does not depend on winning or losing. The winner of the tournament or league is the team or person with the most wins. Figure 15.1 is an example of a round robin tournament organizational format. Round robin tournaments have certain advantages over other formats:

- Teams are not eliminated.
- Every person or team gets an equal chance to play every other person or team.
- Organization ahead of time is easy, and players easily understand the format.
- If games have to be rescheduled or made up, this does not interfere with the other decisions as to who will play whom.

The example in figure 15.1 showing eight teams would take seven *rounds* to complete. If there were 16 teams, it would take 15 rounds. When you have an odd number of teams, you schedule one of the lines of the bracket as a *bye*. The ideal number of teams for a round robin tournament is between four and eight. When you have many teams and the games take a long time to be played, you may have to consider other alternatives. Round robin tournaments are not useful when you have many teams, limited space, or time so limited that it would be difficult to have every team play every other team. One way to deal with the time issue is to reduce the duration of games (e.g., 20-minute basketball games, one game to 11 points rather than regulation scoring that includes multiple games and sets in tennis. Regulation-length games and scoring are not always possible in intramural sports.

Round robin tournaments also have other disadvantages. One of these (although for most school sports it may not be a problem) is that toward the end of the tournament, teams with a low win record may just decide not to participate because they know they don't have a chance of winning. Then the team that they were supposed to play doesn't get a chance to play. To prevent this problem, contracts should include the requirement to play out the tournament. In other types of formats, the losing teams would be eliminated and the winning teams would complete the tournament.

Modified Round Robin

When you have more than eight teams or more teams than your facilities and time schedule will

Week 1	Week 2	Week 3	Week 4	Week 5	Week 6	Week 7
8-7	8-6	8-5	8-4	8-3	8-2	8-1
1-6	7-5	6-4	5-3	4-2	3-1	2-7
2-5	1-4	7-3	6-2	5-1	4-7	3-6
3-4	2-3	1-2	7-1	6-7	5-6	4-5

Figure 15.1 Round robin tournament for eight teams.

allow, you can modify the round robin by running several separate round robin leagues. You may or may not have the winners of each league play each other. An advantage of having leagues that do not play each other is that you can specify the skill level, grade level, or gender of a league and more easily meet individual needs in relation to competition.

Scheduling Round Robin Leagues and Tournaments

You will want to schedule each team to play at least twice a week in order to get the physical activity benefits from participation. You may need to run the program three or more days a week and make sure that each team plays at least two times per week. If you have open time for the facilities, allowing each team to choose to come to a practice day or clinic would also be helpful, particularly for the middle school. The master schedule should be posted and if possible all players given a copy so that they can circle the days they will play.

Elimination Formats

A bracket is a graphic illustration of who plays whom to arrive at a "winner." Many athletic tournaments are organized with elimination formats. The single elimination tournament (figure 15.2) and the double elimination tournament (figure 15.3) are common formats for tournaments in which the goal is not necessarily to maximize participation but rather to choose a winner in the quickest way possible. In the single elimination bracket there are only three rounds for our eight-team tournament, and a team could be eliminated from play in the first round. In the double elimination tournament, a team that lost in the first round would get one more chance and could be eliminated after two games. The multilevel format in figure 15.4 puts teams that lose into a different bracket and allows them to play for four out of the five rounds of the tournament. For most school settings and particularly for intramural programs, you will not want to use these formats. Choosing a winner is not as important as maximizing participation. These formats may be appropriate for a special tournament that you might want to hold for a short period of time.

Challenge Tournaments

Although challenge tournaments can be designed as *ladder, pyramid,* or *king,* the idea is the same. Players or teams get to challenge each other, and the player

or team in the top position at the end of the tournament is the winner. Figure 15.5 illustrates a ladder tournament used for tennis that is designed with three levels of play. The players decide which level they want to participate in.

In challenge tournaments, the players can be ranked or can be placed in the ladder according to when they sign up to play. When players defeat a position at a higher level, they take that position. It is usually best to make rules such as the following to govern the procedures of a challenge tournament:

- Players cannot challenge a player more than two rungs above where they are.
- All play must be complete within a week.
- Players cannot challenge the same player twice in a row, that is, until at least one other match has been played.
- The winner must take the responsibility for recording or turning in the score to the appropriate organizer.

Although challenge tournaments can be run at scheduled times, they are ideal for use in situations in which players can set up their own times to play before school, after school, or on weekends. They are also well suited for activities in which strict supervision or officiating is not critical. Organizers need to establish an official beginning and ending date for the competition.

Standards for Participant Behavior

Sport has been identified as a potential laboratory for the development of values. In reality, sport can develop both positive and negative values depending upon how the experience is conducted. As daily newspapers and other media continuously report, professional sport and to some extent intercollegiate sport are riddled with examples of displays of values we would not want our youth to emulate. It thus becomes difficult for school sport to challenge youth to act differently. Intramural programs can do much to communicate and develop the values we want students to acquire by addressing these values directly and applying them very specifically to a setting.

Teaching Values

Although everyone talks about positive values, they are not easy to define, particularly in specific sport and play settings. It can be easier to convey what

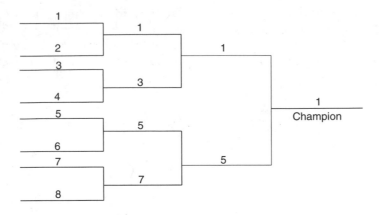

Figure 15.2   Single elimination tournament.

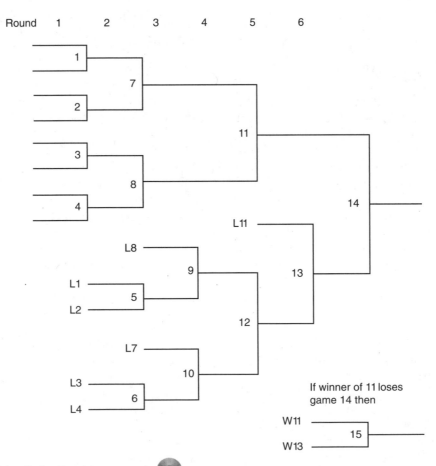

Figure 15.3   Double elimination tournament.

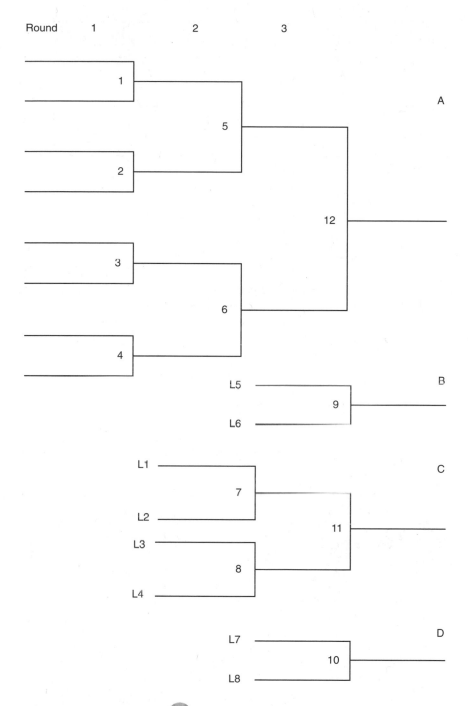

Figure 15.4   Multilevel bracket tournament.

Shark Tournament	Whale Tournament	Dolphin Tournament
Name: E-mail:	Name: E-mail:	Name: E-mail:
Name: E-mail:	Name: E-mail:	Name: E-mail:
Name: E-mail:	Name: E-mail:	Name: E-mail:
Name: E-mail:	Name: E-mail:	Name: E-mail:
Name: E-mail:	Name: E-mail:	Name: E-mail:
Name: E-mail:	Name: E-mail:	Name: E-mail:
Name: E-mail:	Name: E-mail:	Name: E-mail:
Name: E-mail:	Name: E-mail:	Name: E-mail:

Figure 15.5 Tennis ladder tournament: three levels of challenge.

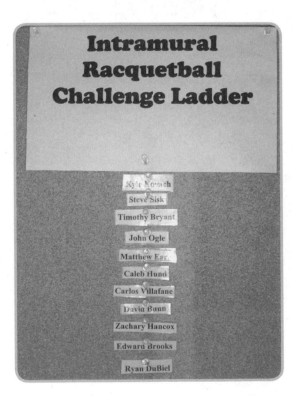

Challenge tournaments allow for flexibility in time and location.

something is not than to explain what it is. Figure 15.6 display the kinds of behaviors we do not want to see from participants in sport.

How do we deal with these behaviors displayed in figure 15.6? In three easy steps. First and foremost, you do not let the behavior go unnoticed or let it continue. Schools are educational settings, and the school has a responsibility to develop student character. You need to be clear about what you expect from participants. You need to be prepared—to know ahead of time what behaviors you will accept and not accept and what behaviors you will try to develop. Second, you need to communicate your expectations for program participation so that there is no question about what they are. Third, you need to reinforce your expectations and hold participants accountable.

What Are My Expectations?

Schools have their own standards of conduct that are usually written down and shared with students. These need to be reinforced in the physical activity program. Physical activity programs also have unique expectations that must be made explicit and

Ima Special

All of us are familiar with Ms. Special. The rule says not to kick volleyballs. Ima Special knows the rule and chooses to ignore it. Every time she is in a position to send the ball to the other team, she kicks it over the net.

Denial Danny

The rule says that you can't use your hands. Everyone knows that Denial Danny used his hands, but he insists that he did not and pouts for the rest of the game because he didn't get his way.

Demolition Debbie

Demolition Debbie is like a Mack truck on any field or court. She is so out of control that most defenders would rather move away from her than risk injury. Her aggressive play is a danger to herself and everyone else on the field.

Ego Eddie

Ego Eddie bases his self-esteem on winning and always has a lot of excuses when he loses.

Harvey Ball Hog

We all know Harvey Ball Hog. Advanced team play is not possible with these people because they have to try to score every time they touch the ball. It never enters their mind to look for a teammate who may have a better shot.

Loudmouth Larry

Loudmouth Larry never lets a moment pass in silence. Instead he fills it with warnings to the officials, jeers at the other team, or admonishes to his own team to "get with it." He rarely misses the opportunity to shout out an unkind word.

Exclusive Evelyn

Exclusive Evelyn came to participate, but when she was assigned a team without all of her friends, she decided to make things difficult for her team and not to demonstrate any effort or display any enjoyment.

Figure 15.6 Each of these characters represents a problem that is common in school sport settings.

shared with students. This means that program planners must decide on and communicate expectations *ahead of time*. Too often, students learn what an expected behavior might be by doing something wrong.

Expectations for student behavior during an intramural program will probably revolve around these themes:

- Following and respecting the rules of play (honesty, respect for officials' calls, playing by the rules)
- Respecting the equipment
- Participating in a way that is safe for others as well as oneself
- Being a gracious winner and loser and valuing participation for its own sake
- Supporting other participants including opponents (treating others as you would have others treat you, appreciating a good play even when made by the opponent, encouraging teammates, behaving inclusively)
- Being in control of one's body and one's emotions (no swearing; no reckless behavior, either verbal or physical)
- Doing one's best

Under each of these themes, program planners might come up with examples that would help get across to students the specific positive behaviors they are looking for, as well as examples of behaviors that are not appropriate. This becomes a code of conduct for the program and can be interpreted specifically for each activity if necessary.

How Do I Communicate Program Expectations?

A code of conduct can be communicated in a variety of ways:

- It can be posted in a place where students can read it.
- It can be printed out for distribution to all participants, and students can be asked to sign an agreement to abide by it.
- The role of the captain in communicating and enforcing the code of conduct can be emphasized at the captains meeting.
- The code can be posted on the physical activity Web page or the school Web site.
- It can be taught in physical education classes.

Initially it may take program time and effort to communicate your expectations. With time, the students will become "socialized" into a way of behaving that is consistent with the code, and they will learn from others the standard of conduct that you have set.

Accountability for a Code of Conduct

Even if you do a good job establishing a code of conduct and sharing it with students, unless it is enforced and reinforced it will not be effective in changing student behavior. Students will learn that it doesn't make any difference what they do because there are no consequences for breaking the code. There are many ways to reinforce what you are trying to do.

- **Officiating.** The foundation of your efforts at reinforcement is the work of the officials and the supervisor of the program. They must understand the code of conduct and specifically what behaviors they will permit and not permit, as well as what positive behaviors they will be looking for to reinforce. The code of conduct should be a major part of training of officials. But while student officials can be expected to reinforce positive behavior, you do not want to put them in a position of having to deal with difficult participants or participants who continuously break the code. Student officials should communicate with the captain of the team or, in the case of more serious or disciplinary issues, go directly to the supervisor of the activity.

- **Awards.** Another, more positive way to reinforce the code of conduct is to reward players who exemplify the code in their own behavior. This is probably more effective with middle school students than with high school students and should not be overdone, as giving out too many awards can trivialize them.

- **Establishing policy to warn or remove a participant.** Repeated or severe breaches of the code of conduct should be handled quickly and decisively, or the wrong message will be sent to students. Programs should have a policy of a warning given to the participant by the supervisor, followed by a decision to remove the player from the program. To prevent problems with parents, this policy should be approved by the school administration, established as school policy, and communicated with the code of conduct to participants. Administrators should be given the "heads up" regarding any situation in which a student has had to be removed from participation.

SUMMARY

1. Intramurals provide an opportunity to play competitive sport within the school for any student who wants to participate.

2. Intramurals can be held before school, after school, or at lunchtime.

3. The number of players, equipment, court and field sizes, time of play, and rules can all be modified to accommodate more players and the needs of an age group.

4. Intramural programs should develop opportunities for student leadership and student officiating.

5. Organizers of intramural programs need to train and work with officials and team captains.

6. Competition can be organized in various formats, including round robin, elimination formats, and challenge tournaments.

7. Intramural programs need to establish, communicate, and hold participants accountable for standards of behavior.

CHECKING YOUR UNDERSTANDING

1. How is an intramural program different from athletics?

2. For each of the times during the day when intramurals can be held, what are the advantages and disadvantages?

3. How can play be modified for the needs of different programs and participants?

4. How can programs develop student leadership?

5. How can program administrators enhance the quality of student officials?

6. What should be the responsibility of team captains?

7. Identify three different organizations for competition and list the advantages and disadvantages of each.

8. What should be the standards for participant behavior, and how can they be communicated and enforced?

RESOURCES

National Intramural-Recreational Sports Association
www.nirsa.org

Jensen, C., & Overman, S. (2003). *Administration and management of physical education and athletic programs* (4th ed., chapter 14, "Intramural Recreation"). Long Grove, IL: Waveland Press.

Stewart, C. (2005). Has the decline of intramural sports contributed to the youth obesity epidemic? *Journal of Physical Education, Recreation and Dance*, 76, 11-13.

Wade, D., & Mayhew, S. (2005). *Everything I know about intramurals, I learned from Gary Cahen*. Sebastopol, CA: Iota Press.

16

Conducting Secondary Health-Related Fitness Programs

OVERVIEW

Fitness is a growing concern for all ages. Secondary students are at an age when they can begin to take responsibility for their own fitness levels. The purpose of this chapter is to describe the components of fitness and how they might be developed in ways appropriate and motivating for the secondary student.

CHAPTER OUTCOMES

This chapter will help you

- describe the components of fitness;
- describe the components of the physical activity program designed to develop fitness, including aerobic capacity, muscular strength and endurance, flexibility, and body composition; and
- provide guidelines for developing the leadership necessary for conducting the program.

There are two kinds of fitness, skill-related and health-related fitness. Skill-related fitness components are those having to do with strength, power, agility, balance, coordination, reaction time, and speed—all of which are qualities essential for high levels of skilled motor performance. Health-related fitness components are those associated with health benefits and are identified as aerobic capacity, muscular strength, muscular endurance, flexibility, and body composition. The health-related components are essential for high levels of skilled performance, but the skill-related components are not necessarily related to health. This chapter concerns the development of the components of health-related fitness.

Health-related fitness is an outcome of physical activity. There are two main approaches to developing health-related fitness. One is through physical activities that the participant finds enjoyable and will do on a regular basis. The other is a conditioning and exercise approach. Most school-aged children and youth are attracted to an activity orientation to developing fitness. They will be "turned off" by training and exercise approaches that focus on planned and repetitive movement targeting a specific fitness component. There is, however, a growing population of students who will want opportunities to "work out."

The increased interest in exercise approaches can be attributed to several factors. Among these are greater awareness of the health benefits of being fit; an increase in the types of programs and equipment that make the development of fitness more appealing; and, particularly for high school students, an increased awareness of the role of fitness in weight control and body image, as well as the role of conditioning in sport performance. The "no pain, no gain" notion of exercise has been replaced by the idea that people can achieve the health benefits of exercise through moderate to vigorous activity.

While the conditioned athlete still needs to work at vigorous levels of activity, people can achieve major health benefits by getting "off the couch" and increasing their amount of activity rather than reaching a strenuous level of activity.

Components of Health-Related Fitness

Well-rounded fitness programming provides opportunities for students to develop each of the components of fitness.

- **Aerobic capacity:** The ability of the body to sustain large-muscle vigorous activity over time
- **Muscular strength:** The amount of force a muscle can produce with a single effort
- **Muscular endurance:** The ability of a muscle group to repeatedly contract or stay contracted
- **Flexibility:** The range of motion of a joint
- **Body composition:** The percentage of body fat

Each of these components can be developed through different activities as well as through different exercises. Table 16.1 lists the components of fitness and gives examples of the exercises and activities that develop them.

Programming for Secondary Fitness Activities

Fitness programming can be extensive, ranging from "boot camp" types of comprehensive programs to individual consultations with students, special programs on weight control, fitness testing, and other opportunities. In schools, much of

TABLE 16.1

The Components of Fitness and the Exercises and Activities That Develop Them

Health-related fitness component	Exercises	Activities	Sport activities
Aerobic capacity	Jogging, walking, running, step climber, treadmill	Aerobic activities, rope jumping, water aerobics	Swimming, basketball, soccer, in-line skating, cross-country skiing, racquetball
Muscular endurance	Push-up, curl-up, chin-up, weight training	Aerobic activities, rope jumping	Swimming, backpacking, bicycling (lower body)
Muscular strength	Push-up, curl-up, chin-up, weight training	Pilates, resistance bands	Swimming, backpacking, gymnastics
Flexibility	Flexibility exercises by muscle group	Yoga, calisthenics, aerobic activities	Gymnastics, dance
Body composition	Jogging, walking, running, step climber, treadmill	Aerobic dance, rope jumping	Any aerobic activity

the instruction and individualization of fitness testing and individual program design should be done in the physical education class as part of the instructional program. The physical activity program of the school should provide opportunities for students to carry out their own personal fitness program through either an activity approach or an exercise (fitness) approach. The intramural and club activities for the physical activity program give students opportunities to become physically active and develop fitness, through an activity approach of "fun" activities. Most schools will want to program for fitness activities and exercise by beginning with four types of opportunities:

- Cardiorespiratory opportunities
- Muscular strength and endurance opportunities
- A fitness class or club that includes strength and endurance training, flexibility, and cardiorespiratory activities
- Aerobic activities such as kick boxing, aerobic dance, geo aerobic activities, step aerobics, fitness geocaching, and Wii Fitness

While they do not represent the complete range of types of activities, these are the opportunities that are most likely to attract the students in a secondary school looking to begin a program. Most of

the program will be designed as self-directed informal activities, meaning that the facilities are open and that students can use them when they choose. Programs may help students keep track of their progress and provide materials for doing so.

Most experts in the field recommend that cardiorespiratory activities be done three times a week (for at least 20 minutes) and that strength and endurance programs be done two times a week to achieve training benefits. Most students will not want to commit themselves to daily training but should have the opportunity to do so.

Cardiorespiratory Activities

Implementing cardiorespiratory activities can be as simple as organizing a walk or jog club or can be more complex, for instance when programs schedule access to an equipment room with step climbers and treadmills or to a pool for aerobic swimming. Walking/jogging clubs are obviously the least expensive and have the advantage of sending the message to students that they can do this activity at home. Machine rooms are probably more motivating for students. New machines available for cardiorespiratory endurance allow students to work specifically at the appropriate heart rate and for the appropriate time. Some students will be motivated to engage in these types of activities (e.g., using step climbers, treadmills, ellipticals). New technology in the form of pedometers and heart rate monitors allows students to store data on their workouts that can be downloaded to a computer. Students may also be motivated by geocaching, which can be used as a fitness activity.

The advantage of cardiorespiratory programs is that students can "mix" activities (cross training). They do not have to do the same program each time they choose to be active as long as they keep their heart rate in the target zone for the level of training they have selected. Being able to do different activities rather than having to stick with only one may be more motivating for this age group. Students should come in to a cardiovascular program knowing their target heart rate. The sidebar "Determining Your Target Heart Rate for Cardiorespiratory Activities" is a quick summary of how to arrive at this figure. What you do not want to do is pressure students to exercise at the upper end of the continuum. They should stay at the lower end for three to six weeks and then gradually move toward the upper end. They should work out for anywhere from 12 to 40 minutes depending on their health and beginning level of fitness.

Physical activity programs can be designed so that opportunities for walking/jogging, aerobic swimming, fitness geocaching, and so on are informal (open opportunities) or structured (club). The good thing about these activities is that you can have students participating in both informal and structured experiences using the same facilities and equipment at the same time. Before school, after school, and lunchtime are all good times to make the facilities available and to schedule opportunities for walking and jogging. Setting up a club for students that offers help in designing personal programs, has a specific time slot, provides a mechanism for students to track their progress, and rewards progress has many advantages over just providing the facilities.

One strategy for schools that have limited facilities and resources is to connect students to community groups. Numerous Web sites for local walking clubs in just about every state and county provide information about scheduled walks with a group to interesting places, computer programs to establish a personal program and track progress, chat rooms for sharing experiences, and competitions and rewards for those who achieve their goals. These programs

Secondary students can be taught to be responsible for their own fitness.

Determining Your Target Heart Rate for Cardiorespiratory Activities

1. Estimate your maximum heart rate (MHR):

208 – (.7 of your age)
Example: 208 – .7 (15) = 198

2. Determine the training intensity zone:

MHR × 65% (for example, 198 × .65 = 129)
MHR × 90% (for example, 198 × .90 = 178)

This individual would exercise at a heart rate between 129 and 178 to get the fitness benefits of the exercise. Extremely unfit people may need to start out lower.

Note: Children younger than 14 should be engaging in vigorous activity without using exercise heart rate thresholds unless they choose to do so. Middle school children should check their heart rate but should not be expected to maintain an exercise heart rate.

are offered through state and local parks and recreation organizations, as well as more commercial organizations such as www.mapmywalk.com and www.walkstyles.com. Lists of walking clubs in your area can also be located through an Internet search. An advantage of walking clubs is that the events are social and develop in participants a sense of responsibility to "show up."

Motivating Students to Become Participants

You can motivate students to choose to participate in aerobic activities, and more importantly maintain their participation, in a variety of ways. These are some suggestions:

- Set up a program with different levels of intensity and help students choose an appropriate level at which to begin their program.
- Make it clear that where students begin is not important.
- Provide students with forms or a computer program to record their progress for walking or jogging distances or for the step climber or treadmill.
- Have students sign up in teams and develop a competition for "progress."
- Use online competitions like those on PE Central or local competitions.
- Have students challenge the faculty.
- Give certificates when students reach a certain level.
- Change the route for walking/jogging and schedule some field trips to different places to jog.
- Combine walking with map work in American or European history.
- Help students learn to use heart rate monitors and pedometers and make them available.

Safety Issues in Cardiorespiratory Activities

Cardiorespiratory activities present their own set of safety issues, particularly when conducted outside.

Hot weather: Hot weather is a problem because it dehydrates the body and because in very hot weather and humidity, the body is not cooled sufficiently through sweat. Schools are not always good about providing participants with water. Encouraging students to drink before participation and having water available, particularly during hot weather, are very important. Heatstroke and heat exhaustion are life-threatening conditions.

Cold weather: Exposure to extremely cold weather for long periods of time can lead to hypothermia and frostbite. In climates that are regularly below freezing, students should not be permitted to be outside in temperatures below 10 degrees Fahrenheit in windy conditions or −5 degrees Fahrenheit in calm conditions. They should also be expected to dress appropriately. Sometimes high school students get a mindset to prove that they can do something and act foolishly (e.g., go out for a run without the proper clothing). Adults need to prevent that from happening.

Muscular Strength and Endurance Activities

Weight training activities used to be reserved for the athletic program. Information on the benefits of weight training for both men and women, athletes and nonathletes, has led to a major increase in the use of weight training in a well-rounded fitness program. Muscular strength and endurance help to improve performance in physical activities, prevent injury, prevent muscle and nerve degeneration, enhance self-image and body image of both men and woman, and prevent and manage chronic disease.

- **Improved performance of physical activities.** Most people are aware that strength is important to athletes. What they do not realize is that muscular strength and endurance are also important for everyday life skills and the enjoyment of recreational activities. You can do everything more easily when you have the muscular strength and endurance for the activity.

- **Injury prevention.** Strength and endurance play a major role in injury prevention in both everyday activities and recreational activities. Training can enhance strength in tendons, ligaments, and postural muscles that is critical to preventing injury.

- **Prevention of muscle and nerve degeneration.** With age, people lose muscle mass, and strength and muscle responses become slower. For older women, osteoporosis is a life-threatening problem. A lot of this loss can be attributed to a lack of physical activity. Strength training and conditioning can lessen these problems. Most of these problems do not manifest themselves until later in life, but high school students who begin to engage in strength and endurance training and who value it will be more likely to do so as adults.

- **Enhancement of self-image and body image.** When boys reach puberty, they increase muscle mass. Looking muscular and strong is important to many boys who associate these characteristics with being masculine. Girls typically do not want to look muscular. What most girls do not realize is that because they do not have the number of muscle fibers of boys, strength training, though it will increase muscle tone, cannot increase the number of muscle fibers. Girls also tend to put on body fat with age. Muscle burns more calories than fat does, so increasing the amount of muscle versus fat in the body is a big part of a weight loss program. Strength training is just as important to a girl's body image as it is to a boy's.

■ **Prevention and management of chronic disease.** Strength training is important to the prevention of heart disease, osteoporosis, and diabetes. Because stronger people do not place the demands on the cardiovascular system that weaker people do, the body is not as stressed by strenuous activity. Strength training also acts to change body composition in ways that are critical to the prevention and management of osteoporosis and diabetes.

Free Weights Versus Machines Versus Body Weight

Most weight training programs use machines. Machines are easy to use, are safe, and seem to be more motivating than use of one's body weight (e.g., curl-ups, push-ups) or free weights. Use of machines can develop strength and endurance more quickly than simply participating in physical activity. Machines do not require spotters and call for less skill than training with free weights. On the other hand, they are expensive, and the number of participants is usually limited to the number of machines available. Machines also do not provide the "real-task" training that free weights or body weight approaches do; they tend to use the same muscle groups and muscle fibers each time a given exercise is performed. In contrast, movements that are not done the same way each time (real-task training) have an advantage in that they involve different parts of the muscle each time. Machines also send the message that you have to go somewhere to work out. Free weights and other methods of strength conditioning (exercises) are much less expensive and can therefore accommodate more students. They also have some transfer value to real-life tasks that machines do not, but they require a spotter and involve some safety issues.

If your program can afford machines, you should consider using them. If not, free weights, resistance bands, exercise balls, yoga, Pilates

Weight training is not the only way to develop strength.

(www.pilatesmethodalliance.org), and calisthenics can accomplish similar goals but will require more instruction and perhaps a structured program with a "leader." Users need to learn how to do these exercises safely. The following lists typical exercises used in weight rooms for machines and free weights.

Machine Exercises

- Bench press
- Leg pullover and pull-down
- Leg flexion and extension
- Abdominal muscle and trunk exercises
- Triceps exercises
- Chest exercises
- Leg press
- Biceps curl

Free Weight Exercises

- Triceps extension
- Military press
- Biceps curls
- Bent rowing

Designing a Successful Strength Training Program

No attempt is made in this text to give you all the information you need to establish a safe and effective weight training program for students. Resources listed at the end of this chapter are good ones to use to help students plan programs and to conduct them safely. Your physical activity program will have two approaches to muscular strength and endurance training. Most students will want to use the weight room without having to commit to a structured program. Others will want some help and structure to their work.

Nonstructured Programs Students participating in a nonstructured program that permits them to work out before school, after school, or at lunchtime will need to have prior instruction in safety and in the design of a personal program. This should occur in physical education. If it does not, this group of students should be required to initially attend a structured weight training program that will give them the safety and program design essentials they will need to get started. Figure 16.1 summarizes this information. These safety ideas and techniques should be posted in the weight room and enforced by the supervisor or attendants on duty. Even if unstructured, good student strength training programs can be facilitated if program cards and written materials are available for students to use to plan and carry out their individual programs. Figure 16.2 is an example of a program (workout) card for an individual.

Structured Programs Some students will want to attend structured programs that have an "instructor" and not just a supervisor. They will want assistance in planning their programs and keeping track of their progress, as well as feedback that will help motivate them to continue. Weight training should be offered in an elective physical education program if it is not part of the normal curriculum. These "classes" can be organized around methods other than machines so that students can continue their programs at home. If an instructional program isn't offered as part of the normal physical educa-

tion curriculum, it should be offered as part of the school's physical activity program.

Flexibility Activities

The development and maintenance of flexibility should be a part of all fitness programs offered within the physical activity program, whether the focus is on cardiorespiratory, muscular strength and endurance, or comprehensive fitness activities. Flexibility refers to the range of motion of a joint. The development and maintenance of flexibility are important because a lack of flexibility makes injury more likely with participation in physical activity. Light stretching or getting into an activity slowly is usually associated with a warm-up. Stretching before strenuous exercise loosens up the muscles and is likely to help keep them from tearing.

Flexibility exercises differ from a warm-up and are designed to increase the range of motion of a joint. Back, shoulder, knee, and ankle pain, particularly in sedentary people, is in part a result of a lack of flexibility. Fitness experts talk about two kinds of flexibility:

1. *Dynamic flexibility* refers to the ability to perform movements over the full range of motion of a joint (e.g., swinging a bat, twisting from side to side, or kicking an imaginary ball). Dynamic flexibility depends to some extent on static flexibility but also on factors such as strength, coordination, and resistance to movement.

2. *Static flexibility* refers to the ability to assume and maintain (hold) a position at one point in the range of motion of a joint (e.g., split in gymnastics). Static flexibility depends on the structure of the joint; the tightness of muscles, tendons, and ligaments; and the tolerance of the individual for a stretched muscle.

Flexibility programs cannot change the structure of a joint. What they do is increase the elasticity and length of muscle and the connective tissue. Flexibility is improved best when the muscle is warm (from activity or heat) and when the stretch is applied slowly and gradually. What you don't want to do is perform sudden and hard stretches, which can lead to injury. People are continuing to use ballistic stretching—forceful and "bouncy" movements like rapid toe touches. Ballistic stretches can cause injury and are not recommended. A flexibility training program should use the following types of stretching:

- *Dynamic stretching:* Move the joint through its full range of motion in a functional movement in

FIGURE 16.1

The Basics of Weight Training

Safety

1. Use proper lifting technique.
   a. Pay attention to the right way to do an exercise.
   b. Make the action smooth and use good form.
   c. Use a 3-second concentric (muscle shortening to lift resistance) and 3-second eccentric (muscle lengthening to lower resistance) contraction.
   d. Lift or push forcefully and lower slowly with control.
   e. Perform all lifts through the full range of motion.
   f. Exhale during the lift and inhale as you lower the lift.
   g. Rest between sets.

2. Free weights
   a. Use spotters and collars with free weights.
   b. Pick up a weight from the floor with your back straight.
   c. Don't bounce weights against your body during a lift.
   d. Use a closed grip.

3. Machines
   a. Keep away from moving stacks and parts of the machine.
   b. Adjust each machine to your body so you are not in an awkward position.
   c. Clean the machine so it doesn't harbor germs.

4. Don't exercise an injured muscle.

5. Alternate muscle groups.

Training

1. Exercise at least two or three nonconsecutive days.

2. Determine your maximum capacity for weight and work at 70% of that level to build endurance; or choose a weight based on the number of repetitions of an exercise you can perform with a given resistance.

3. To improve your level of strength, you must perform enough repetitions to fatigue the muscle. More weight and fewer repetitions build more strength. Lighter weight and more repetitions build endurance.

4. At the end of a set (10-15 repetitions) your muscle should be fatigued. For most people, three sets of 10 repetitions is sufficient (fewer to begin a program).

5. Rest between sets.

6. Include your neck, upper back, shoulders, arms, chest, thighs, lower back, abdomen, buttocks, and calf muscles for well-rounded fitness.

FIGURE 16.2

Program (Workout) Card for Strength Training

Exercise	Date	9/4	9/6	9/8	9/10	9/12	9/14	9/16	9/18	9/20	9/22	9/24	9/26	9/28	9/30	10/2
Knee extension (quadriceps)	Wt	50	50	50	50	50	50	50	50	50	55	55	55	60	60	60
	Sets	1	1	1	2	2	2	3	3	3	2	2	2	3	3	3
	# Reps	8	10	12	8	10	12	8	10	12	10	12	12	10	10	12
Knee flexion (hamstrings)	Wt	40	40	40	40	40	40	40	40	40	45	45	45	50	50	50
	Sets	1	1	1	2	2	2	3	3	3	2	2	2	3	3	3
	# Reps	8	10	12	8	10	12	8	10	12	10	12	12	10	10	12
Leg press	Wt	90	90	90	95	95	95	95	100	100	100	100	100	100	105	105
	Sets	1	1	1	2	2	3	3	2	2	2	3	3	3	2	2
	# Reps	8	10	12	10	10	12	12	10	10	12	10	10	12	8	8
Calf raise with dumbbells	Wt	10	10	10	15	15	15	20	20	20	20	25	25	25	25	30
	Sets	3	3	3	3	3	3	3	3	3	3	2	2	3	3	2
	# Reps	15	15	15	18	18	18	18	18	20	20	20	20	20	20	20
Bench press	Wt	45	45	45	45	45	45	45	45	45	45	50	50	50	50	50
	Sets	1	1	1	1	2	2	3	3	3	3	2	2	2	3	3
	# Reps	8	8	10	12	10	10	12	10	10	12	10	12	12	10	10
Biceps curl	Wt	8	8	8	8	8	8	12	12	12	15	15	15	15	20	20
	Sets	1	1	1	2	2	3	2	2	2	3	3	3	3	1	2
	# Reps	8	10	12	10	12	12	10	10	12	10	10	12	12	10	8
Triceps extension	Wt	5	5	5	5	5	5	5	8	8	8	10	10	10	10	10
	Sets	1	1	1	2	2	3	3	2	2	3	2	2	2	3	3
	# Reps	8	10	12	10	10	10	12	10	12	10	12	12	10	12
Upright rowing	Wt	15	15	15	15	15	15	20	20	20	25	25	25	30	30	30
	Sets	1	1	1	2	2	3	2	2	3	2	2	3	2	2	3
	# Reps	10	10	12	10	12	12	10	10	12	12	12	12	10	12	12
Abdominal curl	Wt	–	–	–	–	–	–	–	–	–	–	–	–	–	–	–
	Sets	1	1	2	2	2	3	3	3	2	2	1	1	2	2	1
	# Reps	45	45	30	30	40	25	25	30	50	50	100	100	55	55	110
Spine extension	Wt	–	–	–	–	–	–	–	–	–	–	–	–	–	–	–
	Sets	1	1	2	2	2	2	1	1	2	2	1	1	2	2	1
	# Reps	12	12	10	10	12	12	20	20	15	15	30	30	18	18	35

an exaggerated but controlled manner (e.g., lunge walk using exaggerated step size and slow, controlled movement). This is useful for warming up and cooling down.

■ *Static stretching:* Stretch a muscle and hold the stretch for 15 to 30 seconds. Stretch to the point that you feel a "pull" but not pain. This method is most recommended for increasing flexibility of a joint.

■ *Proprioceptive neuromuscular facilitation (PNF):* Another person, a "helper," pushes on the joint in the direction of the desired movement. The person being stretched "resists" the force by pushing in the opposite direction for 4 or 5 seconds and then totally relaxes the muscle before the helper begins again with a stronger "push." The process is repeated two to five times.

Recently we have seen increased emphasis on using an outside force (passive stretching) as opposed to using opposing muscle groups to develop flexibility (active stretching). Passive stretching allows the imposition of more force on the stretch when you cannot generate the needed force with use of the opposing muscle group. You can do passive stretching using your own body to apply more force (e.g., using your arms to pull on your legs), a partner (who pushes your toes toward your knees, for example), or special equipment.

Aerobic Activities

Aerobic activities are a fun way for students to develop fitness and are likely to appeal to students who normally would be more sedentary. Aerobic activities can include aerobic dance, step aerobics, Dance Revolution, GeoFitness, aerobic swimming, or water aerobics. Any activity that involves moderate to vigorous effort sustained over a period of time (uses oxygen) is considered an aerobic activity. This section addresses those activities designed specifically to improve fitness that are "fun" things to do.

Some of the more popular and motivating forms of aerobic activities for secondary students involve moving to music. Music is a powerful motivator for aerobic activities for all, but especially for today's youth if it is "their music." Most people associate music with dance, but music can usefully accompany any kind of aerobic activity and should be chosen such that its tempo is consistent with the speed of the activity (e.g., swimming at 60 strokes a minute should use music at 120 beats per minute). You can program music to progress from warm-up speed to your **target heart rate** and then back to a cool-down resting pace to finish. Aerobic routines should not exceed 120 to 140 cadences per minute (number of beats in a minute).

Aerobic activities often combine cardiorespiratory, strength, and flexibility elements into routines performed to music of various kinds. Types of music that may be appropriate for particular groups include hip-hop, disco, country, jazz, popular tunes, and ballet music. Aerobics done to music is far more motivating for many students than calisthenics, walking, or jogging programs.

Some of the more popular forms of aerobic activities for secondary students are hip-hop workouts (exercising to contemporary music), GeoFitness (using a mat with stations on which to perform fitness exercises), kick boxing, boxing training exercises, and step aerobics. Many commercial companies have capitalized on the popularity of fitness aerobics and have produced good DVDs and music exclusively for this purpose.

For aerobic conditioning, the American College of Sports Medicine recommends aerobic exercise done for a minimum of 20 minutes, three times a week, at 60% of the maximal heart rate. This makes aerobic activities a perfect program for before school, after school, and lunchtime. Most physical education teachers should be able to teach aerobic fitness. There are probably also people in the community who have certification to teach and conduct an aerobics program, as well as video and online resources to aid or substitute for instructors. Students can be encouraged to buy one of many books and videos available for working out at home and to use the resources available online.

Levels of Intensity

Basic guidelines for applying the FITT principles (frequency, intensity, time, and type of activity) to aerobic activity are presented in table 16.2. Aerobic fitness activities can be conducted at three levels of intensity. The low-impact type is designed to lessen the stress placed on the lower extremities and feet. Steps and routines are designed so that one foot remains in contact with the ground at all times, thereby minimizing the likelihood of injuries such as shinsplints. However, a low-impact routine is not vigorous enough to increase the heart rate to an optimal level. A low-impact routine will not improve the efficiency of the heart and lungs in people who are already fit, but is a good choice for beginners. The intermediate level benefits the heart and lungs and assists in achieving overall strength and flexibility. Advanced classes, also called high impact, are for fit people who want a hard workout (one foot is off the floor in every exercise), but carry with them the risk of injury. Injury may result from the impact experienced when the feet hit the floor or ground. This risk can be minimized through the use of good aerobic footwear, as well as with specially designed

TABLE 16.2

FITT Guidelines Applied to Aerobic Fitness

	Children (5-12 years)[a]	Adolescents (11+ years)[b]	Middle and high school youth who participate in athletics[c]
Frequency	■ Developmentally appropriate physical activity on all or most days of the week. ■ Several bouts of physical activity lasting 15 min or more daily.	■ Daily or nearly every day ■ Three or more sessions per week	5 or 6 days per week
Intensity	■ Mixture of moderate and vigorous intermittent activity. ■ Moderate includes low-intensity games (hopscotch, Four Square), low-activity positions (goalie, outfielders), some chores, and yard work. ■ Vigorous includes games involving running or chasing and playing sports (level 2 of activity pyramid).	■ Moderate to vigorous activity; maintaining a target heart rate not expected at this level ■ 12-16 rating of perceived exertion (RPE)[d]	■ 60-90% heart rate max (MHR) or 50-85% heart rate reserve (HRR) ■ 12-16 RPE[d]
Time	■ Accumulate at least 60 min, and up to several hours, of activity. ■ Up to 50% of minutes should be accumulated in bouts of 15 min or more.	■ 30-60 min daily activity ■ 20 min or more in a single session	20-60 min
Type	■ Do a variety of activities. ■ Activities should be selected from the first three levels of the activity pyramid. ■ Continuous activity should not be expected for most children.	■ Play, games, sports, work, transportation, recreation, physical education, or planned exercise in the context of family, school, and community activities ■ Brisk walking, jogging, stair climbing, basketball, racket sports, soccer, dance, lap swimming, skating, lawn mowing, and cycling	Activities that use large muscles and are used in a rhythmical fashion (e.g., brisk walking, jogging, stair climbing, basketball, racket sports, soccer, dance, lap swimming, skating, and cycling)

[a]National Association for Sport and Physical Education. (2004). *Physical activity for children: A statement of guidelines for children ages 5-12,* 2nd ed. (Reston, VA: Author).

[b]Corbin, C.B., and Pangrazi, R.P. (2002). Physical activity for children: how much is enough? In G.J. Welk, R.J. Morrow, & H.B. Falls (Eds), *Fitnessgram Reference Guide* (p. 7 Internet Resource). Dallas, TX: The Cooper Institute.

[c]American College of Sports Medicine. (2000). *ACSM's guidelines for exercise testing and prescription,* 6th ed. Lippincott, Williams, and Wilkins: Philadelphia.

[d]Borg, G. (1998). *Borg's perceived exertion and pain scales* (Champaign, IL: Human Kinetics), 47.

floors that absorb the shock (not usually available in schools). A combination of impact levels is the most popular, as this type of routine begins with a warm-up, low-impact period and then increases the heart rate using high-impact exercise.

Routines

For nonathletic girls and boys, one of the problems related to aerobic dance is concern about learning the "dance steps." While aerobic dance used to include many of the more complex dance steps,

Fitness activities should be a choice for students.

routines today involve minimal dance steps and more calisthenic types of movements. Aerobic fitness activities (e.g., GeoFitness, hip-hop, kick boxing) other than "dance" do not require high levels of rhythmic ability or the memorization of complicated steps. This shift in focus has made aerobic exercise routines more popular among nonactive students and boys, too. Beginners should be asked to follow the lead of the instructor and need not be concerned about "keeping up," about what comes next, or about how many times they need to do what step pattern. They should also be encouraged not to be self-conscious about what they look like; the important thing is the benefits of what they are doing.

Aerobic fitness activities are usually measured in beats, using patterns of 32 or 64 of a particular step before changing to a different pattern. In keeping time, people need to count only in intervals of four and eight. A typical aerobic activity exercise is performed in four or eight counts followed by a separate segment using four or eight counts. Ultimately the steps will add up to 32 or 64.

Step Aerobics

Step aerobics uses a 4- to 12-inch (10- to 30-centimeter) stepping platform or step. The 4-inch platform is for beginners and the 12-inch platform for more advanced levels. You step up to and down from the platform at specific intervals, alternating the lead leg. Step aerobics increases a cardiorespiratory workout without putting undue stress on the joints as with high-impact aerobics. The stress on the joints of the leg is similar to that with walking. The workout you get is similar to that for jogging or running but without the stress on the knees and ankles. The intensity level can vary depending on the arm movements used. Large movements that bring the arms overhead result in a higher-intensity cardiorespiratory workout.

Proper form for step aerobics includes the following:

- Step up onto the platform utilizing the entire sole of your foot, using a heel-to-toe motion, and step down using a toe-to-heel motion.

- Position yourself close to the step when stepping up.

- Alternate the legs, performing no more than five consecutive step-ups per leg.

- Do not allow your knee to lock.

- Step up and down softly.

Stepping platforms can be purchased or can be made easily in a district wood shop. A variety of heights would be valuable. If only one height is available, it should be 6 to 8 inches (15 to 20 centimeters). The only requirements are that it be sturdy enough to provide support without slipping and convenient to store and move into and out of the space where it is to be used.

Safety in Aerobic Activities

Injuries occur in aerobic activities because of overuse of muscles, use of the wrong type of floor (too hard or too soft), or stickiness of floors. The best clothing for aerobic activities is light in weight and allows freedom of movement. Participants should wear a shoe that gives good support and cushioning to the ball of the foot. Shoes should slide on the floor without sticking, but should not slip. For safety, participants should follow these guidelines:

- Execute exercise routines properly.

- If you use hand, wrist, or ankle weights to add extra stress to the joints, they should not weigh more than 1 pound (0.45 kilograms).
- For step aerobics, use proper form to step up to and down from a platform that is the proper height, and do not exceed a 120 to 140 cadences per minute.

Leadership for the Fitness Components of the Program

Most physical education teachers will have the skills to administer all the fitness aspects of the physical activity program. The program may want to hire specialists in the field as well. These people do not necessarily have teacher certification and are usually specialized in the aspects of the program they can lead and supervise. Table 16.3 lists the types of certification that are available from various

TABLE 16.3

Certification for Fitness Specializations

Name of organization	Type of certification	Web site
American College of Sports Medicine	Health and fitness instructor	www.acsm.org (ACSM)
American Council on Exercise	Personal trainer Group fitness instructor Clinical exercise specialist	www.acefitness.org (ACE)
Aerobics and Fitness Association of America	Fitness practitioner Kick boxing Primary group exercise Step certification Personal trainer Advanced personal trainer	www.afaa.org (AFAA)
National Strength and Conditioning Association	Certified strength and conditioning specialist NSCA certified personal trainer	www.nsca-cc.org (NSCA)
YMCA	Group exercise instructor Cardio and step aerobics instructor Pilates instructor Group cycling instructor Walk Reebok Premier Instructor Personal trainer Fitness testing and assessment specialist Personal fitness program director Get Real Weight Management Instructor	www.ymca.com (YMCA)

organizations. Preparation for certification varies considerably from one organization to another.

SUMMARY

1. Well-rounded fitness programs provide opportunities for the development of each of the components of fitness.
2. Cardiorespiratory fitness can be achieved by mixing different types of activities.
3. Connecting students to community groups is one strategy that can be used to help them develop fitness.
4. Programs need to find ways to maintain student motivation to continue to participate in fitness programs on a regular basis.
5. Muscular strength and endurance are critical to all ages and participants, not just athletes.
6. Free weights have advantages over machines for developing muscular strength and endurance.
7. Opportunities for both structured and unstructured muscular strength and endurance programs need to be provided.
8. Flexibility is the range of motion of a joint and is critical to injury prevention.
9. Dynamic, static, and PNF are common types of recommended flexibility exercises.
10. Aerobic dance can be conducted at three levels of intensity.
11. Students should be taught the proper use of step platforms for an aerobic workout.

CHECKING YOUR UNDERSTANDING

1. What components should be included in a well-rounded fitness program?
2. What activities can be used for cardiorespiratory development?
3. What are the safety issues with aerobic activities?
4. What are the benefits of developing muscular strength?
5. What are the advantages and disadvantages of machines and free weights?
6. What are the advantages of structured and unstructured strength development programs?
7. What are the two types of flexibility?
8. What are the different types of stretching that should be included in a flexibility program?
9. Why would a fitness program want to include aerobic dance?
10. How are aerobic dance routines of today different from those taught in the past?

RESOURCES

Fitness Certification

www.acefitness.org (ACE)
www.acsm.org (ACSM)
www.afaa.org (AFAA)
www.nsca-cc.org (NSCA)
www.ymca.net (YMCA)

Strength Training

www.pilatesmethodalliance.org

Aerobic Dance Music and Equipment

www.cardiomixes.com
www.dynamixmusic.com
www.FitnessAV.ca
www.fwonline.com
www.technosweat.com

Aerobic Dance Programs by Location

www.AerobicsSearch.com

Walking Web Sites

www.About.com (search engine)
www.mapmywalk.com
www.walkstyles.com

Fahey, T.D. (2004). *Basic weight training for men and women* (5th ed.). Boston: McGraw-Hill.

Hoeger, W., & Hoeger, S. (2000). *Lifetime physical fitness and wellness.* Englewood, CO: Morton.

Howley, E., & Franks, D. (2007). *Fitness professional's handbook* (5th ed.). Champaign, IL: Human Kinetics.

National Association for Sport and Physical Education. (2004). *Physical education for lifelong fitness: The physical best teacher's guide.* Champaign, IL: Human Kinetics.

Sharkey, B. (1997). *Fitness and health.* Champaign, IL: Human Kinetics.

PART IV

Wellness Programs

17

Parent, Staff, and Faculty Physical Activity Programs

OVERVIEW

The purpose of this chapter is to help you develop physical activity programs for the people who work at your school and district, as well as provide educational opportunities for families. Teachers and the staff members of schools are likely to participate in physical activity if they have convenient opportunities to do so. The physical activity of students, particularly in the elementary school, is largely dependent on the physical activity levels of families. A comprehensive school physical activity program will address both.

CHAPTER OUTCOMES

This chapter will help you

- plan and conduct a staff and faculty physical activity program, and
- plan and conduct educational opportunities for parents and family activity programs.

IN THIS CHAPTER

As part of a comprehensive school effort, many schools have made the decision to offer wellness and physical activity programs to staff, faculty, and parent groups. The many advantages of doing this include the following:

- Faculty and staff who have opportunities to maintain health and to engage in physical activity at the workplace are absent less often and are more positive about their work experiences. Many corporations have found that work wellness centers are a good financial investment.
- Faculty and staff who participate in work fitness and wellness programs are good role models for students.
- Parents who participate in school programs are more likely to support not only efforts to increase the physical activity of their children but also other school programs.

What Is a School Staff, Faculty, and Parent Wellness Program?

There is great diversity in the services provided by school faculty and staff wellness programs, ranging from creating time for adults to use the facilities to extensive educational and instructional programming. The publication *School Employee Wellness: A Guide for Protecting the Assets of Our Nation's Schools* (2007) is available from the School Employee Wellness Organization (www.schoolempwell.org). This publication establishes the idea that employee wellness programs should be initiated by the school wellness council and presents a comprehensive health promotion perspective on the development of a program. This chapter focuses on establishing the physical activity part of a more comprehensive program. The sidebar lists some examples of other components that can be included in a comprehensive program. A school physical activity program might simply organize a walking club after school for faculty and staff, or a night when parents can come and "exercise" using the facilities. District programs might consider more extensive programs supported by the district, or outsourcing the program to a local fitness or recreational center. The type of program you design will depend on the resources you have and the interest you can generate in the program.

Alternative Programs and Services for Faculty and Staff Wellness

Fitness testing

Conditioning programs

Weight control and nutrition programming

Walking/jogging clubs

Weight training

Sport programs, intramural and club

Aerobic activities (e.g., aerobic dance, kick boxing, step aerobics, GeoFitness)

Fitness consultation

Family fitness education

Family physical activity opportunities

Yoga

Pilates

Beginning a Program

One of the first things that organizers of any program must do is to get administrative support for a program. If the program is to be a school district program, it will need the support of the superintendent. If it is to be a school-based program, it will need the support of the principal. Support is more easily obtained if the decision makers are given data showing the positive effects of such programming and presented with a well-thought-out plan that initially does not require too many resources.

Organizers need to define the long-term and short-term goals of the program and the target audience. Clearly, staff and parent audiences are different and will initially require a different set of plans, although these may later be combined into overlapping services. You may want to begin with just a walking club for faculty and staff or a "parent night" and then extend the services that your program provides as interest and resources grow. Programs run on a district level may have more resources but may not be as attractive because they do not have the "bonding" and convenience advantages of programs run at individual schools. Initial planning should include the following considerations:

- Who are we going to target—staff, faculty, parents, families?
- Should the program be at the district or school level?
- How are we going to determine interest?
- What program elements should we offer to begin the program?
  - Opportunity for physical activity
  - Instruction in physical activity
  - Educational programming
  - Individual consulting
- What is the potential to expand the services of the program?
- What will the school or district provide (staffing, resources, or organizational support)?
- Who should make these decisions (physical education teacher with administrator, district wellness council, appointed committee)?

Determining Interest

Before schools and districts invest a lot of resources in a program, they need to determine interest. Figures 17.1 and 17.2 on pages 317 and 318 are examples of short surveys that can be used with

Many adults will find participation in fitness activities more enjoyable if they have someone to do it with.

faculty and staff and parents to ascertain interest. Surveys can be sent home with students to parents or may be linked to the school Web site to be returned electronically. Interest is likely to grow if the beginning participants find their participation rewarding. Programs should not be afraid to start small with only a few participants.

While conditioning and walking/jogging programs can be conducted all year and will probably maintain interest, other activities ought to be considered on a seasonal basis (e.g., cycling in the spring or fall, basketball in the winter). Seasonal programs have a clear beginning and ending point during the school year. Fitness programming and opportunities to use the facilities tend to be provided year-round.

Once you have determined interest in the program, you will need to set priorities for what services you will provide. The programs that the survey identifies as being needed will have to be balanced with what you consider most important and realistic in terms of the resources you identify.

Administering the Program

Administration of programs for parents, staff, and faculty begins with obtaining the needed resources. Once the resources are in place, administrators will need to arrange for staffing, for publicizing the program among those who may wish to sign up, and for ongoing communication with participants.

Obtaining Resources for the Program

School districts will have the qualified personnel to conduct a school wellness program. Extensive and comprehensive programs will require financial resources. Resources for a school wellness program can be obtained from community partners (hospitals, local health departments, parent organizations, local businesses, YMCA/YWCA, local media, and civic organizations). District revenues, participant fees, and private and public agencies are also good sources of funding (see resources listed at the end of this chapter for specific sources of funding).

Staffing the Program

Some program components are likely to need more staff involvement than others. A walking program or a conditioning program for faculty and staff is likely not to need a great deal of staff participation after its initial organization. Other programs that require equipment or leadership will necessitate the attendance of a program staff member. This person is most likely going to be the physical education teacher or another faculty member with skills and knowledge in the activity. Often this person volunteers his or her services and even participates in the program. In other situations, schools and districts need to consider a small salary supplement paid from school or district funds, grant funds for physical activity, or a small charge to participants (e.g., $30 per semester).

Programs that meet outside normal school hours will probably need either custodial help, to let participants in and out of the facility without compromising security, or give the staff person in charge of the program the authority to fulfill this responsibility. For programs that use physical education facilities or equipment but that are not conducted by the physical education faculty, the personnel will need to be given keys. The personnel will also need to understand the importance of caring for the facilities and equipment they use in order to maintain positive relationships with the physical education faculty and receive their continued support.

Communication

Once you have determined that there is interest in your program, you will need to make sure that all potential participants are given the opportunity to sign up. You can do this through school and district Web sites, flyers in faculty and staff mailboxes, presentations at beginning-of-school orientations for parents, notes sent home to parents via students, teacher Web sites, or posters set up in the school lobby.

It is important to set up a quick means to communicate with the program participants. You will need a way to communicate quickly when weather is an issue for outdoor events, when holidays and school events interfere with the program's regular schedule, when staff will not be available, or when venues need to be changed. Although this is not as much of a problem for faculty and staff programs within a school, it is a major problem for programs with participants from outside the school. What you don't want is for people to show up for an event that has been canceled.

Establishing a Web site or e-mail listserv is one of the best ways to get information out quickly to participants when it can be assumed that all participants have access to e-mail and a computer. When they do not, participants should be given a telephone number they can call to check whether events are going to be conducted; and a telephone chain should be established to let participants know of any schedule changes (each participant is assigned to call another after he or she has been notified).

Working With the Adult Population

Physical activity has the same benefits for adults that it has for children and youth; and because adults are less likely to get the amount of physical activity they need, it is even more important. Adults can achieve the aerobic activity recommendation through one of the following options:

- A minimum of 30 minutes of moderate-intensity physical activity per day, such as brisk walking, on most days of the week
- A minimum of 20 minutes of vigorous-intensity physical activity, such as jogging or running, three days a week (see table 17.1)

Physical activity helps adults to

- lower their stress and boost their mood;

TABLE 17.1

Examples of Moderate to Vigorous Activity Levels

Indoors	Outdoors	Indoors or outdoors
■ Dancing, general (Greek, hula, flamenco, Middle Eastern, swing) ■ Riding a stationary bike ■ Actively playing with children ■ Taking Jazzercise ■ Scrubbing the floor	■ Mowing lawn, general ■ Frisbee playing, general ■ Playing golf, walking the course ■ Shoveling light snow ■ Downhill skiing with light effort ■ Raking leaves ■ Hand washing, waxing a car	■ Playing basketball, shooting hoops ■ Walking, brisk pace (mall, around a track, treadmill) ■ Doing water aerobics ■ Jogging-walking combination (in a 30-minute period, you should be jogging for at least 10 minutes)

- increase strength, endurance, balance, and flexibility;
- control blood pressure and blood sugar;
- build healthy bones, muscles, and joints;
- help the heart and lungs work better;
- improve self-esteem; and
- boost energy during the day and aid in sleep at night.

Physical education teachers spend most of their time working with children and youth who are healthy and for the most part in good physical condition. Many adults are not in good physical condition and have physical limitations. Programs need to be adapted to their level of fitness.

- Men over age 40 and women over age 50, as well as men or women who have a chronic health problem, should talk to their health care provider before starting a vigorous physical activity program. They do not need to talk to their provider before starting an activity like walking. Figure 17.3 on page 319 is a test for activity readiness established by the American Heart Association.

- Adults typically have many reasons for not participating regularly and for not engaging in physical activity on a regular basis. Some of these issues are common to all ages, but many are unique to the adult population. To get adults to be regular participants in physical activity, you will need to address these issues. Figure 17.4 on page 320, from the USA.gov Web site on adult fitness, lists some of the reasons adults usually give for being nonparticipants and some potential solutions.

- Some of the adults you work with may be overweight and in poor physical condition. Motivation may be a big issue for these participants. Figure 17.5 on page 323 provides some guidelines

for working with adults and with women who may be pregnant or who have a disability or a chronic health condition.

- For many adults, walking will be the exercise of choice. Counting steps with a pedometer is one way to monitor the amount of physical activity each person is getting each day and is motivating and inexpensive. The normal activity level for adults is about 900 to 3,000 steps per day. The recommended number of steps per day just to maintain some level of fitness is 10,000 steps. This means that adults will need to intentionally increase the amount of activity they get each day. Adults may need help on how to use a pedometer. For more information on the 10,000 steps program, go to www.shapeup.org/shape/steps.php.

- Although safety is a concern for all ages, in many respects the adult population is more at risk for injury and health threats resulting from exercise. Figure 17.6 on page 324 provides some guidelines for safe participation.

- Schools should have a risk management plan to deal with the liability issues involved in working with nonprofessional employees on school property. At the very least, participants should be asked to fill out a health questionnaire that is screened for potential problems and should sign a waiver of liability for normal risks associated with participation in physical activities. An example of an assumption of risk form is provided in figure 17.7 on page 325.

Family Programs

Child care responsibilities interfere with the efforts of many families to get more exercise. One of the big challenges is to get an entire family committed to spending time together in physical activities. This strategy not only has the benefit of increasing

Good physical activity programs will educate parents to involve the entire family in physical activities.

physical activity, but also encourages families to "play" together. One of the best ways to get children involved in physical activity is through efforts to increase the physical activity level of families.

The school physical activity program can be considered as having two different kinds of responsibilities. The first and most important is probably the education of parents regarding the importance of physical activity for their children, along with some help and ideas for how to make physical activity a "family affair." The second, providing direct services to parents by conducting family opportunities for physical activity on a regular basis, is important but probably not within the resources of most schools.

Schools can do much to "kick start" family physical activity by conducting events that are designed for parents to participate in with their children (e.g., walking programs, family nights at the gym). They can also schedule PTO or PTA programs that

inform parents of the importance of physical activity and family physical activity, as well as providing educational materials and suggestions regarding what parents can do to help their children and themselves. The Shape Up America! Web site (www.shapeup.org/fittips) provides great tips for family fitness fun. At the Web site you can find additional information as well as links to handouts you can give to parents. Most health and fitness centers and recreation centers in communities have begun to design programs for families. The resources listed at the end of this chapter are also good places to start, both to help parents think about the importance of family fitness and to give them ideas for making it happen.

Schools can establish family fitness programs through a school Web site that alert parents to community opportunities on a monthly or weekly basis, help parents keep track of their participation, and reward families for their efforts.

SUMMARY

1. There are many advantages to a school that runs wellness programs for faculty, staff, and parents.

2. The nature of the program that you design for adults will largely depend on the resources you have. The more resources, the better the program.

3. Planning for a wellness program includes making a decision about the target audience, determining participant interest, deciding what program elements to include, and identifying the resources and support available for the program.

4. Interest can be determined through surveys of potential participants.

5. Some compensation for staff is essential for the success of a program and can be funded by participant fees or supported by the school or district.

6. Programs need a standard way to communicate with participants and potential participants.

7. Physical activity has the same benefits for adults that it does for children and youth.

8. The program will need to adapt to the physical limitations of some adults.

9. Family programs have the potential to contribute to the physical activity levels of both the adults and their children and to develop school support.

CHECKING YOUR UNDERSTANDING

1. Why are wellness programs for faculty and staff a good investment for schools?

2. What are the potential components of a comprehensive wellness program for faculty and staff?

3. What decisions should planners of a program make before the onset of efforts to develop a program?

4. What are the potential methods that can be used to communicate with participants?

5. What unique advantages are there for adults from participating in physical activity?

6. Identify four of the most common reasons adults give for not being physically active and describe how you would respond to these reasons.

7. Identify 10 physical activities that families can do together.

RESOURCES

The Directors of Health Promotion and Education. (2007). *School employee wellness: A guide for protecting the assets of our nation's schools.* Washington, DC: DHPE.

Adult Fitness-Related Publications

Active Living Every Day: 20 Weeks to Lifelong Vitality. Steven N. Blair, Andrea L. Dunn, Bess II. Marcus, Ruth Ann Carpenter, and Peter Jaret. Human Kinetics, 2001. This book offers a step-by-step plan for getting and staying active. The information, suggested activities, and self-help tools in each chapter were successfully tested with people who followed the plan and learned to make activity a part of their daily lives. The 20 chapters correspond to the 20 weeks of the program, but readers are encouraged to go at their own pace. Available from www.humankinetics.com or your local or online bookstore.

Don't Weight: Eat Healthy and Get Moving NOW! Kelly Bliss. Infinity, 2002. This book provides motivation and information for healthy eating and plus-size fitness. It also teaches problem-solving techniques. It offers information that can help the larger person plan and achieve a fitness program that can be sustained for a lifetime. Available from KellyBliss.com, P.O. Box 572, Lansdowne, PA 19050; 610-394-2547; www.kellybliss.com; or your local or online bookstore.

Easy Does It Yoga. Alice Christensen, American Yoga Association. Fireside, 1999. This book presents a program of exercises, breathing, meditation, philosophy, and nutrition for older adults and those with physical limitations. Simple chair exercises and more challenging standing and floor exercises are described. Available from the American Yoga Association, P.O. Box 19986, Sarasota, FL 34276; 941-927-4977; www.americanyogaassociation.org; or your local or online bookstore.

Great Shape: The First Fitness Guide for Large Women. Pat Lyons and Debby Burgard. iUniverse, 2000. This book urges women to be physically active for fun, fitness, and positive body image instead of for weight loss. The authors describe a healthy lifestyle program including walking, swimming, dancing, martial arts, bicycling, and more. Available from www.iuniverse.com or your local or online bookstore.

Just the Weigh You Are: How to Be Fit and Healthy Whatever Your Size. Steven Jonas and Linda Konner. Houghton Mifflin, 1998. This book presents a plan for total fitness and healthy living no matter what your size. Chapters focus on accepting oneself, improving nutrition without dieting, managing stress, and doing moderate physical activity. Available from your local or online bookstore.

Real Fitness for Real Women: A Unique Workout Program for the Plus-Size Woman. Rochelle Rice. Warner Books, 2001. This book describes a six-week introductory fitness program that includes warm-ups, aerobics, strength training and stretching techniques, and meditation. Photos of plus-size women illustrate the exercises. The book also addresses getting motivated, creating support, evaluating current abilities, and increasing self-acceptance. Available from www.rochellerice.com or your local or online bookstore.

Tips to Help You Get Active. Weight-control Information Network (WIN). National Institutes of Health (NIH) Publication No. 06-5578, 2006. This booklet provides ideas and tips for becoming physically active. It focuses on overcoming common barriers and setting goals. Available from WIN, www.win.niddk.nih.gov.

Walking . . . A Step in the Right Direction. WIN. NIH Publication No. 03-4155, 2001. This pamphlet explains how to start a walking program, presents a sample program, and shows stretches for warming up and cooling down. Available in English and Spanish from WIN, www.win.niddk.nih.gov.

Water Exercise. Martha D. White. Human Kinetics, 1995. This book presents water exercises for fitness and muscle tone as well as exercises for injuries, postsurgical rehabilitation, and other special needs. Available from www.humankinetics.com; Human Kinetics, P.O. Box 5076, Champaign, IL 61825; 1-800-747-4457; www.humankinetics.com; or your local or online bookstore.

Funding Sources for School Wellness Programs

www.fdncenter.org
www.fundsnetservices.com/main.htm
www.grants.gov
www.healthinschools.org
www.schoolgrants.org

Videos

BIG MOVES: Yoga for Chair and Bed. Mara Nesbitt. This video is designed for people who have difficulty getting down to or up from the floor. Led by a plus-size instructor, it includes stretches that are done standing, sitting, and lying on a bed, plus a guided meditation. Available from Mirage Video Productions, P.O. Box 19141, Portland, OR 97280; or www.miragevideos.com.

Chair Dancing. Jodi Stolove. This no-impact video series is designed to improve muscle tone, flexibility, and cardiovascular endurance without putting stress on your knees, back, hips, or feet. Available from Chair Dancing International, Inc., 2658 Del Mar Heights Road, Del Mar, CA 92014; 1-800-551-4386; or www.chairdancing.com.

Tai Chi Chuan. Dawn Fleetwood. This 50-minute instructional video features slow, gentle movements and breathing exercises that involve all of the muscles and organs in the body. Available from Orchid Leaf Productions, P.O. Box 72, Flint, MI 48501; 810-235-9864.

Yoga for Round Bodies, Volumes 1 and 2. Linda DeMarco and Genia Pauli Haddon. These videos offer a fitness system based on Kripalu yoga to promote strength, flexibility, stress relief, and cardiovascular health. Round-bodied instructors tailor classic yoga postures to large people at both beginner and intermediate levels in each video. Available from Plus Publications, P.O. Box 265-W, Scotland, CT 06264; 1-800-436-9642; or www.amazon.com.

Organizations and Programs for Adult Physical Activity

Council on Size and Weight Discrimination, Inc. The Council on Size and Weight Discrimination (CSWD) is a nonprofit organization that seeks to improve health care and access to services for large people through educational programs, media monitoring, and medical conference attendance. Contact CSWD at P.O. Box 305, Mount Marion, NY 12456; 845-679-1209; or www.cswd.org.

YMCA and YWCA. The YMCA and YWCA offer physical fitness and health awareness programs in many locations throughout the United States. Contact YMCA of the U.S.A., 101 North Wacker Drive, Chicago, IL 60606; 312-977-0031; or www.ymca.net. Contact YWCA of the U.S.A., 1015 18th Street, NW, Suite 1100, Washington, DC 20036; 1-800-679-1209; or www.ywca.org.

FAMILY FITNESS RESOURCES

99 Tips for Family Fitness Fun

www.cdc.gov/family/springbreak/
www.cdc.gov/healthyyouth/physicalactivity/brochures/pdf/parent.pdf
www.familyfitness.about.com
www.aahperd.org/NASPE/ or www.shapeup.org

WEB SITES

Active at Any Size

http://win.niddk.nih.gov/publications/active.htm

Body Positive

This site addresses issues ranging from self-esteem to fitness to finding respectful health care providers. It includes resources and links to related sites. www.bodypositive.com

Getting Started

Fitness Fundamentals: Guidelines for Personal Exercise Programs
www.fitness.gov/fitness.htm

Healthy Living With Bliss

This site provides information on walking, swimming, aerobics, stretching, and other fitness activities for large and very large people. A resource section offers information on fitness wear, books, exercise equipment, classes, and where to buy fitness videos for large people. Included are an online workbook, e-newsletter, and a chat with plus-size personal fitness trainer Kelly Bliss. www.kellybliss.com

Just Move

Just Move is a personalized, Internet-based fitness program of the American Heart Association.

It features an online activity diary for monitoring your progress, frequently asked questions, health information, and many fitness links and resources. www.justmove.org

Mayo Clinic Fitness Center

This Web site offers a set of articles about walking for fitness and includes a shoe-buying guide and a pedometer guide. It also contains slide shows for strength training and stretching exercises. www.mayoclinic.com/health/fitness/SM99999

Physical Activity in Your Daily Life

www.americanheart.org/presenter. jhtml?identifier=2155

Shape Up America! 10,000 Steps

www.shapeup.org/shape/steps.php

Tips to Help You Get Active

http://win.niddk.nih.gov/publications/tips.htm

FIGURE 17.1

Faculty and Staff Interest Survey

District 5 is thinking about organizing a faculty and staff wellness and physical activity program. If you have any interest in participating in such a program, please fill out this survey and return it by September 14th to Rhonda Burly at the district office.

Please check the activities below that you have an interest in and would participate in if they were offered.

	Walking club			Jogging club			Bicycling	
	Weight training			Softball			Backpacking	
	Fitness testing			Volleyball			Conditioning	
	Aerobic dance			Weight control			Tennis	
	Basketball			Nutrition education			Other—list	

Please indicate the time and days that would be best for you (two days a week).

_____ Before school (6:30-7:30)

_____ After school (4:00-5:00)

_____ Evenings (7:00-8:00)

_____ Monday

_____ Tuesday

_____ Wednesday

_____ Thursday

_____ Friday

_____ Saturday morning

_____ Sunday afternoon

_____ Sunday evening

FIGURE 17.2

Parent Interest Survey

District 5 is thinking about organizing a parent wellness and physical activity program. If you have any interest in participating in such a program, please fill out this survey and return it by September 14th to Rosa Cassidy at the district office.

E-mail: RCassidy@northdell2.k12.ms.us
Address: 321 Loddy Lane, Northdell, Mississippi
Fax: 555-555-7885

Please check the activities below that you or your family have an interest in and would participate in if they were offered. Indicate whether the participation would be personal with a P or family (F), meaning this would be a family event.

_____	Walking club		_____	Jogging club	
_____	Weight training		_____	Weight control	
_____	Fitness testing		_____	Backpacking	
_____	Aerobic dance		_____	Stress management	
_____	Conditioning		_____	Nutrition education	
_____	Hiking		_____	Fitness counseling	
_____	Bicycling		_____	Other—list	

Please indicate the time and days that would be best for you (two days a week).

_____ Evenings (7:00-8:00)

_____ Evenings (8:00-9:00)

_____ Monday

_____ Tuesday

_____ Wednesday

_____ Thursday

_____ Friday

_____ Saturday morning

_____ Sunday afternoon

_____ Sunday evening

FIGURE 17.3

American Heart Association Physical Activity Readiness Questionnaire

If you mark any of the following statements, please talk with your physician or other appropriate health care provider before engaging in exercise.

___ I have a heart condition and my health care professional recommends only medically supervised physical activity.

___ During or right after I exercise, I often have pains or pressure in my neck, left shoulder, or arm.

___ I have developed chest pain within the last month.

___ I tend to lose consciousness or fall over due to dizziness.

___ I feel extremely breathless after mild exertion.

___ My health care provider recommended that I take medicine for high blood pressure or a heart condition.

___ I have bone or joint problems that limit my ability to do moderate-intensity physical activity.

___ I have a medical condition or other physical reason not mentioned here that might need special attention in an exercise program.

___ I am pregnant and my health care professional hasn't given me the OK to be physically active.

FIGURE 17.4

Solutions to Adult Barriers to Exercise

Barrier: Between work, family, and other demands, I am too busy to exercise.

Make physical activity a priority. Carve out some time each week to be active and put it on your calendar. Try waking up a half hour earlier to walk, scheduling lunchtime workouts, or taking an evening fitness class.
Build physical activity into your routine chores. Rake the yard, wash the car, or do energetic housework. That way you do what needs to get done and move around too.

Make family time physically active. Plan a weekend hike through a park, a family softball game, or an evening walk around the block.

Barrier: By the end of a long day, I am just too tired to work out.

Break your workout into three 10-minute segments each day. Taking three short walks during the day may seem easier and less tiring than one 30-minute workout, and is just as good for you.

Find another time during the day to work out. If evening workouts are not for you, then try a bike ride before breakfast or a walk at lunchtime.

Sneak physical activity into your days. Take stairs instead of elevators, park farther away in parking lots, and walk in place while watching TV.

Barrier: I think my weight is fine, so I am not motivated to exercise.

Think about the other health benefits of physical activity. Regular physical activity may help lower cholesterol and blood pressure, and also lower your odds of having heart disease, type 2 diabetes, or cancer. Research shows that people who are overweight, active, and fit live longer than people who are *not* overweight but are inactive and unfit. Also, physical activity may lift your mood and increase your energy level.

Do it just for fun. Play a team sport, work in a garden, or learn a new dance and make getting fit something fun.

Train for a charity event. You can work to help others while you work out.

Barrier: Getting on a treadmill or stationary bike is boring.

Meet a friend for workouts. If your buddy is on the next bike or treadmill, your workout will be less boring.

Watch TV or listen to music or a book on tape while you walk or pedal indoors. Check out music or books on tape from your local library.

Get outside. A change in scenery can relieve your boredom. If you are riding a bike outside, be sure to wear a helmet and learn safe rules of the road. For more information about bike safety, read *Bike Safety Tips* from the American Academy of Family Physicians.

Barrier: I am afraid I will hurt myself.

Start slowly. If you are starting a new physical activity program, go slow at first. Even if you are doing an activity that you once did well, start up again slowly to lower your risk of injury or burnout.

Choose moderate-intensity physical activities. You are not likely to hurt yourself by walking 30 minutes per day. Doing vigorous physical activities may increase your risk for injury, but moderate-intensity physical activity is low risk.

Take a class. A knowledgeable group fitness instructor should be able to teach you how to move with proper form and lower risk for injury. The instructor can watch your actions during class and let you know if you are doing things right.

Choose water workouts. Whether you swim laps or try water aerobics, working out in the water is easy on your joints and helps reduce muscle soreness and injury.

Work with a personal trainer. A certified personal trainer should be able to show you how to warm up, cool down, use fitness equipment like treadmills and weight training machines, and use proper form to help lower your risk for injury. Personal training sessions may be cheap or costly, so find out about fees before making an appointment.

Barrier: I have never been into sports.

Find a physical activity that you enjoy. You do not have to be an athlete to benefit from physical activity. Try yoga, hiking, or planting a garden.

Choose an activity that you can stick with, like walking. Just put one foot in front of the other. Use the time you spend walking to relax, talk with a friend or family member, or just enjoy the scenery.

Barrier: I do not want to spend a lot of money to join a gym or buy workout gear.

Choose free activities. Garden, take your children to the park to play, lift plastic milk jugs filled with water or sand, or take a walk.

Find out if your job offers any discounts on memberships. Some companies get lower membership rates at fitness or community centers. Other companies will even pay part of an employee's membership fee.

Check out your local recreation or community center. These centers may cost less than other gyms, fitness centers, or health clubs.

Choose physical activities that do not require any special gear. Walking requires only a pair of sturdy shoes. To dance, just turn on some music.

Barrier: I do not have anyone to watch my kids while I work out.

Do something physically active with your kids. Kids need physical activity too. No matter what age your kids are, you can find an activity you can do together. Dance to music, take a walk, run around the park, or play basketball or soccer together.

Take turns with another parent to watch the kids. One of you minds the kids while the other one works out.

Hire a baby-sitter.

Look for a fitness or community center that offers child care. Centers that have child care are becoming more popular. Cost and quality vary, so get all the information up front.

Barrier: My family and friends are not physically active.

Do not let that stop you. Do it for yourself. Enjoy the rewards—such as better sleep, a happier mood, more energy, and a stronger body—that you get from working out.

Join a class or sport league where people count on you to show up. If your basketball team or dance partner counts on you, you will not want to miss a workout, even if your family and friends are not involved.

Barrier: I would be embarrassed if my neighbors or friends saw me exercising.

Ask yourself if it really matters. You are doing something positive for your health, and that is something to be proud of. You may even inspire others to get physically active too.

Invite a friend or neighbor to join you. You may feel less self-conscious if you are not alone.

Go to a park, nature trail, or fitness or community center to be physically active.

Barrier: The winter is too cold or the summer is too hot to be active outdoors.

Walk around the mall.

(continued)

(continued)

Join a fitness or community center. Find one that lets you pay only for the months or classes you want, instead of the whole year.

Exercise at home. Work out to fitness videos or DVDs. Check a different one out from the library each week for variety.

Barrier: My neighborhood does not have sidewalks.

Find a safe place to walk. Instead of walking in the street, walk in a friend's or family member's neighborhood that has sidewalks. Walk during your lunch break at work. Find out if you can walk at a local school track.

Work out in the yard. Do yard work or wash the car. These count as physical activity, too.

Barrier: I do not feel safe exercising by myself.

Join or start a walking group. You can enjoy added safety and company as you walk.

Take an exercise class at a nearby fitness or community center.

Work out at home. You don't need a lot of space. Turn on the radio and dance or follow along with a fitness show on TV.

Barrier: I have a health problem (diabetes, heart disease, asthma, arthritis) that I do not want to make worse.

Talk with your health care professional. Most health problems are helped by physical activity. Find out what physical activities you can safely do, and follow advice about length and intensity of workouts.

Start slowly. Take it easy at first and see how you feel before trying more challenging workouts. Stop if you feel out of breath, dizzy, faint, or nauseated, or if you have pain.

Barrier: I have an injury and do not know what physical activities, if any, I can do.

Talk with your health care professional. Ask your physician or physical therapist about what physical activities you can safely perform. Follow advice about length and intensity of workouts.

Start slowly. Take it easy at first and see how you feel before trying more challenging workouts. Stop if you feel pain.

Work with a personal trainer. A knowledgeable personal trainer should be able to help you design a fitness plan around your injury.

FIGURE 17.5

Physical Activity Guidelines for Americans—Adult Recommendations for Safe Physical Activity

Key Guidelines for Safe Physical Activity

To do physical activity safely and reduce the risk of injuries and other adverse events, people should:

- Understand the risks and yet be confident that physical activity is safe for almost everyone.

- Choose to do types of physical activity that are appropriate for their current fitness level and health goals, because some activities are safer than others.

- Increase physical activity gradually over time whenever more activity is necessary to meet guidelines or health goals. Inactive people should "start low and go slow" by gradually increasing how often and how long activities are done.

- Protect themselves by using appropriate gear and sports equipment; looking for safe environments; following rules and policies; and making sensible choices about when, where, and how to be active.

- Be under the care of a health care provider if they have chronic conditions or symptoms. People with chronic conditions and symptoms should consult their health care provider about the types and amounts of activity appropriate for them.

Key Guidelines for Women During Pregnancy and the Postpartum Period

- Healthy women who are not already highly active or doing vigorous-intensity activity should get at least 150 minutes of moderate-intensity aerobic activity a week during pregnancy and the postpartum period. Preferably, this activity should be spread throughout the week.

- Pregnant women who habitually engage in vigorous-intensity aerobic activity or who are highly active can continue physical activity during pregnancy and the postpartum period, provided that they remain healthy and discuss with their health care provider how and when activity should be adjusted over time.

Key Guidelines for Adults With Disabilities

- Adults with disabilities, who are able to, should get at least 150 minutes a week of moderate-intensity, or 75 minutes a week of vigorous-intensity aerobic activity, or an equivalent combination of moderate- and vigorous-intensity aerobic activity. Aerobic activity should be performed in episodes of at least 10 minutes, and preferably it should be spread throughout the week.

- Adults with disabilities, who are able to, should also do muscle-strengthening activities of moderate or high intensity that involve all major muscle groups on two or more days a week, as these activities provide additional health benefits.

- When adults with disabilities are not able to meet the guidelines, they should engage in regular physical activity according to their abilities and should avoid inactivity.

- Adults with disabilities should consult their health care provider about the amounts and types of physical activity that are appropriate for their abilities.

Key Messages for People With Chronic Medical Conditions

- Adults with chronic conditions obtain important health benefits from regular physical activity.

- When adults with chronic conditions do activity according to their abilities, physical activity is safe.

- Adults with chronic conditions should be under the care of a health care provider. People with chronic conditions and symptoms should consult their health care provider about the types and amounts of activity appropriate for them.

FIGURE 17.6

Safe Participation in Physical Activity for Adults

Slow down if you feel out of breath. You should be able to talk during your activity without gasping for breath. Drink water when you are thirsty to replace the water you lose by sweating. Drink water before activity to hydrate.

Wear suitable clothes:

- Wear lightweight, loose-fitting tops so you can move easily.
- Wear clothes made of fabrics that absorb sweat and remove it from your skin.
- Never wear rubber or plastic suits. Plastic suits could hold the sweat on your skin and make your body overheat.
- Women should wear a good support bra.
- Wear supportive athletic shoes for weight-bearing activities.
- Wear a knit hat to keep you warm when you are physically active outdoors in cold weather. Wear a tightly woven, wide-brimmed hat in hot weather to help keep you cool and protect you from the sun.
- Wear sunscreen when you are physically active outdoors.
- Wear garments that prevent inner-thigh chafing, such as tights or spandex shorts.

Stop your activity right away if you:

- Have pain, tightness, or pressure in your chest or neck, shoulder, or arm.
- Feel dizzy or sick.
- Break out in a cold sweat.
- Have muscle cramps.
- Are extremely short of breath.
- Feel pain in your joints, feet, ankles, or legs. You could hurt yourself if you ignore the pain.

Ask your health care provider what to do if you have any of these symptoms.

FIGURE 17.7

Assumption of Risk Form

Date _____

School District #23
For Participants in School Wellness Activities

Participant name: (print)

Home address:

Phone:

The undersigned participant does hereby execute this Assumption of Risk for himself (herself) (themselves), and his (her) (their) heirs, successors, representatives and assigns, and hereby agree(s) and represent(s) as follows:

I am aware that during my participation in: (name of specific event or activity), certain dangers may occur, including but not limited to: (e.g., running or walking on roads and other surfaces, including injuries from surface conditions, injuries from activity in general, injuries from other participants or other spectators or nonparticipants, and the forces of nature).

I understand that (name of specific event or activity) is an inherently dangerous activity and that the risks associated with this activity are generally recognized as dangerous. In consideration of, and as part payment for, the right to participate in the specific event referenced above, and arranged for me by School District #23, I have and do hereby hold School District #23 harmless from any and all liability, actions, causes of action, debts, claims, demands of every kind and nature whatsoever which may arise from or in connection with the specific event/activity referenced above.

The terms thereof shall serve as a release and assumption of risk for my heirs, executor and administrators, and for all members of my family, including minors accompanying me.

I understand that the specific event or activity referenced above has many inherent risks from the standpoint of being basically a physical sport and/or activity. I acknowledge these risks and voluntarily agree to participate in this event/activity as referenced above at my own risk.

I, the undersigned, have read this Assumption of Risk and understand its terms and the risks involved and accept these risks. I understand and agree by my signature hereon that I have had the opportunity to discuss this document with anyone that I might choose and that I freely sign it.

I declare under penalty of perjury of the laws of the State of _____ that the foregoing is true and correct.

Signature of participant (print name)   Date

_____   _____

Signature of witness (print name)   Date

_____   _____

Credits

Tables

Table 5.2: Adapted from NASPE, 2000, *Appropriate practices for elementary school physical education* (Reston, VA: NASPE).

Table 9.2: From *Appropriate instructional practice guidelines for elementary school physical education: A position statement from the National Association for Sport and Physical Education.* 3rd ed. (2000), with permission from the National Association for Sport and Physical Education (NASPE), 1900 Association Drive, Reston, VA 20191-1599, USA.

Table 9.4: From *Appropriate instructional practice guidelines for elementary school physical education: A position statement from the National Association for Sport and Physical Education.* 3rd ed. (2000), with permission from the National Association for Sport and Physical Education (NASPE), 1900 Association Drive, Reston, VA 20191-1599, USA.

Table 16.2: Reprinted, by permission, from National Association for Sport and Physical Education, 2004, *Physical education for lifelong fitness: The physical best teacher's guide* (Champaign, IL: Human Kinetics), 69.

Figures

Figure 1.2: Reprinted, by permission, from Lori Rose Benson.

Figure 1.3: From *Moving into the future: National standards for physical education*, 2nd ed., 2004 (Reston, VA: National Association for Sport and Physical Education), 11.

Figure 2.2: U.S. Department of Agriculture and the U.S. Department of Health and Human Services.

Figure 3.1: From *Moving into the future: National standards for physical education*, 2nd ed., 2004 (Reston, VA: National Association for Sport and Physical Education).

Figure 4.1: Based on information from Meg Greiner.

Figure 5.10: Reprinted, by permission, from T. Purcell-Cone et al., 2009, *Interdisciplinary teaching through physical education* (Champaign, IL: Human Kinetics), 13.

Figure 6.2: Reprinted, by permission, from, L. Masser, 1990, "Teaching for effective learning in physical education," *JOPERD* 61: 19.

Figure 9.1: Reprinted, by permission, from T. Ratliffe and L. Ratliffe, 1994, *Teaching children fitness: Becoming a master teacher* (Champaign, IL: Human Kinetics), 97.

Figure 9.2: Reprinted, by permission, from T. Ratliffe and L. Ratliffe, 1994, *Teaching children fitness: Becoming a master teacher* (Champaign, IL: Human Kinetics), 37-39.

Figure 9.3: Reprinted, by permission, from Cooper Institute, 2006, *FITNESSGRAM/ACTIVITYGRAM test administration manual*, 4th ed. (Champaign, IL: Human Kinetics), 64.

Figure 10.1: © Cindy Wilkerson

Figure 11.3: Reprinted, by permission, from Cooper Institute, 2006, *FITNESSGRAM/ACTIVITYGRAM test administration manual*, 4th ed. (Champaign, IL: Human Kinetics), 78.

Figure 12.1: From *Moving into the future: National standards for physical education*, 2nd ed., 2004 (Reston, VA: National Association for Sport and Physical Education).

Figure 12.2: From *Moving into the future: National standards for physical education*, 2nd ed., 2004 (Reston, VA: National Association for Sport and Physical Education).

Figure 12.3: Reprinted, by permission, from R. Mull, K. Bayless, and L. Jamieson, 2005, *Recreational sport management*, 4th ed. (Champaign, IL: Human Kinetics), 19.

Figure 15.2: Reprinted, by permission, from R. Mull, K. Bayless, and L. Jamieson, 2005, *Recreation sport management*, 4th ed. (Champaign, IL: Human Kinetics), 119.

Figure 15.3: Reprinted, by permission, from J. Byl, 2002, *Intramural recreation: A step-by-step guide to creating an effective program* (Champaign, IL: Human Kinetics), 200.

Figure 15.4: Reprinted, by permission, from J. Byl, 2002, *Intramural recreation: A step-by-step guide to creating an effective program* (Champaign, IL: Human Kinetics), 201.

Figure 17.3: Reprinted with permission
www.americanheart.org
© 2009 American Heart Association, Inc.

Figure 17.4: From Centers for Disease Control and Prevention.

Figure 17.5: From Centers for Disease Control and Prevention, 2008, *Physical Activity Guidelines for Americans.*

Photos

Photo on pages 5, 11, 27, 34, 37, 93, 96, 106, 122, 130, 169, 200, 210, 213, 217, 223, 256, 276, 288: Courtesy of the Authors.

Photos on pages 8, 23, 52, 60, 67, 69, 77, 81, 83, 99, 112, 119, 136, 144, 150, 172, 175, 184, 188, 212, 223, 226, 227, 228, 240, 245, 269, 277, 281, 296, 298, 304, 314: © Human Kinetics

Photo on page 260: Reprinted by permission of Stevenson High School.

Photo on page 311: Photodisc/Getty Images

Sidebars

Sidebar on page 15: U.S. Department of Health and Human Services, Centers for Disease Control and Prevention. (1997). Guidelines for school and community programs to promote lifelong physical activity among young people. *Morbidity and Mortality Weekly Report*, 46 (RR-6), 1-36.

Sidebar on page 58: Adapted from National Association for Sport and Physical Education. (2004). *Moving into the future: National standards for physical education* (2nd ed.). Reston, VA: Author.

Sidebar on page 76: Adapted from Department of Health and Human Services, *2008 Physical Activity Guidelines for Americans*

Sidebar on page 84: Adapted from www.kidchecker.org/tips.

Sidebar on page 221: Reprinted, by permission, from Kathy Kent.

Sidebar on page 222: Reprinted, by permission, from Kathy Kent.

Sidebar on page 243: Reprinted from *Co-curricular physical activity and sport programs for middle school students [Position paper]*, with permission from the National Association for Sport and Physical Education (NASPE), 1900 Association Drive, Reston, VA 20191, USA.

Sidebar on page 261: Reprinted, by permission, J. Byl, 2002, *Intramural recreation: A step by step guide to creating and effective program* (Champaign, IL: Human Kinetics), 44. Based on S. May, 2000, Volunteering – Back to basics. Profile (June-July).

Text

Standards listed on pages 53-54: From *Moving into the future: National standards for physical education*, 2nd ed., 2004 (Reston, VA: National Association for Sport and Physical Education).

Text on page 164: Reprinted from *Appropriate instructional practice guidelines for elementary school physical education: A position statement from the National Association for Sport and Physical Education*. 3rd ed. (2000), with permission from the National Association for Sport and Physical Education (NASPE), 1900 Association Drive, Reston, VA 20191-1599, USA.

Text on page 238: Adapted from NASPE, 2009, *Appropriate practices for middle school physical education: A position statement from the National Association for Sport and Physical Education*, 3rd ed. (Reston, VA: National Association of Sport and Physical Education).

Text on page 240: Adapted, by permission, from NASPE, 2009, *Appropriate practices for high school physical education: A position statement from the National Association for Sport and Physical Education*, 3rd ed. (Reston, VA: National Association of Sport and Physical Education).

Index

About the Authors

Judith E. Rink, PhD, began her career as an elementary physical education teacher in 1965. She is a distinguished professor in the physical education department at the University of South Carolina, where she taught for nearly 30 years and served as department chair for more than 10 years. She has received numerous awards throughout her career, including the Teacher Educator Honor Award from the National Association for Sport and Physical Education (NASPE) in 2007 and the NASPE Hall of Fame Award in 2000.

Rink has authored or coauthored six other physical education and physical activity books and has written dozens of articles for refereed publications. She has presented numerous papers at state, national, and international conferences, and she serves as the South Carolina physical education assessment program director. She also serves on the NASPE Assessment Task Force and served on NASPE's board of directors from 2003 to 2006.

Tina J. Hall, PhD, is an assistant professor in the physical education department at the University of South Carolina. She taught elementary and middle school physical education for 18 years and conducted several programs similar to those addressed in this book. She has conducted numerous workshops and in-services for physical education teachers, encouraging them to take a leadership role in promoting schoolwide physical activity, and has also conducted workshops and in-services for classroom teachers to help them provide opportunities for physical activity throughout the school day.

Hall has taught physical education for elementary classroom teachers since 2002 and has taken a lead role in physical activity training for physical educators and classroom teachers in South Carolina. She is a member of NASPE and the American Alliance for Health, Physical Education, Recreation and Dance (AAHPERD). She was named the Tennessee AHPERD Teacher of the Year in 1995.

Lori H. Williams, PhD, is an assistant professor at the Citadel in Charleston, South Carolina. She has taught physical education at the elementary, middle school, and college levels and has taught other subject matter at the elementary and middle school levels. Her 25 years of teaching experience includes 14 years in public schools. She served as president of the South Carolina Association for Physical Education and Sport in 2006; during her tenure as president she developed material and initiated workshops for physical activity directors in South Carolina elementary schools.

CD-ROM Instructions

System Requirements

You can use this CD-ROM on either a Windows-based PC or a Macintosh computer.

Windows

- IBM PC compatible with Pentium processor
- Windows 2000/XP/Vista
- Adobe Reader 8.0
- 4x CD-ROM drive

Macintosh

- Power Mac recommended
- System 10.4 or higher
- Adobe Reader
- 4x CD-ROM drive

User Instructions

Windows

1. Insert the *Schoolwide Physical Activity* CD-ROM. (Note: The CD-ROM must be present in the drive at all times.)
2. Select the "My Computer" icon from the desktop.
3. Select the CD-ROM drive.
4. Open the file you wish to view. See the "00Start.pdf" file for a list of the contents.

Macintosh

1. Insert the *Schoolwide Physical Activity* CD-ROM. (Note: The CD-ROM must be present in the drive at all times.)
2. Double-click the CD-ROM icon located on the desktop.
3. Open the file you wish to view. See the "00Start" file for a list of the contents.

For customer support, contact Technical Support:
Phone: 217-351-5076 Monday through Friday (excluding holidays) between 7:00 a.m. and 7:00 p.m. (CST).
Fax: 217-351-2674
E-mail: support@hkusa.com